THE FIRST POP AGE

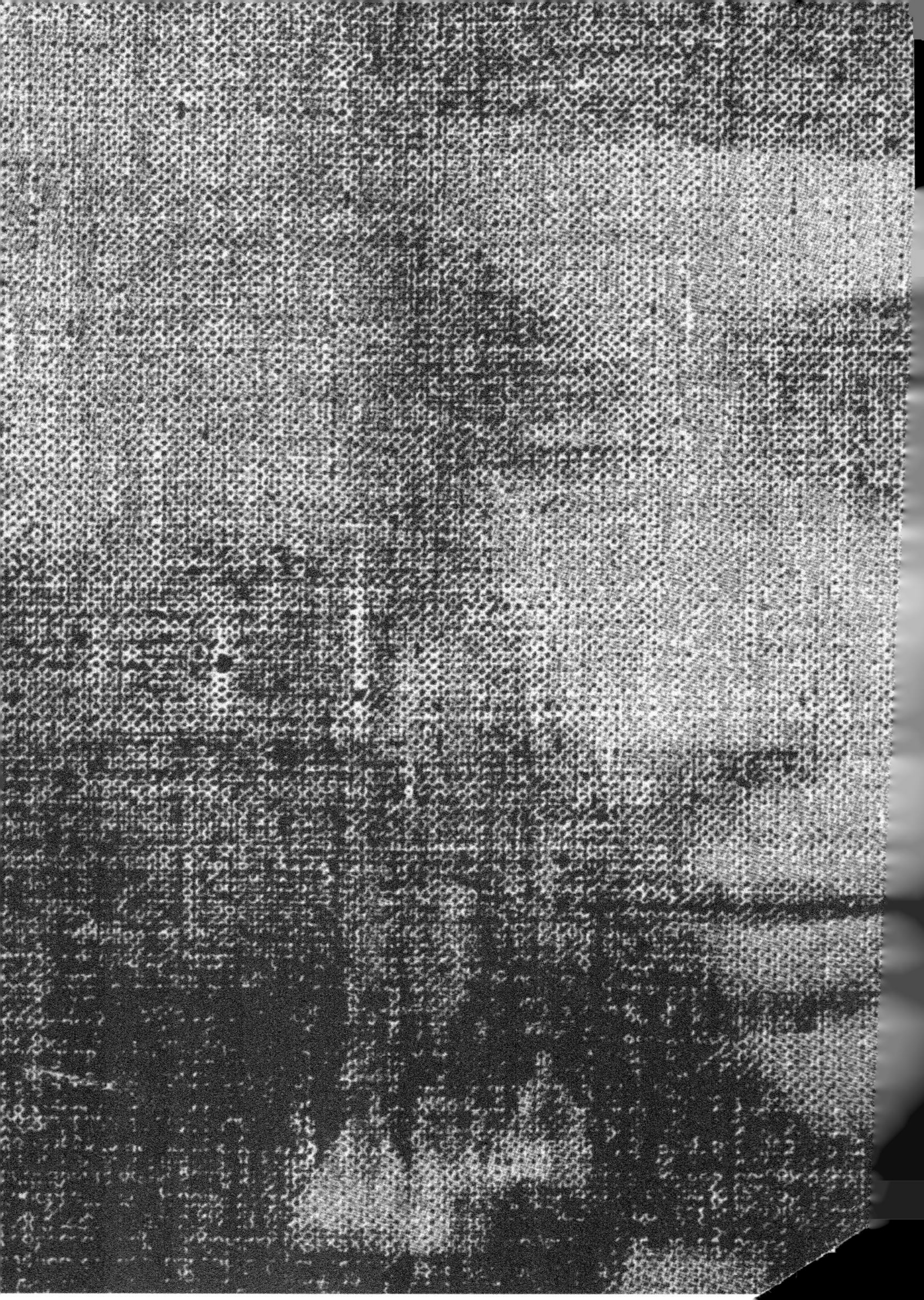

THE FIRST POP AGE

Painting and Subjectivity in the Art of Hamilton, Lichtenstein, Warhol, Richter, and Ruscha

Hal Foster

PRINCETON UNIVERSITY PRESS

PRINCETON AND OXFORD

Published by Princeton University Press,
41 William Street, Princeton, New Jersey 08540
In the United Kingdom:
Princeton University Press,
6 Oxford Street,
Woodstock, Oxfordshire OX20 1TW
press.princeton.edu

Jacket photograph is courtesy of and © Richard Hamilton, *Swingeing London 67—* poster, 1968. Offset lithograph, 27½ × 19¾ in.

Frontispiece: Detail from Andy Warhol, *Liz as Cleopatra*, 1963. © 2012 The Andy Warhol Foundation for the Visual Arts, Inc. / Artists Rights Society (ARS), New York

Second printing and first paperback printing, 2014
Paperback ISBN 978-0-691-16098-6

The Library of Congress has cataloged the cloth edition of this book as follows
Foster, Hal.
    The first Pop age : painting and subjectivity in the art of Hamilton, Lichtenstein, Warhol, Richter, and Ruscha / Hal Foster.
        p. cm.
    Includes bibliographical references and index.
    ISBN 978-0-691-15138-0 (hardcover : alk. paper) 1. Painting, Modern—20th century. 2. Pop art. I. Title. II. Title: Painting and subjectivity in the art of Hamilton, Lichtenstein, Warhol, Richter, and Ruscha.

    ND196.P64F67 2012
    759.06'71—dc22

                                                        2011008603

British Library Cataloging-in-Publication Data is available

This publication is made possible in part from the Barr Ferree Foundation Fund for Publications, Princeton University.
This book has been composed in Adobe Garamond with Trade Gothic display
Printed on acid-free paper. ∞
Printed in the United States of America
10 9 8 7 6 5 4 3

CONTENTS

THE FIRST POP AGE

Homo Imago

On February 12, 1967, local police raided a party at the Sussex home of Keith Richards and arrested Mick Jagger and Robert Fraser for drug possession (Fraser was a prominent art dealer in London at the time). Coverage of the story ran in the tabloids for weeks, and several months later, Richard Hamilton sampled the clippings in a lithograph that featured such racy headlines as "Stones: 'A Strong, Sweet Smell of Incense,'" "Story of a Girl in a Fur-Skin Rug," and "Tablets Were Found in a Green Jacket" (fig. 0.1). Among the press photos of the Rolling Stones and others included in this montage is one of Jagger and Fraser shot through the window of a police van as they were taken to the Chichester courthouse for arraignment. Over the next two years, Hamilton used this one photograph as the basis of no less than seven silk-screened paintings, heightening its effects in different ways: the grainy image is blurred, the lurid colors are blanched as though by a sudden flash of cameras, and in all but one version, the window frame is removed, so we seem to be thrust into the van by the sheer avidity of our own look (fig. 0.2).[1] As if in reaction, the two celebrities, who otherwise thrived on such visibility, attempt to deflect it, lifting their hands, manacled together, to hide their faces and to ward off our gaze.

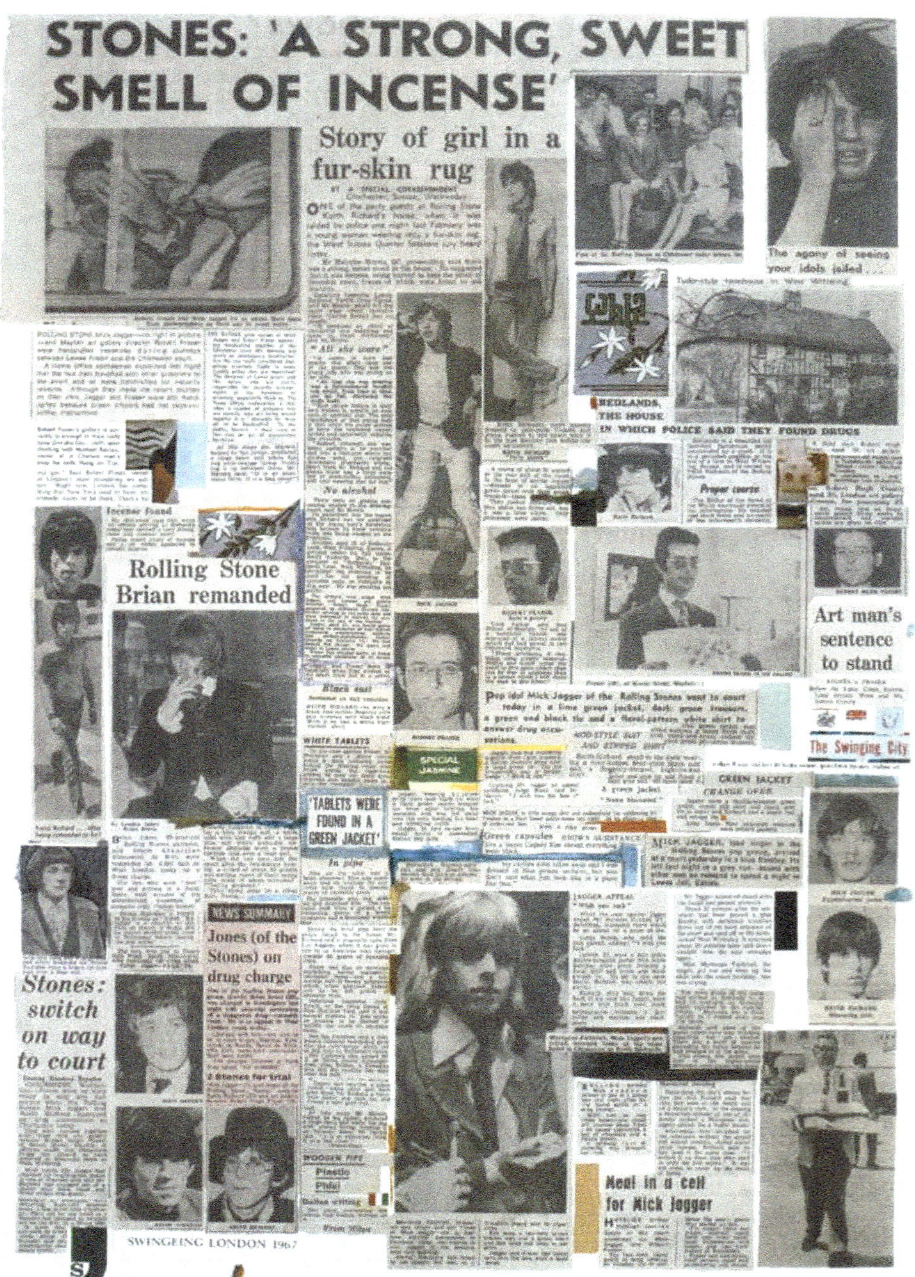

0.1 Richard Hamilton, *Swingeing London 67—poster*, 1968. Offset lithograph, 27½ × 19¾ in.

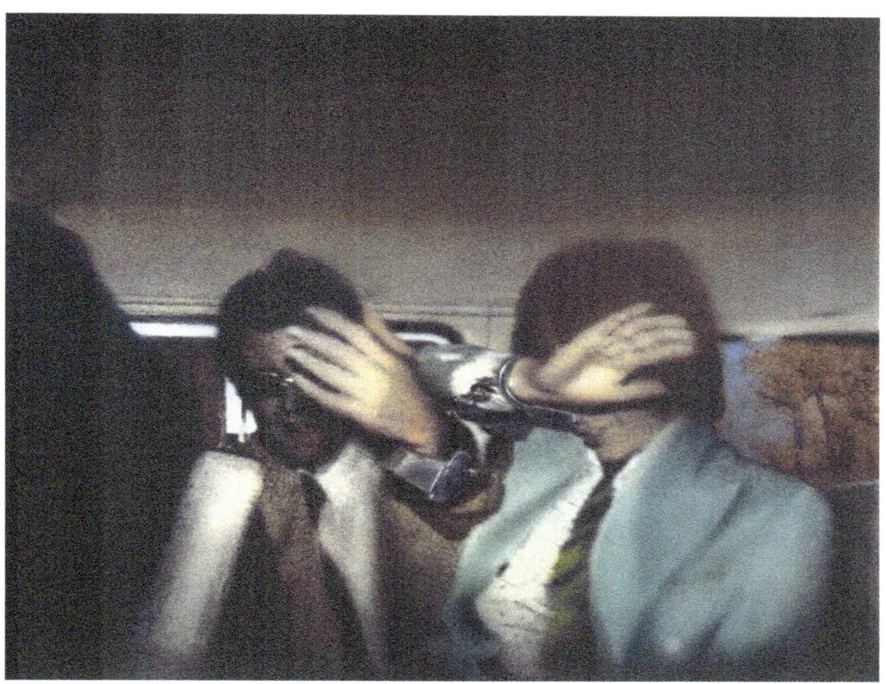

0.2 Richard Hamilton, *Swingeing London 67 (f)*, 1968–69. Silkscreen and pastel on paper, 26½ × 33½ in.

The title of the paintings, *Swingeing London 67*, plays on the hip party-goers (the phrase "Swinging London" was a recent coinage) as well as the severe judgment passed on Fraser in particular ("There are times when a swingeing sentence can act as a deterrent," the judge intoned, dispatching the art dealer to six months of hard labor), but the image is less a protest against retributive justice than a reflection on the vicissitudes of celebrity.[2] In this light, the gesture of hands covering faces might recall the archetypal expression of aggrieved shame that Masaccio bestowed on Adam in his *Expulsion from the Garden of Eden* (1424; fig. 0.3)—it would be like Hamilton to spike a pop-contemporary scene with an art-historical allusion in this way—yet, typically too, he injects an ambiguity here, for Jagger seems to smile, even to smirk, under his palm, and the handcuffs double as bracelets displayed for the benefit of press photographers (in one version

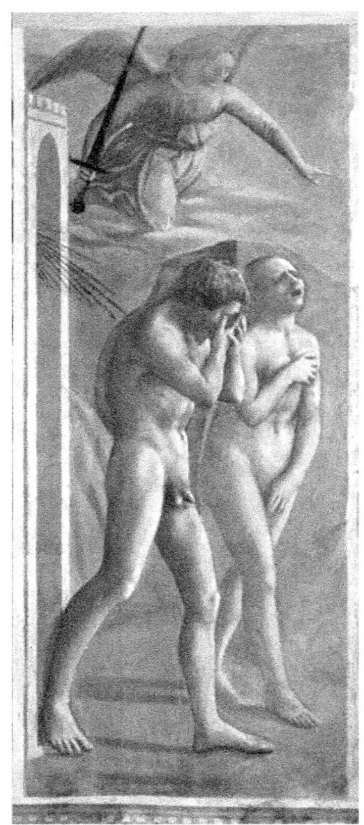

0.3 Masaccio, *Expulsion from the Garden of Eden*, 1424. Fresco.

of the painting, they are built up in globs of shiny aluminum). In fact, like other Pop artists, Hamilton is concerned less with the event than with its mediation—how it is produced for us precisely as an image—and it is this mediation that he both exposes and elaborates. For *Swingeing London 67* is an early reflection on a media world that has become second nature to us today, one in which transgression and adoration are hardly opposed, manacles are often forged into bling, and sheer visibility, desired or not, trumps everything else.

Swingeing London 67 crystallizes several of the concerns of this book: how Pop art often folds painting and photography into each other; how, in doing so, it combines the effect of immediacy with the fact of mediation; how, in this combination, Pop might evoke artistic tradition even as it foregrounds contemporary subjects (*Swingeing London 67* is a history painting of sorts, one that captures a dramatic moment no less); how, in this treatment of image culture, it strikes an ambiguous attitude, neither critical nor complicit strictly; and finally, how Pop indicates, through such ambiguity, not only a heightened confusion between publicity and privacy but also a deepened imbrication of image and subjectivity. I focus my reflections on five artists—Richard Hamilton, Roy Lichtenstein, Andy Warhol, Gerhard Richter, and Ed Ruscha—because they evoke, more graphically than any others, the changed conditions of painting and viewer in the first age of Pop, which here I take to have begun in the mid to late 1950s. Stripped to its essentials, my thesis is this: a shift occurred during this time in the status of image and subjectivity alike, and the signal work of these five artists registers it most suggestively.

Already by the early 1950s, members of the Independent Group (IG) in London, a motley collection of young architects, critics, and artists such as Eduardo Paolozzi and John McHale, had begun to delve into popular culture, and they were quick to use its images in various projects of the mid-1950s. At the same time, Robert Rauschenberg, Jasper Johns, and others in New York and California had begun to elaborate the devices of the found image and the readymade object in ways that also prepared the way for Pop.[3] All these figures advanced a collage practice that Pop then adapted to painting; in this respect, a key moment occurred when Hamilton moved from the collage format of *Just what is it that makes today's homes so different, so appealing?* (1956), which was produced as a poster for the celebrated show, "This is Tomorrow," to the easel format of *Hommage à Chrysler Corp.* (1957), which inaugurated his own "tabular pictures." In this regard, Pop art does not much participate in the neo-Dadaist disruption of the pictorial surface found in British as well as American precedents like Paolozzi or Rauschenberg. (Even for Hamilton, whose pictures are pieced together out of fragments, what was distinctive about Pop painting was its move in composition from juxtaposed parts to given images often treated as wholes.)[4] To be sure, Pop puts painting under pressure—mostly in order to register the effects of consumer culture at large (glossy magazine ads, iconic movie images, blurry television screens, and so on)—but even as it does so, it sometimes looks back to the tradition of the tableau.[5] And in this interplay of low and high, Pop remains in touch with "the painting of modern life," defined a century before by Charles Baudelaire as an art that strives "to distill the eternal from the transitory."[6] On the one hand, at the moment of Pop, mass media seemed to trump artistic mediums, and Pop suggests that almost anything can be reformatted as an image and shuttled across various modes of presentation. On the other hand, Pop resists any teleology of media (as promoted by Marshall McLuhan, for whom the fate of a medium like radio was to become the content of a subsequent medium like television) and uses painting to reflect on the transformations wrought on both popular culture and fine art by photography, film, television, and so on. Thus, at a time when painting seemed to be overturned not only in mass culture but also in avant-garde art (already in Happenings, Fluxus, and Nouveau Réalisme, and soon in Minimalism, Conceptual art, and Arte Povera), painting returned, in the most impressive examples of Pop, almost as a meta-art, able to assimilate some media effects and to reflect on others precisely because of its relative distance from them.

From the start, the involvement of Pop art in popular culture led commentators to concentrate on its content. "I cannot yet see the art for the subject," no less a critic than Leo Steinberg remarked in a symposium held at the Museum of Modern Art on December 13, 1962; "formal or aesthetic considerations are temporarily masked out."[7] This masking out was more complete for commentators who were less well disposed to Pop, and this made them all the more reactive.[8] The artists were sensitive to this focus on content, which they saw as secondary to their work on form, and here, too, critics failed them, for if they regarded the content of Pop as obvious, they dismissed its form as facile—easy in its making and easy in its viewing (this reception was thus a matter less of masking out than of reading through both content and form as if they were transparent). Today, however, we see how elaborate the compositions of Hamilton and Lichtenstein are, and how Richter and Ruscha also complicate our looking in multiple ways. In short, even as these artists aim for impact (Lichtenstein uses this term in early interviews), they also offer complexity, and this is true, too, of Warhol, whose distressed images, however iconic they might appear, are often difficult to assimilate. This book, then, is an attempt to give these artists more formal due, and more theoretical respect, than they are usually afforded, to demonstrate the nuances of their imaging and their understanding alike. I want to offer them the attention to paradigms of picture making that Steinberg offered Rauschenberg and Johns more than forty years ago, when they first rethought painting as a "flat documentary surface that tabulates information." Pop has its "other criteria," too, and each of my five artists puts forward a distinctive model of the image that projects a particular profile of the subject.[9]

That said, some of the leitmotifs of Pop criticism will be found here. I have already mentioned a few of these, such as the pairs high and low, form and content, and immediacy and mediation, and there are other binaries as well, such as representation and abstraction, painting and photography, manual and machined, private and public, contemplation and distraction, and critique and complicity, all of which have structured most readings of Pop art (indeed of modern art at large). In my view, however, Pop renders these oppositions unstable, a matter of convergence and conflation, and puts this confusion to its advantage. For example, Pop does not oppose painting and photography, the manual and the mechanical, so much as it confounds them (early on, the critic Brian O'Doherty pointed to this hybrid with the paradoxical formulation "handmade readymade").[10] In a similar way, Pop does not return art, after the difficulties of abstraction, to the verities of representation; rather, it combines the two categories in a simulacral mode that not only differs from both but disturbs them as well.[11] Then, too, there is the ambiguous position of Pop as neither critical nor complicit. Already in the mid-1950s, IG members had advocated a nonjudgmental approach to popular culture, and in his "sieved reflections" of media representations, Hamilton in particular sought an "ironism of affirmation" that might mix "reverence and cynicism" equally.[12] In their imaging of the lived conditions of consumer society, my other Pop figures produced different equations of delight and disdain, contemplation and distraction, distance and immersion, which we viewers are left to work through as best we can.

This reflection raises the question of the subject in Pop, which is a primary concern here. As is often said, the portrayed subject in this art tends to be superficial, even flat, psychologically as well as physically. The comic-book figures of Lichtenstein are the chief case in point, but hardly the only one, and this blank pose is often adopted in Pop personae, too: "If you want to know all about Andy Warhol," the great Pop cipher claimed in a famous remark, "just look at the surfaces of my paintings and films and me, and there I am. There's nothing behind it."[13] This interest in the superficial, the banal, and the neutral, which is also strong in Richter and Ruscha, is not merely an aesthetic reaction to the deep subjectivity still encoded in residual forms of Surrealism and Abstract Expressionism. Like much literature and criticism of the time (the first novels of J. G Ballard, for example), Pop proposed that subjectivity had surfaced into the world, with the psychological interiorities of bourgeois selfhood now confused with the everyday exteriorities of consumerist life.[14] For all its emphasis on surfaces, however, Pop still registers the subjective (even, I argue, the traumatic), and perhaps nowhere more so than in its manifold moves to *suspend* the subjective: not only in its persistent use of inexpressive gestures and neutral styles, of banal motifs and stupid photos, but also in its mimetic exacerbation of a mass culture calculated to manipulate the subject, which was once understood to be autonomous.[15] As a result, Pop art often suggests paradoxical structures of feeling, looking, and meaning: an affect that is flat one moment and intense the next; a gaze that is deadpan at times and desirous at others; a significance that seems all but absent at first glance and superabundant a second later, with the viewer positioned as a blank scanner one moment and a frenetic iconographer the next.[16]

As initial commentators sensed, the superficiality of the subject in Pop art is bound up with the inflation of the image in consumer society at large. This inflation was much discussed in sociological discourse at the time; in North America alone, one thinks of such texts as *The Mechanical Bride: Folklore of Industrial Man* (1951) by McLuhan, *The Human Persuaders* (1957) by Vance Packard, and *The Image: A Guide to Pseudo-Events in America* (1961) by Daniel Boorstin. So, too, psychological discourse—not only Gestalt theory and ego psychology but also, very differently, Lacanian psychoanalysis—highlighted the importance of the image in the formation of the self. "In its most essential aspect," Jacques Lacan announced in his seminar of December 1, 1954, "the ego is an imaginary function."[17] There is a related proposition in Pop, one with its own psychoanalytical insight, namely, that if the ego can be understood in part as an image, then the image might be seen in part as an ego, that is, as a surface or screen for psychological projections. Often in Pop, especially as practiced by Warhol, people are regarded as a species of image and vice versa, with both people and images thus subject to the vicissitudes of the imaginary (which, in the Lacanian account, is a volatile realm where narcissistic impulses vie with aggressive ones).[18] This view of a vexed relation between subject and image in Pop goes against the usual association of this art with the easy iconicity of media celebrities and brand-name products. On the contrary, Pop in general and Warhol in particular sometimes underscore the sheer difficulty of our status as *homo imago,* the great strain of achieving and sustaining coherent images of self and other at all. This strain speaks to a telling doubleness that often obtains in Pop paintings and personae alike, an oscillation between the iconic and its opposite—the evanescent, even the ghostly. So it is, for example, that Warhol could operate as both superstar and specter in art and life alike (he once proposed "figment" for his epitaph), or that, despite his emphatic style, Lichtenstein could present the self in *Self-Portrait* (1978) as an absence, an empty T-shirt topped by a blank mirror.[19]

In no small measure, this doubleness has to do with the paradox that, even as the Pop subject is formed by images and circulated through them, he or she can also be disarticulated by images and dispersed through them. The serial image alone can produce this strange double effect, as in the *Elvis* paintings made by Warhol in 1963 (fig. 0.4). With the help of his assistant Gerard Malanga, Warhol silk-screened, on a single thirty-seven-foot canvas, sixteen iterations of the same image of Elvis, which he then sent to the Ferus Gallery in Los Angeles, where it was first shown on one wall (the roll was later divided into five canvases, and other *Elvis*es were on display as well). Across this newfangled frieze, Elvis appeared, with frequent overlaps, in various densities of black silk-screen ink on sprayed silver paint, as if in a giant strip of misprinted film. The source of the image was indeed a movie, a Don Siegel western titled *Flaming Star* (1960), in which Elvis plays Pacer Burton, the son of a Texas rancher and a Kiowa mother caught in the crossfire between white and Indian worlds. And in the silk screens, he does appear as a gunslinger, full-blown in the canvas, slightly bigger than life, with legs spread out and six-shooter in outstretched hand, eyes intense, nostrils flared, and luscious lips ready to deliver the kiss of death—classic Elvis, in short. Yet, despite this iconicity, Warhol suggests that Elvis is still subject to the instabilities of the imaginary: at once narcissistic and aggressive in pose, singular and emphatic as an icon but multiple and ghostly as an image, both immediate and faded, present and simulacral—precisely a flaming star.[20]

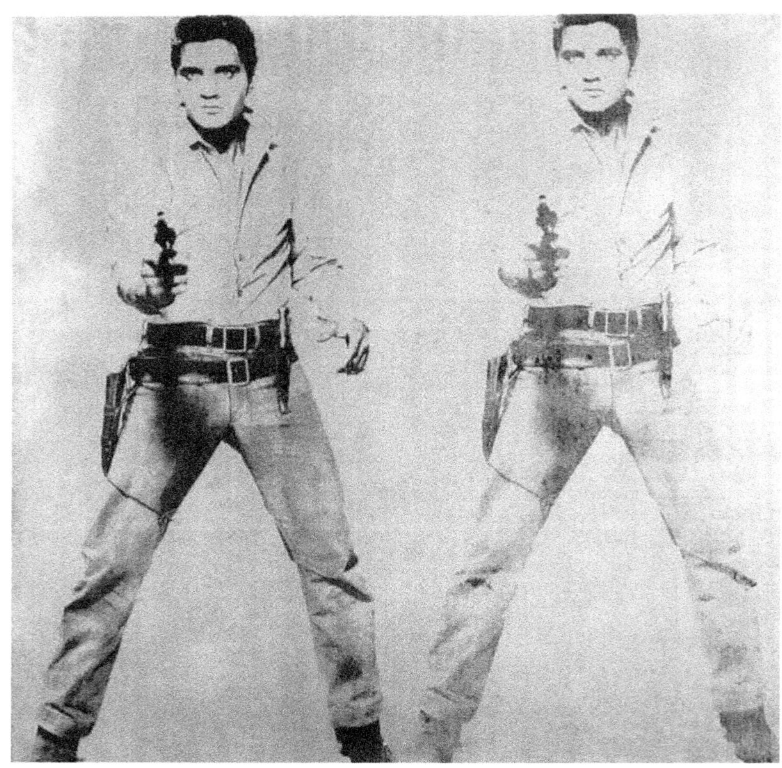

0.4 Andy Warhol, *Elvis II*, 1963. Silkscreen ink and spray paint on linen, 82 × 82 in. © 2012 The Andy Warhol Foundation for the Visual Arts, Inc. / Artists Rights Society (ARS), New York.

"Another nature . . . speaks to the camera rather than to the eye," Walter Benjamin wrote in "Little History of Photography" (1931).[21] A generation later, Hamilton, Lichtenstein, Warhol, Richter, and Ruscha explored some of the changes that new image technologies wrought on human nature, too, in particular the training and testing of the subject by cameras that are photographic, cinematic, and televisual. In doing so, they not only elaborated on the subject-effects of these technologies, but also pointed to a signal shift in the cultural fashioning of the individual. For the acculturation of the expanded middle class of the postwar period, Pop suggests, occurred less through the "Great Tradition" of historical art and literature (as critics such as F. R. Leavis and Clement Greenberg had still hoped) than through the "Plastic Parthenon" of popular culture and mass media; moreover, consumer subjects, Pop intimates, are formed in identification with celebrities and commodities more than through inculcation in any "ideological state apparatuses" such as schools or churches.[22] Pop delights in this new symbolic order, to be sure, but not always: there is also a dark side to its mimesis of consumer society. This is starkest in Warhol, especially in his "Death and Disaster" silk screens of roadside accidents and tuna fish poisonings, but in various ways, the other artists also detail how image culture has refashioned the postwar subject. Yet this penetration is not presented as outright subjection. For instance, in its reworking of image culture, Pop suggests a shift in the function of the artist: the artist neither as a romantic creator nor as a rationalist engineer (many prewar modernists divided along these lines) but as a trained designer (Hamilton and Lichtenstein once worked as draftsmen, Warhol as an illustrator, and Ruscha as a graphic designer). And in this shift in role, a new project also emerges: to treat the artistic image as a mimetic probe to explore this given matrix of cultural languages—to take apart the clichés of celebrity and commodity, to see how they work (that is, how they have transformed personhood and objecthood alike), and to put them back together with differences that (as Lichtenstein once put it) do not appear "great" but might yet be "crucial."[23] Implicit here, too, is that this capacity might extend to the viewer—that *homo imago* is not simply subject to cultural representations, but that, for better and worse, we are all codesigners of our images, each of us (as Hamilton once remarked) "a specialist in the look of things."[24]

However, critics on the Left are also right to remark on the conservative dimension of Pop. Above all, why were these artists committed to the traditional medium of painting despite its displacement in advanced art of the late 1950s and early 1960s? Pop affirms painting, to be sure, but it also pressures painting, which largely serves Pop as a foil with which to register the new forces on image and subject alike. The question of the relation between painting and subjectivity has run deep in aesthetic discourse at least since Kant and Hegel, with the ideal composition of the image often modeled on the ideal composure of the person; the two are explicitly correlated in the definition of aesthetic experience as one of disinterested contemplation and free thought, which Kant and Hegel passed on to count-less followers—philosophers, artists, art critics, and art historians.[25] In light of this aesthetic tradition, Pop and painting would appear to be in funda-mental tension, for in its engagement with a mass culture given over to media and market alike, Pop mostly promotes interested, not disinterested, looking, and celebrates desirous, not detached, being. In its concern with both screened (print) and scanned (electronic) representations, Pop registers technical changes in image production that affect painting too, but more importantly, it also mimics the distractive seeing elicited by such images, and so puts the old unities of pictorial composition and point of view under intense strain. As a result, many Pop compositions teeter between falling apart and holding together, and they seem to involve desublimation as much as sublimation (here are two more oppositions that Pop complicates). Often enough, like the Pop subject, the Pop image is distressed; Richter speaks of some of his pictures as "wounded," and Warhol of some of his as "diseased."

I suggested above that Pop remains in contact with the Baudelairean no-tion of the painting of modern life. Hamilton alludes to this notion in his early writings, and it motivates his signal question of 1962: can popular culture "be assimilated into the fine art consciousness?"[26] Richter and Ruscha also indi-cate its continued relevance when they move to square landscape painting with amateur photography and to abstract art with graphic design respec-tively, and Lichtenstein does the same when he derives his play with pictorial clichés from Walt Disney as much as from Pablo Picasso and Joan Miró. Only with Warhol does the tableau tradition appear to be ruined, and there not in every instance, for some of his "Death and Disaster" images might qualify as history paintings, and no artist in the postwar period refashions the category of portraiture quite as he does. In an ambiguous compliment, Baudelaire once wrote that Édouard Manet was the first in the "decrepitude" of his art; in my view, these Pop painters are the last in this great line.[27]

If painting persists in Pop, then, so do the pressures of modern life. It is for this reason that I draw on concepts proposed long ago to describe the effects of this modernity, concepts like "reification," "fetishization," and "distraction." As they appear in Pop, these effects are heightened by the technological advances of modernity in the postwar period, and in its mimesis, Pop makes them even more emphatic. Thus Pop shows us how, in a consumerist economy, objects and images tend to become serial and simulacral, and how commodities tend to operate like signs and vice versa. Indeed, Pop works to capture a shift in appearance whereby the commercial world appears as a second nature shot through with photographic, filmic, and televisual visualities.[28] In this condition, reification, which once described the routine objectification of human relations in capitalist production and consumption, comes to look like its apparent opposite, that is to say, less a becoming thing-like than a becoming liquid or light, as though what Karl Marx and Friedrich Engels had only imagined in *The Communist Manifesto* (1848) about the capitalist dynamic at large—"all that is solid melts into air"—had actually come to pass.[29] As Pop attempts to paint this changed semblance (which Hamilton once described as photographic "phloo," and Ruscha as "celluloid gloss"), it sometimes makes this appearance more seductive than it is; Pop does so out of sheer delight, to be sure, but its demonstration has cognitive value too. For in its representation of this glossy world, Pop exposes a general drive not only to pictorialize everything but also to fetishize the images that result, that is, to invest them with a powerful life of their own. Such is the theory of consumer capitalism that Pop implies: its political economy depends on a compounding of sexual, commodity, and semiotic fetishisms, a "super-fetishism" in which the making of products, images, and signs becomes evermore obscure while our investment in these phantoms becomes evermore intense.[30]

Pop, then, points to a modernity raised to a second degree with the capitalist expansion of the postwar period, and this book highlights aspects of this demonstration. If, for Baudelaire and his followers, modernity was a wondrous fiction to celebrate, it was also a terrible myth to interrogate, and often the great painters of modern life—from Manet to my Pop five—are its great dialecticians: they are able to celebrate and to interrogate its effects in turn.[31] Methodologically, then, I aim not to historicize Pop in relation to its social context so much as to periodize it, through its paradigms of painting and subjectivity, in relation to capitalist modernity.[32] This is where my allusion to the "painting of modern life" intersects with my title, which echoes

an inaugural text of the first Pop Age by the architectural critic Reyner Banham. In *Theory and Design in the First Machine Age* (1960), conceived in
the midst of the Independent Group, Banham exploits his distance, both
historical and ideological, from the initial framers of modern architecture.[33]
He does so in order to challenge the functionalist or rationalist biases of such
figures as Walter Gropius, Le Corbusier, Nikolaus Pevsner, and Siegfried
Giedion—namely, that form follows function or technique—and to recover
the Expressionist and Futurist imperatives of modern architecture that they
had neglected. In so doing, Banham advances the imaging of technology
as the principal criterion for modern design—for design in his own second
Machine Age (as he called it), or the first Pop Age (as I term it here), as well.

I attempt a similar parallax with Pop in order to clarify its models of
painting and subjectivity. Yet just as Banham also looked back at the first
Machine Age in part to illuminate certain tendencies in his cultural moment, so I look back at the first Pop Age in part to highlight certain tendencies in our present condition. Among the questions I ask (tacitly, without
answers) are these: What of significance has changed concerning the look
and feel of screened and scanned images, the capacity of consumerist and
technological worlds to be represented, and the formation of subjects in a
media environment—and how are these changes treated in art? Is painting
still in a position to reflect on these matters, or is it deluded to believe that
it ever was? Is the symbolic order that Pop limns still in force in the same
ways today? In short, have we moved beyond this first Pop Age, or do we
live in its aftermath?[34] No doubt if this line of inquiry is pursued, mistakes
in self-understanding will be made, but these, too, can be instructive: if
Banham showed the creators of modern architecture to be too charmed by
instrumental reason ("form follows function"), and we see the stars of Pop
art as too seduced by media culture ("it's a global village"), what might our
own blind spots be?[35]

• • • • •

The selection of my five artists is an exclusion of many others, and I especially regret the lack of women and minorities in this book. To be sure,
there were female artists involved in Pop (for example, Pauline Boty, Vija

Celmins, Niki de Saint Phalle, Rosalyn Drexler, Lee Lozano); yet, finally, women could not act as its principal subjects in large part because they were conscripted as its primary objects, even its primary fetishes—and although my artists often reiterate this objectification, they also sometimes probe that fetishization.[36] If women were almost too visible as objects in Pop, minorities were not visible enough as subjects, and only recently have artists of color engaged in Pop begun to attract sustained attention.[37] Such is the limitation of an artistic practice like mainstream Pop, which finds its materials in a mass culture that treats some subjects in a stereotyped manner and others not at all. To make matters worse, mine is a small canon only of white men who have been excessively rewarded in museum and marketplace alike. The art world was transformed in the consumerist society of the mid to late 1950s, and my artists were among the prime beneficiaries of this commercialization—though it is also the case that my five artists do not compose the usual roster in most readings of Pop.

Moreover, with my emphasis on painting, I discuss sculpture only briefly, and mostly as it bears on the different models of the image developed by my artists. This focus leaves out such key figures as Claes Oldenburg, and I would have liked to treat other painters as well.[38] On the other hand, some of my favorites do not fit neatly within the category of Pop. For instance, though I concentrate on early work associated with the movement, I sometimes discuss later work that exceeds it—in part to push back on restrictive definitions of Pop as well as to resist the ready assumption that the work of these artists declines over time (this opinion still shadows the reception of Lichtenstein and Warhol in particular). Again, I trust that today we have enough distance from Pop to see it anew, and that this distance might allow a parallactic view of its effects on contemporary art as well.

Most of the chapters in this book began as essays—in the etymological sense, too, as first attempts to come to terms with the work—but with the expectation that I would revise, extend, and connect them later. Many people have helped with both kinds of labor during the last decade. For advice on initial versions, I thank my editors at the *London Review of Books*, the *New Left Review*, and *Raritan* as well as my colleagues at *October* (especially Benjamin Buchloh and Yve-Alain Bois, with whom I am sometimes in dialogue in what follows). I conceived this project at a conference on Pop at Princeton University in spring 2002 and shaped it at the Courtauld Institute, where I was Research Forum professor in fall 2007; my thanks go to Deborah Swallow and Mignon Nixon for the invitation to lecture there. I am also grateful to participants in my spring 2008 seminar on Pop, as I am to those who read the manuscript in whole or part (Graham Bader, Mark Francis, Kevin Hatch, Gordon Hughes, Alex Kitnick, and Lisa Turvey) and to those who helped to produce it as a book (Hanne Winarsky, Maria Lindenfeldar, Christopher Chung, Terri O'Prey, and Kip Keller). Once again, I thank Sandy for her love, and Tait and Thatcher for their wit.

Richard Hamilton, or the Tabular Image

"[Walter] Gropius wrote a book on grain silos, Le Corbusier one on aeroplanes, and Charlotte Perriand brought a new object to the office every morning; but today we collect ads."[1] This little prose poem appeared in an essay by the English architects Alison and Peter Smithson in November 1956, three months after the landmark exhibition "This is Tomorrow" at the Whitechapel Gallery in London, which included members of the Independent Group (IG), an energetic crew of young British architects, artists, and critics. Forget that Gropius, Le Corbusier, Perriand, and others were also media savvy; the point here is polemical: *they*, Gropius and company, the protagonists of modernist design, were inspired by functional structures, modern transport, and refined products, whereas *we*, the Smithsons and friends, the celebrants of popular culture, look to "the throw-away object and the pop-package" for our models.[2] This was done partly in delight, the Smithsons suggest, and partly in desperation: "Today we are being edged out of our traditional role by the new phenomenon of the popular arts—advertising . . . We must somehow get the measure of this intervention if we are to match its powerful and exciting impulses with our own."[3]

Others in the IG, such as Richard Hamilton and Reyner Banham, shared this urgency.

Who were the prophets of this epic shift? Perhaps the first artist in the group "to collect ads" was Eduardo Paolozzi, who called the collages made from his collection "Bunk" (fig. 1.1).[4] Although this tackboard aesthetic was also practiced by Nigel Henderson, William Turnbull, and John McHale, it was Paolozzi who, one night in April 1952, projected his ads, magazine clippings, postcards, and diagrams at the new Institute of Contemporary Art, in a celebrated demonstration that underwrote the distinctive method of the IG, an antihierarchical juxtaposition of select archival images that appear disparate, connected, or both at once. Performed in early collages by the aforementioned artists, this mode of presentation was first proposed as a curatorial strategy by Hamilton in his 1951 exhibition, "Growth and Form," inspired by *On Growth and Form* (1917), the classic book by the Scottish biologist D'Arcy Wentworth Thompson, and then developed in such shows as "Parallel of Life and Art," directed by Paolozzi, the Smithsons, and Henderson in 1953; "Man, Machine & Motion," produced by Hamilton in 1955; and "This is Tomorrow," which grouped artists, architects, and designers in twelve teams in 1956. As an artistic strategy, however, it is elaborated most significantly in the "tabular" images of Hamilton.

If Paolozzi and Hamilton suggested an aesthetic paradigm that served both collage and curatorial practices, it was Banham who provided the theoretical argument for a Pop Age. "We have already entered the Second Machine Age," he writes in *Theory and Design in the First Machine Age* (1960), "and can look back on the First as a period of the past."[5] Banham conceived this dissertation in the midst of the IG, which reinforced his ideological distance from the initial historians of modern architecture (including Nikolaus Pevsner, his advisor at the Courtauld Institute, who authored *Pioneers of the Modern Movement* in 1936). Committed though he was to modern architecture, Banham was skeptical of the rationalist canon of Gropius, Le Corbusier, and Mies van der Rohe as laid down by Pevsner, Siegfried Giedion, and others, which is to say that he challenged this version of modern architecture according to the criterion of how best to express the Machine Age, and so advanced the imaging of technology as the

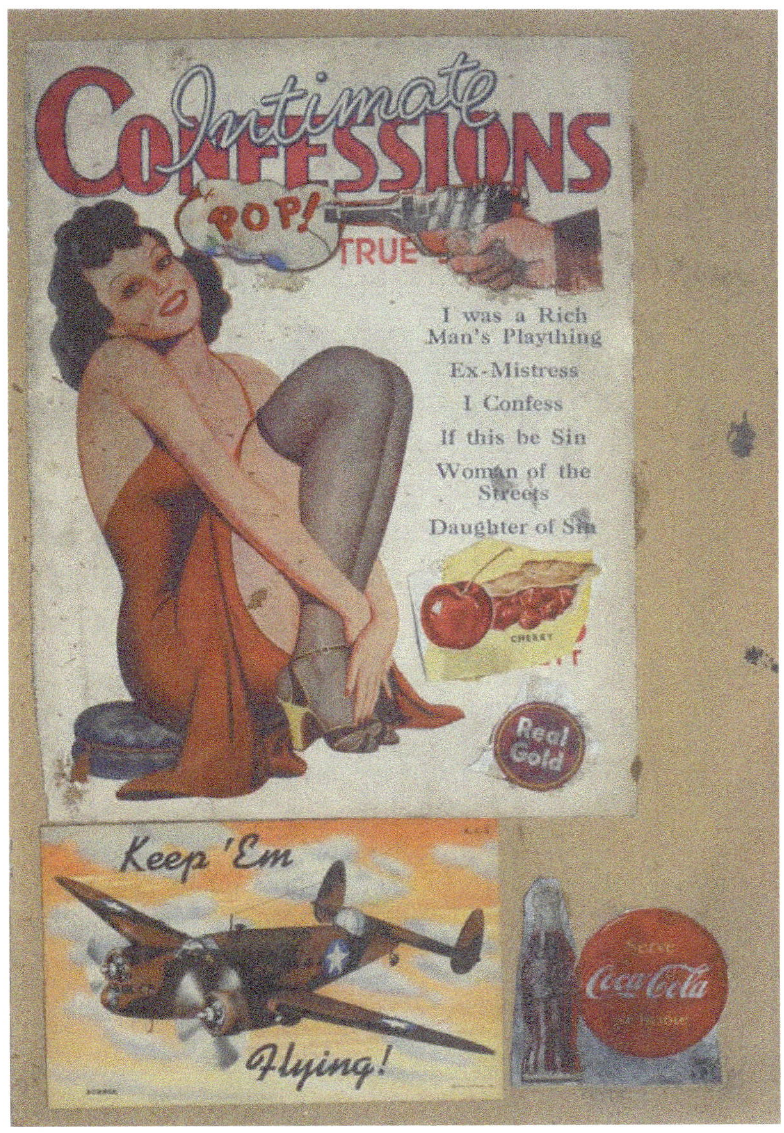

1.1 Eduardo Paolozzi, *I Was a Rich Man's Play Thing*, 1947. Collage, 14 × 9¼ in.
© 2012 Trustees of the Paolozzi Foundation, Licensed by DACS / Artists Rights Society (ARS), New York.

principal criterion for modern design—for design in the second Machine Age, or first Pop Age, too. According to Banham, Gropius and company imitated only the superficial look of the machine, not its dynamic principles: they mistook the simple forms and smooth surfaces of the machine for the kinetic operations of technology. This vision was too "selective"; it was also too orderly—a "classicizing" aesthetic dressed up in the guise of the machine.[6] Le Corbusier acknowledged this classicism-through-the machine when he juxtaposed a 1921 Delage sports car with the Parthenon in his *Vers une architecture* (1923). For Banham, this comparison was absurd: cars are Futurist "vehicles of desire," not Platonic type-objects, and only a subject who thrilled to the machine as "a source of personal fulfillment and gratification" could truly embody its modern spirit.[7]

In this regard, Banham the pop prophet was not at odds with Banham the revisionary modernist. Like others in the IG, he was raised on the popular culture of American magazines, comics, and movies before the war. This is what "pop" meant after the war, not "folk" in the old sense of native culture, or "Pop" in the current sense of Pop art (the former no longer existed for them, the latter did not yet exist for anyone). As magazine and movie buffs, IG members were near enough to this American culture to know it well, but far away enough to desire it still, especially in an impoverished Britain short on attractive alternatives (such as the elite civilization represented by Kenneth Clark, the academic modernism championed by Herbert Read, and the working-class tradition studied by Richard Hoggart).[8] The result was that the IG did not question this popular culture much; hence the apparent paradox of a youthful group in the 1950s that was at once pro-American and pro-Left. At this time, then, a first, Fordist "Americanism," one of mass production, which swept through Europe in the 1920s with important effects on Gropius and company, was supplanted by a second, consumerist "Americanism," one of imagistic impact, sexy packaging, and speedy turnover of products. These values became the design criteria of the first Pop Age.

This revision of modern design was thus not only an academic matter; it was also a way to reclaim an "aesthetic of expendability," first proposed in Futurism, for art and architecture in the Pop period, one in which "standards hitched to permanency" were no longer relevant.[9] In this experiment, Banham had two laboratories: IG activities (discussions, lectures, and exhibitions) and his own many essays, in which he applied to commercial products the iconographic methods developed for high culture at the Courtauld Institute. More than any other figure, Banham guided design theory away from a modernist concern with abstract forms to a pop semiotics of cultural images, in a way that followed the shift from the master architect as arbiter of industrial production to the advertising stylist as instigator of consumerist desire. "The foundation stone of the previous intellectual structure of Design Theory has crumbled," Banham writes in 1961; "there is no longer universal acceptance of Architecture as the universal analogy of design."[10] In this account, it is not the book that killed architecture, as Victor Hugo prophesied in *Notre-Dame de Paris* (1831); it is the chrome fender and the plastic gizmo that displaced it as the center of design. In different ways, the Smithsons (followed by Cedric Price, Archigram, and others) took "the measure of this intervention" in architecture; Hamilton did the same in art.[11]

Hamilton shared many of these enthusiasms with Banham. He, too, delighted in the machine by dint not of its functional fitness but of its affective power, its mythic force. In the introduction to his 1955 exhibition, "Man, Machine & Motion," a gridded display of more than 200 images of mechanomorphs under sea, on land, in the sky, and in outer space (fig. 1.2), Hamilton went so far as to recycle the old trope of a man-machine centaur put forward by F.L.T. Marinetti as an ideal in "The Founding and Manifesto of Futurism" (1909). Yet as Hamilton well knew, by 1955 the machines in "Man, Machine & Motion" were largely obsolete, the mechanical centaurs almost campy, and the techno-futurism on offer a little absurd.[12] Never quite as zealous as Banham, Hamilton already practiced an "ironism of affirmation" toward popular culture and high art alike—a phrase he borrowed from his mentor Marcel Duchamp and glossed as a "peculiar mixture of reverence and cynicism" (Hamilton, *Collected Words, 1953–1982*, 78). This attitude is key, and I return to it below; suffice it to say here that Hamilton never purported to be strictly critical, to stand apart from popular culture or high art, much less to be truly radical (his version

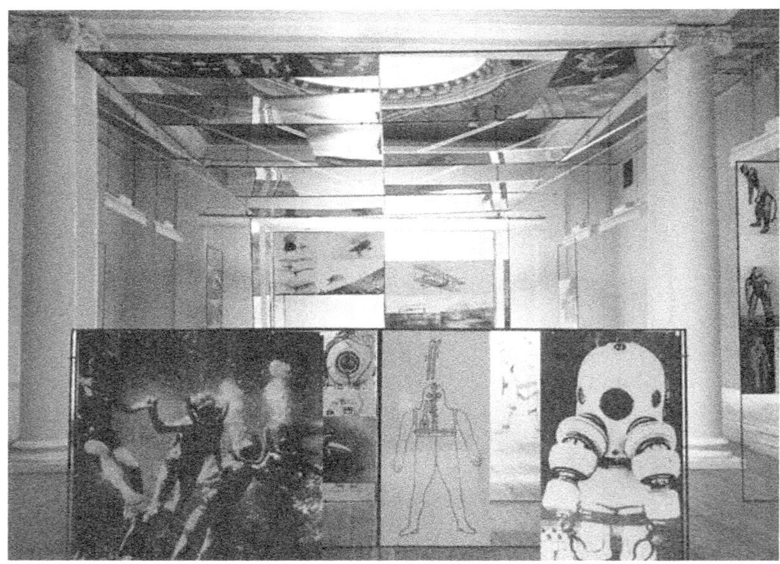

1.2 Installation view of "Man, Machine & Motion" at Hatton Gallery, Newcastle, 1955.

of the Independent Group was hardly the Frankfurt School, let alone the Situationist International), but neither was he merely celebratory. Rather, steeped in both popular culture and high art, Hamilton was concerned to rehearse, indeed to test, the signal operations of each; at once reverential and cynical, he seeks to explore, indeed to exploit, the changed relationship, the charged overlap, between the two.[13]

"Ironism of affirmation" was already evident in "This is Tomorrow," where Hamilton was grouped with artist John McHale and architect John Voelcker (fig. 1.3). His team (Group Two among twelve in all) decided that new kinds of "imagery and perception" required new strategies of representation, and it was for the catalogue that Hamilton constructed his famous little collage *Just what is it that makes today's homes so different, so appealing?* (fig. 1.4), to the first end of the new imagery—to tabulate the emergent Pop iconography of "Man, Woman, Humanity, History, Food, Newspapers, Cinema, TV, Telephone, Comics (picture information), Words (textual

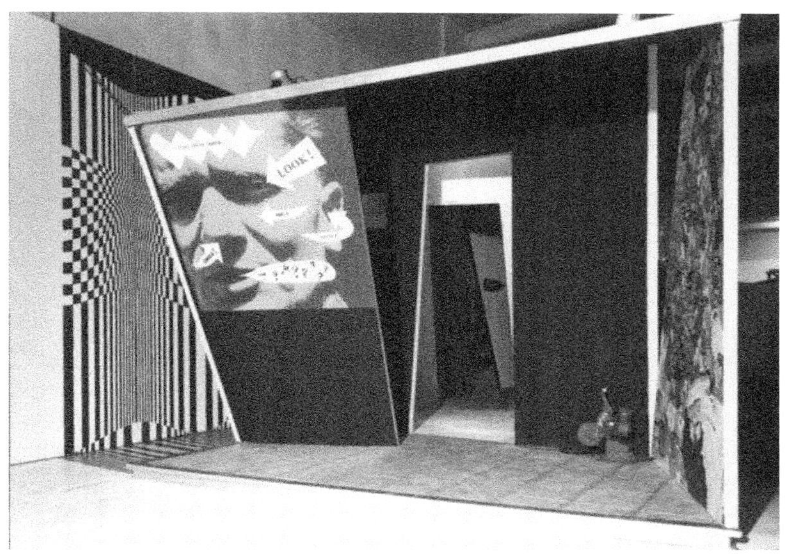

1.3 Group Two display in "This is Tomorrow," at Whitechapel Art Gallery, London, 1956.

information), Tape recording (aural information), Cars, Domestic appliances, Space."[14] Although indebted to the "Bunk" collages of Paolozzi, *Just what is it . . .?* anticipated his own distinctive version of the Pop image, a world of pumped and primped figures, commodity representations, and media emblems, an image that, in his own description, is "tabular as well as pictorial" (24): tabular in the sense that it is a programmatic compilation of the product-people of this world, pictorial in the sense that it still offers a quasi-illusionistic space for these entities—that is, though its juxtaposition of materials is disruptive, its space remains semicoherent.[15]

Two months later, in a January 1957 letter to the Smithsons, Hamilton summed up his interests in IG research to date: "technological imagery" (as explored in "Man, Machine & Motion"), "automobile styling" (he credits Banham in particular), "ad images" (he singles out Paolozzi, McHale, and the Smithsons), "Pop attitudes in industrial design" (as exemplified by "The House of the Future" [1956] by the Smithsons), and "the Pop Art/

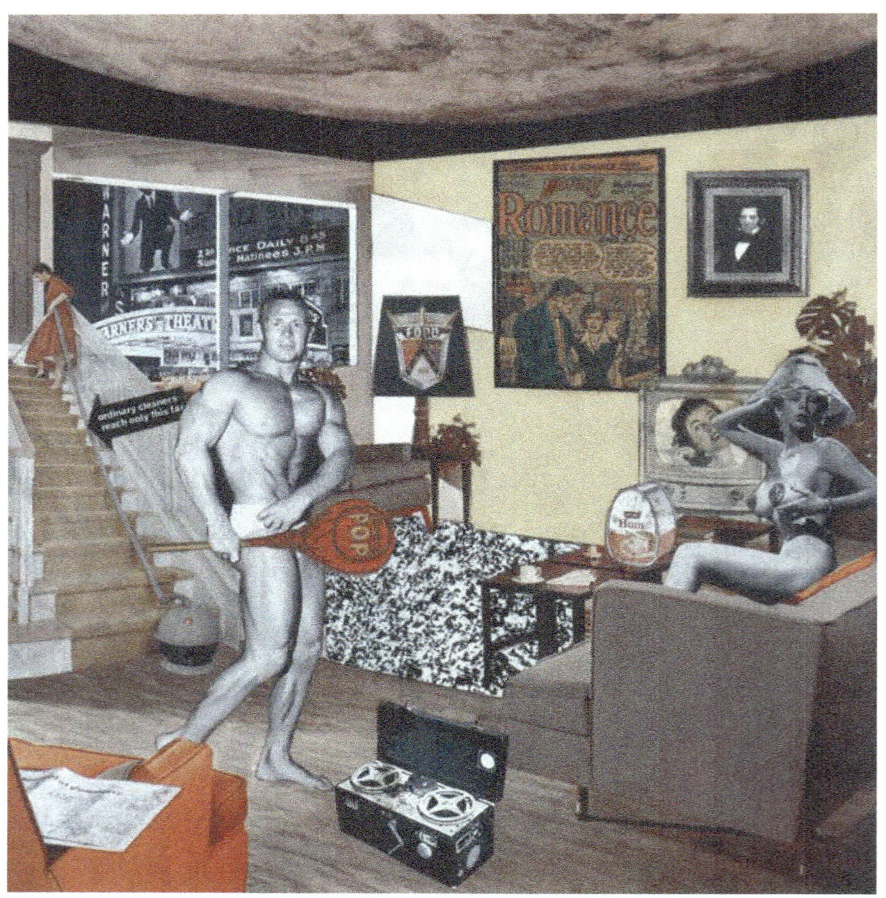

1.4 *Just what is it that makes today's homes so different, so appealing?* 1956. Collage, 10¼ × 9¾ in.

Technology background" (the IG in general and "This is Tomorrow" in particular) (28).[16] Hamilton carried these interests over directly into his tabular paintings, which run from 1957 until 1964, when Hamilton showed them, for the first time as a group, in an exhibition at the Hanover Gallery in London. His most important works, they constitute a distinctive model of the image for the first Pop Age.[17]

A Lush Situation

The letter to the Smithsons, Hamilton tells us, provided "the theoretical basis" (29) for *Hommage à Chrysler Corp.* (1957; fig. 1.5). This painting began his intrigue with the automobile as the core design commodity of the twentieth century (until the personal computer came along), and for Hamilton, the car was more metamorphic "vehicle of desire" à la Banham than Platonic type-object à la Le Corbusier.[18] "It adopts its symbols from many fields and contributes to the stylistic language of all consumer goods," he wrote in 1962. "It is presented to us by the ad-man in a rounded picture of urban living: a dream world, but the dream is deep and true—the collective desire of a culture translated into an image of fulfillment. Can it be assimilated into the fine art consciousness?" (35)

Hommage was his first response to this persistent question, and here his "ironism of affirmation" is not paradoxical, for Hamilton is so affirmative of automobile imaging at midcentury, so mimetic of its moves, that he is led to ironize its fetishistic logic. That is, he exposes the breakup of each body on display—the new Chrysler in the foreground and the vestigial showgirl behind it—into erotic details (as in sexual fetishism according to Freud) whose production is rendered obscure (as in commodity fetishism according to Marx). Not only does Hamilton show these different body parts to be subject to the same process of fragmentation and reification (associated, since Georg Lukács, with industrial production), but he also relates these various parts by analogy (the diagrammatic breast-bra, say, with the car headlight and fin). In so doing, he demonstrates a conflation of the sexual fetish with the commodity fetish, since the two bodies exchange properties, even parts, à la Marx, in a way that invests them with erotic power à la Freud (they thus share the "corp" of the title in more ways than one).[19] This conflation of fetishisms, intuited by Hamilton, was historically novel in the first Pop Age, a function of a consumerist economy in the postwar period in which the actual production of commodities was evermore obscured and our libidinal investment in them evermore intense. Although foreseen in Surrealism, this super-fetishism was first foregrounded in Pop, and the tabular pictures perform it in a playful-parodic way that is both excessive and demonstrative.[20]

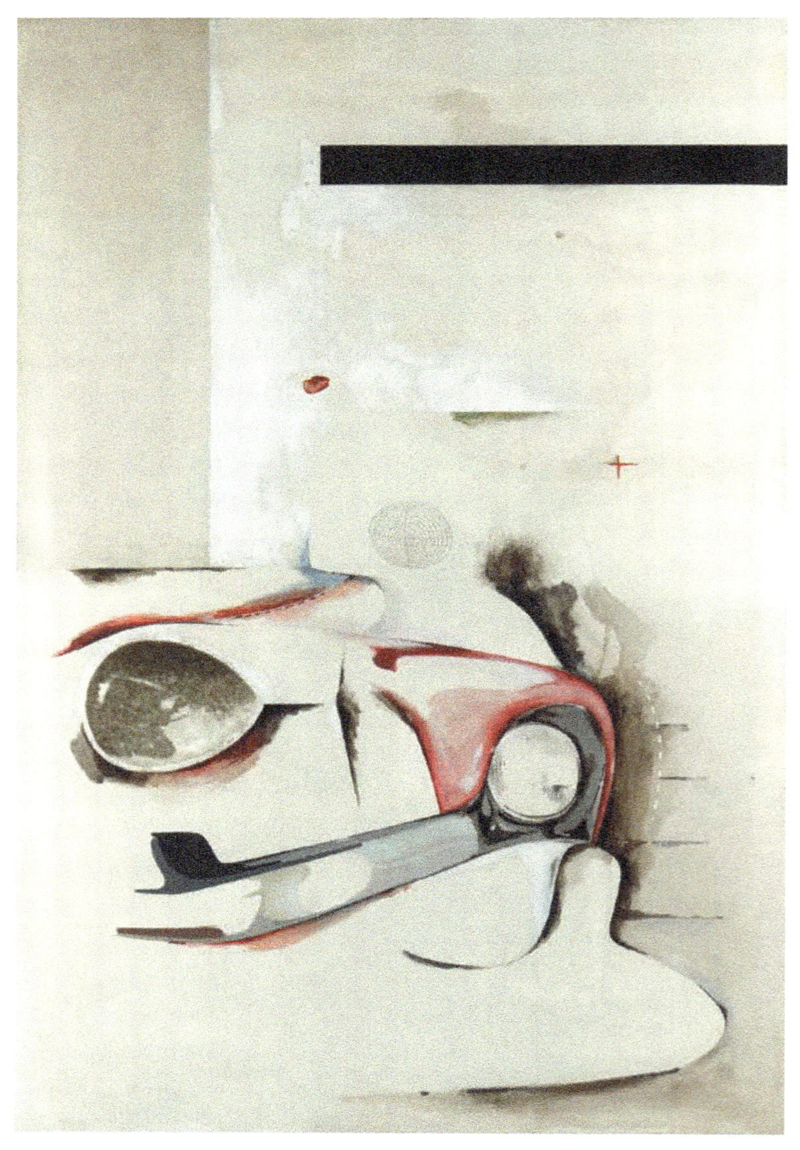

1.5 *Hommage à Chrysler Corp.*, 1957. Oil, metal, foil, and collage on panel, 48 × 32 in.

Signal characteristics of the tabular picture are already apparent in *Hommage*. As Hamilton informs us, the composition is "a compilation of themes derived from the glossies"—several images each for the car, the woman, and the showroom (31). Arranged on a pale ground of flesh tones, the figures seem to emerge from this space and to dissolve back into it; for his own ends, then, Hamilton exploits the imbrication of figure and ground achieved in much modernist painting. Already fragmented, the car is also rotated for display; the headlight and bumper on the right can be read as its front, the fin and fender to the left as its rear (the fin is actually a collaged image of a jet-intake device that was brand new at the time). Like Banham, Hamilton is a detail buff: "Pieces are taken from Chrysler's Plymouth and Imperial ads," he tells us; "there is some General Motors material and a bit of Pontiac" (31). Yet, fetishistically specific though they are, these parts are composed not only into a coherent picture but also into a near abstraction: if the woman caresses the car in the painting, so Hamilton caresses its image in paint, smoothing its rough edges as he does so. Like the car, the woman is reduced, within a faint outline, to erotically charged parts, to breast and mouth, which Freud counted among the secondary sexual characteristics, here represented by a partial diagram of an "Exquisite Form Bra" and a collaged photo of the lips of one "Voluptua," a star of a late-night American television show of the time.[21] This, then, is representation *as* fetishization, a procedure that is extended here to the appearance of the object-world at large—the styling of the car, the posing of the woman, the staging of the scene, and so on. It is a reflexive, almost camp version of what Walter Benjamin once called, in the milieu of Surrealism, "the sex appeal of the inorganic."[22] Such is the chiasmic tabulation performed by Hamilton: a car is (like) a female body, a female body is (like) a car, and the two commingle as if naturally. (This analogy also drove the sexist lingo of the day—"nice chassis," "great headlights," and so on—which Hamilton both acts out in his painting and mimics in his writing.) But the exchange between the two bodies is not equal: the car appears almost animate, while the woman appears almost spectral, drained of life, her carnality all but given over, in fetishistic transfer, to the Chrysler.

The car thus takes on the erotic attributes of the woman, including some of the problematic ones bestowed on the nude in the Western tradition of painting. Consider again the rotation of body parts in the picture. Such rotation is performed often enough on the female body in modern painting; one thinks of the extreme pelvic torsion in *The Blue Nude* by Matisse, not to mention the impossible twisting of the squatting figure in *Les Demoiselles d'Avignon* by Picasso, both painted exactly fifty years before *Hommage*. Picasso also attempted, in many drawings, to capture the female body in a single line, an expression of virtuosity bound up with a drive toward mastery.[23] Indeed, in *Hommage*, Hamilton all but suggests that the skill of Old Master drawing has become a technique of semipornographic surveying. The bodies here are not only offered up to vision but also already mediated for display: "The main motif, the vehicle, breaks down into an anthology of presentation techniques" (31), Hamilton informs us, as he highlights in paint the magazine effects of glossy color and shiny chrome, all previously screened by the photographic lens, as if there were now no other mode of appearance available to anyone. (As we will see in subsequent chapters, this shift in semblance is suggested by other Pop artists, too.) In the process, pictorial space is also transformed: in effect, it becomes display space *tout court*, a showroom based on "the International Style represented by a token suggestion of Mondrian and Saarinen"—the former evident in the residual grid of the painting, the latter in the curvaceous forms of its motifs (32). The black bar is another such "token suggestion," in this case of magazine design, in which the fetishization of things as signs seems complete.[24]

With Édouard Manet in the mid-nineteenth century, Michel Foucault once claimed, the art museum had become the principal frame of reference for painting; with Manet, too, Benjamin added, the primary value of painting had become its exhibition value, its status as a product for sale.[25] Here, with Hamilton, the showroom is mingled with the museum, the frame is purely one of exhibition, and exhibition value is given over to consumption value, whereby to show is to seduce and to seduce is to sell. This is much to suggest, yet Hamilton also rehearses fetishization excessively, in a way that uses its paradoxical logic as a fragment-that-appears-perfect against its own purpose of fixation, its own end of closure—a closure that is at once formal, psychological, and semiotic. For like the tabular paintings that follow, *Hommage* is a pastiche of different techniques, marks, and signs—painterly, photographic, collaged, abstract, figurative, modernist, commercial—a pastiche that works against any final reduction of the body to immaculate fetish. Consider the palette alone: despite its evocation of photographic finish, it is also a calculated mess of fleshy pinks and fecal browns that reasserts bodiliness in the very midst of its apparent dispersion.[26]

This play of fragment and whole occurs at the material level, too. Even as *Hommage* contains bits of photograph and metal foil, it marks a dramatic shift from the total collage of *Just what is it . . . ?* to the painting practice of the tabular pictures proper; nevertheless, the fundamental method remains that of juxtaposition. The composition of the painting is a matter of assembled pieces, and several studies reveal a process of subtraction and addition pushed toward an uneasy unity (fig. 1.6).[27] This combination of artistic techniques in the painting underlies the combination of psychological responses in the viewer. For here as elsewhere in Hamilton, fetishization, which is a displacement in the *object* of erotic interest, no longer seems so distinct from sublimation, which is a displacement in the *aim* of erotic interest. For example, even as both sets of body parts are fetishized, both are also sublimated, pushed toward aesthetic qualities of beauty, and this occurs especially where disjunctive bits are smoothed into painterly passages (around the headlight, say) and where painterly facture plays with photographic effects of gloss and blur (along the bumper).[28] In the process, fetishization takes on the grace of sublimation, as it were, and sublimation assumes the

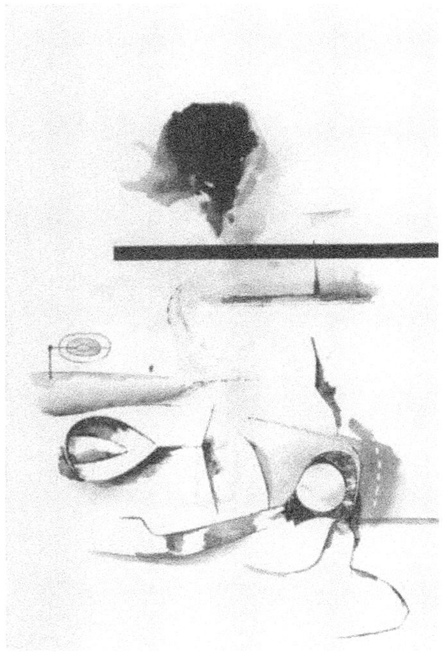

1.6 Study for *Hommage à Chrysler Corp.*, 1957. Pen and ink, gouache, and collage, 13½ × 8½ in.

charge of fetishization. In a sense, Hamilton reimagines sublimation as a "subliming"—that is, as a focusing and priming of erotic intensity, not as its diverting and diminishing (as Freud had suggested).[29] The tabular picture tabulates these intensive displacements, too.

Here Hamilton is close to Duchamp. *The Bride Stripped Bare by Her Bachelors (The Large Glass)* (1915–23) already obsessed Hamilton at the time of *Hommage*: he published his typographic translation of the *Green Box*, a set of notes for the *Large Glass* (the title by which the work is commonly known), in 1960, and followed it with his reconstruction of the *Glass* in 1965–66 (fig. 1.7). Hamilton does mention "a quotation" from Duchamp in *Hommage*, a study for which cites the three panels of the blossoming Bride (they vanish from the final painting). But perhaps he also has in mind a note from the *Green Box* in which Duchamp speaks of the *Large Glass* in terms of an "interrogation of the shop window" and a "coition through a glass pane."[30] If so, Hamilton moves this interrogation along: it is now the enticement of the showroom, where not only traditional line, color, and modeling have become means of product display, but aspects of modernist art and architecture—"Mondrian and Saarinen," diagrammatic marks, and geometric bands—have also become devices of commercial exhibition.[31] Perhaps the allusion to Duchamp is more general, too, to the effect that *Hommage* is, like the *Large Glass*, a "Bachelor Machine."[32] But if Bride and Bachelor are distinct in the *Large Glass*, which is the Bride and which is the Bachelor in *Hommage*? Despite the note about coition, the upper and lower zones do not interpenetrate in Duchamp, yet they do in Hamilton. Given their shared properties, perhaps the car and the woman together compose the Bride as one vehicle of desire, and we the viewers make up the Bachelor (certainly, in the first instance, the spectator of the tabular picture, as of its magazine sources, is presumed to be male). In any case, the shop window mentioned by Duchamp appears to be dissolved in Hamilton, who in *Hommage* shows desire to be transformed too—not quite fulfilled, to be sure, but not as frustrated as it is in the *Large Glass*.

In his next tabular picture, *Hers is a lush situation* (1958; fig. 1.8), which is another tabulation of images from the glossies, Hamilton pushes the association of woman and car beyond formal analogy to actual commingling.

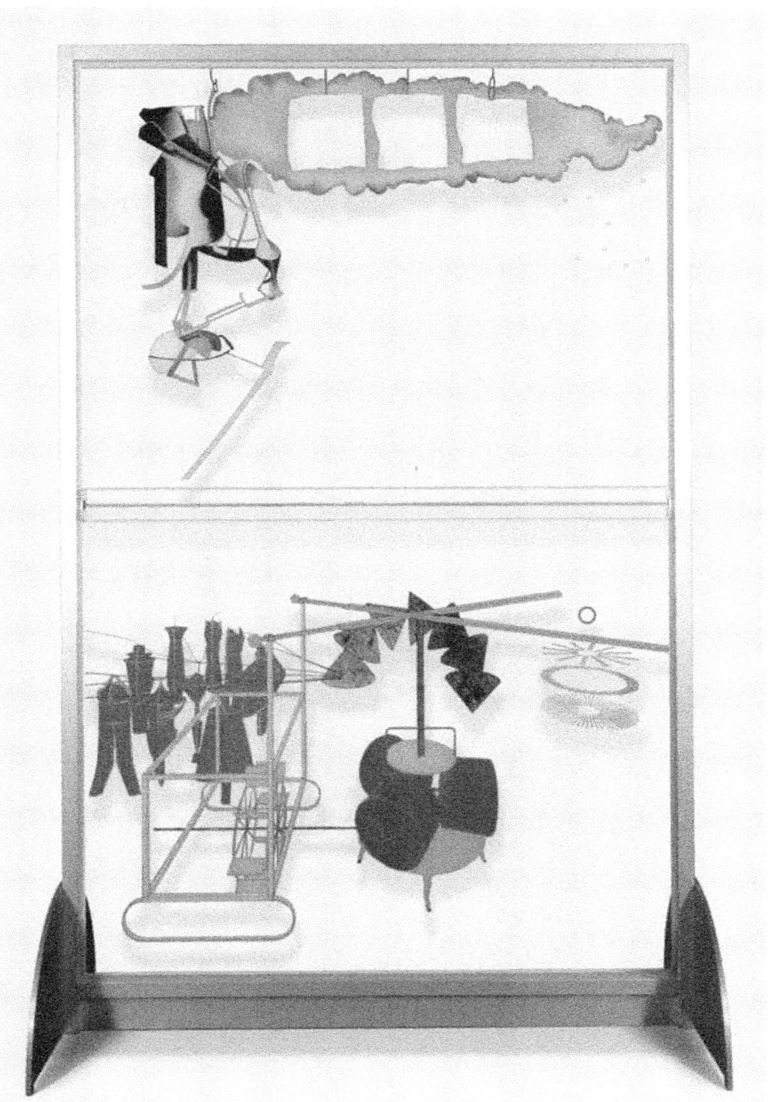

1.7 Marcel Duchamp, *The Bride Stripped Bare by Her Bachelors, Even (The Large Glass)*, 1915–23. Replica by Richard Hamilton, 1965–66 (lower panel remade in 1985). Oil, lead, dust, and varnish on glass, 109½ × 69¼ in. © 2012 Artists Rights Society (ARS), New York / ADAGP, Paris / Succession Marcel Duchamp.

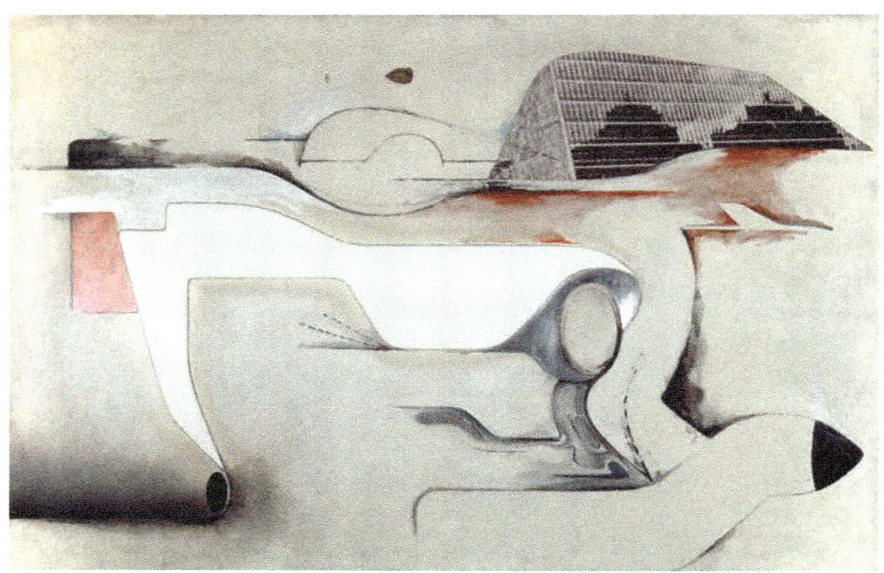

1.8 *Hers is a lush situation*, 1958. Oil, cellulose, metal foil, and collage on panel, 32 × 48 in.

The curves of the implicit driver are imbricated with the lines of bumper, headlight, fin, windshield, and wheel, and in turn this automotive centaur is imbricated with others in the ambient traffic of the implicit city. At the same time, "the driver sits at the dead calm center of all this motion: hers is a lush situation" (32). This is the sentence—from an *Industrial Design* review of a 1957 Buick—that prompted the painting, and the situation in question is a drive on the east side of midtown Manhattan, as signaled by a partial image of the United Nations building collaged to form the windshield (two other skyscrapers are reflected there as well). The setup, then, is similar to that of *Hommage* (like most of the tabular pictures, both paintings are forty-eight by thirty-two inches), but the orientation is different, rotated from the vertical to the horizontal, and the showroom is expanded to the city at large. (Perhaps along with the magazine layout, Hamilton wished to evoke the movie screen, in particular the projective power of the new technology of Cinerama.)[33] Moreover, the notional woman is no longer a salesgirl who proffers the car, but a star who commands it (the lips at the top are those of

Sophia Loren no less). Bed and chariot in one, her Buick is her dais; even the diminished UN bows down before her.[34]

At the same time Sophia is swept up in a sea of different surfaces, steely and fleshy, glossy and grimy; it is, as Hamilton riffs, "a sea of jostling metal, fabulously wrought like rocket and space probe, like lipstick sliding out of a lacquered brass sleeve, like waffle, like Jello" (49). The picture is also a vortex of different spaces, with forms that are concave (the exhaust hole at lower left), convex (the extended fin at lower right), and somewhere in between (the casing around the headlight, which is actual foil meant to evoke pressed steel—part of the hood is also in low relief). In effect, *Lush situation* combines the *Large Glass* and *Les Demoiselles d'Avignon* and redoes them, with car parts, as a traffic jam, as if the world of Duchamp and the bordello of Picasso had become a Manhattan reimagined by Hamilton as automotive-architectural intercourse. In this respect, it is the next stage in his Pop evolution of the Bachelor Machine, one that is more Surrealist in spirit; in fact, Hamilton seems close, momentarily, to the orbit of Hans Bellmer: *Lush situation* as a graphic updating of *Machine Gunneress in a State of Grace* (1937; fig. 1.9), say, in which Bellmer renders woman and weapon as one. Yet what is still perverse, even obscene in Bellmer has become somehow normative, almost beautiful here: a lush situation, not a sadomasochistic threat; *la dolce vita* of Pop, not the praying mantis of Surrealism.[35]

Although Hamilton works to assimilate popular design into "fine art consciousness," the flow of this assimilation runs in the opposite direction, too, and *Lush situation* shows it to be far along, for here the genre of the nude (the odalisque in particular) is subsumed in an ad for a Buick. As with the Cheshire cat, all that remains of the woman is her smile; it is as if a Willem de Kooning drawing were not erased by Robert Rauschenberg but reworked by an automobile stylist. (Both in time and in effect, these lips exist somewhere between those created by de Kooning in his *Woman* paintings and Warhol in his *Marilyn* silk screens [fig. 1.10].) In the process, line, which is still individual and expressive in de Kooning, a medium of human contact between artist and model, also appears, for all its lushness, almost engineered and statistical: "line" becomes "the right line" for "the new line" of Buick—a suturing device by which the stylist-cum-adman captures the

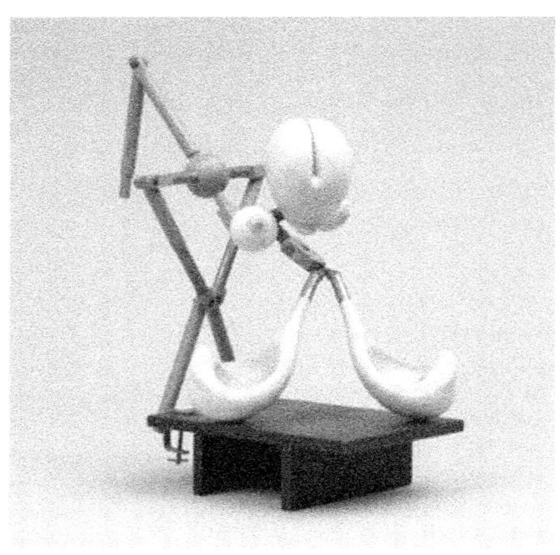

1.9 Hans Bellmer, *Machine Gunneress in a State of Grace*, 1937. Construction of wood and metal, 30⅞ × 29¾ × 13⅝ in. Museum of Modern Art, New York. © 2012 Artists Rights Society (ARS), New York / ADAGP, Paris.

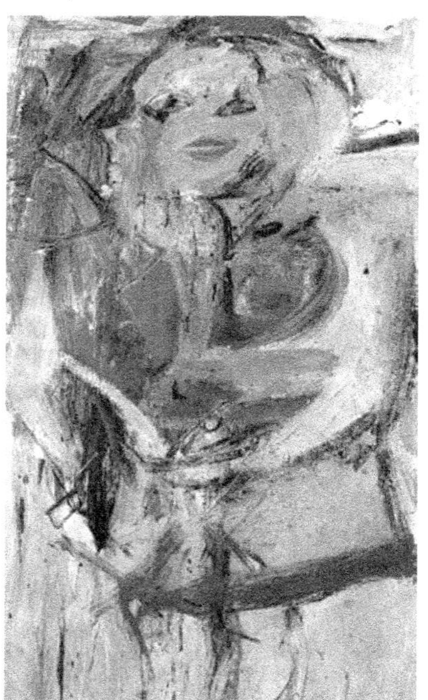

1.10 Willem de Kooning, *Marilyn Monroe*, 1954. Oil on canvas, 50 × 30 in. © 2012 The Willem de Kooning Foundation / Artists Rights Society (ARS), New York.

viewer as consumer. On the one hand, then, line is still eroticized: the situation is indeed lush, a seraglio of curves, and though the female body as such gets a little lost, a female bodiliness still permeates the painting (again it bleeds into other areas, especially in the red tins beneath the windshield).[36] On the other hand, line is also manipulated and manipulative—in a word, reified—and somehow the two processes do not seem contradictory here: like fetishization and sublimation, eroticization and reification are folded into each other. Such, according to Hamilton, was the sex appeal of the inorganic in 1958.

Moreover, as line is revalued in this manner, so is plasticity, in a way that makes two further states, animation and inanimation, also difficult to distinguish. The old Futurist dream of the inorganic world charged with a vital force, first vaunted in fascist culture, comes true, in a different way, in consumerist culture, and Hamilton evokes this uncanny life in *Lush situation* (it has become an everyday event, he suggests, as ordinary as a midtown drive). "More than a substance, plastic is the very idea of its infinite transformation," Roland Barthes wrote in *Mythologies* just a year or two before *Lush situation* was painted; "the whole world *can* be plasticized, and even life itself."[37] This is what reification is like

in the postwar period, Hamilton hints too, "like lipstick . . . waffle . . . Jello";
it is a protean process of new materials, techniques, and effects, one that can
take on the qualities of its nominal opposites—liquefaction, even rarefaction
(note the shimmer of the UN, for example, or the sheen of the bumper).[38]

"Sex is everywhere," Hamilton wrote in 1962, "symbolized in the glamour of mass-produced luxury—the interplay of fleshy plastic and smooth,
fleshier metal" (36). Again, as explored in tabular pictures like *Hommage*
and *Lush situation*, this erotic plasticity is not only fetishistic, a matter of
charged details (often rendered in realistic fashion, such as the collaged lips),
but also sublimatory, a matter of seductive displacements (usually evoked by
abstract means, such as the curvaceous lines). It is as if Hamilton tracks the
desirous eye in its saccadic jumps across associated forms—breasts to headlights, hips to bumpers, and so on, across and around the field of vision—in
movements that seem metonymic at times, as desire is said to be in its shift-
ing from object to object, and metaphoric at other times, as the symptom
is said to be in its logic of association.[39] In any case, together these two sets
of operations—fetishistic detailing and desirous jumping on the one hand,
sublimatory sliding and symptomatic rhyming on the other—inform the
hybrid space of the tabular pictures, which are at once specific and sketchy
in content, broken and seamless in facture, subtractive and additive in composition, and collagist and painterly in medium.

Phloo

In play in *Hommage* and *Lush situation*, these combinations are intensified
in *$he* (1958–61; fig. 1.11), the summa of the tabular paintings, which
Hamilton describes as a "sieved reflection of the ad man's paraphrase of the
consumer's dream" (36). *$he* develops the format of the two prior pictures:
if a magazine image of a Chrysler structures *Hommage*, and a magazine review of a Buick prompts *Lush situation*, here it is a magazine shot of a RCA
Whirlpool refrigerator-freezer, and the implication is that there is no end
to the showroom in consumer society, not even (not especially) at home.
Hamilton lists no less than ten sources for the refrigerator, the woman, and
the hybrid of toaster and vacuum cleaner (which he dubs a "toastuum"), all

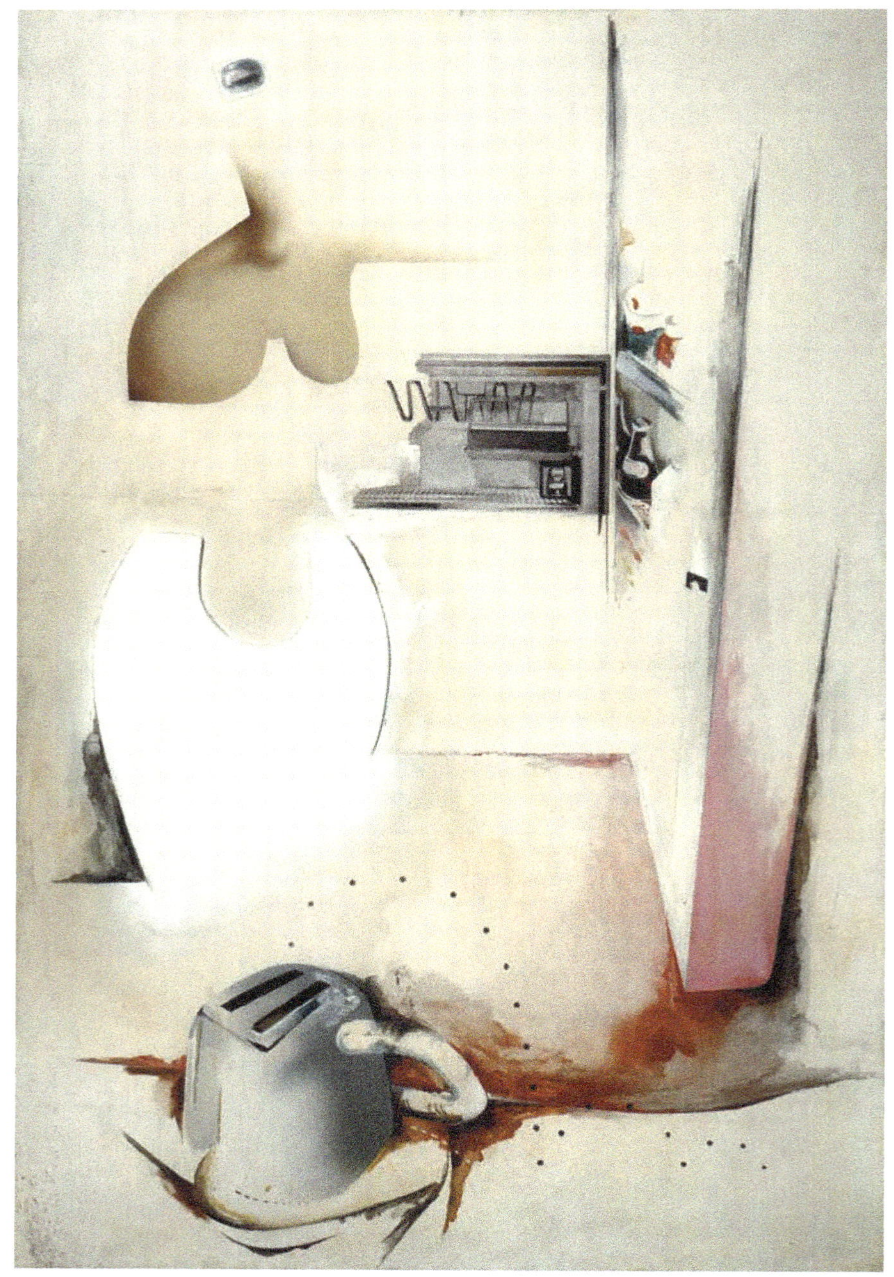

1.11 *$he*, 1958–61. Oil, cellulose, and collage on panel, 48 × 32 in.

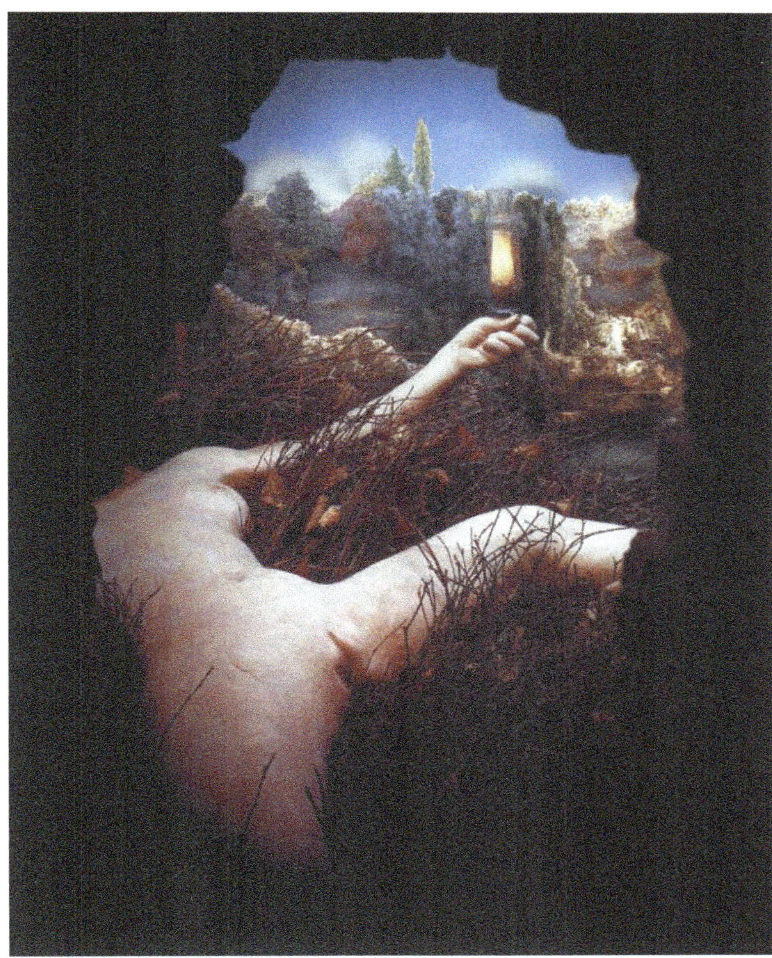

1.12 Marcel Duchamp, *Etant donnés*, 1946–66. Mixed media. © 2012 Artists Rights Society (ARS), New York / ADAGP, Paris / Succession Marcel Duchamp.

credited to specific designers and brands; again, like Banham, Hamilton is a mad iconographer of Pop representations of everyday life. At the same time, in an allusion to the Baudelairean formula of modern painting, he sees, in this evocation of the everyday, an intimation of "the epic" and "the archetypal" (37, 49).[40] Of the repeated scenario of the woman with a commodity, Hamilton notes "the caress" in particular: "Characteristic posture:

inclination towards the appliance in a gesture of affectionate genuflexion. Possessive but also bestowing. She offers the delights of the appliance along with her other considerable attributes" (36).

This "archetype" of a woman with a commodity was already in play in *Hommage* and *Lush situation*, but here the commodity offers the woman for sale as much as the reverse—for sale as an up-to-date accessory (like the defroster collaged to her left) or as a quick consumable (like the bottle of drink in the door rack), a for-sale-ness that is underscored by the dollar sign in the title (both woman and fridge are "white goods").[41] However, though consumerist timesaving is promised here, there is still work to be done: clearly, as Hamilton remarks, Mum has "a job, like Dad's; [she] too has a uniform," evoked by the white apron (36). And though the diagrammatic dots of movement by the toastuum appear to track the flight and crash of a piece of toast, they might also suggest a Taylorist time-motion study of kitchen labor, which is preponderantly female. At the same time, the uniform is shapely, the source of the image is upscale (it comes from *Esquire*), as is the original model, Vikky Dougan, who "specializes in modeling backless dresses and bathing costumes" (37). If the Victorian gentleman was said to split the figure of woman into Madonna and whore, his postwar middle-class descendant, the implied addressee here, projects the double of efficient housewife and elegant sex kitten, with her apron below, in sanded white relief, and her strapless gown above, with "the shoulders and the breasts," Hamilton tells us, "lovingly air-brushed in cellulose paint" (37).[42]

Despite these "loving" touches, the woman is again reduced to an erotic essence, not breast and lips, as in *Hommage* and *Lush situation*, but eye and hips. Once more her body is cut back, only to reappear, associatively, in the pinks and reds that wash down the fridge door onto the tabletop, and once more these colors evoke blood, perhaps menstrual, which return like the repressed in this otherwise superclean image of the refined housewife. But the greatest shock, the one that upsets the sublimatory scene, is the rotation of the body, which, revisited on the woman, is extreme: as with the squatting demoiselle in Picasso, it is her front we see above, her back (her bottom) below. Moreover, with her hips in sanded wood and her eye a plastic one (taped on at the last moment), relief and collage are exploited for fetishistic effects, not for the opposite ends, as they often were in Berlin Dada or Russian Constructivism, in which relief and collage worked to expose the fetishistic operation of traditional figuration. The lenticular eye opens and closes, as a fridge does, turns on and off, as a toastuum does: apparently in this Pop world of animated things, it is not only sardine cans that look back at us.[43] Like the lips in *Hommage* and *Lush situation*, this eye attracts us like a perspectival point affixed to the surface. Could Hamilton have guessed that Duchamp planned a related setup in his final work, *Etant donnés* (1946–66; fig. 1.12), the peephole diorama in the Philadelphia Museum of Art in which the vulva of the spread mannequin in the reeds serves as an outrageous vanishing point of the scene as a whole? In the tabular pictures, Hamilton often suggests a relay between eye or mouth, vagina, and vanishing point, one that recalls the gloss on the perspectival system of *Etant donnés* once offered, pithily enough, by Jean-François Lyotard—*Con celui qui voit* ("he who sees is an idiot," but also, distantly, "he who sees is a cunt"). Yet in Hamilton, the relation between viewer and viewed seems more benign: although, like the sardine can made famous by Jacques Lacan, the eye might carry a hint of threat, a reminder of lack, its gaze in Hamilton is also a winking come-on.[44]

"Art's Woman in the fifties was anachronistic," Hamilton writes in 1962, no doubt with de Kooning in mind,

> as close to us as a smell in the drain; bloated, pink-crutched, pin-headed and lecherous; remote from the cool woman outside fine art. There she is truly sensual but she acts her sexuality and the performance is full of wit. Although the most precious of adornments, she is often treated as just a styling accessory. The worst thing that can happen to a girl, according to the ads, is that she should fail to be exquisitely at ease in her appliance setting. (36)

But is everything so cool and easy in *$he*? Again, there are those pesky pinks and reds, and that odd eye as well; like her predecessors, the woman acts out the contradictory logic of the fetish—at once partial and perfect, castrated and phallic—and in this labor, she is supported, ambiguously, by the strange appliance in the foreground. A mix of General Electric and Westinghouse ads, the toastuum both prepares food and collects waste;

like the fridge, which both chills and defrosts, it is a servomechanism, but an absurd one, a little Bachelor Machine along the lines of the onanistic coffee mills and chocolate grinders by Duchamp (one is included in the *Large Glass*).[45] Once more, then, Hamilton shows us the fetish, but shows it flawed, even failed. Not even the closure of the kitchen is complete; at this point in history, there is no cool and easy separation of home and work or private space and public realm. Indeed, Hamilton produced *$he* at the moment of the kitchen debate between Richard Nixon and Nikita Khrushchev (it occurred on July 24, 1959), in which the kitchen became the focal point of political confrontation, a hot spot in the Cold War. In a sense, *$he* is a history painting of this moment, of "domesticity at war," and it might be argued that the other tabular pictures are as well.[46]

Just as *Hommage* forms a pair with *Lush situation*, so *Pin-up* (1961; fig. 1.13) does with *$he*, and here, too, there is a shift in setting, from a notional kitchen to a notional bedroom, as signaled by the naked woman and the dangled bra as well as by the hybrid appliance, a Princess Bell telephone and Wundergram record player in one. Perhaps *Pin-up* captures the sexy homemaker of *$he* at a later moment, after an evening out on the town; the garter, nylon, and high heel (all in illustrational style) suggest as much, as do the breasts (in low relief) and the bra (a collaged photograph). Yet the social ambiance is different, a change made explicit by the title, which also cues the image source—not the classy *Esquire* as in *$he*, but "girlie pictures" including (Hamilton tells us) "not only the sophisticated and often exquisite photographs in *Playboy* magazine, but also the most vulgar and unattractive to be found in such pulp equivalents as *Beauty Parade*" (40). Here the woman is the sole item on offer: her breasts are not only exposed but doubled (they appear in profile as well), haloed (as is her head), and built up (they are literally padded). In Duchampian terms, the Virgin has long since passed over to the Bride, and she is "stripped bare" in the most explicit sense (we even see her bikini tan line). Indeed, as suggested by the diagrammatic dots, the next move in this staged striptease is a leg kick that might reveal her sex all the more. In this regard, her posture is a strange mix of passive and active: she has agency, but it is the agency of display only.

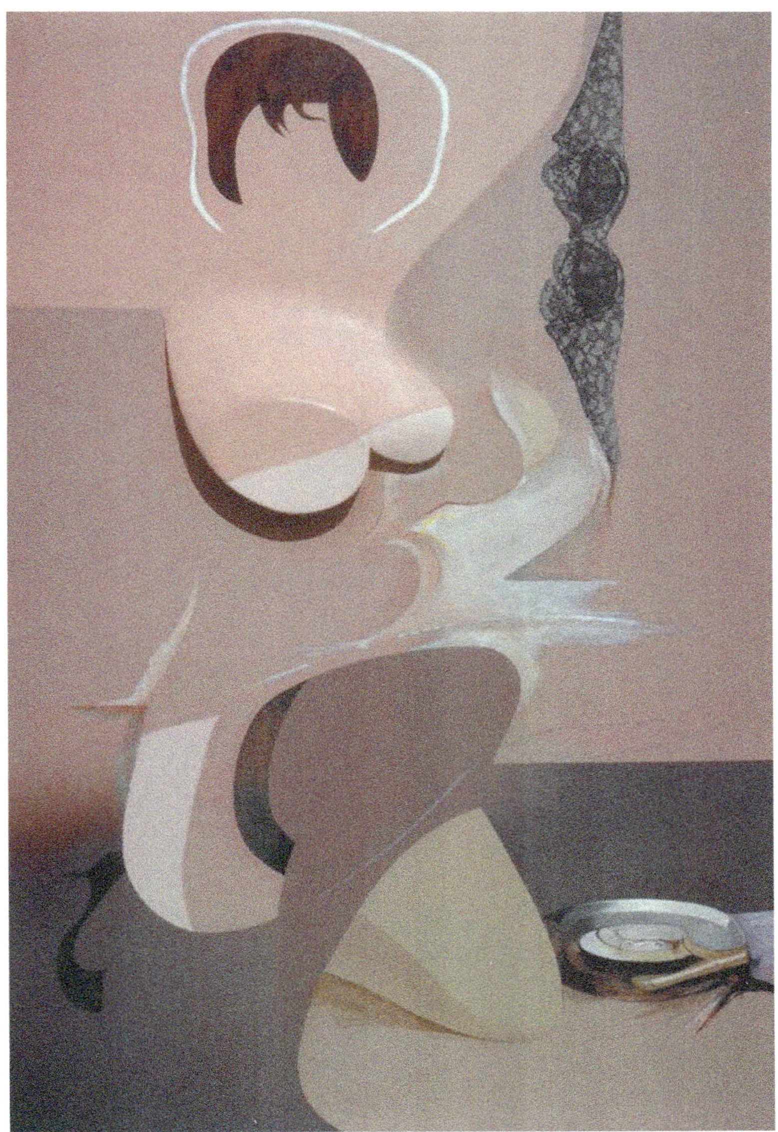

1.13 *Pin-up*, 1961. Oil, cellulose, and collage on panel, 48 × 32 in.

Apart from the usual photo-inflected flesh tones, the brown wig sets the relatively dark palette for the painting, and it replaces the eye and mouth in the prior paintings. Hence the woman cannot look back at us, and nothing much impedes our gaze. Moreover, she is comparatively intact, and the desublimated bodiliness of the other tabular paintings is not felt as strongly here (there are, for example, no blood reds, though the browns retain a faint fecal association). In short, fetishization is less challenged than paraded in this figure as well as in her accoutrements (not only bra and wig but garter, nylon, and heel). Finally, not much transformation is wrought either on the high term, the nude or odalisque (there are echoes of Manet, Renoir, Matisse, and Picasso), or the low term, "the girlie pictures"; the one reinforces more than undercuts the other. Certain studies, which show a Picassoesque (or, again, Bellmerian) confusion of body parts, of breasts and heads, nipples and eyes, are more disruptive in effect (fig. 1.14). In the painting, such confusion is evident only in the midsection, where there is some slippage between breast and buttock, stomach and knee. In a smart touch, however, this logic of body parts turned into part-objects is extended to the object-world at large, where again the bra, wig, heel, and turntable-telephone appear as vital, indeed as erotic, as the woman. Like the toastuum in *$he*, the turntable-telephone is an odd hybrid, a crossing not only of two appliances but also of two media of entertainment and communication. In this light, it might not be so absurd after all, for Hamilton, a close observer of technological developments, might

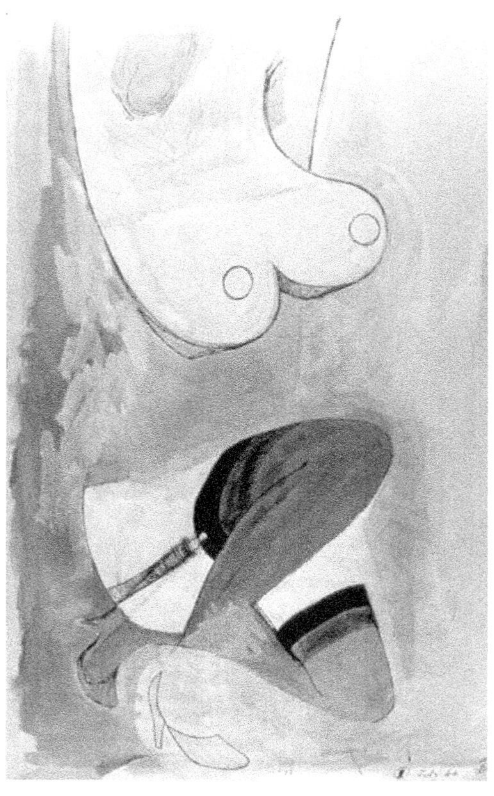

1.14 *Pin-up sketch V*, 1960. Ink, watercolor, gouache, 14½ × 9 in.

imply here a thesis, soon to be associated with Marshall McLuhan, that "the content of any medium is always another medium," and that media technology advances precisely through the combination of devices and the assimilation of functions (a process as accelerated in the early 1960s as it is in our own time).[47] But there is also an irony here, for what possible use is served by a turntable-telephone? Fetishization, both sexual and technological, might not be challenged, but it is underscored, even parodied through an excessive elaboration of an absurd consumerist object.[48]

Glorious Techniculture (1961–64; fig. 1.15) and *AAH!* (1962) form yet another pair of tabular pictures. More intricate than *$he* and *Pin-up*, they return to the woman-car archetype of *Hommage* and *Lush situation* and complicate it—maybe too much so. First called *Anthology, Glorious Techniculture* was originally eight feet high, and its upper two-thirds was given over to a fantasy image of the Manhattan skyline at night, its skyscrapers stretched through photographic multiplication, as if in a Pop update of the classic Fritz Lang film *Metropolis* (fig. 1.16). Near the top of these cellular high-rises, above a silver band, presided a giant horizontal still of Charlton Heston as Moses in *The Ten Commandments* (1956), as though the skyline has become one big Cinerama screen; staff in hand, arms outstretched, Heston-Moses parts the Red Sea and lets the chosen woman-car pass. Commissioned for the Congress of the International Union of Architects in London in July 1961, this version was soon cut down by Hamilton (perhaps the point of its implicit jab at architectural hubris passed with the occasion), the upper half was discarded, and the lower refashioned as the painting that exists today.

Even absent the Gotham towers and the Hollywood Moses, *Glorious Techniculture* is an "anthology" of different myths of popular culture and modes of stylistic representation.[49] Among the Pop motifs are tokens of a car, a rifle, and a guitar at the center, fragments of a large poster at the upper left and of an American flag at the upper right; and among the representational modes are a crooked black line derived from a cross-section of a cooling duct of a Corvair engine, six diagrammatic arrows that might signify this cooling, and swatches of pinks and yellows that seem to represent abstract painting. As with prior tabular pictures, *Glorious Techniculture*

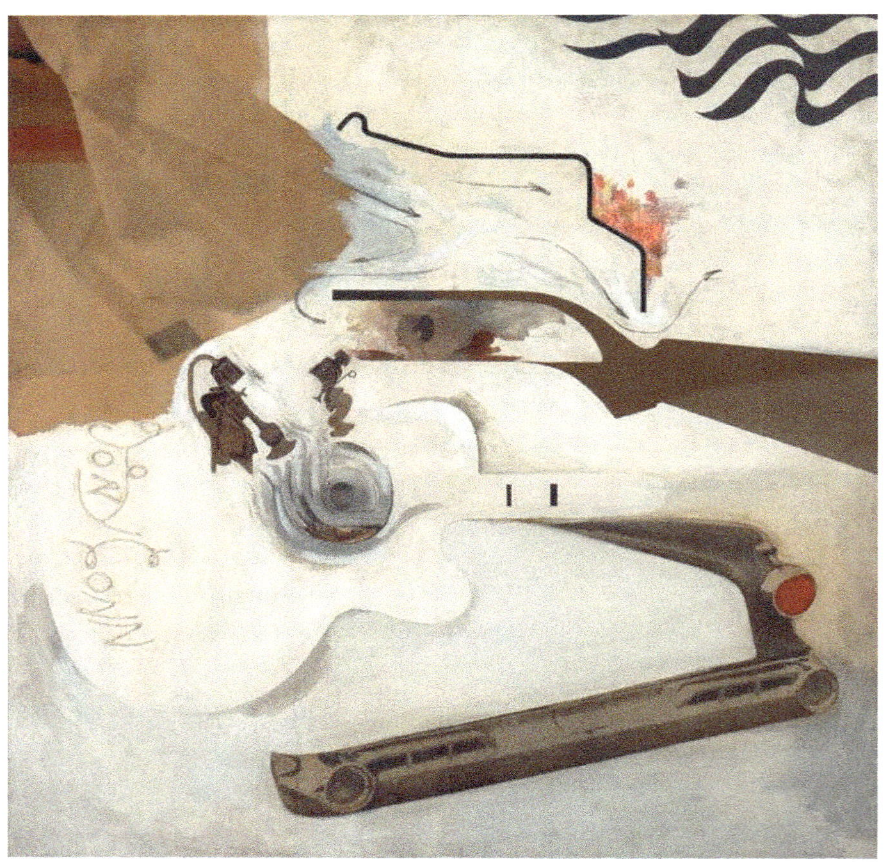

1.15 *Glorious Techniculture*, 1961–64. Oil and collage on asbestos panel, 48 × 48 in.

is essentially a Bachelor Machine, articulated here by the combination of car, rifle, and guitar. Established by a collaged print of the rear fender and fin of a Corvair, the car is framed by the profile of the rifle, which doubles as an interior that houses the Bride, who appears as a little female head, also in profile, with a windswept veil. Opposite her are two Bachelors in the guise of "robotic space men" produced from a cross-section of a car engine imprinted on the surface (with various parts painted out).[50] This weird face-off is doubled by that between the dark rifle on the right and the pale guitar

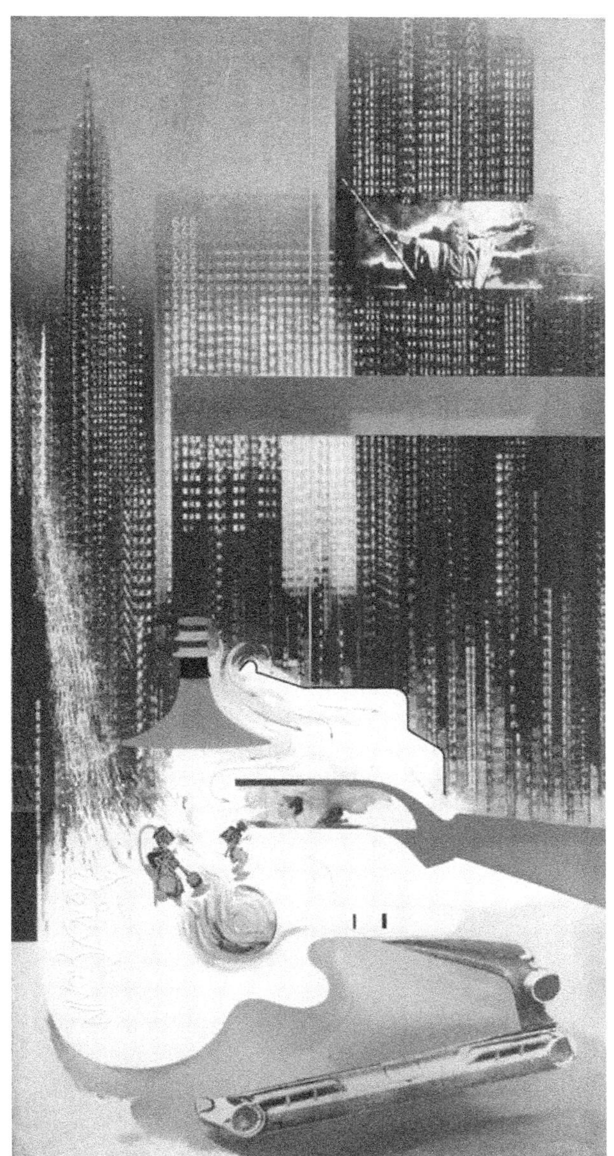

1.16 Original version of *Glorious Techniculture*, 1961.

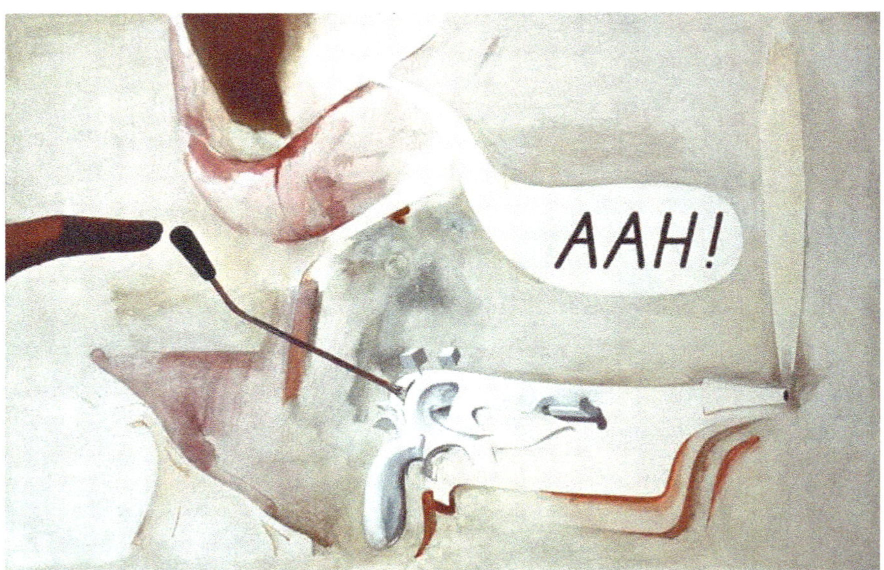

1.17 *AAH!* 1962. Oil on panel. 32 × 48 in.

on the left, its body decorated with the name of the rockabilly singer Tony Conn written cursively in string.

The "glorious techniculture" of the painting, then, is an America given over to flags, cars, and guns, an America that still runs on the myth of the West, old and new, as produced in New York and Hollywood. For Hamilton, the rifle is the key sign: "Guns and hunting is a branch of Pop mythology—symbol of the West, the great outdoors; in an urban context violence, gangsterism and one of the best-loved children's toys."[51] Provocatively, he juxtaposes it with the guitar and the car, as if to imply that the violence represented by the rifle is sublimated in the culture of country music and open-road cruising. This civilizing process has produced some gender confusion, too, for the gun is slight compared with the guitar, and the little Bachelors, as pathetic as any in Duchamp, seem content to bounce along as the joyous Bride drives. The different scales in this painting are indeed weird; they suggest a disorientation, even a delirium, which Hamilton associates with America.

The Bride in *AAH!* (fig. 1.17) is also in control, and her situation is even more lush. The primary shift is in scale, from the panorama of *Glorious Techniculture* to the close-up of a car interior. The source of *AAH!* is an advertisement in *Life* magazine for a 1955 Plymouth that shows a velvet glove on the knob of a transmission lever, the photographic focus so tight that the dashboard is blurred (fig. 1.18). In the painting, Hamilton reduces the hand to an index finger, elongates the lever, turns the transmission into a rifle (car and gun cultures are again associated), and renders the dash as a swirl of bodily reds, browns, pinks, and blues. "When I began work on the panel," Hamilton tells us, "the subject became plainly erotic. Much of the hedonism comes from the lush visual pleasure that only photographic lenses can provide" (44). This pleasure stems in particular from the tactility and visuality of different surfaces and spaces in various states of focus and blur: "Definition swings in and out along a lip length. A world of fantasy with unique erotic overtones. Intimacy, trespass, yet on a purely visual plane. Sensuality beyond the simple act of penetration—a dizzy drop into swoonlike coloured fuzz, clicked, detached and still, for appreciative analysis (50)." Captured here, Hamilton suggests, is the relation not only between photographic and painterly effects but also between such stimuli and our sensuous and sexual responses. Hamilton calls this mix of effects "phloo" (50), a fitting term for the protean nature of postwar reification discussed above, a mode of appearance that can seem seductively fluid, as it is here. At the same time, *AAH!* is an attempt to mitigate this condition, to de-reify line and color a little through the lush array of blurs and tints, to refunction phloo.[52]

Like *Glorious Techniculture*, *AAH!* also reflects on Pop mythology and technological fantasy. The female finger is about to touch the extended trigger of a rifle that is part "Isher weapon" (inspired by the 1951 sci-fi novel

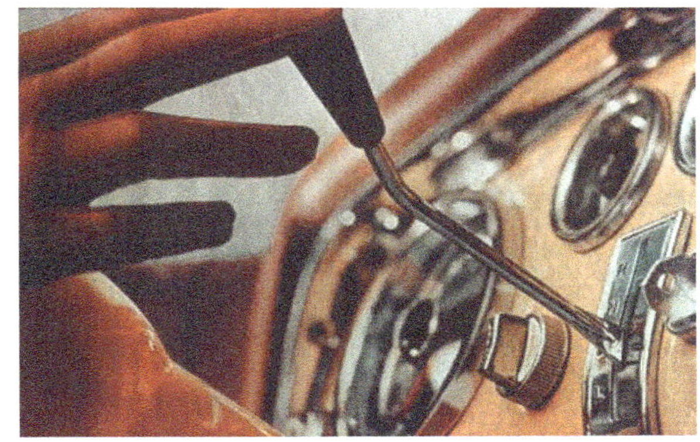

1.18 Source image for *AAH! Life* magazine, 1955.

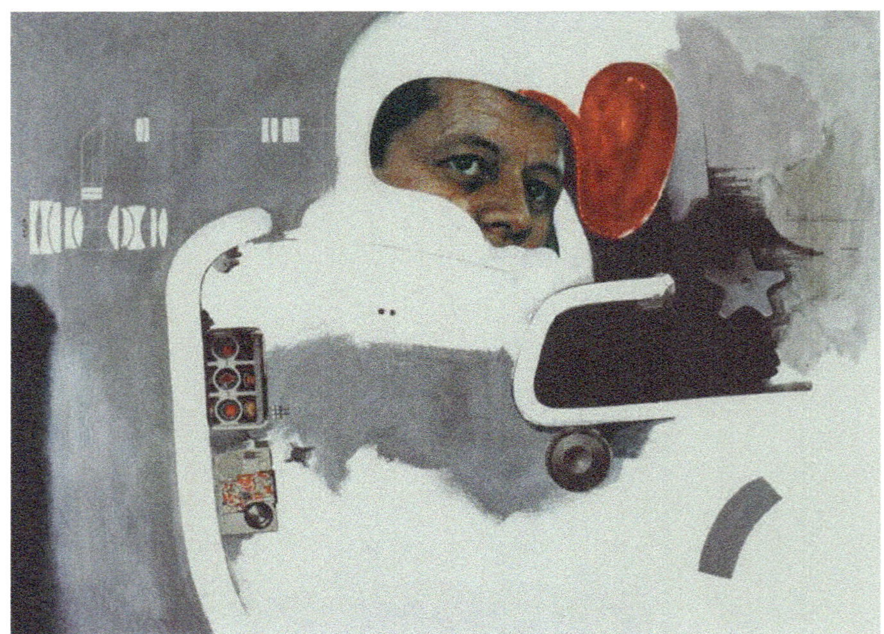

1.19 *Towards a definitive statement on the coming trends in men's wear and accessories (a) Together let us explore the stars*, 1962. Oil and collage on panel, 24 × 32 in.

The Weapon Shops of Isher by A. E. van Vogt) and part cigarette lighter (a Varaflame manufactured by Ronson). This hybrid is even more bizarre than the turntable-telephone in *Pin-up*, but more important here is the erotics of "fingertip control" that it evokes. In his introduction to "Man, Machine & Motion," Banham had underscored how the gearshift had progressed "from gloved grasp of massive lever to naked finger-touch on chromium plant-stem," and car design in general "from an approximate truce with mechanical forces to a pure creation of the human will—the driver no longer dresses for battle, but for the boudoir."[53] This new mediation of technological power also interests Hamilton, and his rendering of this control is at once mythic and comic. Like the God of the Sistine Chapel, the notional woman is about to activate a fantastic mechanism, and in this Bachelor Machine, the men are altogether displaced. The orgasmic flame emitted by the rifle seems to

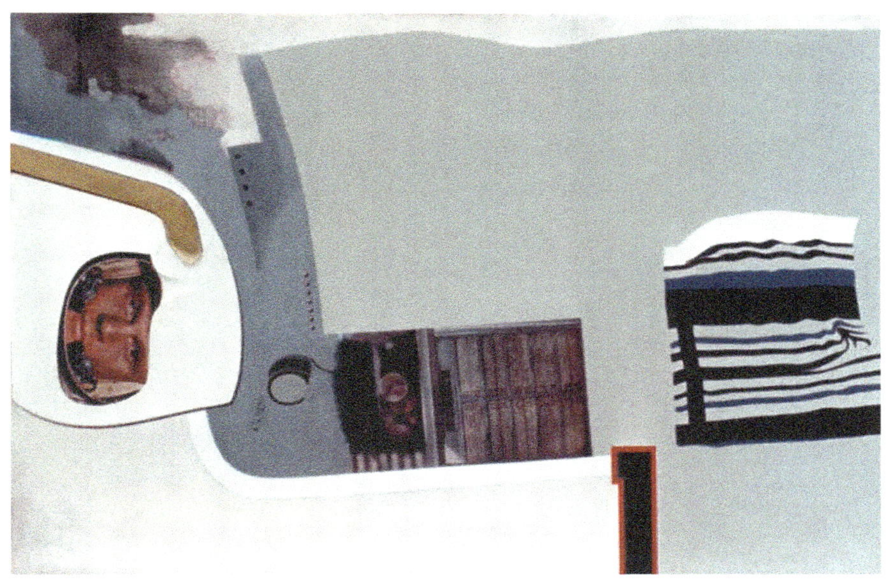

1.20 *Towards a definitive statement on the coming trends in men's wear and accessories (d)*, 1962. Oil, collage, and perspec relief on panel, 32 × 48 in.

be hers (perhaps it is a version of the blossoming of the Bride), as does the "comically dribbled sigh of ecstasy" in the speech balloon (*AAH!*). Even so, her desire is still fetishistically displaced onto a gadget, and the implication is that "fingertip control" is preferable to sex with any human partner.

In the tabular pictures, Hamilton foregrounds women as the key players in postwar consumer culture and uses this new position (which does not reverse the old subjection) as a way to update the female figure in painting. Exceptionally, however, he features men in *Towards a definitive statement on the coming trends in men's wear and accessories* (1962; figs. 1.19, 1.20), a suite of four paintings, the title of which also derives from a magazine, in this case an annual *Playboy* review of male fashion. Hamilton describes *Towards a definitive statement* as a "preliminary investigation into specific concepts of masculinity" (46): specifically, man in "a technological environment," as represented by a not yet assassinated President Kennedy; man in "a sporting ambience," as figured by a Wall Street broker-cum–football player; man in "some timeless aspect of male beauty," as typified by a Hermes-cum-muscleman; and finally, a combination of all three categories, as approximated by astronaut John Glenn (who, on February 20, 1962, became the first man to orbit the earth). Along with tokens of various systems of representation familiar from other tabular pictures, each figure is associated with a particular accessory—a transistor, a telephone, a chest expander, and a jukebox, respectively—which is to say, a particular mechanism of media, communications, exercise, and entertainment, all instruments of spectacle. (Might Hamilton anticipate here our own yoking to cell phones, Blackberries, iPods, and the like, our own status as servomechanistic Bachelor Machines? If so, it is with his usual "ironism of affirmation.")

This shift in gender in the tabular pictures is marked by a change not only in palette (fewer pinks and reds, more blues and grays) but also in accessories: the women appear at home or on display with consumer products, whereas the men appear at work or at play with active devices. Yet even as the women are commingled with their commodities, they appear relatively opened to the world through them, while even as the men are connected to their prostheses, they seem largely closed to the world—in a protected state, with bodies uniformed or heads helmeted, in spaces that are relatively airless.[54] At the same time, the men are as much slaves to fashion as the women are, and this common condition trumps the sexual difference remarked in the title.

"The pageant of fashion" was one of the prime subjects of modern painting for Baudelaire.[55] "By 'modernity,'" he writes in a famous line, "I mean the ephemeral, the fugitive, the contingent, the half of art whose other half is the eternal and the immutable." Yet these two halves are opposed dialectically, not directly: the artist is to seek the epic "in the passing moment," "to distill the eternal from the transitory."[56] Already in the time of Baudelaire, the alleged heroism of this modern life was in doubt; a part of Hamilton still wants to believe in it, however. Of his pageant of men in *Towards a definitive statement*, he writes, "We live in an era in which the epic is realized. Dream is compounded with action. Poetry is lived by an heroic technology" (40).[57] And it is there, in mass culture, that this heroism is to be sought: "Epic has become synonymous with a certain kind of film and the heroic archetype is now buried deep in movie lore. If the artist is not to lose much of his ancient purpose he may have to plunder the popular arts to recover the imagery which is his rightful inheritance" (42). This last line (which harks back to the Smithsons' mandate to "get the measure" of "the popular arts") speaks directly to the interrelationship between high and low, painting and pop, in Hamilton.

Tabular as Well as Pictorial

What, then, are the implications of the tabular picture? To begin with, the word (Hamilton is as particular about terms as he is about images) "tabular" derives from *tabula*, Latin for "table" but also for "writing tablet," in which, in ancient use, painting as well as printing figured as a mode of inscription. Surely this association appealed to Hamilton, who deploys both techniques in his practice (where printmaking is not necessarily secondary to painting); he does so in part because he finds the effects associated with them already imbricated in the media. "Tabular," then, also invokes writing, which Hamilton involves through his generative lists and programmatic titles. It connotes "tabloid" as well, a form that Hamilton takes up directly in *Swingeing London 67* (1968–69), a series of posters and paintings (discussed in the Introduction) based on press coverage of Mick Jagger and Robert Fraser arrested for drug possession. In addition, the tabular pictures contain traces of the visual-verbal hybrid characteristic of magazines and tabloids (as in the implicit narratives in *Hommage, Lush situation, $he, AAH!* and so on).[58] Perhaps in this regard, Hamilton anticipates the mixed sign of information and image that dominates electronic media space today, an often lush picture that carries an often insistent directive ("click here," "submit now," etc.).[59]

Most of the pictures are thus tabular in the sense that they are scripted by a table of terms, as with *Just what is it . . . ?*; of images, as in *Hommage* and *$he*; or of journalistic jingles, as in *Hers is a lush situation* or *Towards a definitive statement*. "To tabulate," the *OED* informs us, is "to set down in a systematic form." Clearly, Hamilton does this too, and not only at the level of content, for again, he is also concerned to effect a precise "overlapping of presentation styles and methods": styles and methods that are commercial, as in the various display techniques he evokes; modernist, as in the various abstract signs he cites; and modernist turned commercial, as in the elements of avant-garde art and mass culture that he treats as already "assimilated" (recall the "token suggestions of Mondrian and Saarinen" in the ad that underlies *Hommage*). In his own words, "photograph becomes diagram, diagram flows into text," and all are transformed by painting (38).[60] In effect, then, Hamilton conjures up a composite media-space in which capitalist exchange has turned once-distinct categories of representation into so many "floating signifiers" (in the late 1950s and early 1960s, this was an important insight, not the misunderstood cliché about postmodernism that it is today).[61] On the one hand, Hamilton wants these "plastic entities [to] retain their identity as tokens," which is one reason why he uses "different plastic dialects," such as photography, collage, and relief (38). On the other hand, he seeks "the unified whole" of painting (38) and uses the flow of its facture not only to connect the different bits but also to slow them down, as it were, for our critical review, which is one reason why Hamilton, for all his media interests, remains committed to painting. Like an adman, then, Hamilton tabulates (correlates) different media and messages, and tabulates (calculates) this correlation for its visual appeal and psychological effect. In so doing, he allows the possibility of "appreciative analysis" for viewers as well.[62]

The import of this redoubling of popular culture is much disputed in the literature on Pop art: when is it truly analytical, and when it is only appreciative, even charmed? This question is especially vexed with Hamilton, whose "ironism of affirmation" attempts to split this difference, to allow him to participate as an agent on both sides. "An art of affirmatory intention is not necessarily uncritical" (52), Hamilton insists, with a double negative that suggests the difficulty here. Certainly, this paradox often promotes a tension between investment in the image and distance from it, one that carries over to his viewers too. In any case, his pastiche (which is not a pejorative term for Hamilton) is not disruptively random, as it is in many collages in Dada or, for that matter, in the Neo-Dada of his peers Paolozzi and Rauschenberg.[63] Another insight of Pop (or "Son of Dada," as Hamilton calls it [42]) is that such "randomizing" had become, by this moment, a feature of the media at large, a logic of distraction within the repertoire of the culture industry.[64] Sometimes Hamilton pushes this logic of the random to a demonstrative extreme; at other times, his tabular pictures are logical in a different sense, one that is almost typological; at still other times, both operations are somehow at work together, as they are, for example, in *Towards a definitive statement*.

Here Hamilton differs most tellingly from his peers. With his British colleagues, he might share a tackboard aesthetic, but his practice is both more programmatic and more compositional than the Bunk collages of Paolozzi, the glutted screens of Henderson, or the striated collages of McHale. Again, intended as they are to test the assimilation of popular culture into "the fine-art tradition," the tabular pictures are necessarily *paintings*. His practice differs from his American peers on similar grounds. Especially in relation to works like *Towards a definitive statement*, Rauschenberg comes to mind, yet the tabular picture should not be confused with his "flatbed picture." For Leo Steinberg, who coined this term in his landmark essay "Other Criteria" (1968/72), Rauschenberg promoted a shift to a horizontal inscription of cultural images that broke with traditional paradigms of painting such as the window, the mirror, or indeed the abstract surface, all vertical frames to be looked at or through as onto a natural scene.[65] Like the flatbed picture, the tabular picture might appear horizontal both in the practical sense of how it is assembled in the studio, sometimes flat on a table or floor, and in the cultural sense that it scans images and texts across "the fine/pop art continuum."[66] Nevertheless, here again Hamilton insists on the pictorial, whereas Rauschenberg disrupts it: for all its horizontal tabulation of found images and texts, the tabular image remains a vertical picture of a semi-illusionistic space, even though this orientation is associated with the magazine layout or the media screen as much as with the painting rectangle.[67] "The newspaper is read more in the vertical than in the horizontal plane," Benjamin once remarked in a rapid genealogy of Western techniques of text and image, "while film and advertisement force the printed word entirely into the dictatorial perpendicular."[68] In part, Hamilton holds to the vertical plane in his pictures because he wants to address the "dictatorial perpendicular" of modern media like film and advertisement (this is most explicit, perhaps, in the original version of *Glorious Techniculture*).

There are other structural differences between Hamilton and Rauschenberg. In its very heterogeneity, the flatbed picture promotes a scattering of the gaze, a "vernacular glance" sometimes associated with the random connections and disconnections of urban as well as televisual space; the tabular picture, on the contrary, focuses our gaze even as it moves it about.[69] Also, the tabular picture is iconographic (maybe to a fault) in a manner that the flatbed picture is not (despite art-historical attempts to track down particular sources so as to impute particular meanings). Indeed, in keeping with his IG formation, Hamilton is communicative, almost pedagogical, in his work, again in a way that Rauschenberg is not; the former has a cognitive purpose, while the latter does not (Steinberg speaks of the "schizophrenic" effects of Rauschenberg combines). Above all, Hamilton holds on to depth—depth that is at once pictorial, psychological, hermeneutic, and historical—whereas his American colleagues tend to dissolve it. In short, there is no American equivalent to the tabular picture that I know.[70] Nor is there a European parallel; for example, the tabular picture attests to systematic research into specific types of cultural images, not an "anomic archive" of a wide range of such images, as suggested by the *Atlas* compendium of photographs by Gerhard Richter.[71]

The cognitive purpose here is key. With the spread of mechanical reproduction in the first Machine Age, László Moholy-Nagy asserted in 1928 (to be seconded by Benjamin in 1931), the test of literacy must include the decoding of captioned photographs.[72] Additionally, in the first Pop Age, Hamilton suggests, literacy must also involve the deconstructing of the mediated image-word that hails us variously from billboards, magazines, tabloids, movies, televisions, and other screens. Of course, this literacy is fundamental to postwar self-fashioning, which has to do far less with any "Great Tradition" of literature and art (as cultural elders such as F. R. Leavis and Clement Greenberg still hoped) than with a diffuse host of commodity signs and media apparitions of the sort that Hamilton lists as his sources—from magazine spreads to Hollywood movies, from Vikky Dougan to John Glenn.[73] Suggestively, in ancient use, the word "tabular" also refers to "a body of laws inscribed on a tablet" (*OED*). Might we understand these tabular pictures as almost pedagogical investigations of a "new body of laws," a new subjective inscription, a new symbolic order, that informs pop society?[74]

Hamilton is self-aware about the preconditions of this new order. Committed to nature, he nonetheless knows that it is "second-hand": "In the '50s we became aware of the possibility of seeing the whole world, at once, through the great visual matrix that surrounds us; a synthetic, 'instant' view. Cinema, television, magazines, newspapers immersed the artist in a total environment and this new visual ambience was photographic" (64). Certainly, he does not attack this second nature from an imagined outside, yet neither does he submit to it. So, too, committed to the figure (his *Collected Words* ends with this statement: "I have never made a painting which does not show an intense awareness of the human figure" [269]), he knows that it is also transformed—not only rearticulated by machines and confused with commodities but designed and redesigned as an image-product as well.[75] Yet here again he neither embraces nor rejects this condition.

Consumer society, Hamilton writes in "Persuading Image," an essay first delivered as a lecture in 1959, depends on the manufacturing of desire through design, on an artificial, accelerated obsolescence of image, form, and style.[76] In this process, the consumer is also "manufactured," designed to the product. "Is it *me?*" Hamilton remarks of the commodities in *$he*, mimicking the adman playing to the buyer: "The appliance is 'designed with you in mind'" (36). The tabular pictures set out to describe and to work over this condition—not only the fetishistic-sublimatory conflation of different objects and aims, but also the social interpellation of subjects by images, in images, indeed *as* images. Today this process has become all but natural to us, each of us, as Hamilton had forecast, a "specialist in the look of things" (136), designer and designed in one, a near servomechanism of consumption.[77] The tabular pictures allow us to step back from this process and to see it analytically.

Hamilton explores this condition most directly in his own version of the great Pop icon Marilyn Monroe, made after his 1963 visit to the States (his first). In *My Marilyn* (1965; fig. 1.21), he adapts, in painting, part of a contact sheet from a photo shoot (by George Barris) that includes her own editorial indications as to which images to cut and what pose to permit—in

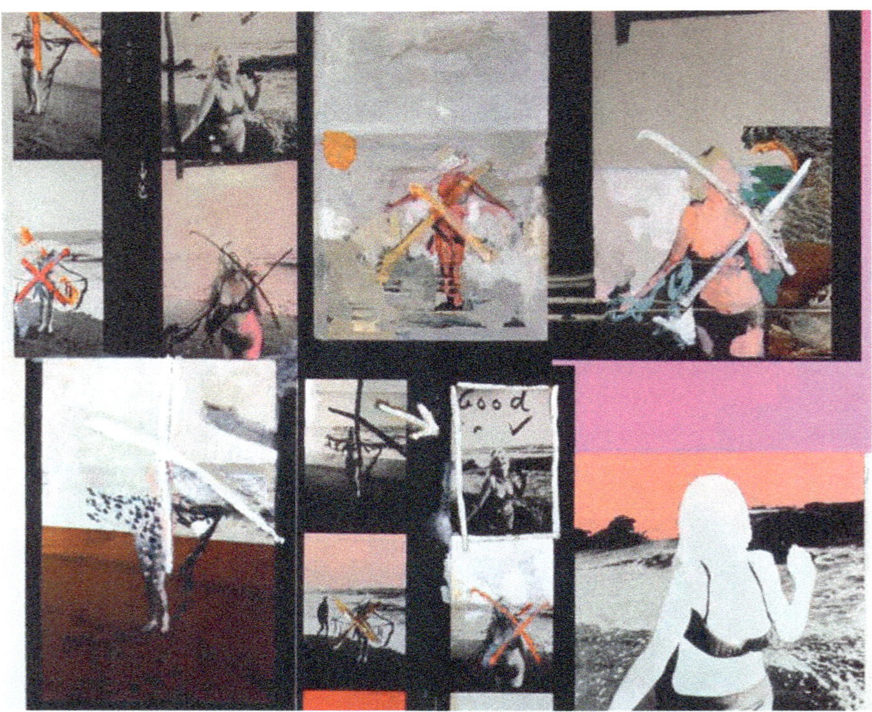

1.21 *My Marilyn*, 1965. Oil and collage on photograph on panel, 40½ × 48 in.

short, how to look, to appear, *to be*.[78] In the rough grid of the painting, a cluster of four images appears twice, with slightly different markings and croppings, once at upper left and again, a little smaller, at center bottom; each of the images also appears, enlarged, with additional alterations by Hamilton, in the other rectangles of the painting. The most dramatic changes are wrought on the one image approved by Marilyn (marked "good"): here the color is that of a deteriorated photograph (the sky and the sea are two bands of lurid pink and orange), and her body is whited out, as if in negative, as though she were already absent (as indeed she was in 1965). The Marilyn commemorated by Hamilton is still a star, but she is less an erotic object than an anxious designer—the stringent artist of her own powerful iconicity. As we can see in the painting, she is a merciless editor of her appearance, and perhaps Hamilton identifies with this editorial rigor; in any case, the implication is that, in the Pop age, being *is* imaging. This relation to Monroe is very different—more pointed, more poignant—than the agitation usually acted out by de Kooning or the thralldom often suggested by Warhol.[79]

Here Hamilton elaborates not only on the semiotic "possibilities" that Marilyn offers up (apparently she would mark her contact sheets with whatever was at hand—lipstick, nail-file, scissors) but also on the psychological states that she evokes—which range, in his words, from the "narcissistic" to the "self-destructive" (65). All at once, Marilyn appears to desire, even to solicit, the gaze (that the gaze of others be captured is, of course, the sine qua non of celebrity), and to fear, even to refuse, the gaze (rightly so, perhaps, given that her masochistic marking seems to anticipate our invasive looking, which might be partly sadistic even when it wishes to be wholly sympathetic). In this regard, *My Marilyn* asks to be compared with that other great essay on the problematic glare of celebrity visibility, *Swingeing London 67* of three years later.

Just as a product is often in excess of function, as Hamilton suggests in his essay "Persuading Image," so demand is often in excess of need. In effect, he sketches a consumerist formula of *demand – need = desire*, one that is not distant from the formula of desire that Lacan developed in the 1950s. In this light, might the Lacanian definition of desire also be historically grounded, a theory of desire inflected by consumerism? Again, the tabular pictures seem to share the Lacanian sense of desire as a metonymic slippage, at once fetishistic and sublimatory, from image to image, a finding of similar objects in ever-new guises. In this respect, the tabular picture not only anthologizes "presentation techniques" but also mimics the distracted attention of the desirous viewer-consumer. Thus, its painterly subsumption of photography, collage, and relief might not seem to be so conservative after all—conservative, say, in relation to the usual reading of Dada as transgressive (about which Hamilton is skeptical in any case, especially regarding accounts of Duchamp). As noted, he assumes the fetishistic effects of traditional bourgeois painting, not to mention of other devices, both modernist (like collage and relief) and commercial (like the magazine spread). He recognizes that all these forms are reworked in a general economy of fetishism—commodity, sexual, and semiotic—and he moves to exploit this new order, which is one of appearance as well as of exchange, and in so doing, sometimes to deconstruct it too.[80] Painting allows for the requisite mixing not only of charged details with blended anatomies, but also of the optical jumpiness of the subject with the erotic smoothness of the object. It is this unresolved combination that makes his early paintings both pull apart and hold together compositionally (this is also true of Warhol, as we will see in chapter 3).[81]

Finally, how does this effect jibe with traditional painting—that is, how does the tabular relate to the tableau? Again, the inaugural move away from the collage practice of *Just what is it . . . ?* means that painting is a primary frame of reference for the tabular pictures. All the media formats and codes in play here (ads, pinups, film stills, photo shoots, and tabloid images) test easel painting, and the core of this test is to see how well the old genres of painting, such as the nude, the still life, and the interior, can absorb these other materials. There is a double risk here: on the one hand, the tableau might be overwhelmed by these materials (as many critics of Pop believed); on the other, these materials might be simply returned to techniques and traditions associated with the tableau. However, the former is not the case with Hamilton, and the latter is not as reactive as it might appear. Indeed, Hamilton believes that painting remains the best way to reflect on new media as they emerge, and it is for this reason above all others that he remains committed to the tableau.

Yet Hamilton has additional motives. "In the mainstream of Western painting (since the Greeks, anyway)," he wrote in 1970, "it has been taken for granted that a painting is to be experienced as a totality seen and understood all at once before its components are examined." "Some twentieth-century artists questioned this premise," he adds, with the heteroglossic pictures of Klee and the prototabular *Glass* of Duchamp foremost in mind (104). Clearly Hamilton is affined with this minor line ("minor" in the sense less of secondary than of insubordinate).[82] But just as clearly, he is also committed to the dominant tradition of painting "as a totality seen and understood all at once"—a tradition that runs, if not from the Greeks, then from Renaissance perspective through the neoclassical tableau to the "modernist painting" championed by Clement Greenberg and Michael Fried (Cézanne, Picasso, Mondrian, Pollock). Moreover, in his own time, in figures like Paolozzi and Rauschenberg, Hamilton saw this dominant tradition cross with his own genealogy, and in the end, the tableau and the tabular might not be so distinct. Indeed, this is how these lines appear in his pictures, which are "views" that are both "instant" and "synthetic" (as Hamilton says, almost oxymoronically). On the one hand, he is committed to the "static" nature of painting (again, so technophilic an artist would have moved on otherwise), and he cherishes its capacity "to project very forcibly a significant instant"—a formulation not distant from the fabled ideal of "the pregnant moment" variously espoused by Gotthold Lessing, Denis Diderot, and others, though Hamilton prefers the term "epiphany" (which he adapts from his beloved James Joyce).[83]

On the other hand, from the early abstractions through the tabular pictures (and beyond), Hamilton is also concerned with the disturbances that arise from movement, and this perceptual interest pressures his epiphanic ideal (which would also seem to be in tension with his interest in Duchampian "delay," let alone "appreciative analysis"). Moreover, in Hamilton as in Joyce, the epiphanic is sometimes riven internally, cleaved by desire and disappointment alike: it is a moment of transcendence that cannot help but pass, even fail. In fact, the epiphanic, once disappointed, can come to debunk the very perfection that it otherwise proposes, in which case, even as the low is brought high, the high is brought low. (This banal high is conveyed by the button slogan "Slip It To Me," which Hamilton found in Venice, California, on his 1963 sojourn, enlarged massively, painted in eye-popping orange and blue, and titled *Epiphany* [1964; fig. 1.22]).[84] So, too, the transpositional logic of so much of his work—many Hamilton images develop not only as sequences (as in *Towards a definitive statement*) but also across mediums ("the processing," as Hamilton puts it, "through photography and printing and back into painting" [62])—pressures his epiphanic ideal. Both the seriality and the exchangeability of the mass image thus complicate his picturing.

In this way, then, Hamilton articulates a convergence, in pictorial spectatorship, between epiphanic presentness and everyday distraction. This

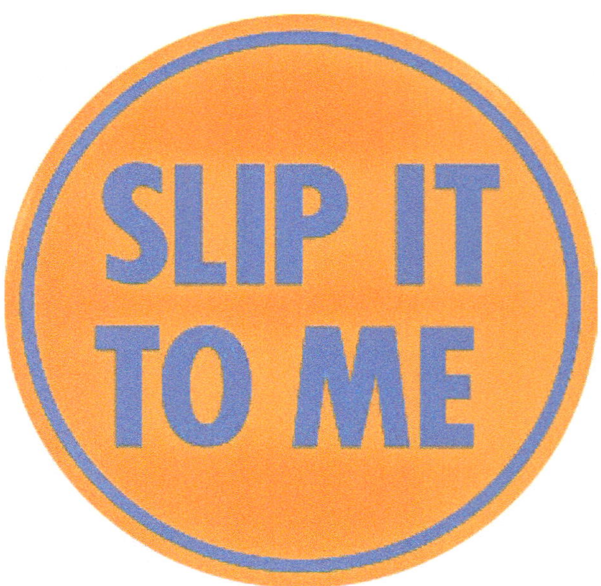

1.22 *Epiphany*, 1964. Cellulose on panel, 48 in. diameter.

convergence is a historical process involving a new formation of the consumerist subject within postwar culture. In "Other Criteria," for instance, Steinberg argues that, for all its claim to autonomy, late-modernist abstraction (such as the stripe paintings of Kenneth Noland and Frank Stella) is driven by a logic of design, in fact by the very logic of Detroit styling so admired by Banham and Hamilton—imagistic impact, fast lines, speedy turnover, and so on—or, in other words, that an ironic identity is forged, under the historical pressure of consumer society, between modernist painting and its other term, whether this other is called "kitsch" (as it was by Greenberg), "theatricality" (by Fried), or "design" (by Banham and Hamilton).[85] In effect, Hamilton recognizes and reflects on this condition for us. In this regard, what Greenberg and Fried theorize as a "strictly optical" space of pure painting, Hamilton pictures as a mostly scopophilic space of applied design; and what Greenberg and Fried theorize as a modernist subject, fully autonomous and "morally alert," Hamilton projects as its apparent opposite, a fetishistic subject openly desirous and perceptually distracted.[86] This is another Pop insight, one that Hamilton shares with Roy Lichtenstein in particular (as we will see in chapter 2): by the moment of Pop, there is often no great difference, in either compositional order or subjective effect, between a good comic or ad and a grand painting. Importantly, however, this demonstration of the decay of the totality unique to painting is made *within* painting, for only there is it fully articulate. Paradoxically, then, this demonstration sustains painting even as it shows painting to be deconstructed, within and without, by historical forces.[87] In 1865, Baudelaire wrote to Manet, in an ambiguous compliment, that he, Manet, was the first in the "decrepitude" of his art.[88] One hundred years later, Hamilton brought this fine tradition of popular decrepitude to a climax.

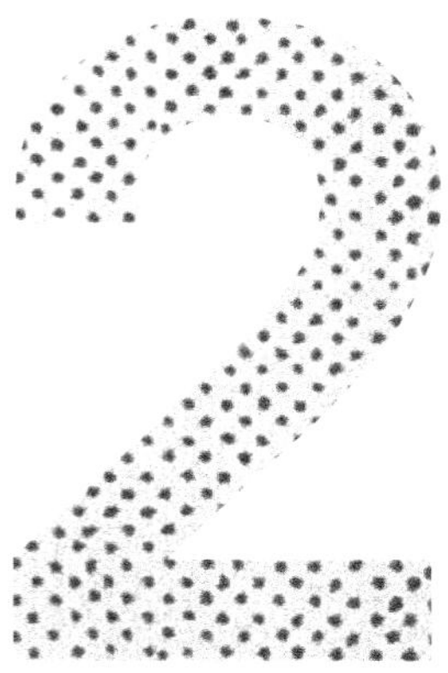

Roy Lichtenstein, or the Cliché Image

"What Lichtenstein makes perfectly clear is that all his subjects are made as one before he touches them," Richard Hamilton wrote in 1968. "Parthenon, Picasso or Polynesian maiden are reduced to the same kind of cliché by the syntax of print: reproducing a Lichtenstein is like throwing a fish back into water."[1] These two artists so crucial to the development of Pop art share the resource of popular culture, of course, but in his brief essay on his peer, Hamilton points to two other affinities as well: like Hamilton, Lichtenstein is concerned less with the object in the world than "with the style of its intermediary treatment," and "the image is always treated as a totality."[2] Here again we confront the seeming paradox of a double commitment to the mediated nature of the mass image and to the immediate unity of the traditional painting. For Lichtenstein, too, to use the mass image to test the tableau was the best way to advance his art—in this respect his painting is also in line with the painting of modern life—and, as Hamilton suggests, the cliché was his primary means of doing so.

The story is now well known. In the late 1950s, Lichtenstein tried out various expressionistic and abstract idioms, with only a hint of popular

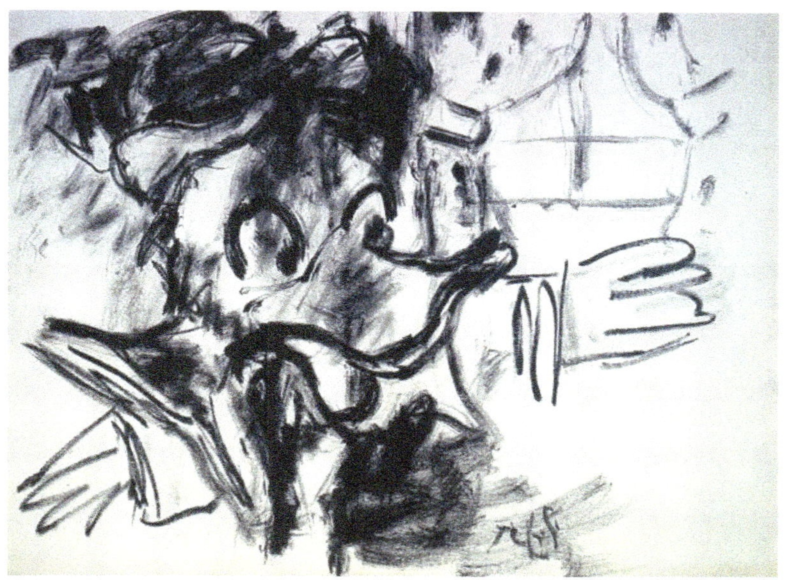

2.1 *Donald Duck*, 1958. India ink on paper, 19¾ × 24½ in.

imagery, such as a smudgy head of Mickey Mouse, Donald Duck, or Bugs Bunny, in some drawings toward the end of this period (fig. 2.1). In fall 1960, he began to teach at Douglass College of Rutgers University in New Jersey, not far from New York, and in this new context, which included colleagues like Allan Kaprow and Robert Watts, who were involved (or were about to be) with the use of everyday objects in Happenings and in Fluxus activities, his way of working changed.[3] In spring 1961, Lichtenstein started to paint pictures based on cartoons and advertisements taken from tabloid newspapers and similar sources—familiar characters like Mickey and Popeye, generic products like tennis shoes and golf balls, and, a little later, domestic appliances like washing machines and refrigerators—all in the clean and cool manner soon to be associated (largely through his example) with Pop art at large.[4]

In February 1962, when Lichtenstein first showed these paintings at the Leo Castelli Gallery in New York, he was charged with "banality"—no term was more pronounced in the initial reception of his work or of Pop in general—and when Lichtenstein focused on paintings based on melodramatic comic strips of war and romance, this condemnation grew only more shrill.[5] Not only did his impersonal surfaces appear to reject the subjective depths of Abstract Expressionism, but his superficial subject matter also seemed to ridicule the very profundity of art, its ethical import as well as its cultural importance, and mainstream critics, who had come around to Jackson Pollock and company, were not pleased by this turn of events.[6] In 1949, *Life* had showcased Pollock under the banner "Is He the Greatest Living Painter in the United States?"; in 1964, the same magazine profiled Lichtenstein under the heading "Is He the Worst Artist in the U.S.?" The question was not entirely tongue-in-cheek: many supporters of contemporary art were upset to see cartoon characters and everyday products in the metaphysical spaces recently reserved for the numinous rectangles of Mark Rothko and the epiphanic zips of Barnett Newman.

The charge of banality directed at Lichtenstein concentrated initially on his Pop subject matter. It was long accepted that modern artists had poached on popular culture (at least since Courbet, even well before), but they had done so, it was thought, mostly to reinvigorate the staid forms of high painting with the feisty contents of low images—that is, in a manner redemptive of the low, which could be justified, even admired. With Lichtenstein, on the other hand, the low content appeared to overrun the high form, despite his repeated insistence that he was a "classical" artist with "traditional" concerns, one who wanted only to adapt his popular sources to the parameters of fine art (this is another key purpose held in common with Hamilton).[7] And as we will see, Lichtenstein did not put his vulgar materials to very contrarian purposes, at least not in formal terms.

Critics soon targeted his Pop procedure, too, which appeared, if anything, worse than banal. Since Lichtenstein appeared to reproduce his cartoons, ads, and comics directly—in fact they were always modified, sometimes extensively—he was thought to lack originality altogether, and in one often-cited instance, he was accused outright of copyright infringement. (In 1962, Lichtenstein modeled a few paintings on diagrams of portraits by Cézanne made by an art historian named Erle Loran in 1943 [fig.

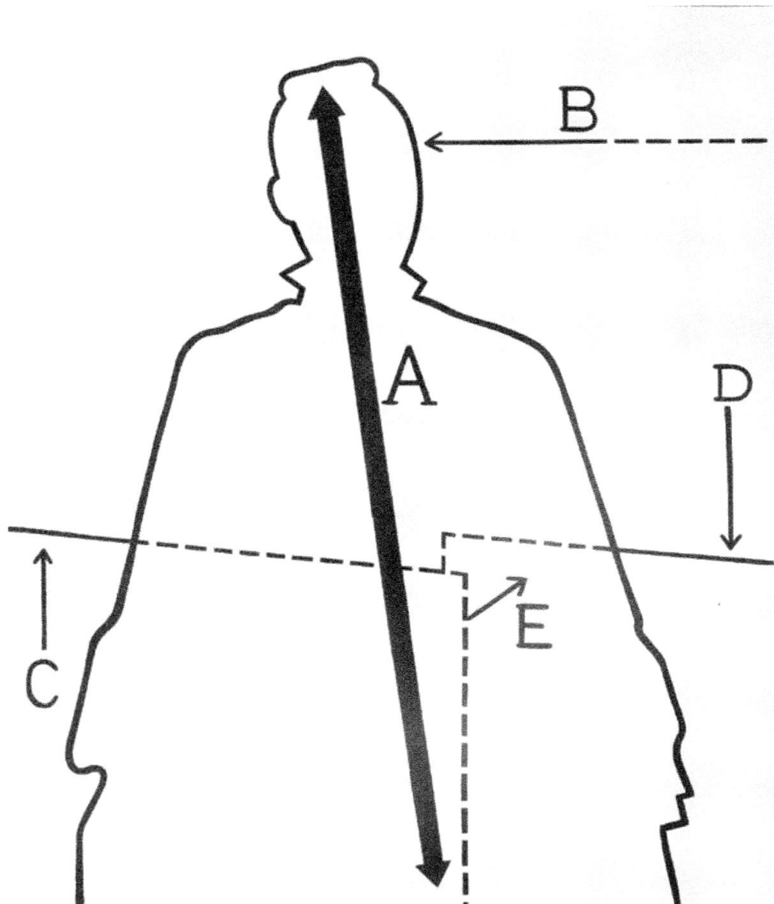

2.2 *Portrait of Madame Cézanne*, 1962. Magna on canvas, 68 × 56 in.

2.2]; a year later, Loran surfaced to protest loudly in simultaneous articles in the art press.)[8] Lichtenstein did copy, it is true, but in a complicated fashion. Typically in the case of the comics, he would select one or more panels from a strip, sketch one or more motifs from these panels, then project his drawing (never the comic) on a canvas with an opaque projector, trace the image in pencil with alterations along the way (usually involving a further

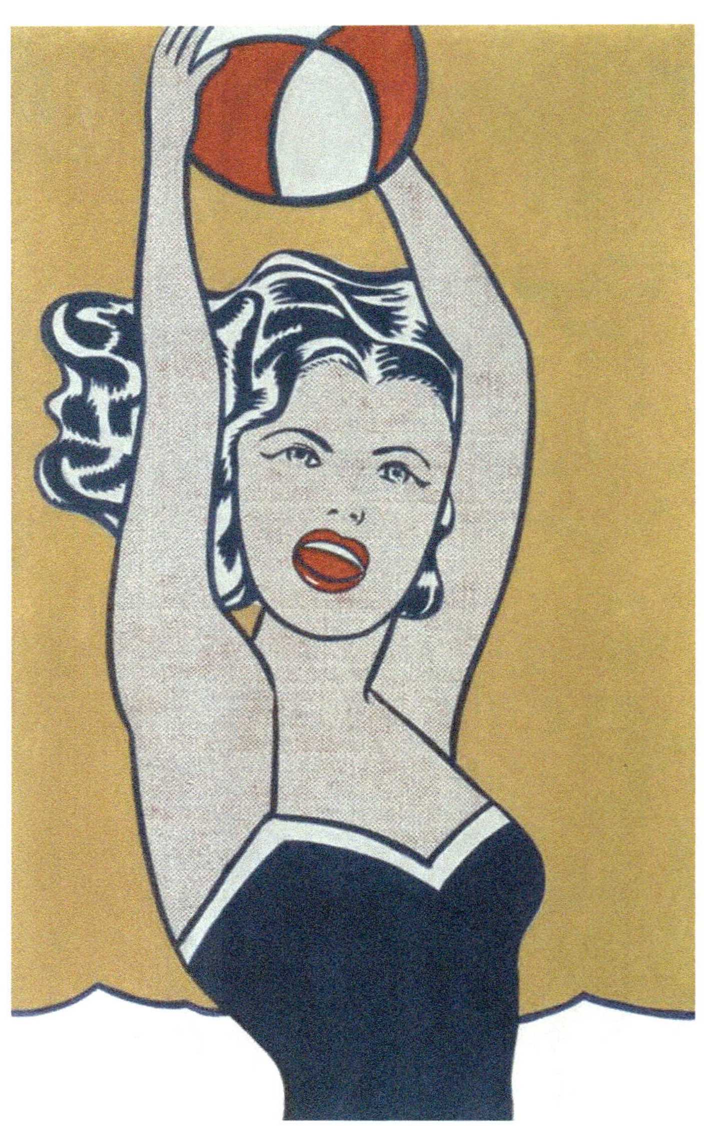

2.3 *Girl with Ball*, 1961. Oil on canvas, 60½ × 36½ in.

suppressing of details and flattening of figures), and then fill in his stenciled dots, primary colors, assorted words (often based on the speech bubbles and onomatopoeic exclamations in the comics), and thick contours—the lighter ground of the dots first, the heavier black of the outlines last (the paintings based on ads were produced in similar fashion: figs. 2.3, 2.4).[9] Thus, while a Lichtenstein painting might appear industrially fabricated, it is actually a layering of mechanical reproduction (comic), handwork (drawing), mechanical reproduction again (projector), and handwork again (tracing, masking, painting), to the point that distinctions between the manual and the mechanical are very difficult to recover. This confounding of the handmade and the readymade, the painterly and the photographic, is effected by most Pop artists, but it is especially thorough in Lichtenstein.[10] Where, for example, are we to locate his stenciled dots on the manual-mechanical continuum? As is well known, they evoke the so-called Benday dots devised by Benjamin Day in 1879 as a technique to reproduce an image through gradations of shading translated into a system of marks. Yet

even as they conjure up this mechanical process of halftone printing, the Lichtenstein dots are always painted; they thus crystallize the Pop paradox of "the handmade readymade."[11] By the early 1960s, the Benday technique was already old-fashioned; it appears in Lichtenstein, then, as a cliché in its own right, and at this remove, it is more than his signature device—it typifies the characteristic operation of his work. This is to suggest, finally, that the Pop image is never as quick and easy as it first appears, and that Lichtenstein in particular, rather than only reiterate the clichéd appearance of his source images, was concerned both to exploit and to complicate it.

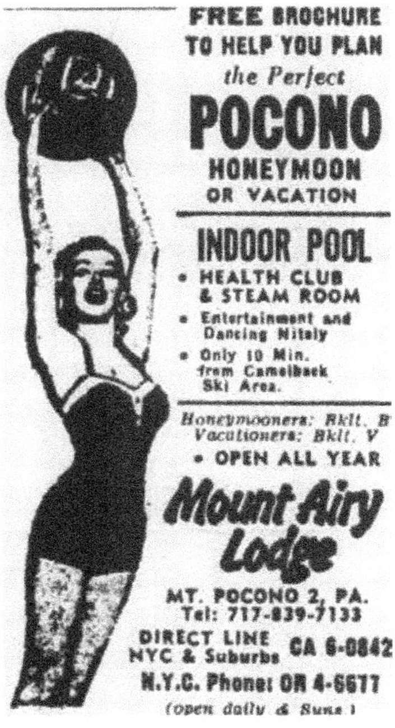

2.4 Source image for *Girl with Ball. New York Times*, 1961.

What I Do Is Form

In 1963, with the accusation of copying in mind, Lichtenstein made this important statement concerning his sources: "What I do is form, whereas the comic strip is not formed in the sense I'm using the word; the comics have shapes, but there has been no effort to make them intensely unified. The purpose is different, one intends to depict and I intend to unify. And my work is actually different from comic strips in that every mark is really in a different place, however slight the difference seems to some. This difference is often not great, but it is crucial."[12] Forming and unifying are, of course, the fundamental concerns of pictorial composition as historically conceived. Alone among early reviewers, Donald Judd, no friend of conventional composition in his emergent work, highlighted this classical aspect of Lichtenstein. "Ironically," Judd wrote in response to the 1962 show at Castelli, "the composition is expert, and some of it is quite traditional."[13] Four years later, Lichtenstein stressed a related point: "I don't feel that my space is anything but traditional"; and again, in a longer view a decade on, he insisted: "The kind of unity that holds the painting together is really the same whether it's done by Rembrandt or David or Picasso or Oldenburg. There's really not that much difference, there never really was."[14] In this remark, Lichtenstein explicitly aligns his painting with the classical tableau and so discloses a primary stake of his practice: to demonstrate that his low sources might be made to serve the same lofty goals set for high painting throughout the long modern period—goals not only of pictorial unity and dramatic focus (associated with the Enlightenment thinkers Diderot and Lessing) but also of "significant form" and "the integrity of the picture plane" (associated with the Anglo-American formalists Clive Bell and Clement Greenberg).[15] This commitment to the tradition of the tableau recalls Hamilton; yet where the different materials and methods in his tabular pictures remain evident as such, pressuring the paradigm of the tableau, Lichtenstein resolves his appropriated elements into a uniform order of facture as well as composition. Clearly, this uniformity distinguishes his work, too, from the disruptive heterogeneity of works by immediate predecessors like Robert Rauschenberg and Jasper Johns, not to mention close peers like his Rutgers associates: in its formal unity, his painting elicits a focused gaze, not the "vernacular glance" that is associated with the "flatbed pictures" of Rauschenberg, let alone the distracted spectatorship effected by Happenings.[16] In effect, Lichtenstein proposes his own model of painting: not strictly a vertical aperture, as in the old window and mirror paradigms (which Hamilton retains with revisions), yet also not a "flat documentary surface that tabulates information" (as elaborated by Rauschenberg, Johns, and others), but rather an unexpected combination of the two—painting as an image that both diagrams a semi-illusionistic space and insists on its already-screened surface.[17]

Yet why this emphasis on forming and unifying, in which regard Lichtenstein exceeds all other Pop artists, including Hamilton? Why abide by such traditional norms of pictorial composition, ones that, as Lichtenstein implies, govern much modernist painting as well? "My work is involved with organization," he insisted in 1966, and then added: "I don't want it to appear to be involved in this."[18] Clearly, Lichtenstein does not seek formal unity for its own sake alone; it also exists as a foil for his brash Pop elements—not only his trashy subject matter, but also his mostly consistent dots, thick lines, and artificial colors, all of which are treated as if transformed, once and for all, by the sea change of mechanical reproduction. Lichtenstein extends this bringing together of high form and low content to his sculpture as well: just as he plays with traditional genres in his painting (where one finds figures, still lifes, landscapes, seascapes, interiors, and studio scenes), so does he recast the bust as a painted shop mannequin, the still life as a diner coffee cup and saucer, and so on. Critically, however, his juxtaposition of high and low modes is not only framed but also controlled by his double attention to compositional norms and traditional genres: Lichtenstein might not redeem his low content entirely, but he also does not seek to desublimate the high forms of painting and sculpture as Warhol and Claes Oldenburg do (here again he is closer to Hamilton). If there remains a critical edge in his work, it lies here—less in his thematic appropriation of cartoons, ads, and comics, and more in his formal superimposition of high and low modes. Even as Lichtenstein indicates how intimate these two orders of culture had become by the 1960s (certainly, he exploits the proximity as well as the distance between them), he never fully reconciles the two; again, as he says, "the difference is often not great, but it is crucial."

This juxtaposition is hardly his alone; both historically and aesthetically, Lichtenstein is flanked by Johns on one side and Warhol on the other. However, with Johns, the proposition that a vulgar image like a barroom target could hold its own, pictorially, with the high pathos of a drip painting by Pollock was ironic, with the light provocation that such irony entails. (As Leo Steinberg remarked in 1963, the Johns targets, flags, and numbers met the Greenbergian criteria for modernist painting—that it be flat, self-contained, objective, immediate—by means that Greenberg found utterly alien to such painting, the everyday images and objects of mass culture.)[19] In contrast, with Warhol, the repeated appearance, in the exalted space of such painting, of a murky news-service photo of a gruesome car crash or a poisoned housewife is scabrous, and its subversive edge still cuts. Lichtenstein takes up the ironic line of Johns and intensifies it, yet not to the point that, as with Warhol, the question of painting becomes all but moot. As with Warhol, his juxtaposition of high and low registers might shock, but only in the first instance; as with Johns, it is the unexpected fit between tableau and its cultural others (cartoon, ad, or comic) that counts—a fit that, paradoxically, disturbs both terms. In this way, Lichtenstein confounds, perhaps more thoroughly than any predecessor or peer, the oppositions on which much modernist painting is structured, oppositions not only of high and low but also of abstract and representational. As Judd commented in his 1962 review, "Lichtenstein's comics and advertisements destroy the necessity to which the usual definitions pretend."[20]

In this light, consider *Golf Ball* (1962; fig. 2.5), a simple circle outlined in black on white and dotted with various marks (some in white, most in black) that signify the dimples of the ball in light and shadow, all set on a light gray ground. A prime token of suburban leisure, a golf ball is an iconic object that is easy to recognize (the source image is a tiny newspaper ad), and yet, as others have noted, the Lichtenstein version recalls the plus-and-minus abstractions of Mondrian (from 1914–18), also painted in black-and-white.[21] On the one hand, the abstract quality of *Golf Ball* tests our understanding of representation, which, here as elsewhere, Lichtenstein

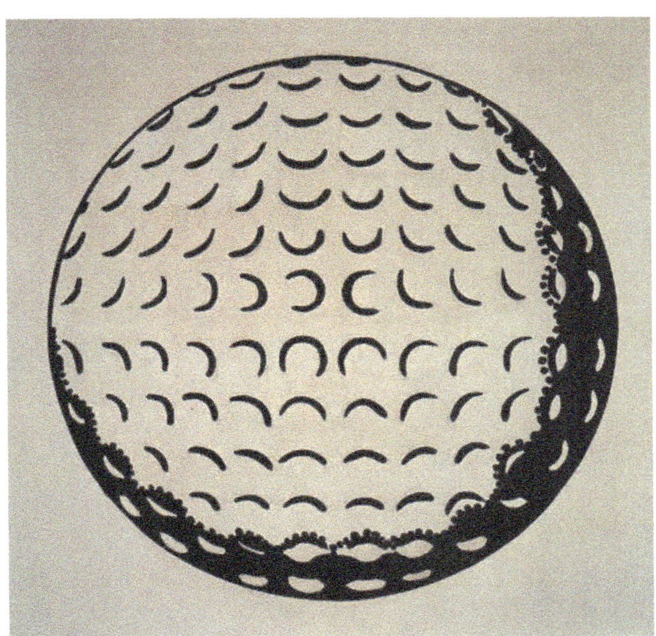

2.5 *Golf Ball*, 1962. Oil on canvas, 32 × 32 in.

shows to be a conventional code, a matter of signs that often bear little resemblance to actual things. (During this period, he may have read *Art and Illusion* [1960], in which Ernst Gombrich argues, influentially, that in the Western tradition of painting, "making" preceded "matching"—that is, that artists followed the codes of representation, the "schema" for making, given to them by artistic precedents, before they matched the results against worldly appearance.)[22] On the other hand, when a Mondrian begins to look like a golf ball, then the category of abstraction, indeed of aesthetic autonomy, is also in trouble. If modernist painters like Mondrian worked to resolve the figure in the painting into the ground of the medium, to check spatial depth with material flatness, Lichtenstein stresses both equally—figure and ground, the illusion of space and the fact of surface, the iconic and the nonobjective—in a juxtaposition that, again, is never quite a reconciliation.[23]

Lichtenstein thus short-circuits such apparent oppositions as mechanical and manual procedures, low and high categories, representational and abstract forms, all of which are turned into ambiguous doubles or unstable relays. We have already touched on a fourth instance of this unsettling: often his work delivers both the mediated look of the print image and the immediate effect of the modernist painting. In this regard, consider another early canvas, *Popeye* (1961; fig. 2.6), which shows the spinach-powered sailor knocking out his cartoon rival Bluto with a roundhouse left. The painting is sometimes read as an allegory of the Pop upstart taking the Abstract Expressionist tough to the canvas with a single blow, yet what is crucial here is the pictorial blow, not the narrative content (Lichtenstein often plays down the source story in the interest of the painting "as a totality"): arguably as instantaneous in its impact as a Pollock, *Popeye* smacks the viewer in the head as well.[24] Thus, at the level of subject-effect, too, Lichtenstein suggests that a Pop painting might not be so different from a modernist one like a Pollock (or, for that matter, given the two simple bands of yellow and red here, like a Color Field painting), that, for all its mediation, both at its source and in his treatment, his painting might project a similar sort of viewer, one who takes in the work in a single flash, an immediate "pop." In this light, *Popeye* is an early manifesto of Pop vision.

As noted in chapter 1, the instantaneity of the modernist painting is sometimes said to induce a transcendental experience of "presentness," even of "grace."[25] Lichtenstein also aims at "impact" (it is as important a term as "unity" in his lexicon), but impact is hardly the same as grace; in a 1967 conversation, Lichtenstein described this kind of response as "immediate, not contemplative," and his source images are too rooted in the everyday world to offer his viewers any transcendence of it.[26] In effect, Lichtenstein rethinks the immediacy of modernist painting from within the condition of mass culture, from which, like Hamilton, he indicates that it can no longer be held apart.[27] As with the classical value of pictorial unity, then, so with the modernist value of visual instantaneity: however affirmed by Lichtenstein, it is also pressured, repositioned, never to be the same again.

As is well known, Lichtenstein absorbed these values of pictorial unity and visual immediacy not through the example of past painting alone; they

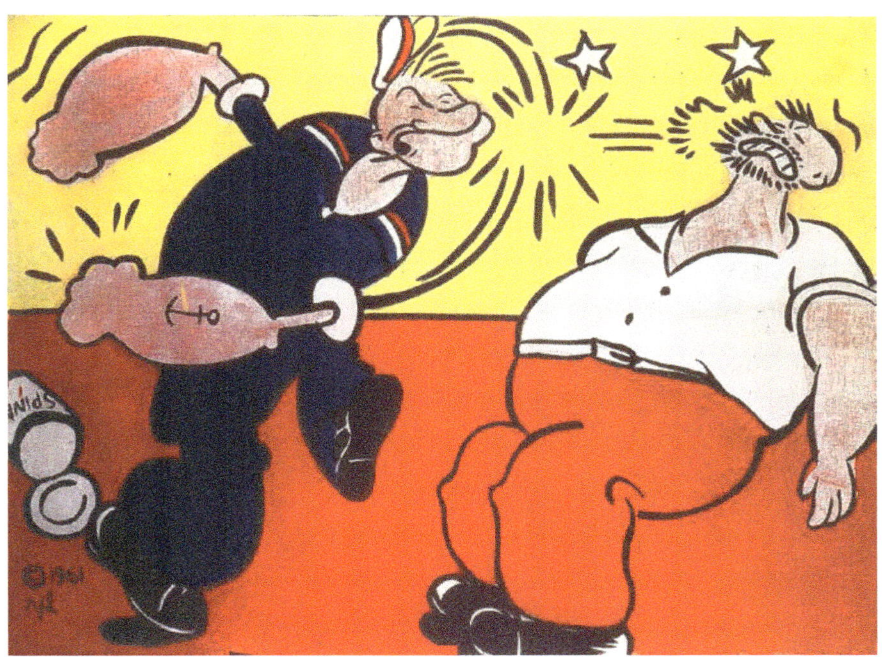

2.6 *Popeye*, 1961. Oil on canvas, 42 × 56 in.

were also fundamental to his studies at the Ohio State University in the 1940s. Except for a few years spent in the army (1943–46), Lichtenstein was at OSU from 1940 to 1949, first as a student and then as an instructor, and there a professor of art and design named Hoyt L. Sherman was "his earliest important influence."[28] Inspired by Gestalt psychology, Sherman had devised a distinctive technique of perceptual training that he dubbed the "flash lab": on a projection screen in a darkened room, he showed rows of students a sequence of flat images, usually abstract, each for a fraction of a second, and had them draw what they had seen (that is, effectively, afterimages of what they had seen) very rapidly with crayon or charcoal on paper. Each sequence included twenty images, which became more complex both as the sequence progressed and as the course developed; eventually, Sherman presented actual objects to his students as well. The purpose of the flash lab was to sharpen aptitudes for visual recognition and pictorial concision—for "organized perception."[29] The flash worked to forestall the saccadic movements of the eyes necessary in the gauging of depth, and so to render vision almost monocular, an effect that Sherman deemed salutary for art "because it facilitated the apprehension of images or objects as 'wholes,' intensified the student's appreciation for the constitutive role that negative space plays in forming an image, and assisted in the process of transposing objects seen in three-dimensional space into the two-dimensional terms of a picture surface."[30] Clearly, this training bears directly on how Lichtenstein undid such apparent opposites as representational and abstract and mediated and immediate, and I return to it below; suffice it to say here that "organized perception" was not only a matter of aesthetics, and that the values of unity and immediacy were also under enormous strain in American culture at large.[31]

The Hardest Kind of Archetype

In the 1950s, after Lichtenstein left OSU, he lived first in Cleveland and then in Oswego in central New York, where he taught briefly before his move to Rutgers. During this time, Lichtenstein worked through various styles of twentieth-century painting, first along expressionistic lines, then in a faux-naif manner (in which he adapted Americana themes, as in *Washington Crossing the Delaware I* [1951; fig. 2.7]), and finally in the abstract modes that preceded his Pop breakthrough. Lichtenstein experimented in much the same way in his early sculpture, which includes archaistic stone and primitivist wood figures. In the process, he became adept in a range of modernist styles and devices, some of which, such as the gestural brushstroke, would reappear in his Pop work, but as secondhand—that is, as already processed, just as his motifs drawn from the cartoons, ads, and comics are.

However, it was harmless enough for Lichtenstein to stress that his print material was mediated beforehand; it was more controversial to imply, as he proceeded to do, that all artistic representations—"Parthenon, Picasso or Polynesian maiden"—were already reproduced or otherwise screened, "made as one," as Hamilton put it, "before he touches them."[32] In part,

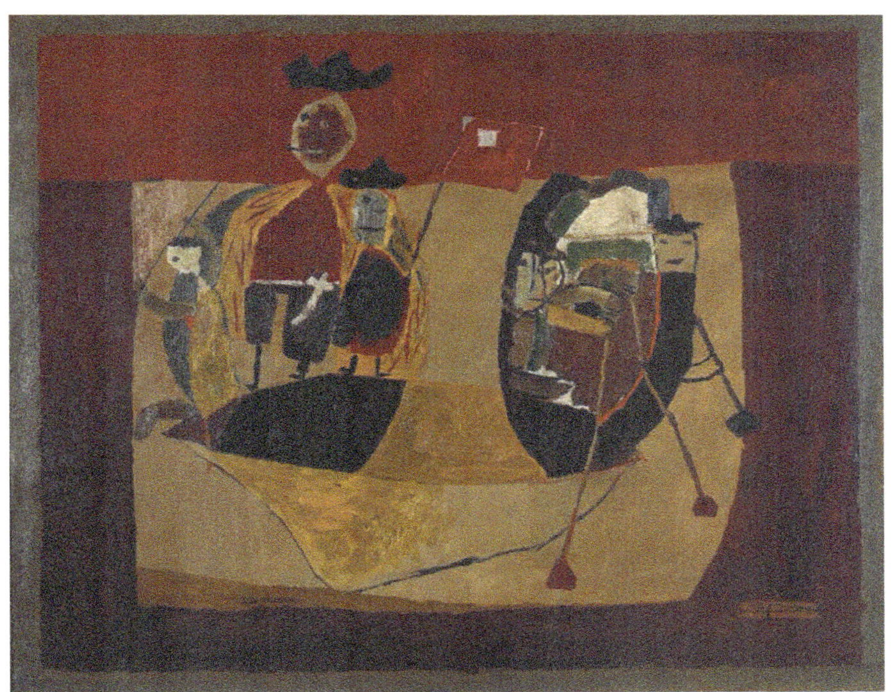

2.7 *Washington Crossing the Delaware I*, 1951. Oil on linen, 26 × 32 in.

modernist forms of expression and abstraction were developed to resist the effects of mechanical reproduction; as though to underscore that these forms could no longer be protected from this pressure, Lichtenstein focused his first Pop renderings of prior art there—in cartoonish reductions of print reproductions of various masters of expression and abstraction that he called "idiot" versions.[33] Thus already in 1963 Lichtenstein had begun to produce parodies of Picasso in his Cubo-Surrealist phase (as in *Woman with Flowered Hat*; fig. 2.8), and in 1964 he did the same with Mondrian in his Neo-Plastic mode (as in *Non-Objective I* and *II*; fig. 2.9). Yet perhaps his most pointed parodies in this regard are his series in 1968–69 after the *Rouen Cathedral*s (1892–94) and *Haystack*s (1890–91) of Monet, in which the differentiated Impressionist brushstroke is replaced by the uniform Benday

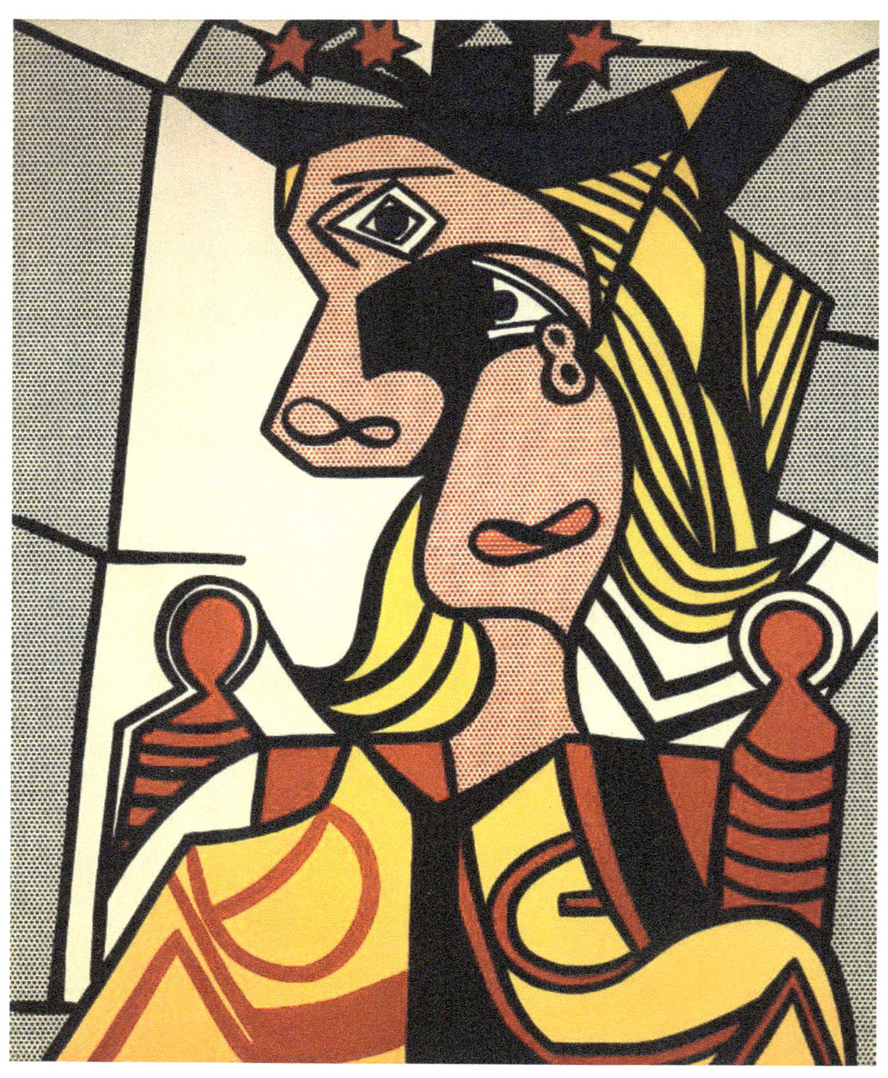

2.8 *Woman with Flowered Hat*, 1963. Magna on canvas, 50 × 40 in.

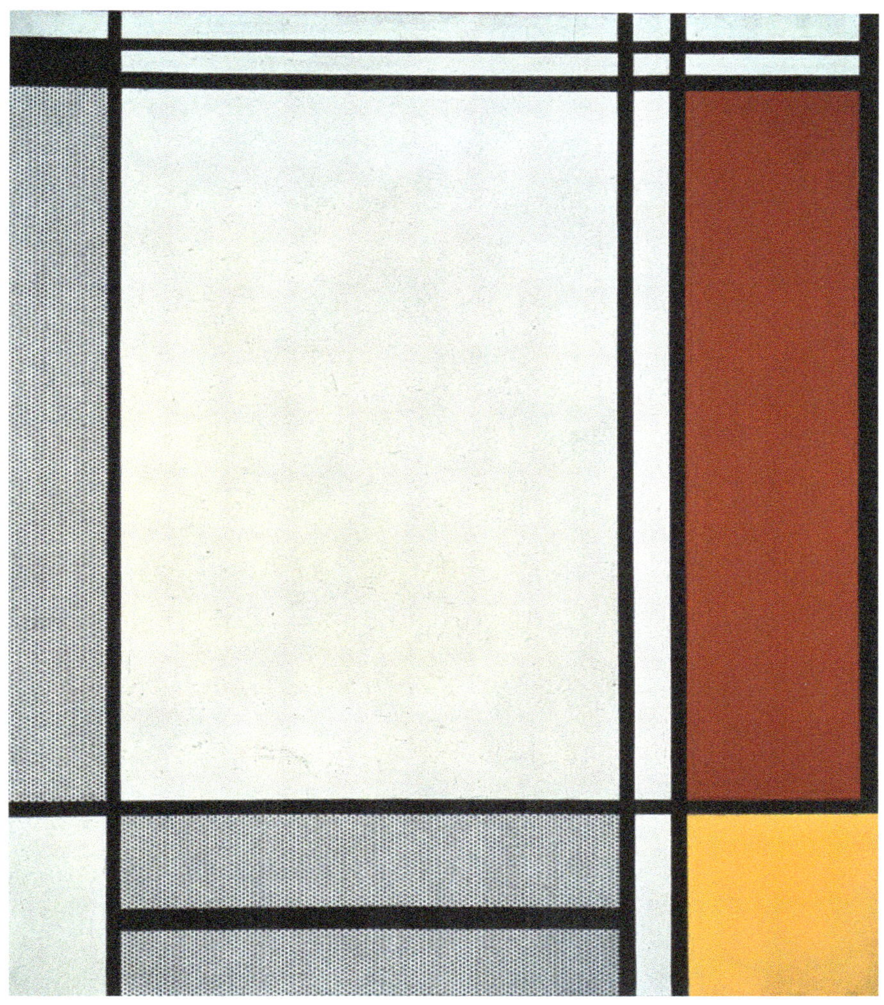

2.9 *Non-Objective I*, 1964. Magna on canvas, 56¼ × 48 in.

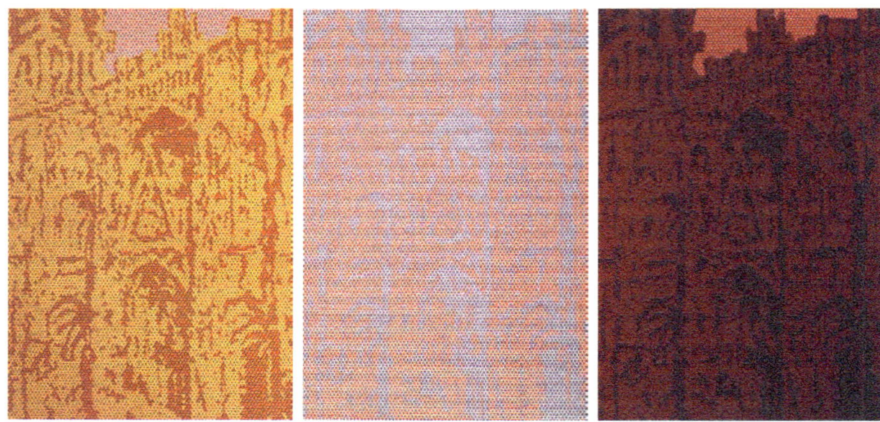

2.10 *Rouen Cathedral*, 1969. Oil and Magna on canvas, 63 × 42 in. each.

dot (fig. 2.10). If the Picasso and Mondrian parodies imply that mechanical reproduction had transformed the reception of what once seemed the most private and the most nonobjective of modernist styles, the Monet parodies suggest that it had also qualified the very production of what once seemed the most immediate of modernist techniques, the one concerned to register optical sensation directly. The mechanical, Lichtenstein intimates, had worked its way into Monet—both technically in the repetition of his strokes and structurally in the seriality of his canvases—and he, Lichtenstein, simply diagrammed what was already there.[34]

Lichtenstein applied his quasi-mediated dots, lines, and colors to motifs of his own invention, too, such as his first landscapes and sculptures, both of which date from the mid-1960s. In doing so, he underscored that the world at large, natural as well as man-made, was no less subject than art to the effects of mechanical reproduction. His initial objects, ceramic female heads and coffee cups (figs. 2.11, 2.12), appear to pop literally from his paintings of the same subjects of the early 1960s; most of his later objects also exist somewhere between painting and sculpture, as though caught between the condition of image and thing, or, more precisely, as though, even as things, they could not fight free of the virtual status of images. (His first *Explosions* [fig. 2.13], jagged shards of enamel and steel, which date from the mid-1960s, hyperbolize this hybrid state also: as these cartoonish signs for various bursts move into three-dimensional space, they carry bits of two-dimensional imagery along with them.)[35] In this way, Lichtenstein implies, mechanical reproduction had not only confounded the definition of artistic mediums like painting and sculpture, but also transformed the appearance of everyday things like glasses, bowls, pitchers, and lights (such are the sculptural motifs that follow his early heads and cups [fig. 2.14]). Thus, during the same time when Marshall McLuhan emerged as an apocalyptic prophet of a revolution in communication technologies, Lichtenstein also suggests that "media" has trumped "medium" and that almost anything might be reformatted as an image.

Lichtenstein points to the causes of this change in general terms too. "In America," he remarked in 1965, "there's just more industrialization, and it permeates everyday life"; as a result, he added in 1967, there exists "a new landscape for us [of] billboards and neon signs and all this stuff . . . to sell products."[36] So, too, Lichtenstein points to the effects of this change, which he does not simply celebrate in his statements (here again, he should not be confused with Warhol).[37] In fact, in his early interviews, Lichtenstein is explicit about the "hard" and "deadening" aspects of the culture; at the same time, he insists, these "brazen and threatening characteristics . . . are also powerful in their impingement on us"; more, they "give a kind of brutality and maybe hostility that is useful to me in an aesthetic way."[38] This point is key to his practice, for implicit here is a strategy that goes beyond a provocative troubling of artistic oppositions (such as manual and mechanical) toward a critical redoubling of lived conditions in consumer capitalism.[39] That is to say, what Lichtenstein intimates is a mimetic troping of "the brazen and threatening characteristics of our culture"—a mimesis of the industrial (he underscores the "hard steely quality" of his work), the informational ("I want my painting to look as if it had been programmed"), and, of course, the commercial ("I got some of these colors from supermarket packaging," he remarked in 1971; "I would look at package labels to see what colors had the most impact on one another").[40] I say "mimetic troping"

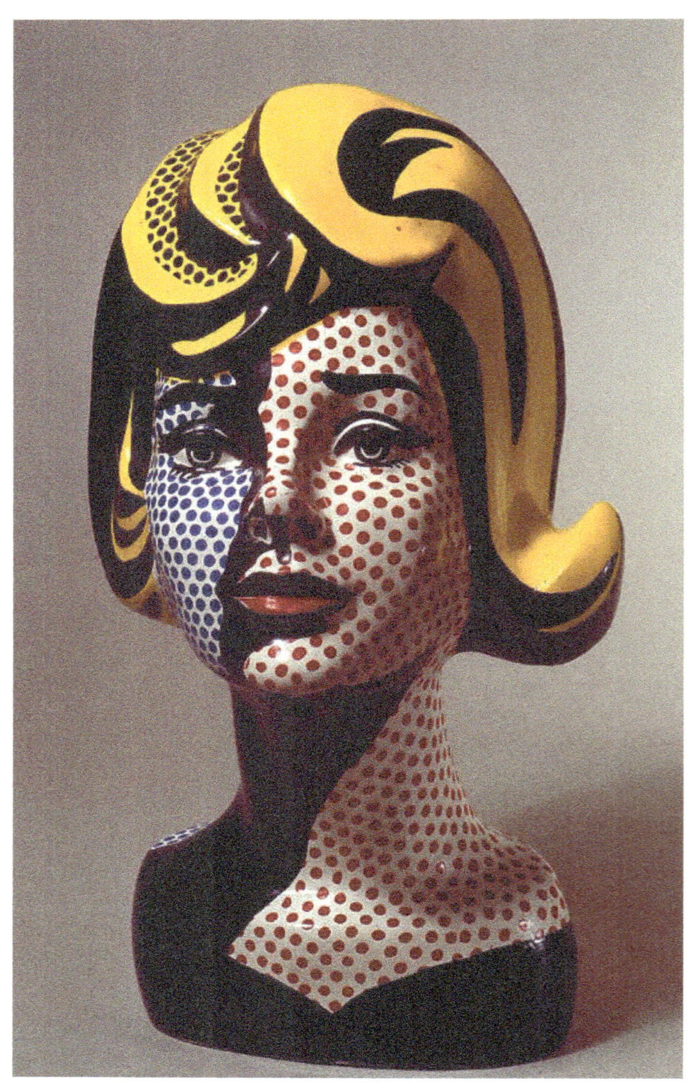

2.11 *Head with Blue Shadow*, 1965. Glazed ceramic, 15 × 8¼ × 8 in.

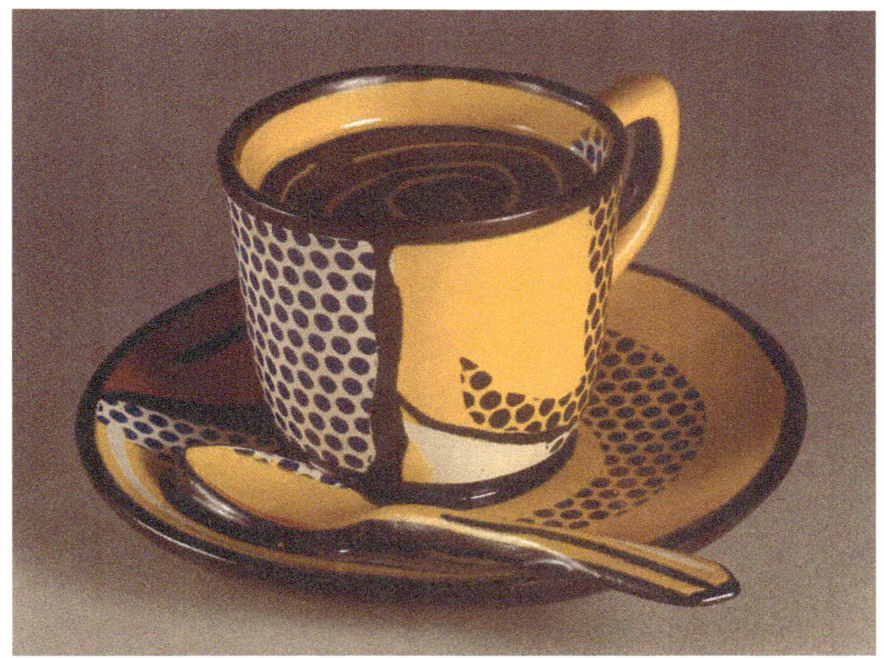

2.12 *Ceramic Sculpture 2*, 1965. Glazed ceramic, 3½ × 7½ in.

because his mimesis of the hard, programmed, and impactful is only part of his operation; just as important is his troping of these qualities, his turning of their "powerful impingement" to his own ends.

In the consumerist world as sampled by Lichtenstein, even the devices and styles of modernist art have hardened into clichés. His primary figure of this hardening of devices is the gestural brushstroke: once a mark of subjective expression, Lichtenstein displays it as a congealed sign in his paintings of the 1960s and 1970s, and he shows it all the more fetishized when it doubles as an abstract nude in his sculptures of the 1980s and 1990s (fig. 2.15). His primary instance of the hardening of styles is Cubism, but a Cubism become "hackneyed," even "senseless," a Cubism stylized sometimes as Purism and sometimes as Art Moderne or Art Deco, as in *Modern Sculpture*

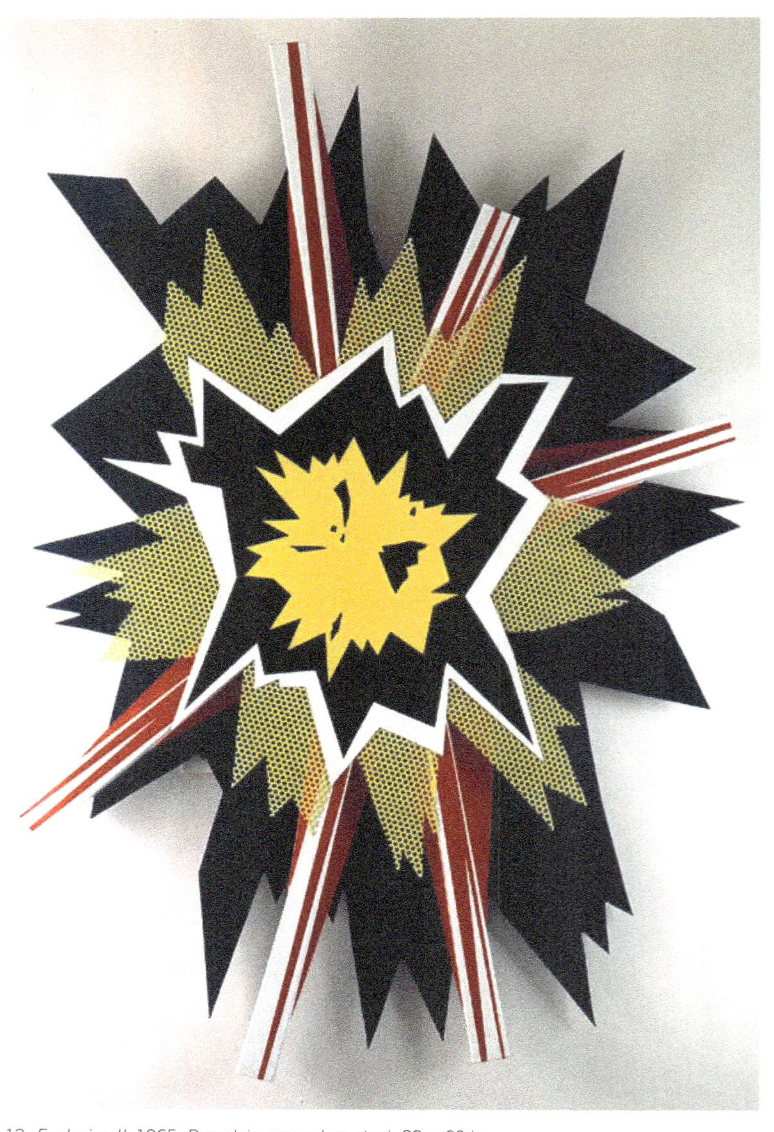

2.13 *Explosion II*, 1965. Porcelain enamel on steel, 88 × 60 in.

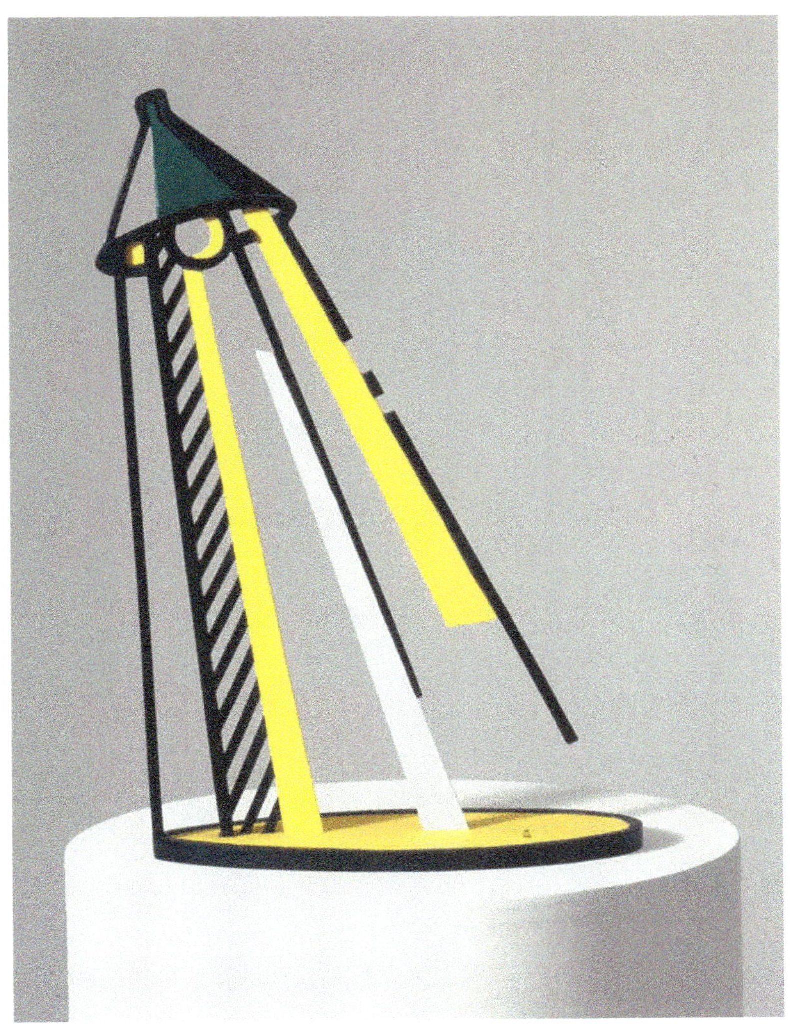

2.14 *Lamp 1*, 1977. Painted and patinated bronze, 28½ × 17⅜ × 8⅜ in.

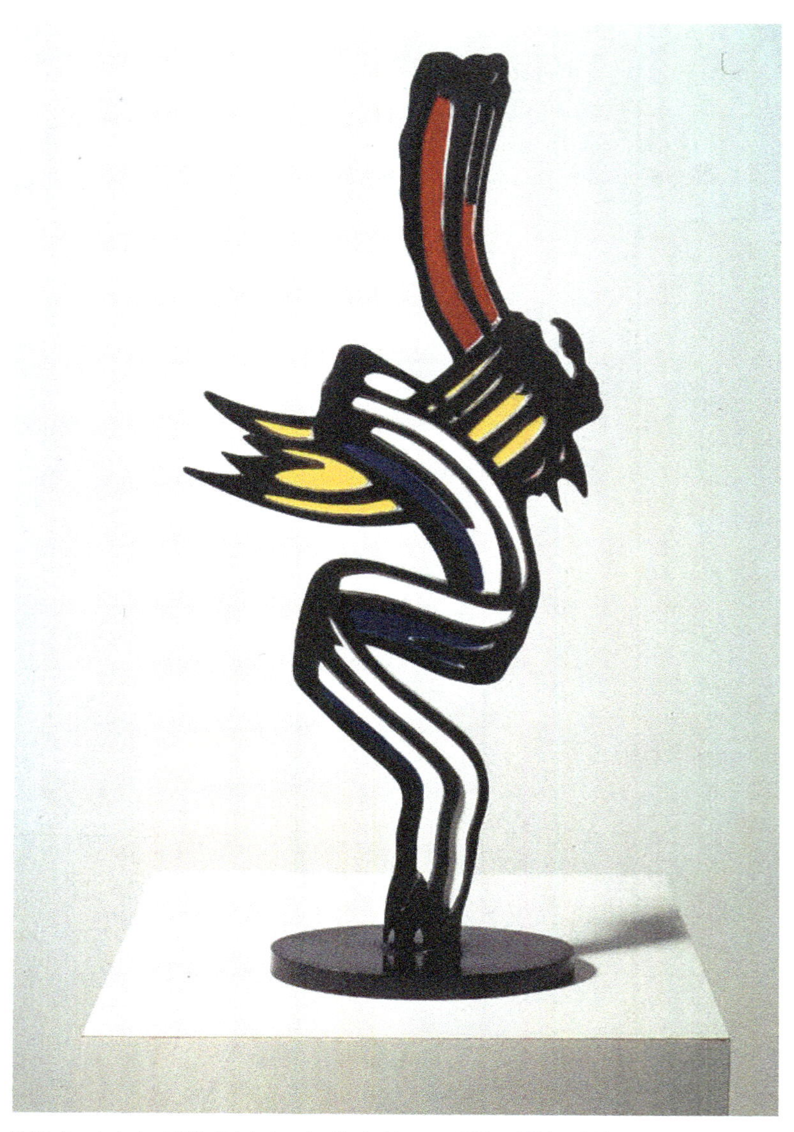

2.15 *Brushstroke*, 1981. Painted and patinated bronze, 31⅜ × 13¾ × 6½ in.

with Horse Motif (1967; fig. 2.16).[41] This is a Cubism reduced to the commodified status of an objet d'art or a decorative ornament (his *Modern Sculpture*s feature such characteristic Deco materials as brass, copper, aluminum mirror, tinted glass, and veined marble), which is perhaps why Lichtenstein often treats this style in sculptural form—though his sculpture, frequently in shallow relief and sometimes in trompe l'oeil, is more pictorial than sculptural.[42] *Modern Head* (1970; fig. 2.17) is a particularly witty example. With positive and negative volumes in shallow relief, this profile in black chromed aluminum evokes a personage somewhere between a classical Athena or Mercury and a comic-book superhero; at the same time, it recapitulates the historical recuperation of both African figures and Cubist portraits in a chic version of streamlined Deco.

Lichtenstein was also drawn to other styles in which art converges with commercial design.[43] For example, in the early 1980s, he made a few sculptures after Constantin Brancusi, an artist who, despite his rhetoric of aesthetic purity, often approached the threshold of design (in an infamous case, U.S. customs once held his *Bird in Space* [1923] for duty as a manufactured thing, a kitchen utensil in fact). With his own version of *Sleeping Muse* (1983; fig. 2.18) in patinated bronze—just a few inches deep, it is more outline than volume; its striated bars alone signify "shading" and thus "depth"—Lichtenstein pushes Brancusi across this decorative line. Sometimes, too, Lichtenstein alludes to Art Nouveau, a style in which the commingling of art and design is

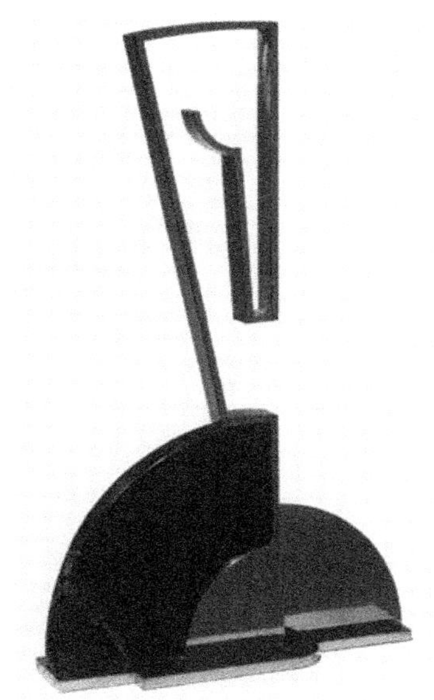

2.16 *Modern Sculpture with Horse Motif*, 1967. Aluminum and marble, 28¾ × 16½ × 5½ in.

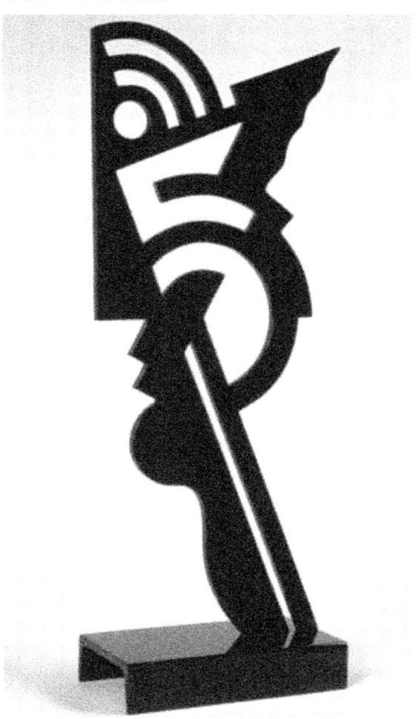

2.17 *Modern Head*, 1970. Black chromed aluminum, 25⅝ × 10¼ × 5 in.

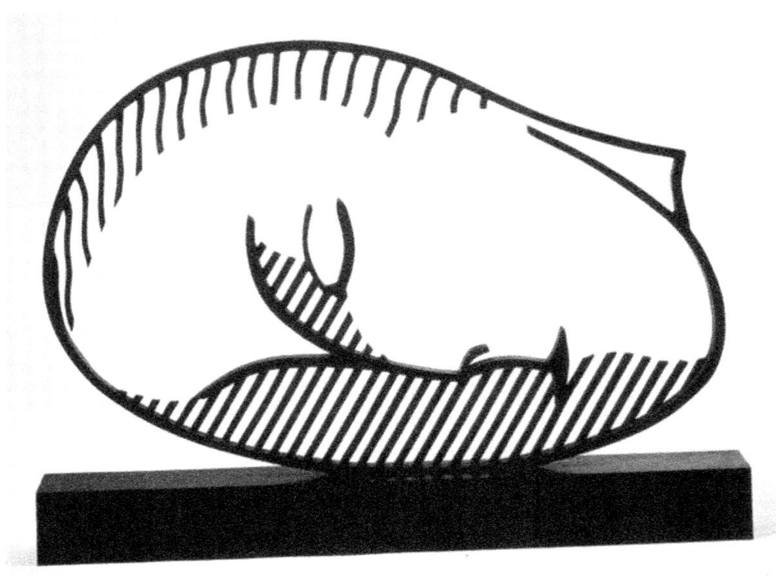

2.18 *Sleeping Muse*, 1983. Patinated bronze, 25½ × 34¼ × 4 in.

programmatic. Here an especially rich instance is *Surrealist Head* (1986; fig. 2.19), in which the florid curves of Art Nouveau are quoted to form the profile of the figure, the outline of her blonde hair and hat (or is it a parasol?), as well as the base of the piece. Walter Benjamin once read this "mediumistic language of line" in Art Nouveau as a desperate attempt, deep into the industrial age, "to win back the forms [of industry] for art"; yet here the appropriation runs in the other direction, in favor of industrial design.[44] The voluptuous line-language of Surrealism, the other style in play in this piece (again Lichtenstein favors the Picassoesque version), might be seen as an equally desperate attempt to win back the forms of eroticism for art. However, as evoked in *Surrealist Head*, this contest, too, is lost: *Surrealist Head* is no more voluptuous than it is mediumistic (it is also far from uncanny in the Surrealist manner). If *Modern Head* suggests that the Cubist play with perception and signification had become hackneyed, *Surrealist*

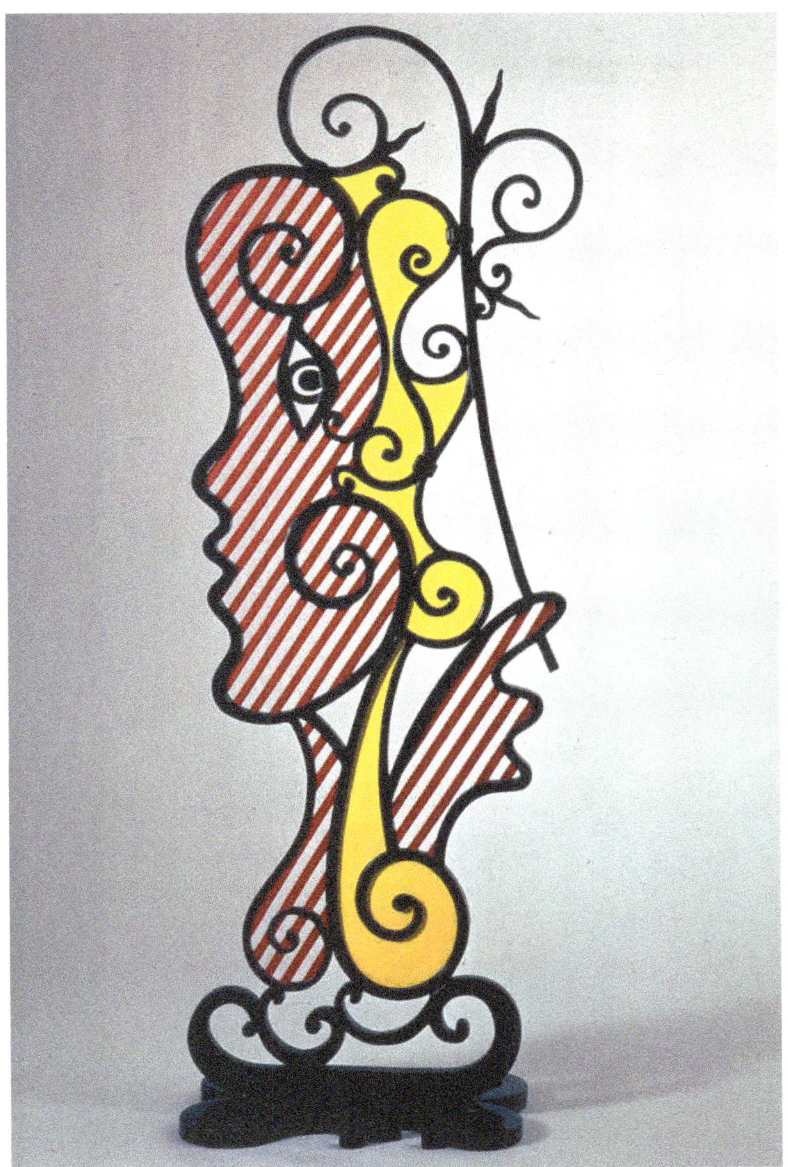

2.19 *Surrealist Head*, 1986. Painted and patinated bronze, 79 × 28 × 17⅜ in.

Head suggests that the Surrealist exploration of the unconscious had become ornamental.

In fact, Lichtenstein implies that no language, artistic or other, is immune from such reification. For example, the expressive utterances in his early romance paintings, even the onomatopoeic words in his early war paintings, are all so many clichés, reproduced for our camp appreciation.[45] And in his later sculptures, Lichtenstein presents entire categories of art as generic—not only *Modern Sculpture* but also *Ritual Mask, Chinese Rock,* and *Amerind Figure*—as if they were so many listings in a catalogue. (With its contraction of words, "Amerind" suggests a corporate brand, and with its abstraction of forms—part Northwest Coast Indian totem, part CBS logo—the 1981 sculpture so titled looks the part, too [fig. 2.20].) These rubrics conflate the most disparate of objects, styles, and practices, and none more so than his *Archaic Head*s (1988; fig. 2.21), which evoke archaic styles from the Egyptian and the Minoan to the Etruscan, as well as modernist adaptations of these styles by the likes of Gauguin and Picasso, only to condense all such allusions into one contoured stereotype (recall Hamilton: "Parthenon, Picasso, or Polynesian maiden are reduced to the same kind of cliché"). Beyond "the museum without walls" initiated, according to André Malraux, by photographic reproduction, what is suggested here is a mediation without limits, in which diverse styles can be processed as one.[46]

One can draw a set of dire conclusions from this commingling of art and commercial design that

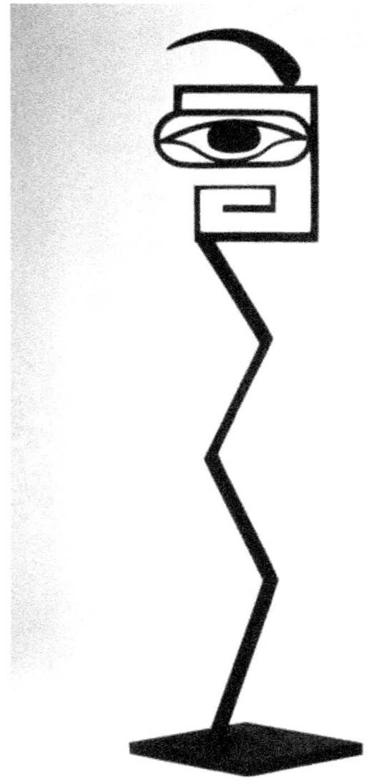

2.20 *Amerind Figure*, 1981. Patinated bronze, 65½ × 20½ × 13½ in.

Lichtenstein rehearses: that, by the moment of Pop, many avant-garde devices and modernist styles had become gadgets of the culture industry; that product and image, commodity and sign, had become conflated, and that Pop paintings merely reiterated this structural equivalence; that, as a medium once uniquely suited to explore object relations, sculpture, too, had become overridden by the commodity, whose effectivity Pop objects could only mimic; and so on.[47] Or one can take the benign view that both art and design often benefit from this exchange of forms, and that traditional values of painting, such as unity of image and immediacy of effect, are updated in the process. In his most provocative doubling of all, Lichtenstein advances both views at once: his mimesis of "brazen and threatening characteristics" points to the reification at work in his culture, even at the level of artistic devices and styles; at the same time, his troping of these characteristics works to invent within this condition and, in so doing, to mitigate it, if only a little, as well.

Here the crucial term for Lichtenstein is indeed "the cliché," which the *OED* defines, in the first instance, as "a metal casting of stereotype" (a piece of printing composed in type) and, in the second, as "a hackneyed phrase of opinion"—a definition on the two registers, technical and rhetorical, that are pertinent to Lichtenstein. "He would tell me that he was most interested in European clichés," his Rutgers colleague Allan Kaprow once remarked of Lichtenstein, "that is, the kind of thing that becomes standard imagery."[48] This standardness is again double: on

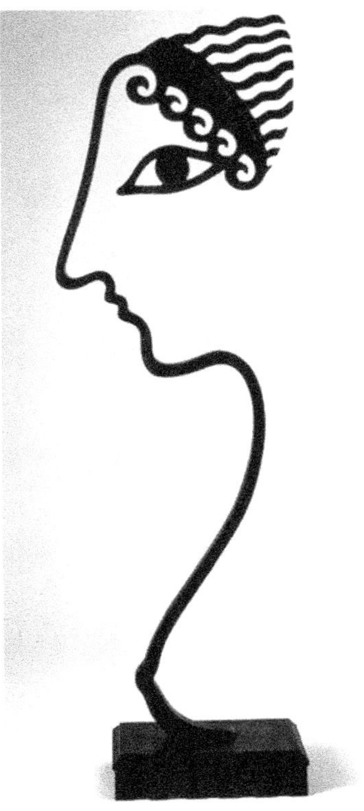

2.21 *Archaic Head VI*, 1988. Patinated bronze, 58½ × 18¾ × 10 in.

the one hand, the cliché is reproduced to the point of utter familiarity, and therefore, as Lichtenstein comments, it is "completely antithetical to art"; on the other, its "visual shorthand" suggests "a kind of universal language," one that can possess a "startling quality," in which case it involves "an esthetic element" that can be developed.[49] It is this doubling within the cliché that Lichtenstein exploits.

The cliché also partakes of both terms in other doubles active in Lichtenstein—high and low, abstract and iconic, and so on. Thus, in his view, the cliché is fundamental to "classical" art and to cartoons alike. Consider this important comment made to the critic David Sylvester in 1966 when Lichtenstein was involved with his *Brushstroke* paintings:

> I'm interested in . . . classical form, an ideal head for instance . . . Well, the same thing has been developed in cartoons. It's not called classical, it's called a cliché . . . I'm interested in my work's redeveloping these classical ways . . . I think that it's to establish the hardest kind of archetype that I can. There's a sort of formidable appearance that the work has when this is achieved . . . I think, really, that Picasso is involved in this. In spite of the fact that it seems as though he could do almost any kind of variation of any kind of eye or ear or head, there are certain ones that were powerful and strong because of the kind of symbolism that he employed.[50]

Note the relay here, permitted by this understanding of the cliché, among classical art, popular forms like cartoons, a modernist painting like Picasso's, and his own practice. "Mine is linked to Cubism to the extent that cartooning is," Lichtenstein commented in a related remark about his pictorial language to the critic John Coplans in 1967. "There is a relationship between cartooning and people like Miró and Picasso which may not be understood by the cartoonist, but it definitely is related even in the early Disney."[51] Here again Lichtenstein connects both mass and modernist styles to his own, implicitly via the cliché, and does so without the usual suggestion of corruption, co-option, or even compromise.

In some respects this notion of the cliché recalls the notion of the schema that, again for Gombrich in *Art and Illusion*, guided the main trajectory of Western art toward ever more perfect representation. "In that sense," Lichtenstein said of the cliché in a 1962 conversation with another Rutgers colleague, Geoffrey Hendricks, "it's like classical art, in that there's a classical eye or classical nose that gets redrawn," and this schema is operative in commercial art as well in as his own:

> I think many people miss the central tendency of the work . . . I don't care what, say, a cup of coffee looks like. I only care about how it's drawn, and what, through the additions of various commercial artists, all through the years, it has come to be, and what symbol has evolved through both the expedience of the working of the commercial artists and their bad drawing, and the reproduction machinery that has gotten this image of a coffee, for instance, to look like through the years. So it's only the depicted image, the crystallized symbol that has arrived. . . . We have a mental image of a sort of the commercialized coffee cup. It's that particular image that [I'm] interested in depicting. I'm never drawing the object itself. I'm only drawing a depiction of the object—a kind of crystallized symbol of it.[52]

Yet why this interest in "the crystallized symbol"? Certainly, as his comments suggest, Lichtenstein values the "impact" of the cliché; this "compelling" aspect compels him in turn.[53] Clearly, too, he is interested in its legibility across subcultures ("classical," commercial, modernist, and so on); it is this range that makes it appear "archetypal." More importantly perhaps, the cliché is a means for Lichtenstein to draw on these different idioms, "hard" and "formidable" though they often are, and invent with them.[54] Finally, Lichtenstein is drawn to the cliché for its artificiality; he works to use and to demonstrate this conventionality, but also, in doing so, to distance us from its power (here again he is close to Hamilton in particular).[55]

This is to suggest that the cliché functions in Lichtenstein not only as a "crystallized symbol" but also as a protean sign—another key double in his work. Consider his own example of the cliché as treated in *Cup of Coffee* (1961; fig. 2.22). The painting uses but one true color, a dirty yellow, to establish the cup and the saucer as well as the wall behind them. However simple they appear, the other elements, the black and the white, are also multivalent: the black signifies at once as tabletop, as shadow on the cup, and as coffee, while the white signifies as light both on the cup and on the surface of the coffee, where it might also evoke milk or cream. Together the two constitute the sign for rising steam, too, crisscrossing curves of

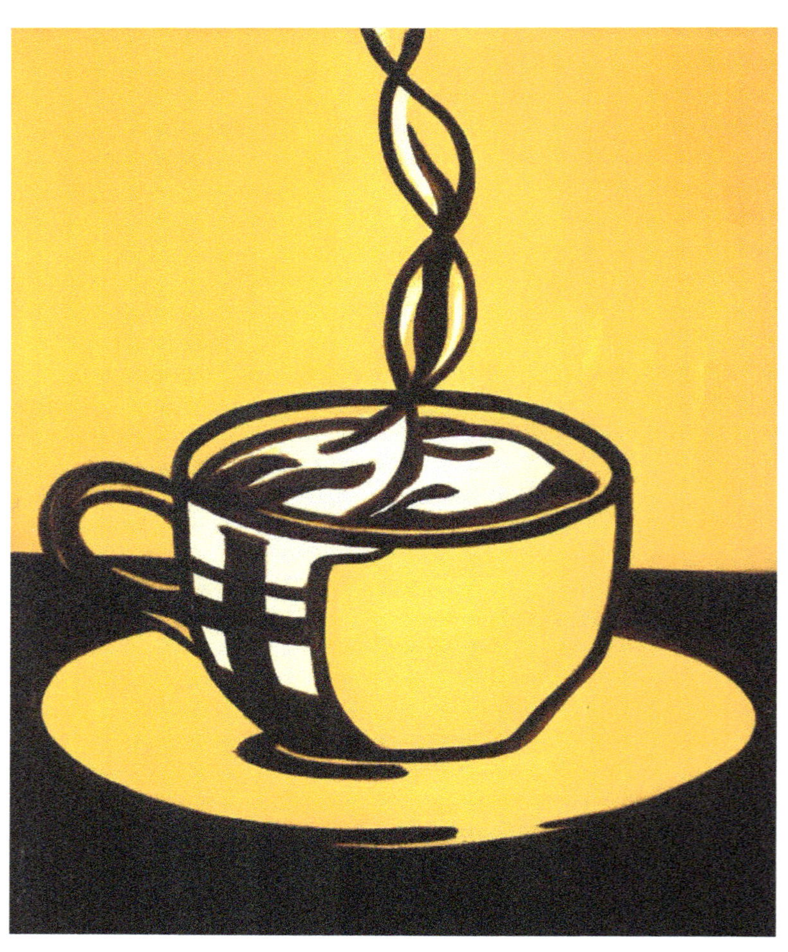

2.22 *Cup of Coffee*, 1961. Oil on canvas, 19⅞ × 15¹⁵⁄₁₆ in.

black and white, which is precisely a cliché as described by Lichtenstein, with little resemblance to the actual phenomenon.[56] *Cup of Coffee* has all the "impact" of the crystallized symbol, yet as Lichtenstein pulls it apart and puts it back together, we see the making of this effect and understand its artifice.

In *Art and Illusion*, Gombrich notes a prime convention in the Western tradition of picture making: "We respond with perfect ease to the notion in which black lines indicate both the distinction between ground and figure and the gradations of shading that have become traditional in all graphic techniques."[57] Lichtenstein often deploys this sign in both these ways—and in others as well. A band of parallel lines might signify "motion" when arrayed horizontally, as in *In the Car* (1963; fig. 2.23), or "window" or "windshield" when disposed diagonally, as in the same painting; elsewhere such lines signify "screen" or, if slightly curved, "mirror." As Rosalind Krauss has shown, this semiotic play was already active in Cubism, especially in the early collages and *papiers collés* of Picasso, and as Michael Lobel has noted, the parallel with Lichtenstein is sometimes suggestive. Picasso might use fragments from the same newspaper page to signify, largely by position, either the material flatness of an object or the atmospheric depth of its surround; often Lichtenstein deploys his dots in this double manner as well.[58] "Dots can mean printed surface and therefore 'plane,'" Lichtenstein remarked to the curator Diane Waldman in 1971, "but in contradiction, particularly in large areas, they become atmospheric and intangible—like the sky."[59] Like Picasso, Lichtenstein finds rich semiotic potential in poor material means.

Lichtenstein also turns inert stereotypes into active signs. Consider his early insistence on the primary colors (he also uses the occasional green): as in Mondrian, his primaries evoke a nonnatural world, but not a transcendental one—they signal the "readymade nature," the second nature, of media. Moreover, though his colors are not always arbitrary (yellow for blonde hair, for example, or blue for fair sky), they do tend to signify differentially, relative to one another (one patch in a painting might be yellow for no apparent reason other than others patches are painted blue or red).[60] Thus in *In the Car*, for example, yellow is credible enough for the woman's hair, but less so for her fur, and blue is credible enough for the man's jacket, but less

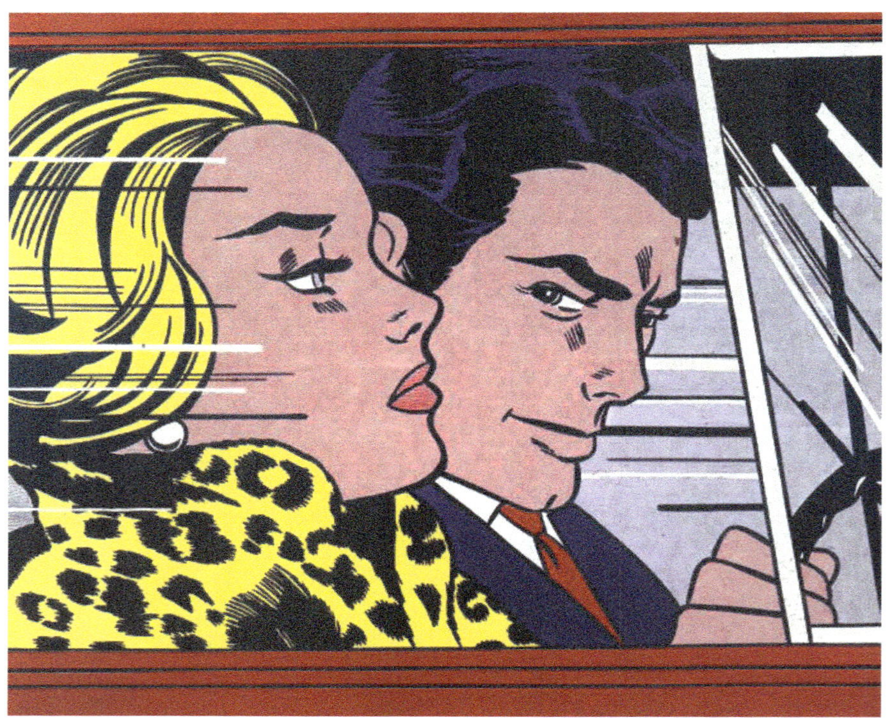

2.23 *In the Car*, 1963. Magna on canvas, 68 × 80 in.

so for his hair. In comics and cartoons of the time, these clichés were dictated by the technical limits of the printing process, but Lichtenstein turns them to his advantage, and out of this commodified condition, he produces a semiotic charge, one not dependent on personal expressivity: "I got some of these colors from supermarket packaging. I would look at package labels to see what colors had the most impact on one another. The idea of contrast seemed to be what advertising was into in this case. An advertisement is so intensely impersonal! I enjoyed the idea that anything vaguely red like apples, lips, or hair would get the same red."[61]

In his remarks on the cliché, Lichtenstein does not mention African sculpture, yet as Yve-Alain Bois has demonstrated, Picasso and Braque developed the semiotic ambiguity of Cubist art in large part through their study of African masks. Daniel-Henry Kahnweiler, the dealer for these art-ists at this moment, articulated their insights as follows:

> These painters turned away from imitation because they had discovered that the
> true character of painting and sculpture is that of a script. The products of these
> arts are signs, emblems, for the external world, not mirrors reflecting the external
> world in a more or less distorting manner. Once this was recognized, the plastic
> arts were freed from the slavery inherent in illusionistic styles. The masks bore
> testimony to the conception, in all its purity, that art aims at the creation of signs.
> The human face "seen," or rather "read," does not coincide at all with the details of
> the sign, which details, moreover, would have no significance if isolated.[62]

Lichtenstein, too, aims at the creation of signs, at a script that is read as much as seen. Consider once more his *Modern Head*, which, again, evokes both African sculpture and Cubist art, even as it also suggests the reification of both in Art Deco. At the same time, it engages semiotic ambiguity in a way that qualifies this reification.[63] Its entire profile can be taken as a simple head if we read the circular hole near the top as its "eye," or it can be seen as a head with a headdress or a helmet in which the "eye" becomes an ornamental element; as often with Picasso, this "modern head" is at least two in one. Or consider a later example, *Ritual Mask* (1992; fig. 2.24), in which the Lichtenstein dots and stripes are punched holes and steel curves. In the context of "mask," such details on the cheeks signify the scarification often represented in African masks as well as the modeling that the Cubists sometimes used these marks to evoke. However, "if isolated," these details would "have no significance," and the same is true of the sharp ovals signify-ing "eyes," the nearly triangular piece signifying "nose," and the nearly rect-angular piece signifying "mouth." Like *Modern Head*, *Ritual Mask* snatches a semiotic dimension out of reified cliché—the hackneyed Cubism of Deco. In both instances, the cliché-as-stereotype flips into the cliché-as-sign, and "the hardest type of stereotype" de-reifies before our eyes.

Paradoxically, then, the primary way that Lichtenstein mitigates reified appearance is through its exacerbation. "It's another case of degrading the thing and then building it back up again," Sylvester commented to Lichten-stein in 1966. "You make a joke about it, but you make it dramatic again."[64]

Again, at the time of this conversation, Lichtenstein was at work on his first *Brushstroke* paintings, and though he inherits this gesture as a crystallized symbol, he also works to reanimate it. In his sculptures of the 1980s and 1990s, for example, he stands the brushstroke up, makes a figure of it, and, in such pieces as *Brushstroke* (1981; fig. 2.15), endows it with a lively Pop contrapposto.[65] Indeed, Lichtenstein treats entire styles in this fashion, as we saw with his *Modern Sculpture*s. By the 1960s, Art Deco had become "a discredited area," Lichtenstein remarked, "like the comics"; however, as such, it acquired the uneasy effects of the démodé, as he also discerned: "I am interested in the quirky results of those derivatives of Cubism and like to push this quirkiness further toward the absurd."[66] This quirkiness is most evident in his "idiot" versions of Picasso, whom Lichtenstein appropriates more often than he does any other artist, especially in the manner of the early 1930s, which combines the semiotic invention of Cubist forms with the "peculiar maneuverability" of Surrealist figures.[67] In *Galatea* (1990; fig. 2.25), which displays his de-reifying energies as vitally as any work, Lichtenstein puts both qualities in play.

Galatea is a sinuous figure in a continuous line of painted bronze; it calls to mind how Picasso, for motives that were erotic as well as aesthetic, sometimes attempted to grasp his female bodies in a single trace, even though the process here is anything but immediate. Depending on size and location (that is, according to the semiotic principle pioneered by Picasso), three different oval areas in identical red stripes signify "belly" and "breasts,"

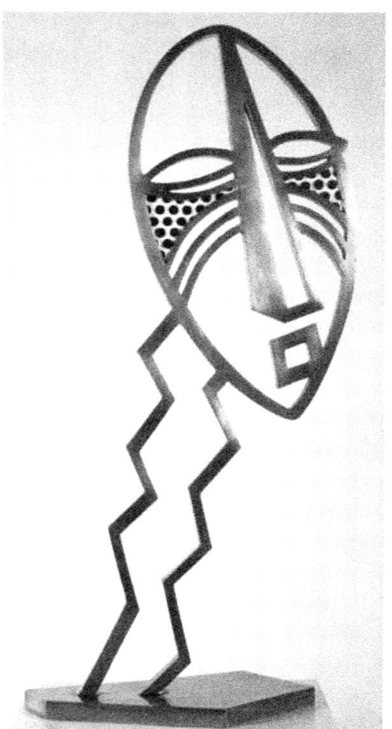

2.24 *Ritual Mask*, 1992. Painted and galvanized steel, 51¼ × 22 × 11⅜ in.

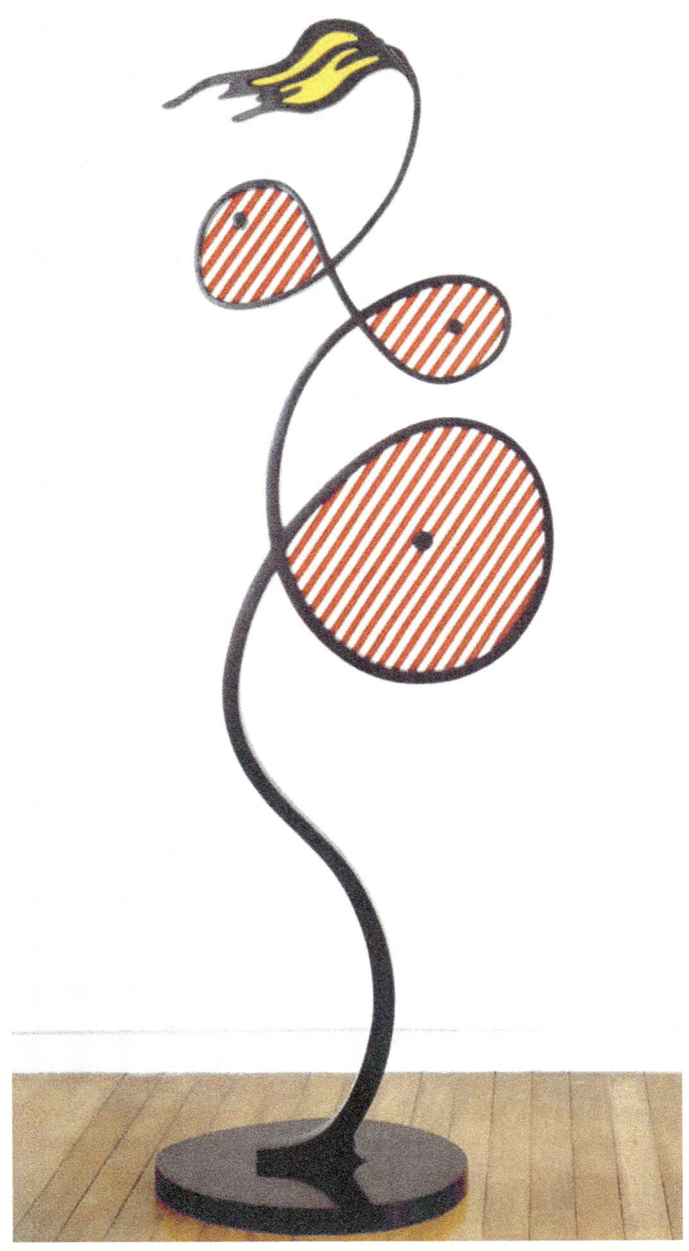

2.25 *Galatea*, 1990. Painted and patinated bronze, 89 × 32 × 19 in.

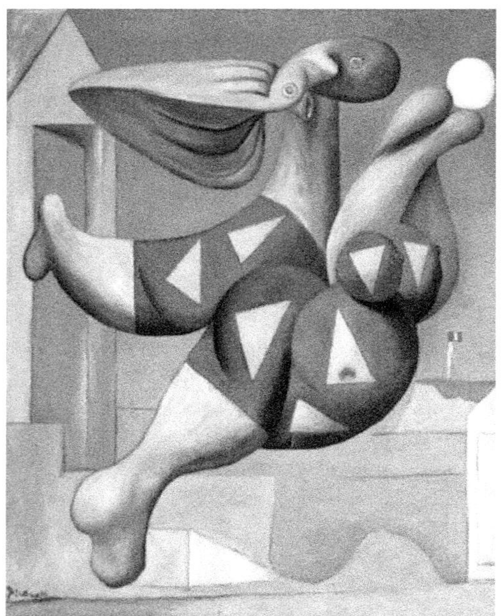

2.26 Pablo Picasso, *Bather with Beach Ball*, 1932. Oil on canvas, 57⅞ × 45⅛ in. © 2012 Estate of Pablo Picasso / Artists Rights Society (ARS), New York.

while three similar cylinders within these areas signify "navel" and "nipples." Lichtenstein then tops his figure with a yellow brushstroke detailed in black that identifies her as a sprightly blonde, perhaps a lithe dancer on a stage or a bikinied girl on a beach. The Picasso that comes to mind is *Bather with Beach Ball* (1932; fig. 2.26), which was a talisman for Lichtenstein as early as *Girl with Ball* (fig. 2.3). On the one hand, then, like these two bathers, *Galatea* might be seen as a late incarnation of the ancient nymphs that so intrigued the art historian Aby Warburg, who traced these recurrent spirits through "the afterlife of antiquity" into modern visual culture; on the other hand, the sculpture is assembled from reified bits and pieces of received artistic styles and cartoonish signs.[68] On the one hand, *Galatea* is brought to life by her Pygmalion, Lichtenstein inspired by Picasso; on the other hand, no artist is more foreign than Lichtenstein to this classical myth about the immediacy of expression, the efficacy of touch, and the identity of art object and love object. Lichtenstein recovers aspects of the semiotic and the erotic in Picasso, even as he points to a reification already evident in his predecessor. At the dawn of the modernist era, the young Marx wrote, "Petrified social conditions must be made to dance again by singing them their own song."[69] Here as elsewhere, Lichtenstein sings his own version of that song.

It Must Leave Me Something to Do

If, ideally, the traditional tableau projects a contemplative response, and the modernist painting a transcendental one, what kind of subjectivity is modeled by a Lichtenstein painting? If, as I have argued, Lichtenstein pressures the privileged terms of both traditional tableau and modernist painting, what sorts of subject—portrayed, viewing, and producing—emerge in the process?

The charge of superficiality that first greeted Lichtenstein was also directed at his figures, which appear flat psychologically as well as physically. In addition, the ones drawn from comic books often face the viewer frontally (this device both invites the reader to relate to the character and condenses as much narrative as possible in a single cell). As Lobel has noted, Lichtenstein tends to push his female figures in particular to the picture plane, where they are sometimes equated with pure image or sheer surface, as they frequently are in classic Hollywood cinema.[70] For Lichtenstein, however, this convention also bears on the actual self-presentation of stylish women. "Women draw themselves this way," he remarked in 1967 in a partial justification of his pictorial treatment of female figures, "that is what makeup really is."[71] Here Lichtenstein refers less to the artificiality of all maquillage than to the flatness of the Pop face (think of Edie Sedgwick or Twiggy, who emerged as a star model not long before this comment); in this account, life copies art in a manner that Lichtenstein redoubles in his painting (fig. 2.27).

In the 1960s, these flat surfaces were taken as a sign of a cool sensibility, an affectless condition, which was associated with the culture of Pop, especially the Warhol scene. Affect is not absent from Lichtenstein—on the contrary—but it is relocated away from emotional depth toward melodramatic surface, from Action Painting to action scenes of romance and war in the comics (fig. 2.28). To a degree, this is a camp move on his part, but it carries a serious proposition about postwar society, one that Hamilton also advances: codes of femininity and masculinity are primarily learned from mass-cultural media, and subjects are socialized through such popular

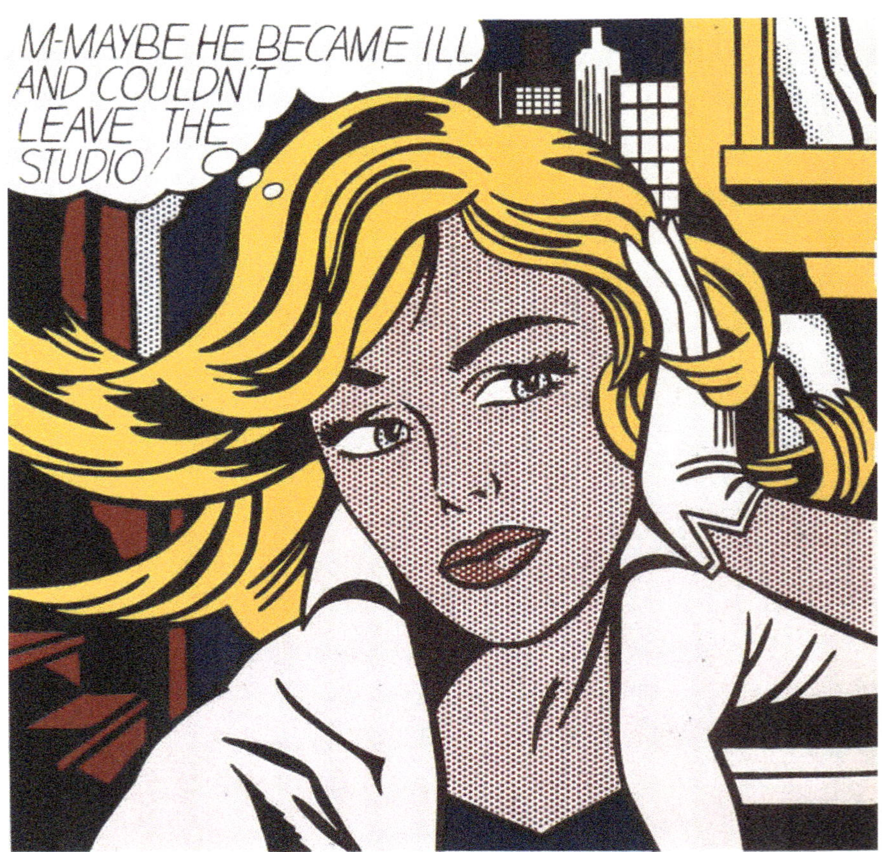

2.27 *M-Maybe*, 1965. Oil and Magna on canvas, 60 × 60 in.

forms as comic books, ads, magazine stories, and television shows more than through any elite tradition of art and literature. At the same time, with the satirical streak in his paintings, Lichtenstein renders these codes comical; the stereotype of the passive woman lost in romance, say, or of the macho man bloodthirsty in war is inflated to an absurd point, the point of deflation. "The heroes depicted in comic books are fascist types," Lichtenstein commented in 1963, "but I don't take them seriously in these paintings—maybe there is a point in not taking them seriously, a political

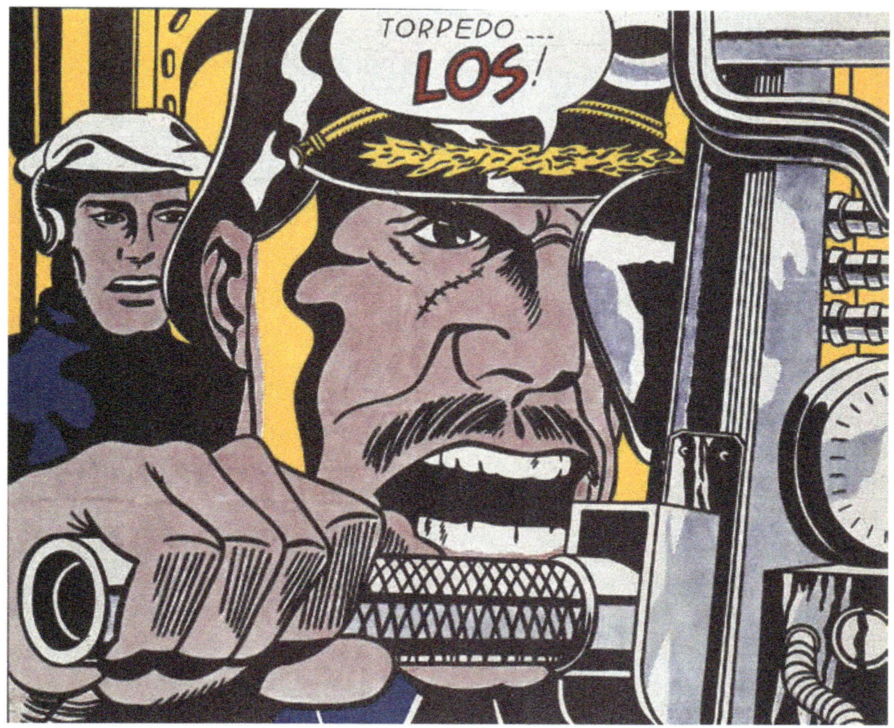

2.28 *Torpedo Los*, 1963. Oil on canvas, 68 × 80 in.

point."[72] In short, his artistic manipulations of his media sources introduce an element of *dis*identification into the very mechanisms of mass-cultural identification. At the same time, Lichtenstein points to an important shift in the ground of subject formation—a shift away from the old notion of a self-made ego (whether of the romantic or the existentialist type) toward a new view of the individual as structured by a symbolic order that precedes him or her. And in turn, this view suggests a different project for the artist (one also proposed by Hamilton): to treat the artistic image as a mimetic probe to explore this given matrix of cultural languages—to take apart its clichés and to put them back together, with differences that, though "not great," may yet be "crucial."

Here we pass from the portrayed subject to the viewing subject. On this score, again, the Sherman flash lab at OSU was an early testing ground for Lichtenstein. As others have argued, the quickening of vision taught by the flash lab was also an instrumentalizing of vision. One can see this instance as only another moment in the long history of the disciplining of the distracted subject in the modern world, yet this particular training had a special importance in the United States of the 1940s and 1950s, for heightened skills of visual recognition were essential to soldiers in World War II and the Korean War, especially pilots and gunners.[73] Lichtenstein knew as much from his own experience: in 1943 he was posted at Camp Hulen in Texas, an anti-aircraft training base, and in 1944 at Keesler Air Force Base in Mississippi, which specialized in pilot training. Nearly twenty years later, just as the American involvement in Vietnam had begun to deepen, he made aerial warfare a prominent subject of his paintings. What is key here, however, is not his biographical connection to the subject but his pictorial association between the visual acuity prepared by modernist art and the perceptual aptitude demanded by modern war.[74] Especially in his pictures of fighter pilots, submarine captains, and the like, Lichtenstein suggests that there is but a fine line between a fast "pop" eye and a futurist "killer" eye; his paintings point to a shared aggressivity in these ways of seeing.[75]

The Sherman ideal of "organized vision" bears on consumerist vision, too. If flash-lab training was "object-directed," as Lichtenstein remarked, it was also product inflected, for the apprehension of images as wholes was essential to commodity identification, especially during the postwar boom in marketing.[76] Some of his early paintings of products, such as *Tire* (1962; fig. 2.29), play on this eidetic kind of consumerist recognition: usually presented starkly in black on white, these images already possess the graphic power of company brands and corporate logos. This is another aspect of the historical convergence between late-modernist painting and commercial design noted above, and in this regard, Lichtenstein saw a link between his own work and contemporaneous abstraction: "It's maybe the same kind of thing that you find in [Frank] Stella or in [Kenneth] Noland," he remarked to Sylvester in 1965, "where the image is very restricted."[77] Here

Lichtenstein aligns the impact of late-modernist painting with the impact of media images; both elicit a response that he elsewhere describes as "immediate, not contemplative."[78] In short, the implication is that a targeting subject has arisen in the military-consumerist complex of postwar America in a way that complicates, even negates, the contemplative subject of the traditional tableau as well as the transcendental subject of the modernist painting.[79]

However, this point must be qualified somewhat. First, the very need for such training as occurred in the flash lab presupposes the recalcitrance, even the resistance, of the distracted subject, and Lichtenstein does not merely reproduce this disciplining in any case. The viewer of a Lichtenstein painting is hardly one with the fighter pilot, the stylish consumer, or even the reader of comic books devoted to such figures; again, Lichtenstein renders them often comical and sometimes preposterous, and we "don't take them seriously." As for the paintings of products, not only does Lichtenstein efface the brand names of his sources, but more importantly, he often breaks down the cliché of the image.[80] For example, however iconic they might appear, *Golf Ball* (fig. 2.5) and *Tire* are also quite abstract, and *Turkey* (1961) and *Standing Rib* (1962; fig. 2.30), say, are more shapeless blobs than "crystallized symbols." Here pictorial schemata are loosened from referential grounding and brand recognition alike, and the suitability of painting to these ends is exploited accordingly.

Second, in several paintings of the early 1960s, Lichtenstein places his figures in front of windshields, dashboards, gun sights, and televisual monitors in a way that asks us to compare or "correlate" the canvas with such surfaces.[81] We can thus measure our own looking against the scanning, tracking, and targeting that such prosthetic screens demand of the subject. However, even as Lichtenstein compares these different surfaces, he hardly conflates them: convergences are intimated, but discrepancies persist. The same is true of the different kinds of images in his work, whether "screened" or "scanned" (to borrow a distinction from Hamilton). Clearly, Lichtenstein focuses on the first (print) mode, already somewhat dated in the 1960s, but he also looks to the second (electronic) mode, dominant in our age of the

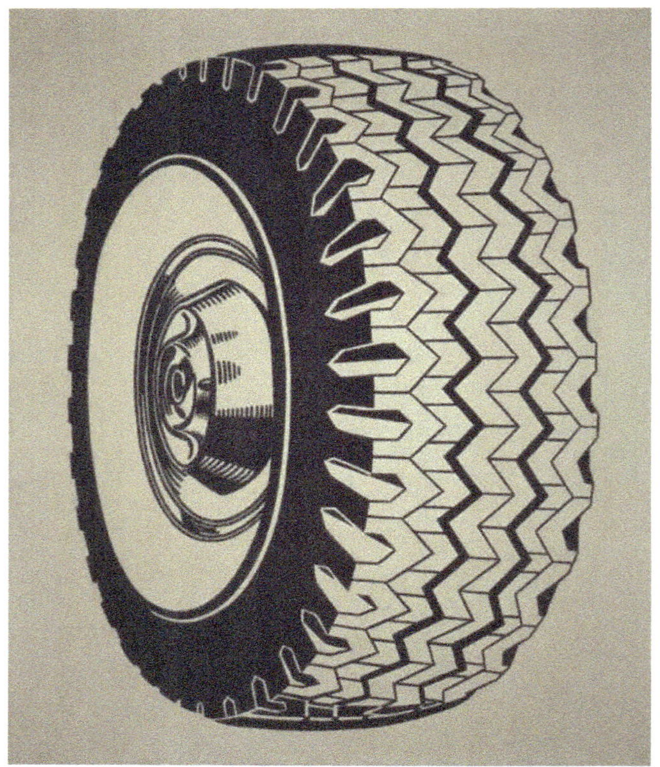

2.29 *Tire*, 1962. Oil on canvas, 68 × 56 in.

computer, a mode that mixes the visual and the verbal in data that we are trained to see and read at once, precisely to scan. (Such is how we are instructed to sweep through information that is at once image and text: we scan it as it records us, counting our keystrokes, tracking our website hits, and so on.) Lichtenstein points to this important shift in semblance and in viewing, yet in doing so, he does not elide the differences between them: the contradictions remain for us to consider.

What, finally, of the producing subject? Initially, Lichtenstein all but invites the charge that he is neither original nor expressive; at the same time, he "Lichtensteinizes" his sources, as Lobel comments, and works "to

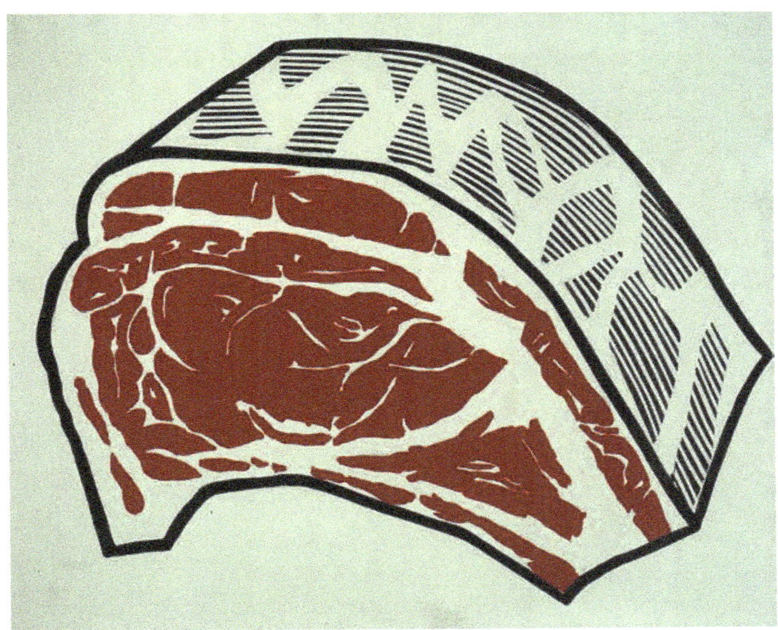

2.30 *Standing Rib*, 1962. Oil on canvas, 21 × 25 in.

make the comics look like *his* images."[82] (This paradox is condensed in his signing of early Pop paintings with a copyright symbol, which might be construed, equally and oppositely, as an emptying out of invention or as a claiming of all within the image as his own.) Later, too, according to Lobel, Lichtenstein "oscillates between an erasure of self and an attempt—however conflicted or provisional—to reconstitute a semblance of authorial presence."[83] Yet this is less a contradiction than it seems, for Lichtenstein creates a signature style out of given forms that appear to preclude this individuation. Moreover, if he did feel a conflict here, it did not disturb him much. "I am not against industrialization," Lichtenstein remarked, modestly enough, in 1967, "but it must leave me something to do." "I don't draw a picture in order to reproduce it—I do it in order to recompose it. Nor am I trying to change it as much as possible. I try to make the minimum amount of change."[84] More than oscillate between signs of erasure and presence, then, Lichtenstein hews closely to this fine line: to adapt images from print media to the demands of advanced painting, in the interest not only of pictorial unity but also of distinctive style, in a way that might affirm these values and, at the same time, register them as threatened or transformed by the very forces of mechanical reproduction, commercial design, and mass culture that he otherwise engages. This threat or transformation is less an existential dilemma for Lichtenstein than a historical problematic that all Pop artists faced. (Indeed, it is the apparent implacability of this problematic that the relative impersonality of Pop canvases conveys most vividly to us today.)

Lichtenstein evokes this threat or transformation regarding the producing subject in a distinctive way. It is suggested, for instance, in his mirror paintings of the 1970s, which are mostly blank except for his favorite signs for light and shadow, reflection and refraction; that is to say, these paintings capture the most fleeting of phenomena in the most fixed of representations—his stereotyped dots, lines, and colors. In *Self-Portrait* (1978; fig. 2.31), the self in question is represented only by a T-shirt sans a body or a head (which is replaced by a mirror); as a result, the painting is sometimes taken as a portrait of "the death of the artist."[85] Yet if such is the case, it is a comical representation of this "erasure of the self": a self-portrait of the downtown artist in a cheap shirt who, like a vampire, feeds on other images but is unable to project his own. In a light manner typical of Lichtenstein, the threat to the subject is at once presented and parodied.

Parody is indeed the distinctive way that Lichtenstein performs and parries such threats. "In parody there is the implication of the perverse," Lichtenstein stated in a 1964 conversation (that included Oldenburg and Warhol), but not necessarily the implication of the cynical: "The things that I have apparently parodied I actually admire."[86] This perverse admiration is clear enough in his early parodies of Cézanne, Picasso, Mondrian, and other modernist masters; at the same time, he processes these predecessors through his own emergent style. Different effects are thus produced at the same time. On the one hand, Lichtenstein shows how these master styles have hardened into clichés. On the other hand, as Oldenburg added in the same 1964 conversation, "a parody is not the same thing as a satire"; rather,

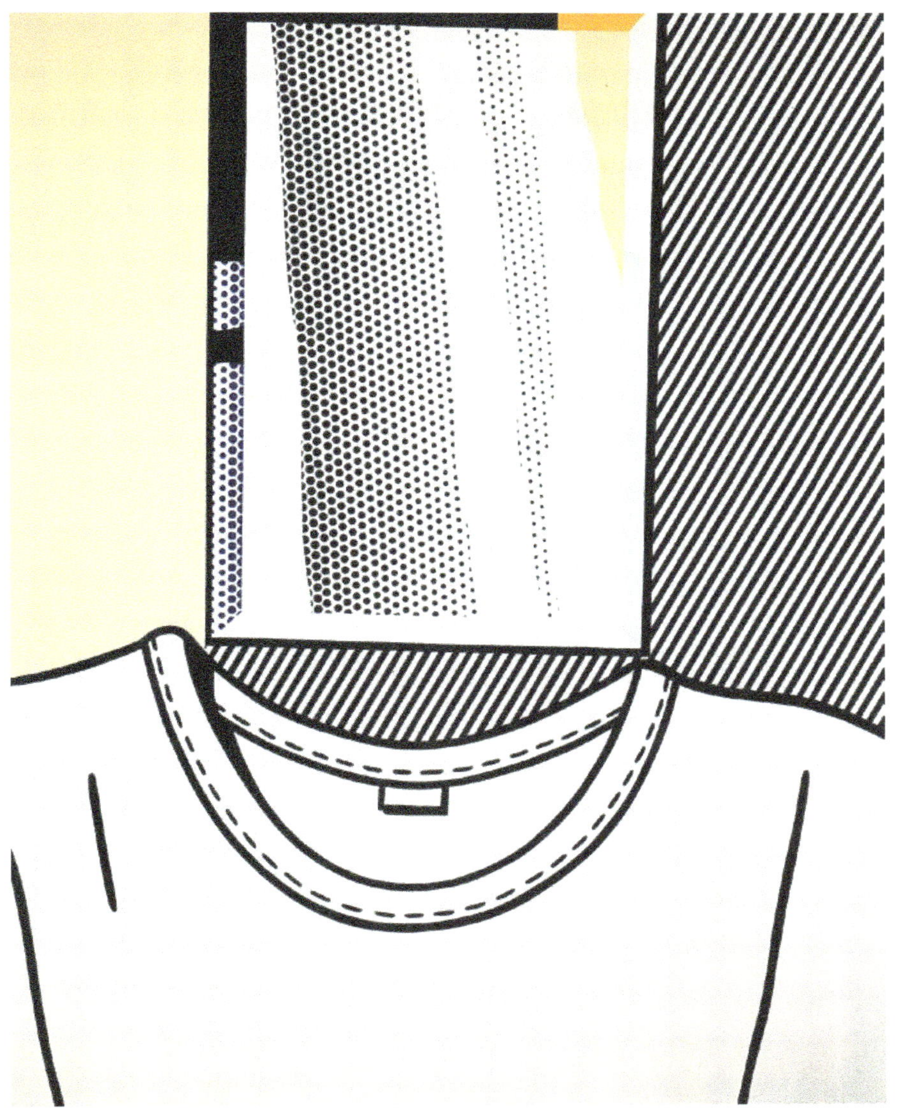

2.31 *Self-Portrait*, 1978. Oil and Magna on canvas, 70 × 54 in.

it is "kind of imitation . . . [that] puts the imitated work in a new context," and this displacement can reanimate these styles too, and individuate Lichtenstein artistically in the process.[87] In short, as with the reification of signs discussed above, he does not simply submit to the styles that he entertains; rather, Lichtenstein finds multiple options—for the artist and the viewer alike—within this array. At the very least, his work helps free us from two automatic habits: obeisance to high art on the one hand, and obedience to mass culture on the other.

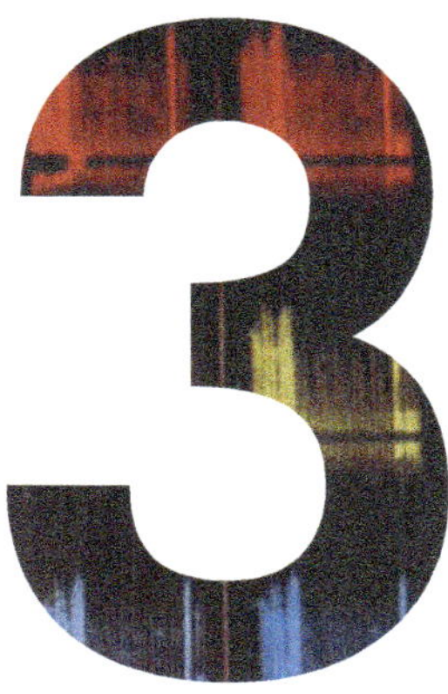

Andy Warhol, or the Distressed Image

"I was an old-fashioned artist compared to him," Roy Lichtenstein once remarked of Andy Warhol, and it is true that Warhol does not aim to assimilate his images from low sources to the parameters of high painting, and thus to maintain the values of pictorial unity and aesthetic totality under the pressures of mass culture, as Lichtenstein and Hamilton do.[1] Even as Lichtenstein and Hamilton test the traditional tableau in ways that register its changed circumstances in consumer society, they also largely preserve its essential formats and effects. Warhol does so far less: in his move to distress his images and viewers alike, he dispenses with most conventions of good composition and proper spectatorship alike.

I Never Fall Together

The Warholian distressing of the image is most evident in his "Death and Disaster" silk screens of the early 1960s.[2] It was in the midst of these pictures, in 1963, that Warhol told the critic Gene Swenson, "Everybody should be a machine," a famous utterance that is usually taken to confirm the relative blankness of the artist.[3] Yet it might indicate less a blank subject than a shocked one, who takes on what shocks him as a mimetic defense against that shock, as if to say "I am a machine too, I make (or consume) serial product images too, I give as good (or as bad) as I get." In this same conversation, Warhol claimed that he had eaten the same lunch every day for the past twenty years (Campbell's tomato soup, of course). "Someone said my life has dominated me," he then remarked. "I liked that idea."[4] Together these two statements—"Everybody should be a machine" and "Someone said my life has dominated me"—indicate an embrace, both casual and calculated, of the compulsive habits of repetition enforced by a capitalist society of serial production and consumption.[5] If you can't beat this system, Warhol implies, join it; more, if you enter it totally, you might expose it: you might reveal the automatism of this compulsion to repeat through your own excessive example. Developed in Dada, this strategy of mimetic exacerbation was performed ambiguously by Warhol—ambiguously because its different degrees of complicity and criticality are notoriously difficult to measure.[6]

These signs of shock and automatism reposition the role of repetition in Warhol. "I like boring things" is another of his famous sayings: "I like things to be exactly the same over and over again."[7] In *POPism* (1980) Warhol glosses his embrace of bored repetition: "I don't want it to be essentially the same—I want it to be exactly the same. Because the more you look at the same exact thing, the more the meaning goes away, and the better and emptier you feel."[8] Here repetition is cast as both a draining of unwanted significance and a defending against excessive affect, and this approach guided Warhol as early as his 1963 interview with Swenson: "When you see a gruesome picture over and over again, it doesn't really have any effect."[9] Clearly, this is one function of repetition: to rehearse a traumatic event in order to integrate it somehow into a psychic economy, a symbolic order. But repetition in Warhol is not often restorative in this way; rarely does it suggest a mastery of trauma, even in the case of his most familiar images. Consider the *Marilyn* silk screens, the first of which (the iconic gold one) was made immediately after her suicide on August 5, 1962 (fig. 3.1), or the *Jackie* silk screens, which were produced in the wake of the JFK assassination (fig. 3.2). Note all the cropping, copying, composing, and coloring of such images: these operations suggest an obsessive fixation on a lost object

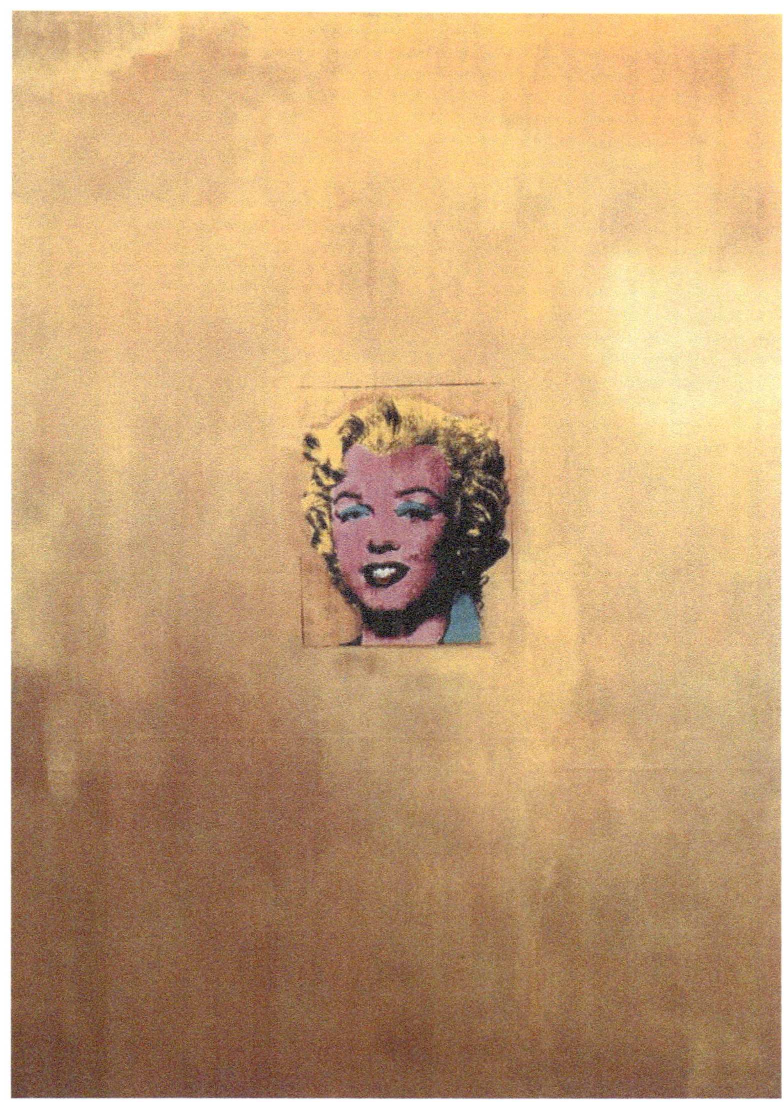

3.1 *Gold Marilyn*, 1962. Silkscreen ink on synthetic polymer paint on canvas, 83¼ × 57 in.
© 2012 The Andy Warhol Foundation for the Visual Arts, Inc. / Artists Rights Society (ARS),
New York.

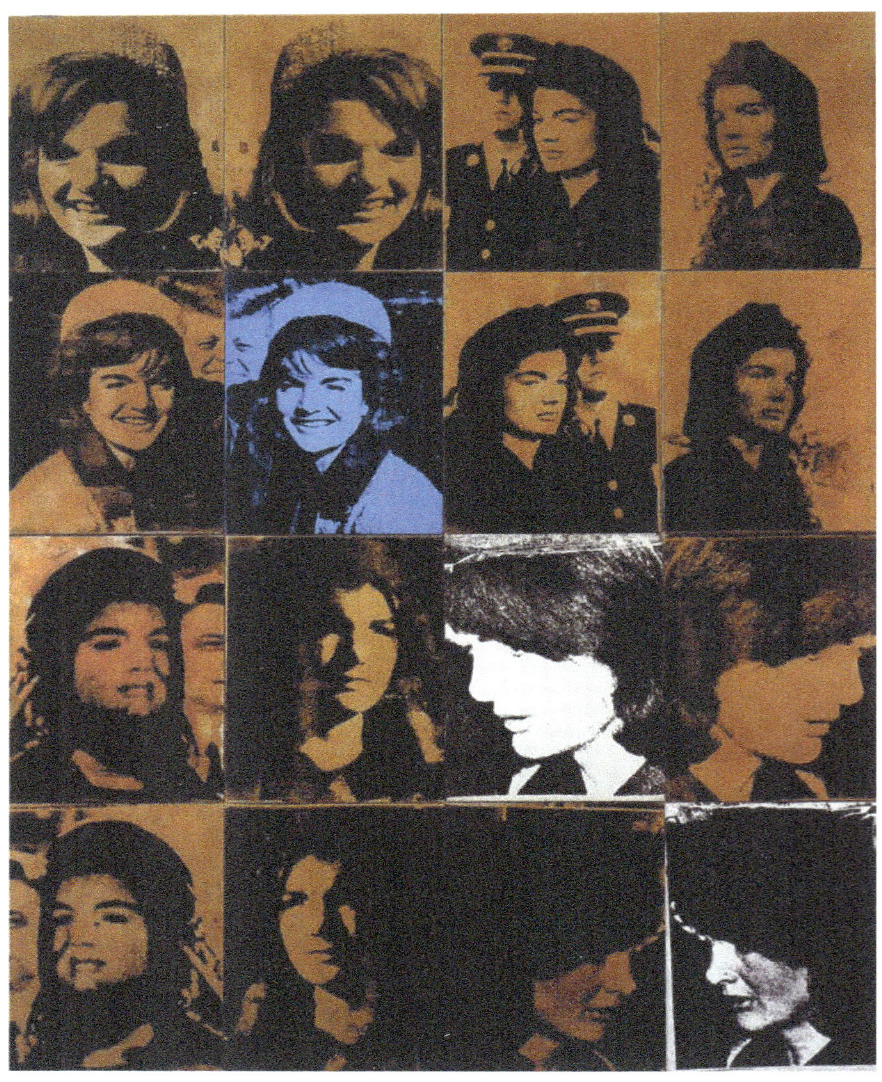

3.2 *Jackie (The Week That Was)*, 1963. Acrylic, spray paint, and silkscreen ink on linen, 80 × 64 in.
© 2012 The Andy Warhol Foundation for the Visual Arts, Inc. / Artists Rights Society (ARS), New York.

in melancholy, or a compulsive repetition of a traumatic event, more than a patient release from this object or that event in mourning.[10] Yet this account is not quite right either, for repetition in Warhol not only reproduces traumatic moments; often enough it produces them as well (I offer a few examples below). In these repetitions, then, several contradictory effects can occur at the same time: a warding off of traumatic significance and an opening to it, a defending against traumatic affect and a producing of it.[11]

In the early 1960s, Jacques Lacan was concerned with rethinking the real in terms of the traumatic. His salient seminar, "The Unconscious and Repetition," was roughly contemporaneous with the "Death and Disaster" images (it ran in early 1964), but its theory of trauma was not influenced by Pop.[12] However, it was informed by Surrealism, which here had its deferred effect on Lacan, a young associate of the movement three decades before, and "traumatic realism" is a category that Warholian Pop shares with Surrealism (it is the basis of such key Surrealist concepts as "the marvelous" and "convulsive beauty").[13] In this seminar, Lacan defines the traumatic as "a missed encounter" with the real, that is, as an encounter that is not registered consciously. In part because it is missed, the traumatic real cannot be represented as such; it can only be repeated—indeed, it must be repeated precisely because it is missed (it is like a blank in experience that continues to misfire). "*Wiederholen*," Lacan writes in reference to Freud, "is not *Reproduzieren*"; repetition is not reproduction.[14] This formula also holds for Warhol, for in his work, repetition is not reproduction in the sense either of a direct representation of a referent lodged in the world or of a superficial simulation of an image detached from it. Rather, repetition in Warhol often serves to *screen* the real understood as traumatic—an effect that is sometimes produced by other devices too, such as his blurring of the image, his washing it with color, or his doubling it with an empty canvas.[15] Yet this very need to screen or otherwise soften the real can also *point* to the real, and sometimes at this point the real seems to rupture the screen of his repetitions and so to poke through the image once again.

In an allusion to Aristotle on accidental causality, Lacan calls this traumatic point the *tuché*, while in *Camera Lucida* (1980), a celebrated study of photography that follows Lacan, Roland Barthes calls it the *punctum*. "It is this element which rises from the scene, shoots out of it like an arrow, and pierces me," Barthes writes. "It is what I add to the photograph and what is nonetheless already there."[16] Somehow, this rupture is both in the image and in the subject at once, or, more precisely, it occurs between the perception and the consciousness of a viewer touched by an image. Thus the confusion about the precise location of the rupture, *tuché*, or *punctum* is also a complication of subject and world, inside and outside, and this confusion is central to trauma (etymologically, "trauma" means "wound"); in fact it might be this confusion, this breaching, that *is* traumatic.[17] (In a 1960 painting of a schematic female torso based on a newspaper ad for surgical trusses, Warhol asks indirectly, "Where Is Yo__ Rupture?" [fig. 3.3], and certainly he was keen to the telling cracks not only in images but also in people, whom he tended to regard as another species of image.)[18] "It's just like taking the outside and putting it on the inside," Warhol once remarked, elliptically enough, about Pop, "or taking the inside and putting it on the outside."[19] Here the traumatic, understood as a confusion of interiority and exteriority, is implicated as the very operation of his art.

Concerned as Barthes is with straight photographs, he relates the *punctum* to details of content. This is not often the case with the traumatic points in Warhol. The accident in *White Burning Car* (1963; fig. 3.4) is appalling, to be sure: thrown out of his vehicle, the crash victim is impaled on a telephone pole (the photo is from the June 3, 1963, issue of *Newsweek*). Yet pierced though this figure literally is, there is no *punctum* here, at least for me (Barthes stipulates that it is a personal effect); the *punctum* lies instead in the indifference of the passerby in the background. This indifference is bad enough, but its repetition is galling (in three versions of *White Burning Car* the image appears five times). Another instance of such galling is the treatment of the two housewives (Mrs. McCarthy and Mrs. Brown by name) in the eleven versions of *Tunafish Disaster* (1963; fig. 3.5), both victims of botulism whose stories Warhol also appropriated from the pages of *Newsweek* (in this case the April 1, 1963, issue): smeared across the surface in one version, their smiling faces become piercing in repetition.

These examples begin to suggest the nature of the *punctum* in Warhol. Content is hardly trivial: to see a white man impaled on a telephone pole (not to mention a black man attacked by a police dog, as in the *Race Riot* silk screens [fig. 3.6]) is a shock. Yet, again, it is this first order of shock that

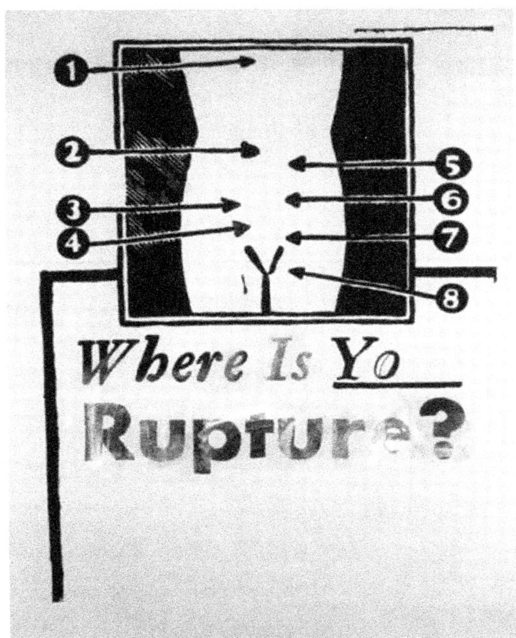

3.3 *Where Is Your Rupture?*
[1], 1960. Water-based paint
on cotton, 69½ × 54 in.
© 2012 The Andy Warhol
Foundation for the Visual Arts,
Inc. / Artists Rights Society
(ARS), New York.

his treatment of the image (its repeating, coloring, smearing, blanking, and so on) often serves to screen, even if in doing so this treatment sometimes produces a second order of trauma, here at the level of technique, where the *punctum* breaks through the screen and allows the real to poke through the image.[20] The *punctum* in Warhol, then, arises less through content than through technique, especially through the "floating flashes" of the silk-screen process, the engineered accidents (the slipping of the register, the streaking of the image, and so forth) that appear as the ink is squeezed onto the canvas and the screen is repositioned.[21] One more example of this effect: there is a *punctum* for me in *Ambulance Disaster* (1963–64; fig. 3.7), at least in one version of the three. The source image is a particularly gruesome UPI photo of a fatal accident involving two ambulances. But the *punctum* arises less from the dead woman slumped over the ambulance door in the upper half of the canvas than from the obscene stain that effaces her head in the same image in the lower half—a stain that was an accidental upshot of the silk-screen process.[22]

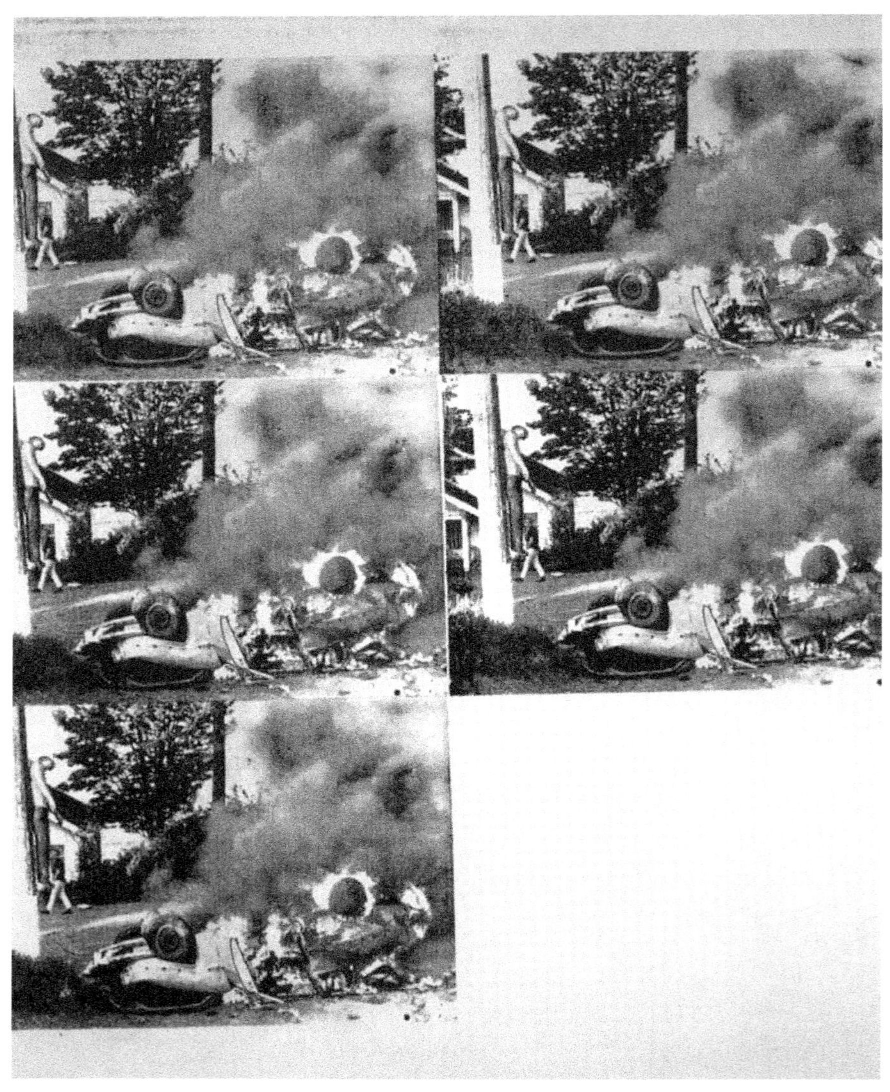

3.4 *White Burning Car III*, 1963. Silk-screen ink on linen, 100½ × 78¾ in. © 2012 The Andy Warhol Foundation for the Visual Arts, Inc. / Artists Rights Society (ARS), New York.

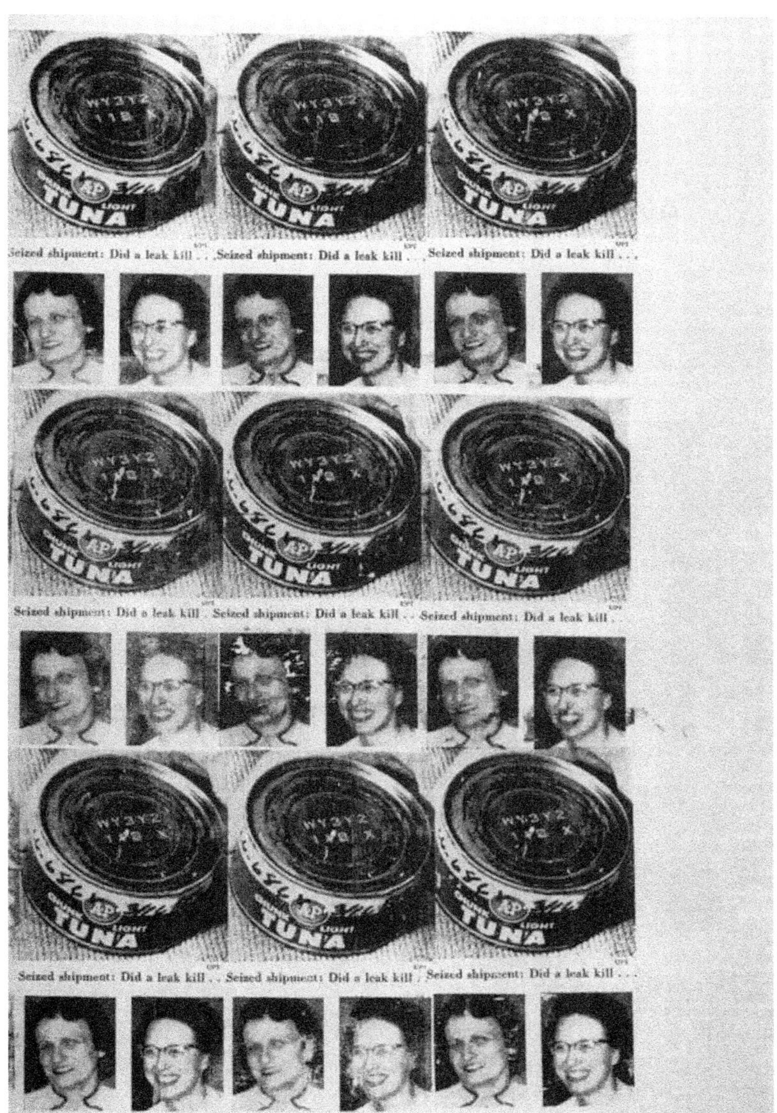

3.5 *Tunafish Disaster*, 1963. Silk-screen ink and silver paint on linen, 124½ × 83 in.
© 2012 The Andy Warhol Foundation for the Visual Arts, Inc. / Artists Rights
Society (ARS), New York.

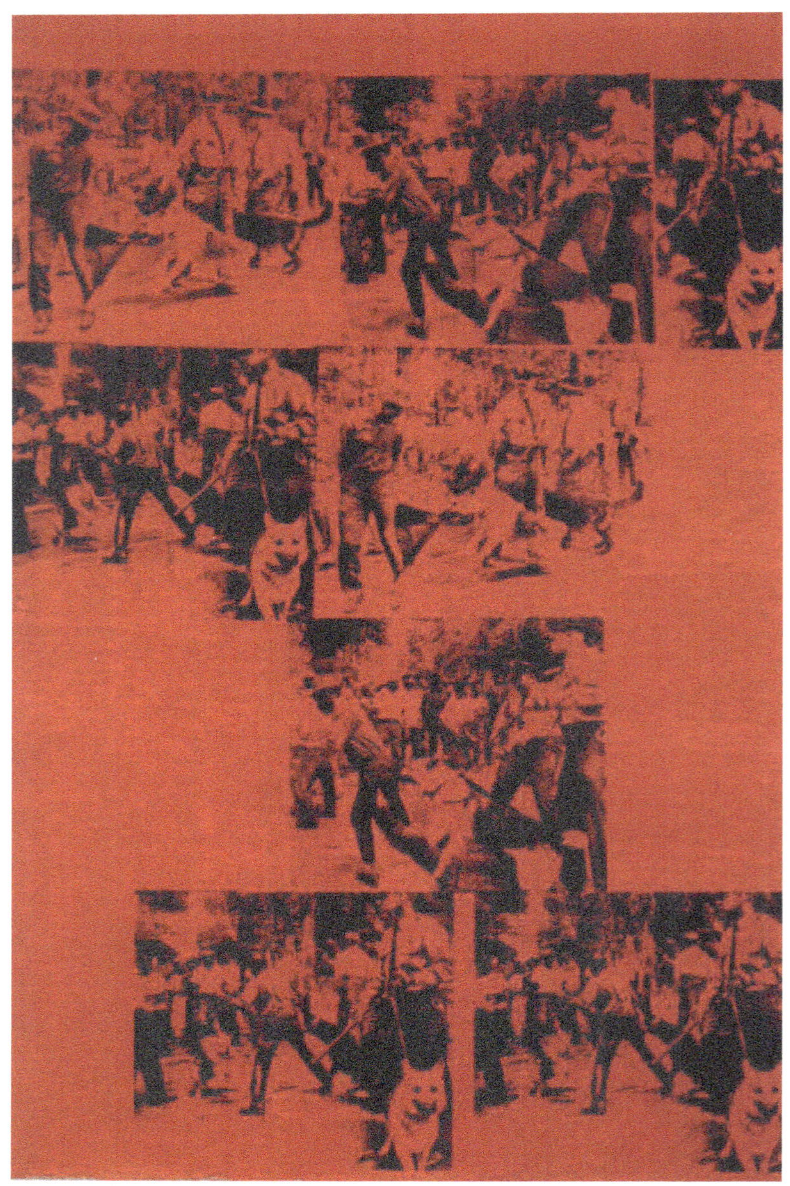

3.6 *Red Race Riot*, 1963. Silk-screen ink and acrylic on linen, 128¼ × 83 in. © 2012 The Andy Warhol Foundation for the Visual Arts, Inc. / Artists Rights Society (ARS), New York.

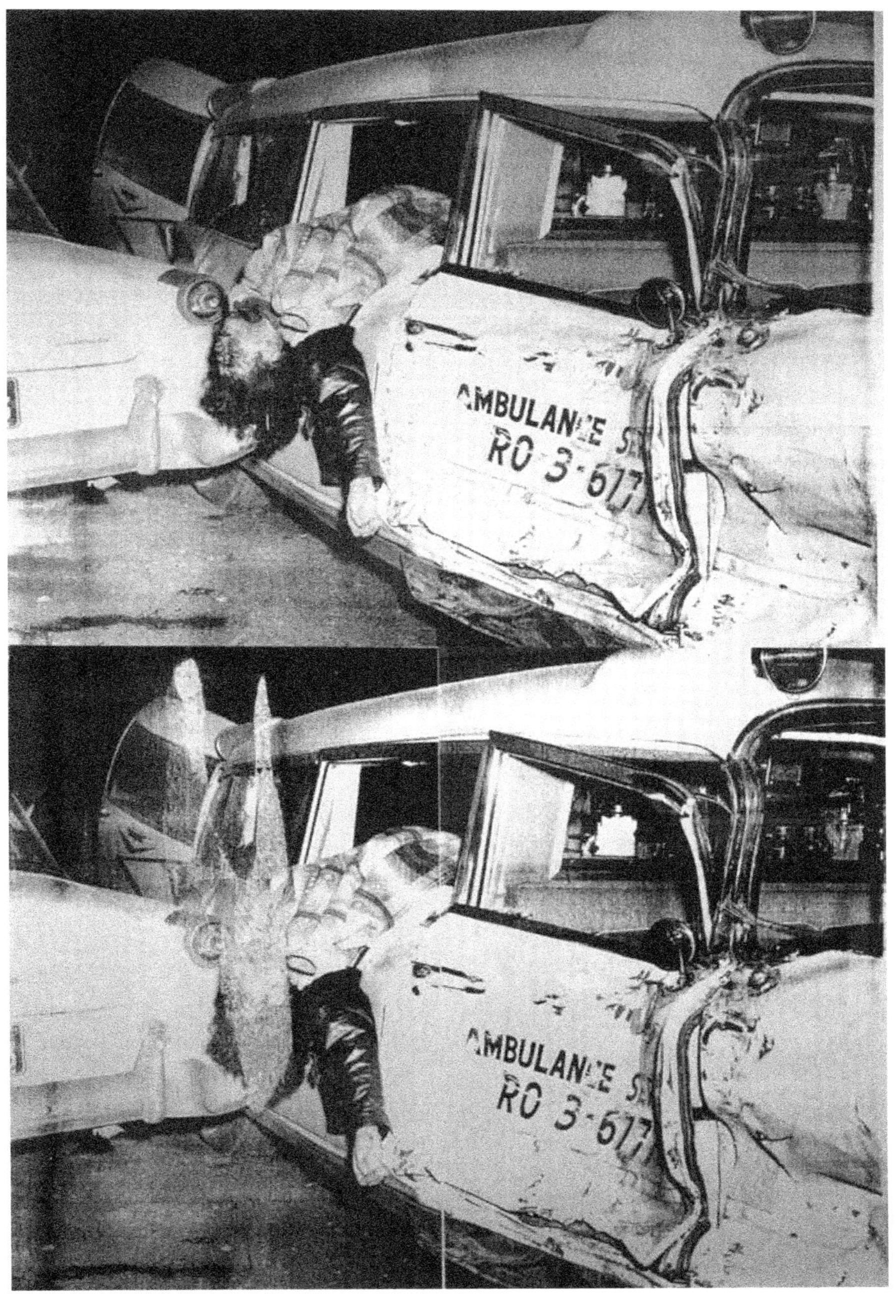

3.7 *Ambulance Disaster*, 1963–64. Silk-screen ink on linen, 119 × 80⅛ in. © 2012 The Andy Warhol Foundation for the Visual Arts, Inc. / Artists Rights Society (ARS), New York.

In short, the *punctum* in Warhol lies chiefly in the frequent flashing and popping of his images. "It was all so simple," he once remarked of his silkscreen technique, "quick and chancy. I was thrilled by it."[23] These flashes and pops are indeed quick and chancy, and sometimes they operate as visual correlatives of our missed encounters with the real. "What is repeated," Lacan writes, "is always something that occurs . . . *as if by chance*."[24] And so it is with the flashes and pops: however accidental, they can also appear repetitive, mechanical, even automatic. Sometimes, through these flashes and pops, we seem almost to touch the real, which the repetition of the image at once distances and rushes toward us; again, the blurring of the image and its washing in color can also produce this strange double effect. In these ways, then, Warhol puts different kinds of repetition into play: repetitions that fix on the traumatic real, that screen it, and that produce it. And this multiplicity makes for the Warholian paradox not only of images that are both affective and affectless, but also of viewers who feel neither composed, as in the ideal of most modern aesthetics (the subject made whole in contemplation), nor dissolved, as in the effect of some popular culture (the subject given over to the schizo intensities of the spectacle). "I never fall apart," Warhol remarked in *The Philosophy of Andy Warhol* (1975), "because I never fall together."[25] Such is the subject-effect of much of his work too; the viewer is left in this limbo as well.

They Were All Diseased

This distressing in Warhol is not restricted to the punctal space between the image and the subject; it also occurs separately in both, and in the next two sections, I consider each instance on its own. Distress in the image is found in Warhol early, middle, and late. According to legend, he broke into his Pop style abruptly in early 1962 when he presented two paintings of a Coca-Cola bottle, one still marked by traces of expressivity (such as drips and stains), the other purged of all such signs, to select friends like Emile de Antonio, who steered him toward the clean and cool version.[26] But this anecdote is misleading: the Warholian image is rarely so simple or secure, and its apparent ease is belied at every turn. Consider the early paintings that foreground the issue of artistic skill, such as the five *Do It Yourself* canvases (1962; fig. 3.8), based on paint-by-number images of banal landscapes and still lifes that Warhol

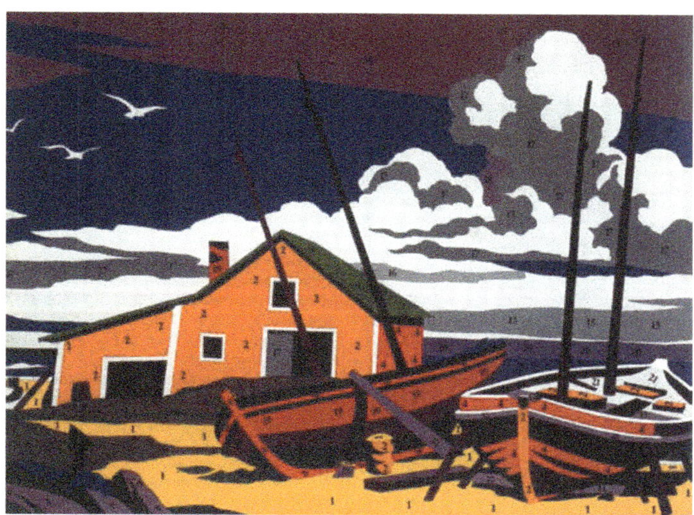

3.8 *Do It Yourself (Seascape)*, 1962. Acrylic, pencil, and Letraset on linen, 54¼ × 72¼ in. © 2012 The Andy Warhol Foundation for the Visual Arts, Inc. / Artists Rights Society (ARS), New York.

appropriated from the Venus Paradise Company (a name almost too good to be true). Like a subpar Sunday painter, he laid down the correct colors in the stipulated areas, yet only one of the patterns, the seascape, qualifies as finished according to the template. Warhol stages failure even in this prosaic, almost robotic kind of picture making.

Moreover, the image had already appeared deteriorated in his 1960–61 paintings based on newspaper advertisements. Here Warhol drew from cheap ads that hawked, among other products and procedures, hernia supports (used in the three versions of *Where Is Your Rupture?*), nose jobs (used in the three versions of *Before and After*), false teeth, wigs and extensions, and corn treatments (fig. 3.9). Significantly, all refer to the vicissitudes of the body and its image, with pain and relief an explicit subject in one work ("Stop Pain" exhorts an ad concerning corns), and desire and desirability in another (an ad showing a couple in evening clothes reads "Make Him Want You"); in the context of these paintings, the cosmetic improvement diagrammed in *Before and After* seems tenuous, to say the least (fig. 3.10).[27] Often in these works, the texts appear as eroded as the images, and this is

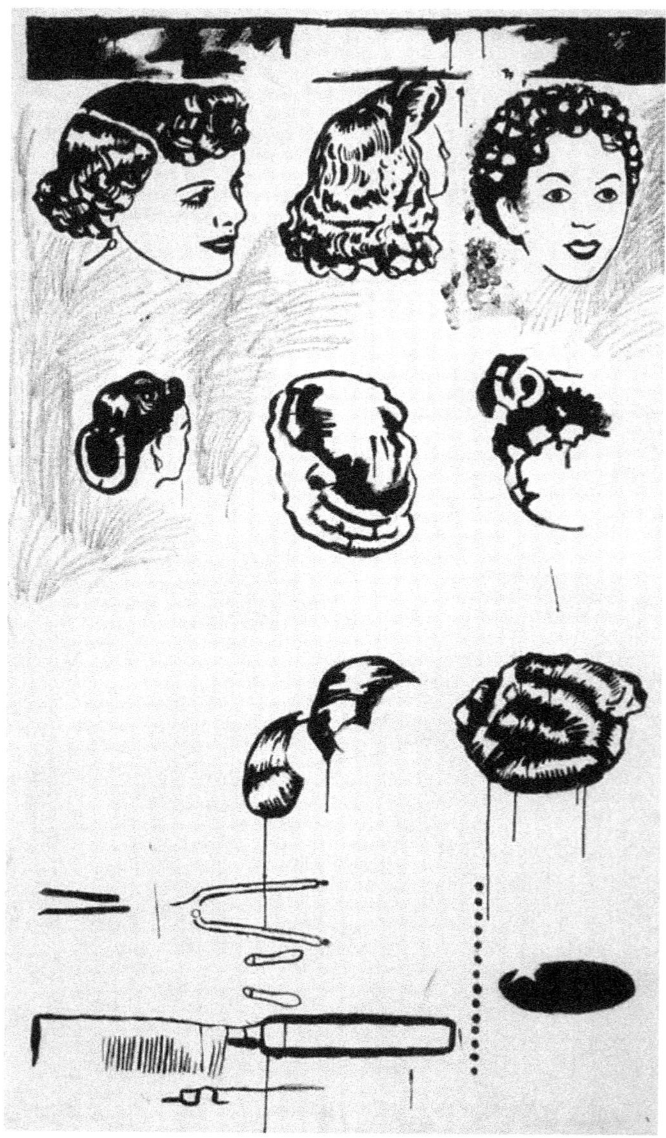

3.9 *Wigs*, 1960. Casein and wax crayon on cotton, 70 × 40 in. © 2012 The Andy Warhol Foundation for the Visual Arts, Inc. / Artists Rights Society (ARS), New York.

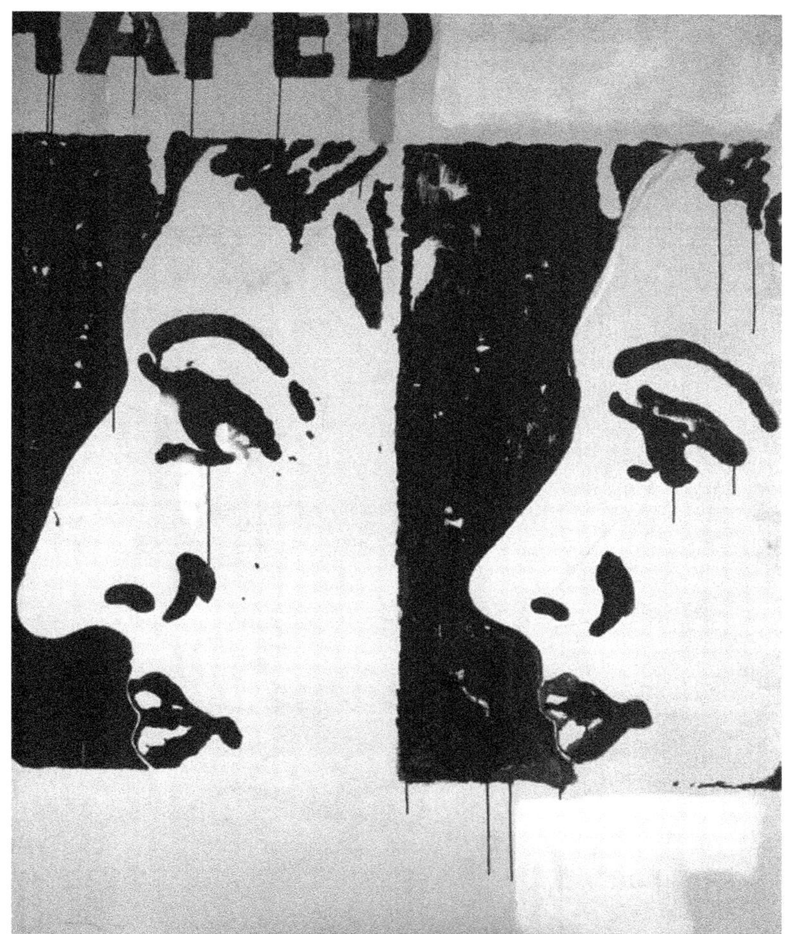

3.10 *Before and After [1]*, 1960. Shiva casein on preprimed cotton duck, 68 × 54 in.
© 2012 The Andy Warhol Foundation for the Visual Arts, Inc. / Artists Rights
Society (ARS), New York.

also the case in the early paintings based on comic strips such as *Dick Tracy* (1960; fig. 3.11)—a breakdown in language as well as in picture to which Warhol would return in his last decade.[28] Subsequent images of consumer products, painted in shiny black and white, are not so distressed, it is true, yet here the chosen items—a turn-of-the-century toilet, a bathtub of the same vintage, a 1928 telephone, a 1936 typewriter (all 1961; fig. 3.12)—are out-of-date, as if nothing could escape outmoding, neither the commodity nor its aesthetic double, the readymade (with the toilet and the typewriter, Warhol alludes specifically to two readymades by Duchamp). Finally, the distressing of the product is overt in those *Campbell's Soup Can*s (1962; fig. 3.13) with torn labels and discolored tins. Given his identification with this commodity in particular, they might be taken as disguised portraits of the damaged artist as a no-longer-so-young man.

Early on, Warhol mooted actual harm to the artwork as well. Thematically, damage is suggested in the fifteen shipping-label paintings, such as *Handle with Care—Glass—Thank You* (1962; fig. 3.14), which point to what they warn against—mishandling and shattering. So, too, the five *Close Cover Before Striking* paintings (1962; fig. 3.15), in which sandpaper bands represent the friction strips on matchbook covers, all but invited viewers to scratch them, and a few were so marked. The seven *Dance Diagram* paintings (1962; fig. 3.16) also imply wear and tear; in fact, first exhibited flat on the floor, they were susceptible to outright damage.[29] And in the same years, Warhol proposed other aggressive measures, such as canvases placed on the sidewalk to be walked on by passersby (the so-called *Footprint* paintings) or on the studio floor to be urinated on by assistants (the so-called *Piss* paintings), which were resumed in earnest with the *Oxidation* paintings of 1978. "In the end I had a lot of dirty canvases," Warhol remarked in retrospect. "Then I thought they were all diseased and so I rolled them up and put them somewhere."[30] For an artist often identified with the sheer superficiality of images, this association not only with active bodiliness but also with mortal corruption might come as a surprise.[31]

Again, Warhol injects smearing and streaking, blanking and washing, flashing and popping, in his early silk screens, but perhaps his key means of

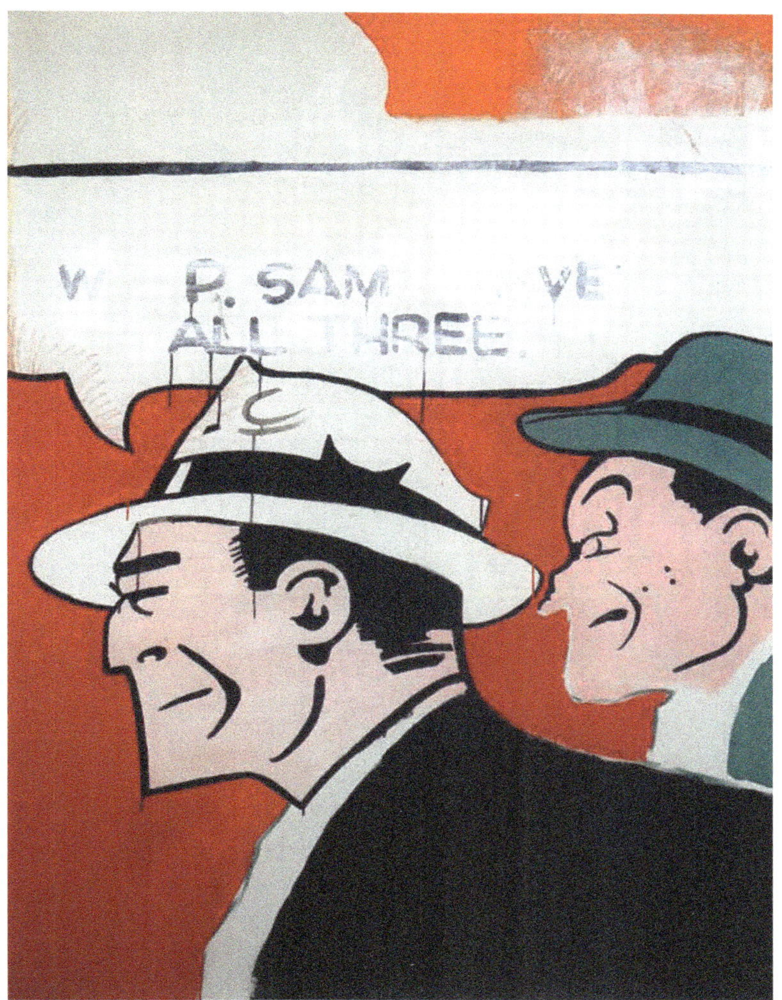

3.11 *Dick Tracy*, 1960. Synthetic polymer paint on canvas, 79 × 45 in. © 2012 The Andy Warhol Foundation for the Visual Arts, Inc. / Artists Rights Society (ARS), New York.

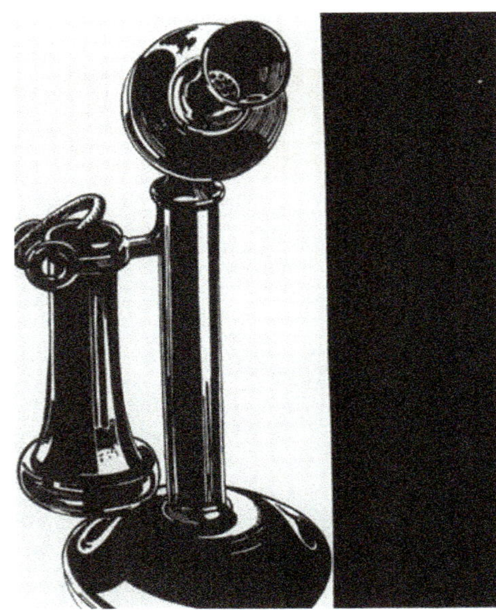

3.12 *Telephone [2]*, 1961. Casein on linen, 69¾ × 54⅛ in. © 2012 The Andy Warhol Foundation for the Visual Arts, Inc. / Artists Rights Society (ARS), New York.

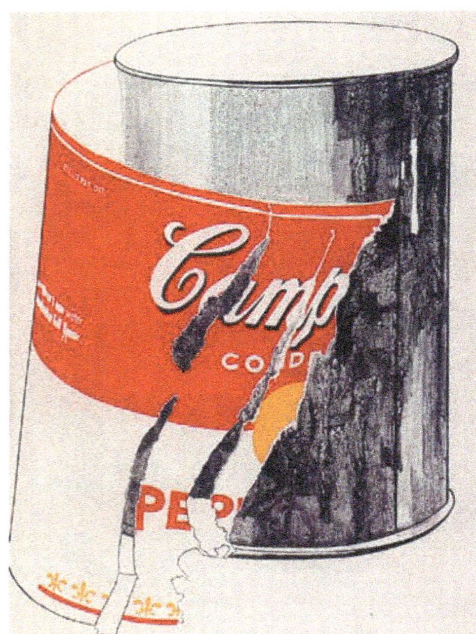

3.13 *Big Torn Campbell's Soup Can (Pepper Pot)*, 1962. Oil, synthetic polymer paint, and Prestype on canvas, 71¾ × 51¾ in. © 2012 Andy Warhol Foundation / ARS, New York / Trademarks, Campbell Soup Company. All rights reserved.

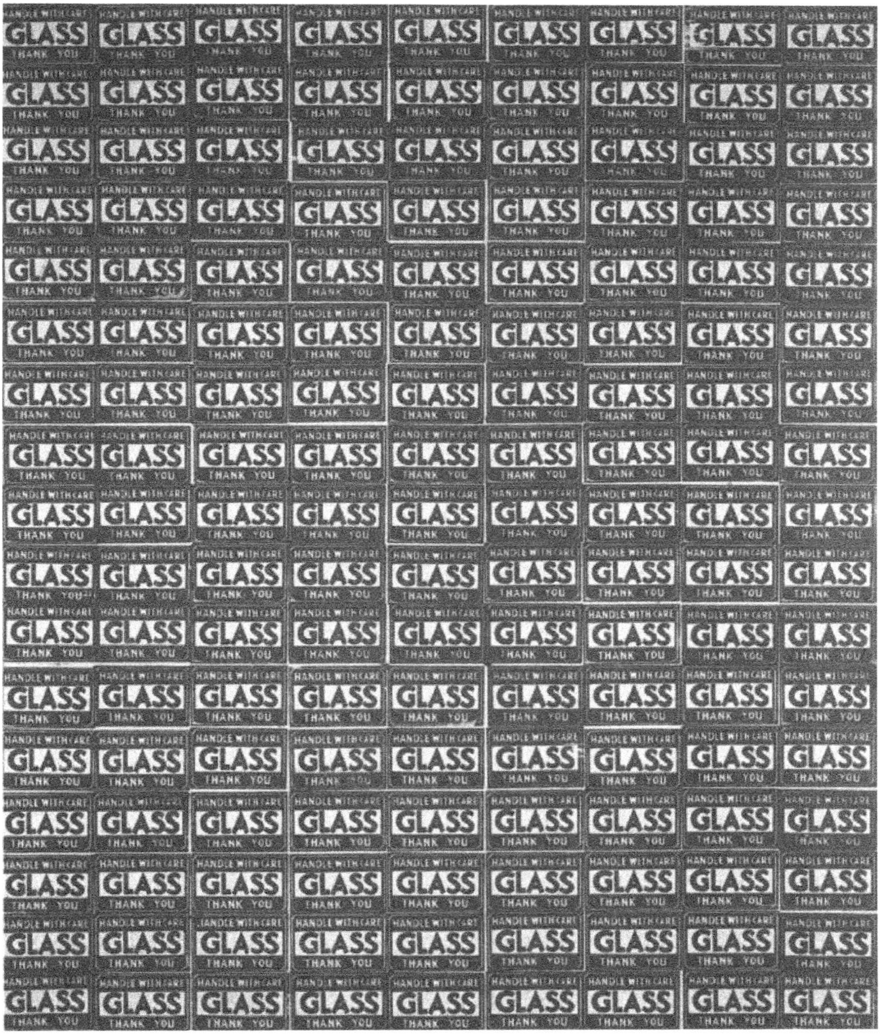

3.14 *Handle with Care—Glass—Thank You*, 1962. Silk-screen ink and pencil on linen, 81¾ × 66½ in.
© 2012 The Andy Warhol Foundation for the Visual Arts, Inc. / Artists Rights Society (ARS), New York.

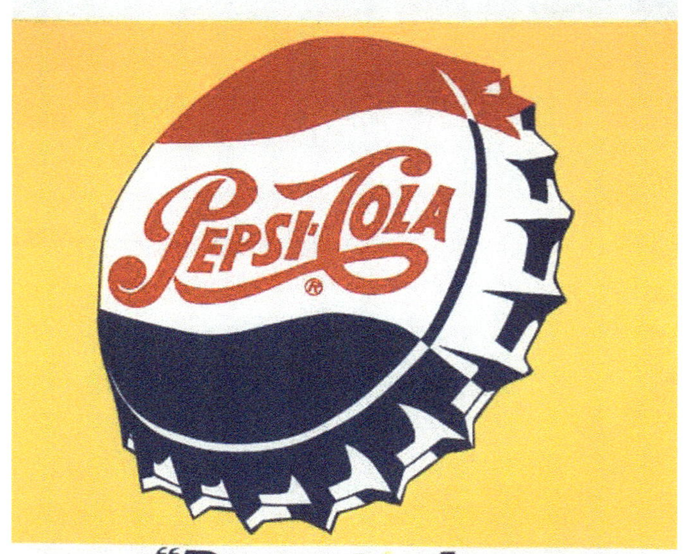

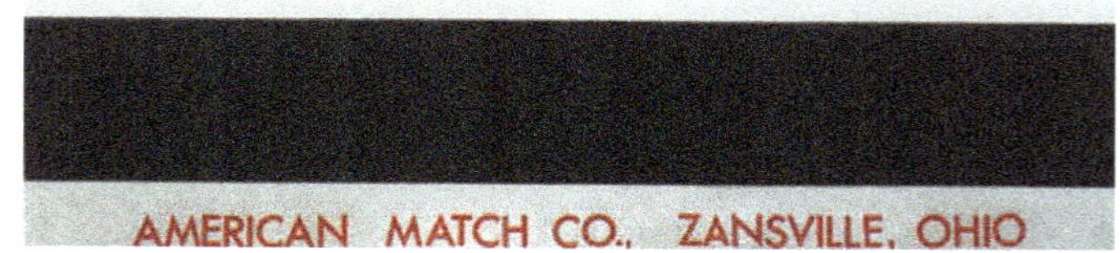

3.15 *Close Cover Before Striking (Pepsi-Cola),* 1962. Acrylic, pencil, Letraset, and sandpaper on linen, 72 × 54 in. © 2012 The Andy Warhol Foundation for the Visual Arts, Inc. / Artists Rights Society (ARS), New York.

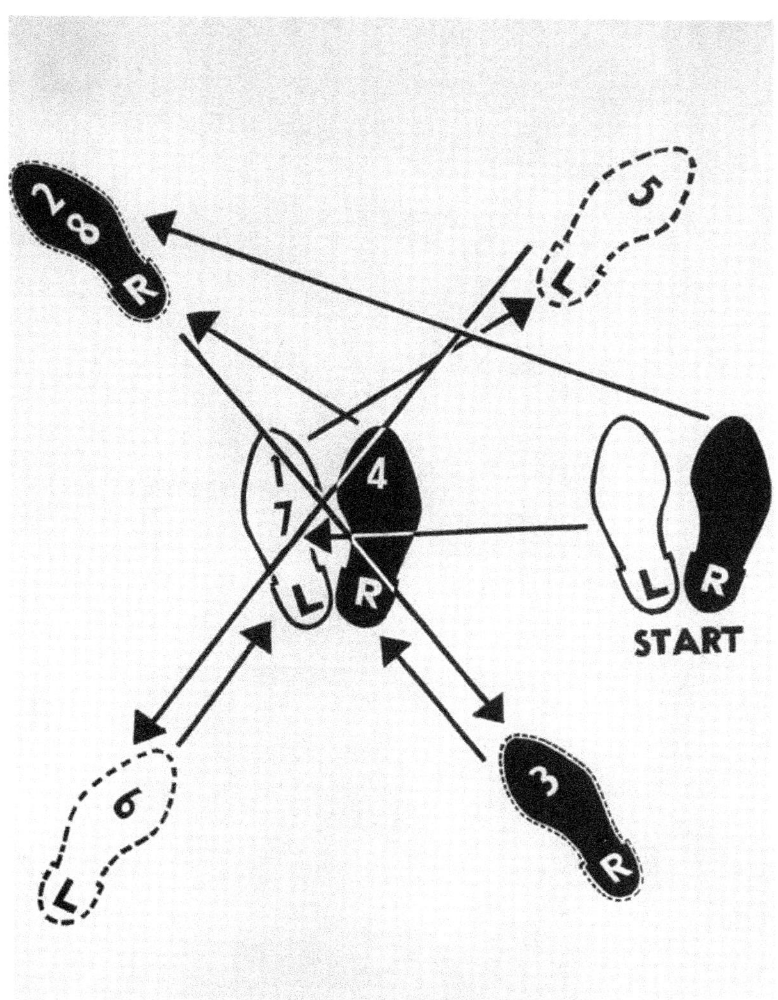

3.16 *Dance Diagram [6] ["The Charleston Double Side Kick—Man and Woman"]*, 1962. Casein and pencil on linen, 71½ × 53½ in. © 2012 The Andy Warhol Foundation for the Visual Arts, Inc. / Artists Rights Society (ARS), New York.

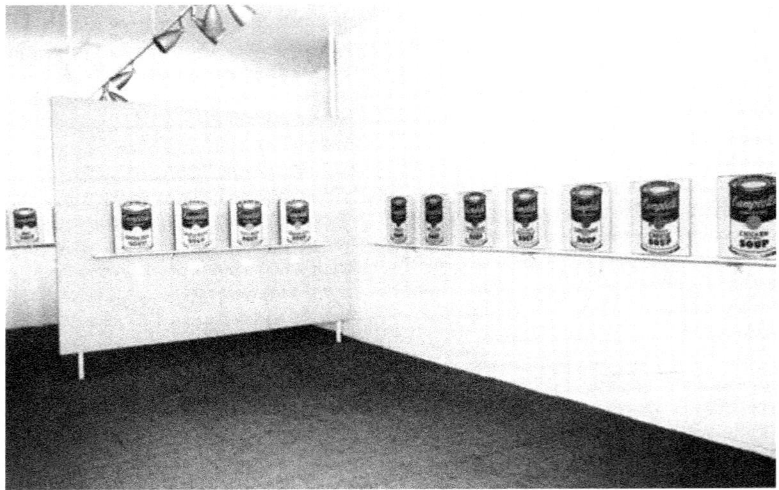

3.17 Installation view of *Campbell's Soup Cans* at the Ferus Gallery, Los Angeles, July 1962.
© 2012 Andy Warhol Foundation / ARS, New York / Trademarks, Campbell Soup Company.
All rights reserved.

distress there is sheer repetition. Serial replication would seem to reinforce the image, not to subvert it, and sometimes, as with the row of thirty-two individual *Campbell's Soup Cans* first shown at the Ferus Gallery in Los Angeles in July 1962 (fig. 3.17), this is the initial effect: canned and sealed twice over, as it were, the images appear perfect as both product and display, with each made and presented in the same manner. Yet even here the re-doubling complicates the image as the singular soups are subsumed by the generic brand, and especially when seriality occurs within a single painting, as in, say, *Two Hundred Campbell's Soup Cans* (1962; fig. 3.18), more be-comes dramatically less as the image approaches the point of abstraction.[32] This is to say that repetition in Warhol often either produces a sameness or

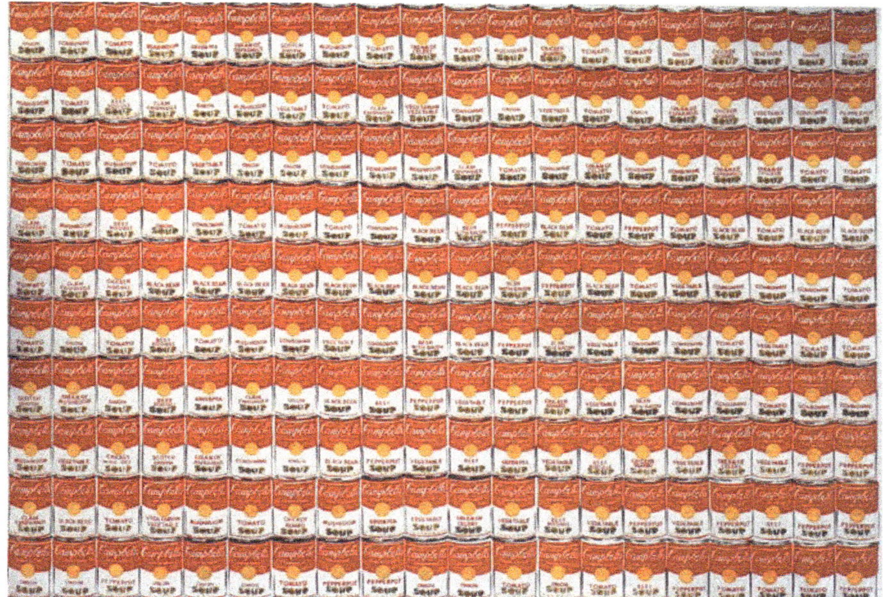

3.18 *Two Hundred Campbell's Soup Cans*, 1962. Synthetic polymer paint on canvas, 72 × 100 in. © 2012 Andy Warhol Foundation / ARS, New York / Trademarks, Campbell Soup Company. All rights reserved.

releases a difference, and that both can be corrosive of the identity of the image. Sometimes, too, the effect is to obscure the image, literally, as the silk-screen ink thins with repeated use of the screen or blots with uneven application on the canvas.[33] An instance of the former phenomenon is *Elvis Six Times* (1963; fig. 3.19), in which the figure becomes spectral in the course of its horizontal iterations; an instance of the latter phenomenon is *Baseball* (1962; fig. 3.20), the first silk screen with a photographic template, in which the figure of the batter, repeated forty-two times, is blotted out midway through the bottom row.

This deterioration of the image through seriality is not limited to the silk screens; it begins with stencil paintings like *Handle with Care* and with

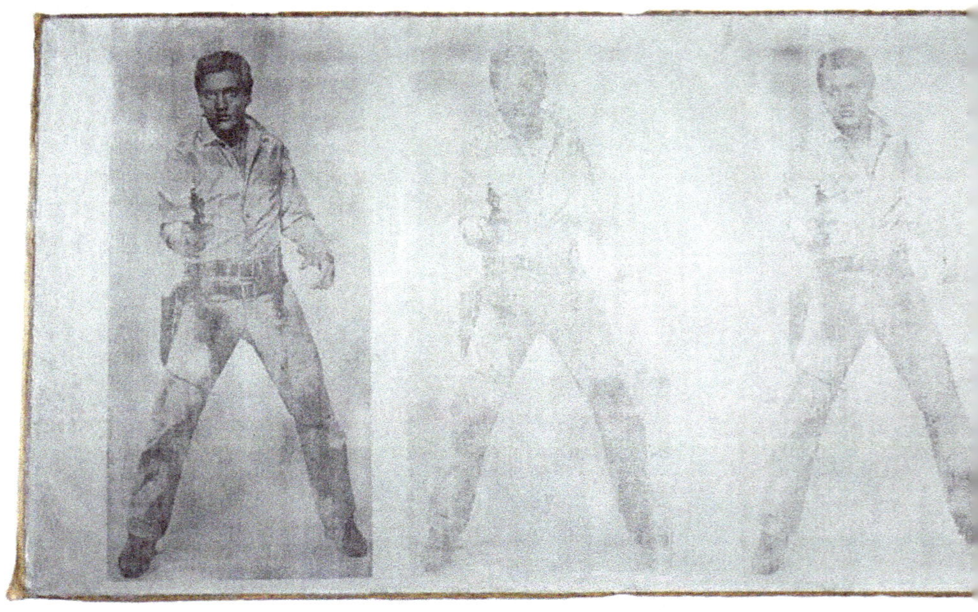

3.19 *Elvis Six Times*, 1963. Silk-screen ink and silver paint on linen, 83½ × 241¾ in. © 2012 The Andy Warhol Foundation for the Visual Arts, Inc. / Artists Rights Society (ARS), New York.

stamp paintings like *Air Mail Stamps* and *S&H Green Stamps* (1962; fig. 3.21), which were produced by means of actual stamps that Warhol carved into art-gum erasers, applied with paint, and printed on canvas. Just as the flag and target paintings of Jasper Johns are given as flat, so these stamp images are given as serial; yet, already imprecise as templates, they also vary in repetition. Another type of deterioration is implied here too, a devaluation through counterfeiting. This issue is raised again, directly, with the very first silk screens, in which Warhol arrayed his own drawings of dollar bills

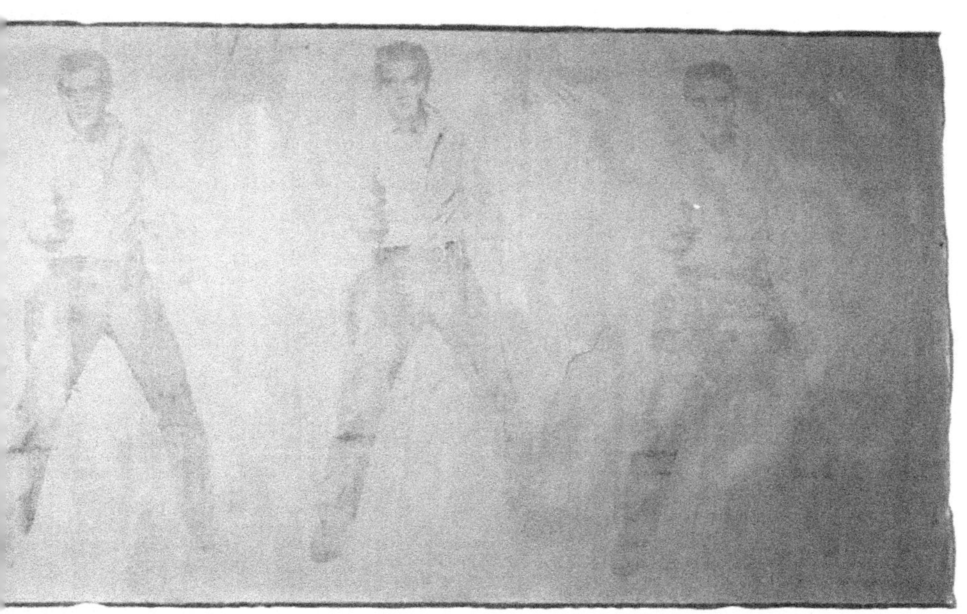

in different ways on the canvas (fig. 3.22). Like the stamp paintings, the bill silk screens invite us to consider the instabilities of value in images—to question what counts as "tender" or "trust" in representation. Finally, the devaluation of the image is also mooted through sheer proliferation. Between 1962 and 1964, Warhol produced some 2,000 paintings, or more than one a day; and his later photographs present an even more extreme statistic: from 1976 to 1986, he exposed on average a roll of film a day, which amounts to more than 100,000 shots.[34]

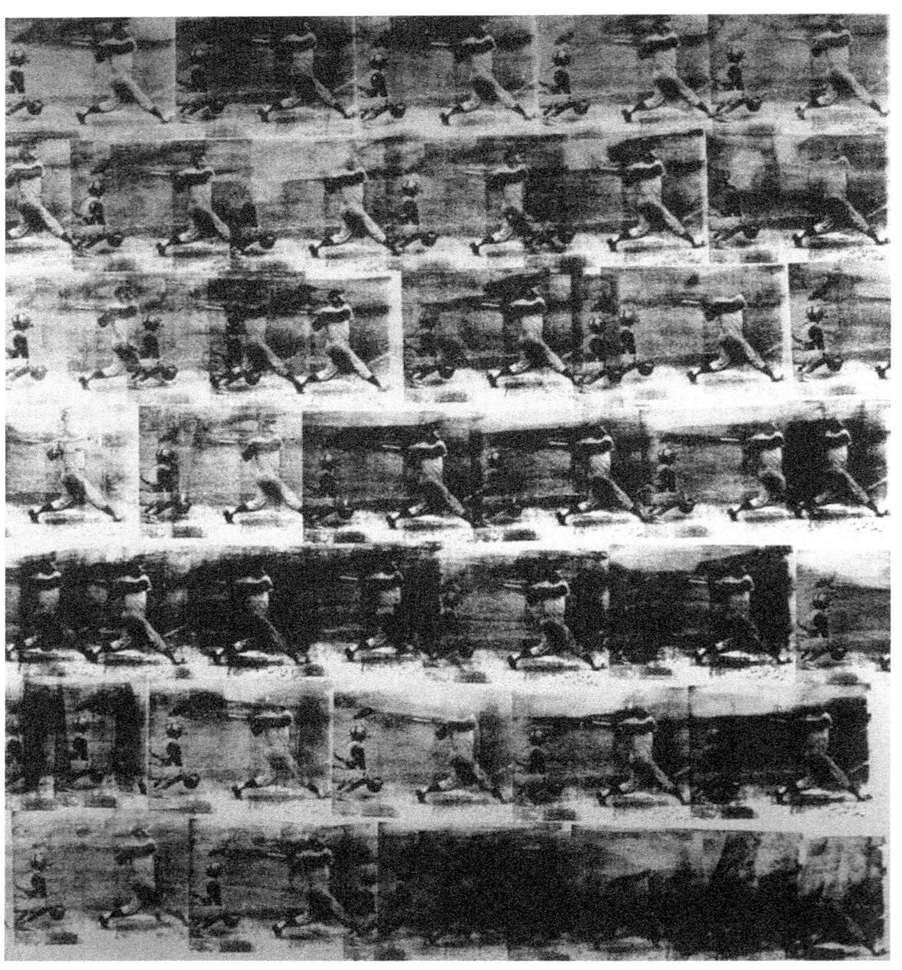

3.20 *Baseball*, 1962. Silk-screen ink on linen, 91¾ × 82 in. © 2012 The Andy Warhol Foundation for the Visual Arts, Inc. / Artists Rights Society (ARS), New York.

Besides the aforementioned dancing, walking, and pissing—all procedures that, again, register bodily desublimation as well—Warhol distressed his images through other indexical procedures: blotting, printing, stenciling, stamping, and screening. This predilection for indexicality cuts across the usual divisions of his work into commercial and artistic modes and early and later periods. In his illustrations from the late 1940s, for instance, Warhol favored the blotted-line technique, in which ink is transferred by contact from support to support, and intermittently he used offset printing from 1953, stamping from 1955, and gold leaf from 1956.[35] So, too, in his initial Pop work, Warhol developed stenciling, stamping, and silkscreening in rapid succession from February to August 1962, with the last his principal technique thereafter. All these procedures can produce images that are emphatic, even iconic; at the same time, their indexicality often works against this iconicity, and sometimes resemblance to any referent is lost altogether. Warhol only deepens this indexical distressing of the image in his later work. Produced by sprays and puddles of urine in contact with canvases coated with metallic paint, the *Oxidation* paintings (1977–82; fig. 3.23) are manifestly indexical, largely automatic (or "autochemical") in process, and mostly amorphous as a result. And as silk screens of photographs of shadows, the *Shadow* paintings (1978–79; fig. 3.24) are doubly, even triply, indexical; in the process, the things used to cast the shadows have all but disappeared, and only rarely can they be conjured up from the obscure traces on the canvases. These two series in particular test not only our definitions of representation and abstraction but also our very understanding of what an image is.[36]

Warhol sustained this testing throughout his later paintings, many of which problematize the distinction between figure and ground, which is fundamental to image production and reception alike. Such dedifferentiation might be the one common characteristic of these otherwise disparate series.[37] Evident in some *Shadow*s and *Oxidation*s, dedifferentiation is explicit in all the *Camouflage*s (1986; fig. 3.25), where the imbrication of figure and ground exists patently on the canvas. A disruptive oscillation between the two can also occur in our eyes, as it were, through an optical pulsation effected by color contrasts. Already active in some *Optical Car*

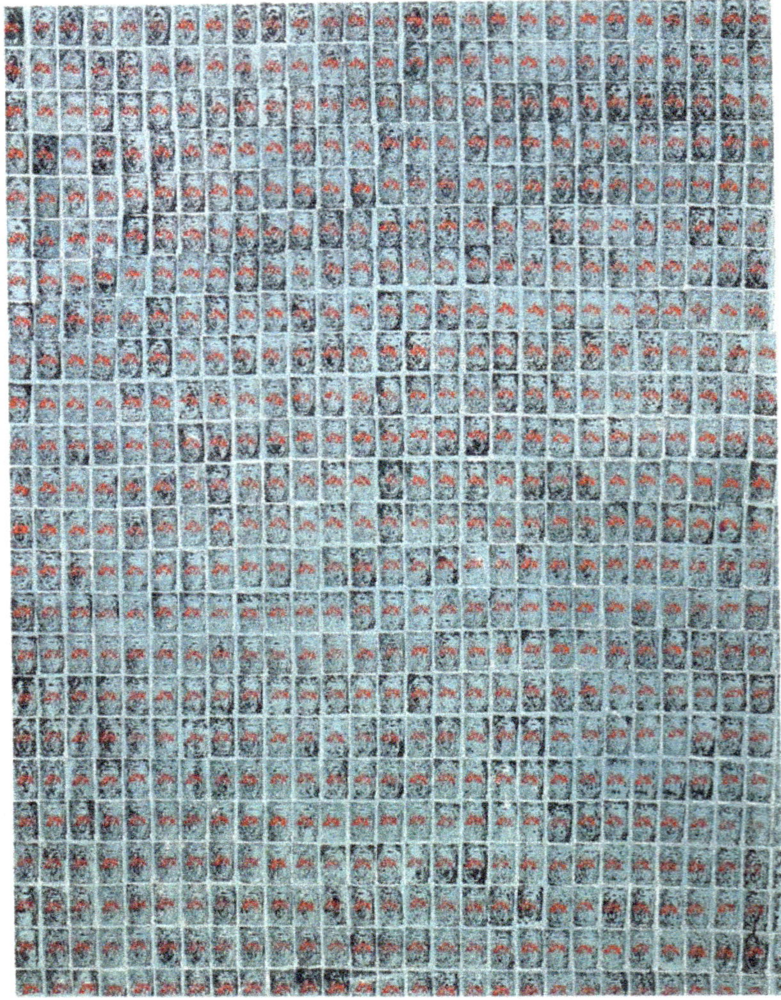

3.21 *S&H Green Stamps*, 1962. Acrylic on linen, 71¾ × 53½ in. © 2012 The Andy Warhol Foundation for the Visual Arts, Inc. / Artists Rights Society (ARS), New York.

3.22 *Many One-Dollar Bills,* 1962. Silk-screen ink, acrylic, and pencil on linen, 52 × 72 in. © 2012 The Andy Warhol Foundation for the Visual Arts, Inc. / Artists Rights Society (ARS), New York.

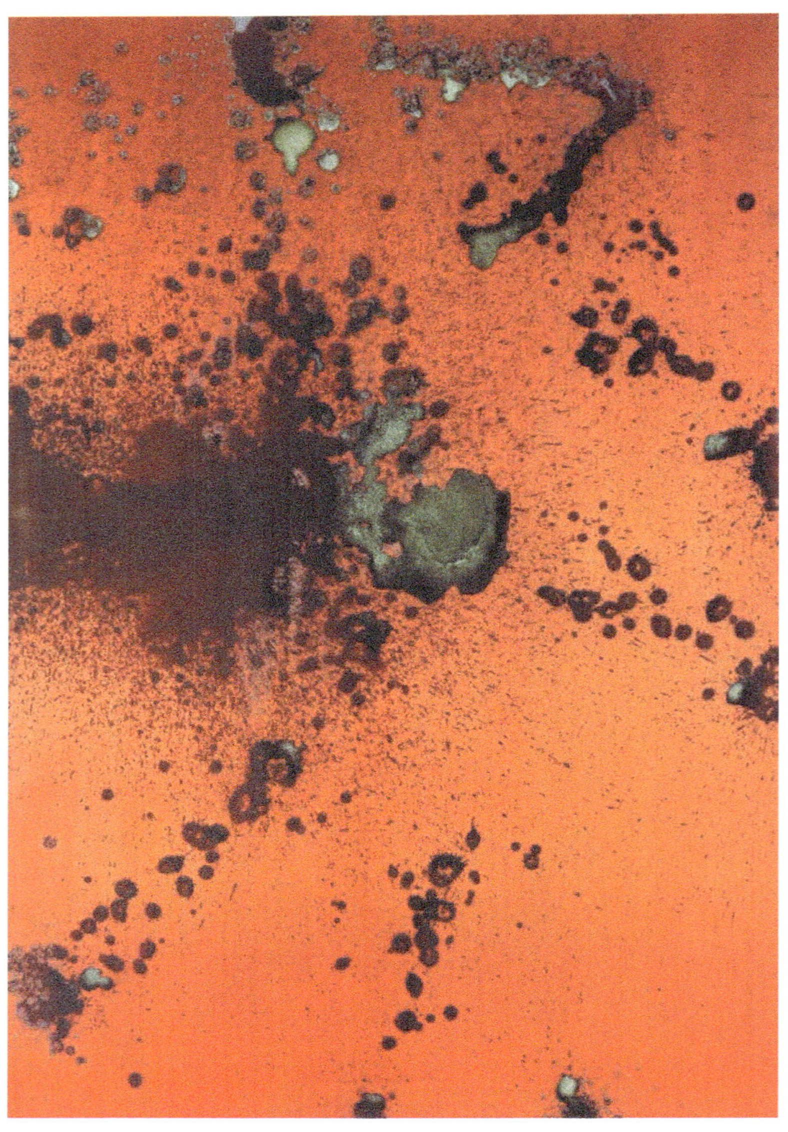

3.23 *Oxidation*, 1978. Copper paint and urine on canvas, 76 × 52 in. © 2012 The Andy Warhol Foundation for the Visual Arts, Inc. / Artists Rights Society (ARS), New York.

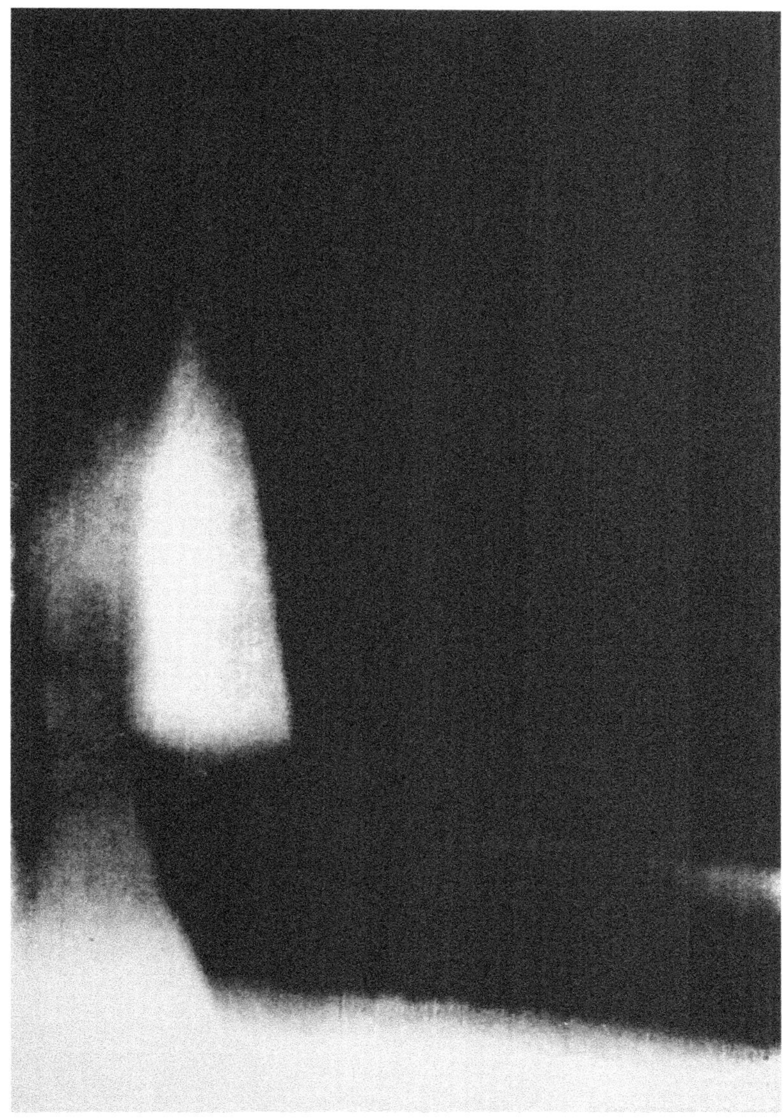

3.24 *Shadow*, 1978–79. Silk-screen ink on synthetic polymer paint on canvas, 76 × 52 in.
© 2012 The Andy Warhol Foundation for the Visual Arts, Inc. / Artists Rights Society (ARS),
New York.

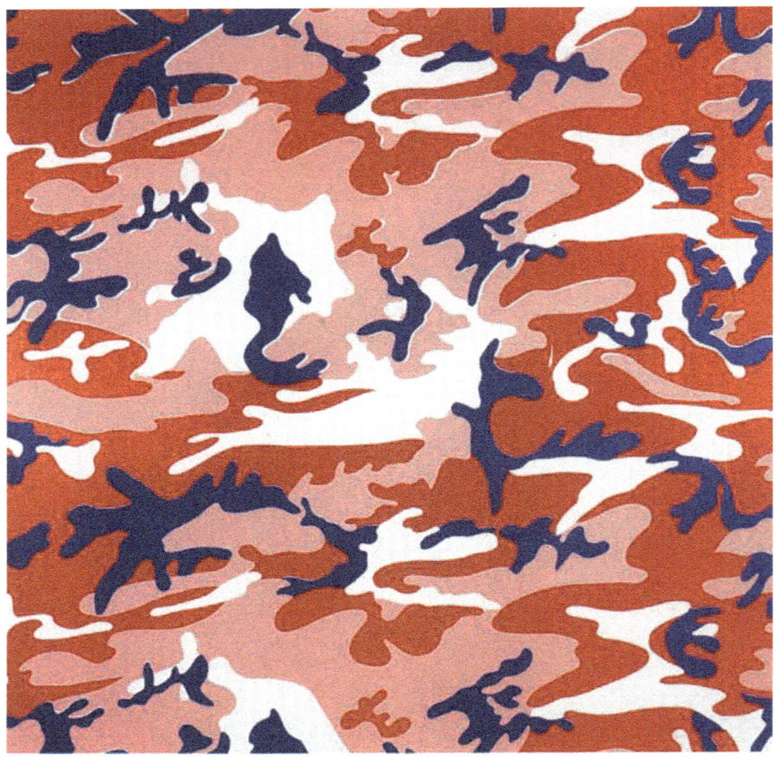

3.25 *Camouflage*, 1986. Acrylic and silk-screen ink on canvas, 80 × 80 in. © 2012 The Andy Warhol Foundation for the Visual Arts, Inc. / Artists Rights Society (ARS), New York.

Crash (1962) and *Flower* (1964) paintings, this pulsatile effect is strong in several *Diamond Dust Shoes* (1980; fig. 3.26), where it is produced by the throbbing of the colored high heels on the rich black ground as well as the dazzle of the diamond dust on the painting surface. It is also in play in some *Reflected (Zeitgeist Series)* paintings (1982; fig. 3.27), in which an image of a colonnade of spotlights in the night sky—the notorious "cathedral of ice" designed by Albert Speer for the Nazi Party rally at Nuremberg in 1937—is silk-screened in electric colors on black grounds (in one instance, in three long rows of bright red, yellow, and blue on deep black). The last two se-ries even hint at the problematic uses of pictorial bedazzlement in political

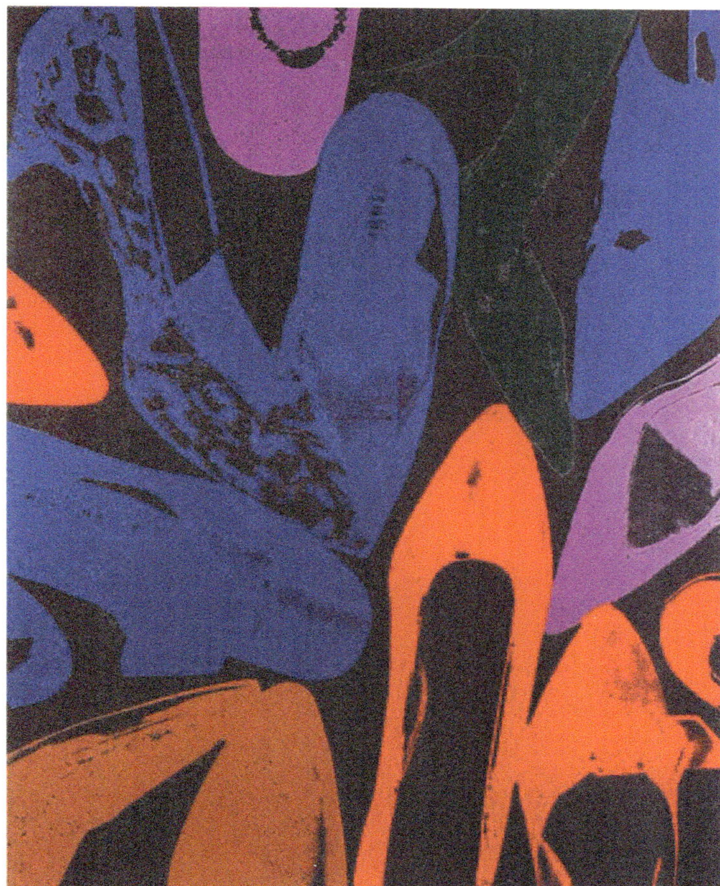

3.26 *Diamond Dust Shoes*, 1980. Silk-screen ink and diamond dust on synthetic polymer paint on canvas, 90 × 70 in. © 2012 The Andy Warhol Foundation for the Visual Arts, Inc. / Artists Rights Society (ARS), New York.

regimes—whether driven by the American cult of glamour, as in *Diamond Dust Shoes*, or the Nazi cult of the techno-sublime, as in *Reflected*.[38]

The two kinds of dedifferentiation at issue here, physical and optical, come together in another late series, the *Yarn* paintings (1983; fig. 3.28), which are scarcely known to this day. Commissioned by a textile company

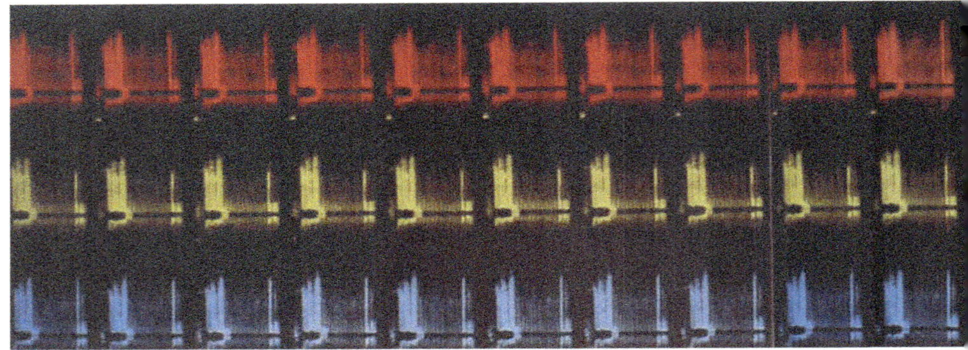

3.27 *Reflected (Zeitgeist Series)*, 1982. Silk-screen ink on synthetic polymer paint on canvas,
84 × 477 in. © 2012 The Andy Warhol Foundation for the Visual Arts, Inc. / Artists Rights
Society (ARS), New York.

in Florence, the *Yarn*s are built up from a single silk screen of one skein of
yarn overprinted multiply on canvas; the results are pulsatile webs that recall
the drip paintings of Pollock, though they are never so dense (the favored
colors are also quite different—reds, yellows, oranges, blues, greens, and
pinks). Many of the *Yarn*s are only a meter square, but a few do approach
the horizontal extent and immersive scale of the great Pollocks. And like
some drip paintings, some *Yarn*s project an optical intensity that flips the
impression of plenitude in the image into a sense of scotoma in the viewer
(scotoma as understood by Freud, too, as a condition in which "the ego has
lost control of the organ" of sight).[39] According to Michael Fried, a few drip
paintings, such as *Out of the Web: Number 7, 1949*, where bits of the canvas
are literally cut away, produce "a kind of blind spot," as if a part of our visual
field has also been excised in the process.[40] A few *Yarn*s suggest a related effect, albeit through a scattering of vision more than a blinding. "Pulsatile,
dazzling, and spread out": such is how Lacan described the gaze, which he
located in the first instance not in any human subject but in the world at

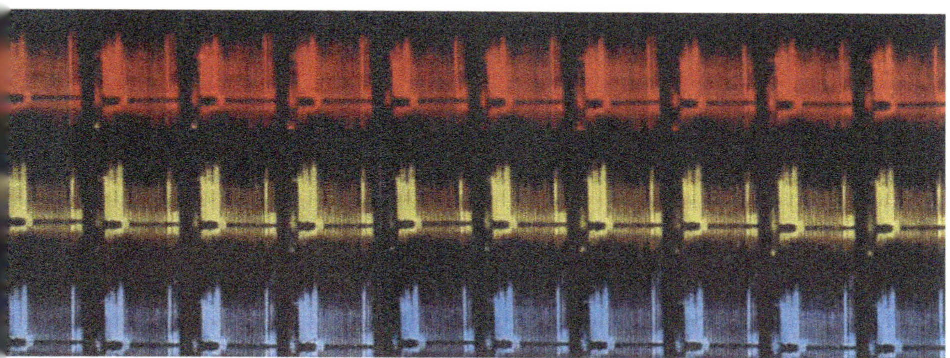

large, in its ambient light before it is tamed by any picture or screen.[41] Some *Yarn*s provoke a similar sort of optical vertigo.

"The point of the gaze," Lacan remarked, "always participates in the ambiguity of the jewel," and jewels figure in yet another late series by Warhol, the *Gem* paintings (1978–79; fig. 3.29), which are also little known.[42] Often large (some are two meters wide), most *Gem*s are near monochromes in pale yellows and greens. A cut gem almost fills the canvas, but ambiguously so: it is difficult to determine where it begins or ends, or whether it advances toward us or recedes from us—an ambiguity that is a combined effect of the lustrous light within the image of the jewel and the thin film of diamond dust on the painted surface. Paradoxically, the *Gems* are at once too bright and too obscure to be perceived properly (their special paint is readily visible only under ultraviolet light). Thus, in the *Gems* as in the *Yarn*s, not only is the image put in distress but our visual apparatus is also put to the test.

This testing suggests a relation to Duchamp, a staple of the literature on Warhol, who encountered Duchamp in Los Angeles in 1963 (Warhol

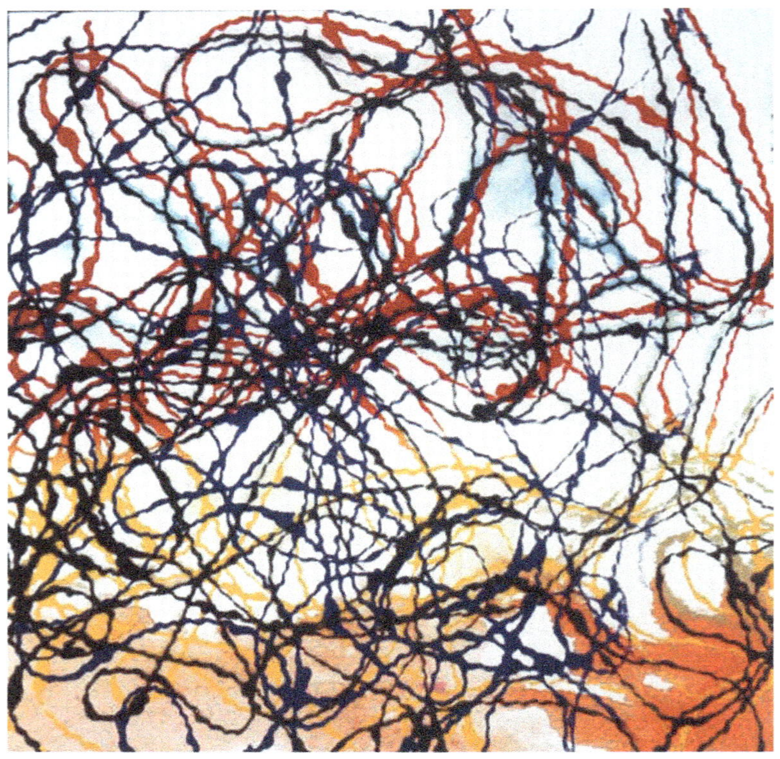

3.28 *Yarn*, 1983. Acrylic and silk-screen ink on linen, 40 × 40 in. Collection of the Andy Warhol Museum, Pittsburgh. © 2012 The Andy Warhol Foundation for the Visual Arts, Inc. / Artists Rights Society (ARS), New York.

was in town to show his *Elvis* silk screens at the Ferus Gallery, Duchamp to open his retrospective at the Pasadena Art Museum). Like his Pop peers, Warhol adapted the Duchampian readymade to the image, and so prompted questions of originality and authenticity in its sphere as well; yet a more precise connection emerges here too, for Duchamp was also interested in the distressed, even diseased work of art. Consider his "Specifications for 'Readymades,'" collected in the *Green Box* notes (1934), in which, in rapid sequence, Duchamp underscores "the serial characteristic of the readymade," then speculates about two other salient possibilities.

3.29 *Gem*, 1978–79. Synthetic polymer paint, diamond dust, and silk-screen ink on canvas, 54 × 85¾ in. © 2012 The Andy Warhol Foundation for the Visual Arts, Inc. / Artists Rights Society (ARS), New York.

The first, which he calls the "reciprocal readymade," is an extreme example of the destructive acts staged by Warhol: "use a Rembrandt as an ironing board." The second is more enigmatic—"make a sick picture or a sick readymade"—and yet this anti-aesthetic impulse, which disturbs the old relation between good composition in an object and proper composure in a subject, also motivated both artists.[43] Again, like Warhol, Duchamp subjected the artwork to damage, fictive and real, as in *Tu m'* (1918), in which a jagged painted tear is held together with actual safety pins. In a few instances, damage effectively becomes the work, as in *Sculpture for*

Traveling (1917), in which colored shreds of bathing caps were turned into a cobweb installation that soon disintegrated, and in *Unhappy Readymade* (1919), a wedding present for his sister Suzanne and brother-in-law Jean Crotti that they were asked to create for him: "It was a geometry book," Duchamp tells us, "which he [Crotti] had to hang by strings on the balcony of his apartment in the rue Condamine [in Paris]; the wind had to go through the book, choose its problems, turn and tear out the pages."[44] Thus exposed, the volume was soon destroyed (one photograph shows its blanched and crumpled pages, and Suzanne painted it in a similar state). Most importantly, damage was visited on his summa, *The Bride Stripped Bare by Her Bachelors, Even* (1915–23), which Duchamp declared "definitively unfinished" only after the *Large Glass* was badly cracked. (It also became a petri dish for "dust breeding," the title of a famous photograph by Man Ray that shows the *Glass* coated with schmutz.)

Two points are key here. First, in Duchamp as in Warhol, this distressing of the object is not separate from its testing. Again, with his stamps and bills, Warhol mooted the question of image deterioration and devaluation—of what counts as tender or trust in representation—which Duchamp also posed with his *Tzanck Check* (1919), a handwritten note of payment to his dentist, and his *Monte Carlo Bond* (1924), which he offered to backers of a system he devised to win at roulette. Second, this testing of the object is not separate from the testing of the subject. For example, Duchamp pressured our visual apparatus with the pulsatile opticality of his rotoreliefs long before Warhol did the same with his *Yarns*. Moreover, the "tear" in Duchamp, like the "rupture" in Warhol, is sometimes referred not only to damage in body images but also to distress in sexual difference (think of the vagina of the spread-eagled manikin in *Etant donnés* [1946–66] and the crotch shot in *Where Is Your Rupture?*). It is to this testing of the subject that I turn now.

To Be Your Own Script

"Taking the outside and putting it on the inside, or taking the inside and putting it on the outside": again, this definition of Pop points to a confusion between private and public, one deepened in the expanded spectacle of the 1960s, which Warhol both exposed and exploited. Certainly, he was porous in a strange, new, near-total way: porous both in his art, with its steady stream of mass-cultural images, and in his life, with the Factory set up as a playground of downtown denizens, uptown divas, and superstars somewhere in between. At the same time, Warhol was the opposite of porous: even before his near-fatal shooting by a crazed Valerie Solanas on June 3, 1968, he countered his vulnerability with physical supports and psychological defenses—opaque looks with his wigs and glasses, protective gadgets such as his omnipresent tape recorder and Polaroid camera, and buffering entourages at hangouts like Max's Kansas City—and after his shooting, he was literally corseted, so damaged was his midsection. Warhol also possessed a weird ability, early on, to attract quasi doubles like Edie Sedgwick (only the most famous of his companions to die young) and Nico (the monotone singer with the Velvet Underground) and, later, to pass as his own simulacrum—even when he was present, Warhol appeared absent or otherwise alien, a paradoxical quality for an omnipresent celebrity. These devices became central to his persona, which is sometimes seen as his ultimate work: Warhol as a blank *Gesamtkunstwerk*-in-person, the spectral center of a flashy scene. Fittingly, he once proposed "figment" for his epitaph, and once suggested that "the best American invention" was "to be able to disappear."[45] His own image, then, also oscillated between the iconic and the ghostly.

Whereas his contemporary Marshall McLuhan viewed media technologies as prostheses, Warhol used them as shields, ones that could also be deployed aggressively. From the early days of the Factory, he recorded talkative associates like Ondine, and visitors were often placed before a stationary movie camera for a three-minute "screen test" that served as an initiation to the scene. And in his later years, Warhol collected compulsively, to the point that his eastside townhouse became filled with great piles of kitschy things like cookie jars (10,000 items were auctioned after his sudden death in 1987). Such endless taping and filming, buying and bagging, point to a subconscious plan to "conquer by copying" or to control by gathering.[46] Here what counts as put in or taken out, porous or trussed, open or closed, is not clear; like the psychological states that underlie them, these operations are bound up with one another in Warhol. In this light, perhaps his copying and collecting was another way to be porous to the world, and his being porous another way to defend against images, objects, and people—to treat them as indifferent, to drain them of affect. When Warhol worked as an illustrator in the 1950s, sometimes he carried his portfolio in a sack, and was called "Andy Paperbag" for the affectation, a nickname that captures both his compulsion to contain and the fragility of this protective device. In this sense "Where Is Your Rupture?" is the Warholian question par excellence.[47]

Putting in and taking out, falling apart and falling together, Warhol was vexed by his own image. As a young person, he failed to work up a coherent look for the camera, and well into his time in New York, he often appears uncertain, even abashed, in photographs.[48] In various shoots in the 1950s by Otto Fenn, Leila Davies Singeles, Edward Wallowitch, and Duane Michaels, Warhol often struggles to adopt the signature poses of Greta Garbo, Marlene Dietrich, and Truman Capote (fig. 3.30), and even in his Pop self-portraits in the 1960s, he strives to inhabit given looks, as in his "confrontational" *Self-Portrait*s of 1964 (fig. 3.31), with his head up and eyes fixed, and his "reflective" *Self-Portrait*s of 1967 (fig. 3.32), with his fingers on his chin. Eventually, of course, Warhol did produce a public image, but he did so largely through his "baffles" of wigs and glasses and his doubles like Edie and Nico, so here again iconicity was in tension with its opposite.[49] Perhaps this difficulty with his own image made Warhol aware of the same difficulty in others, and appreciative of still others who were skilled at self-fashioning—hence, in part, his fascination not only with movie stars but also with accomplished transvestites like Candy Darling.

With others, too, Warhol explored an array of poses associated with various genres of photographic portraiture—in particular, the histrionic mugging of the friend in the photo-booth picture, the blank look of the criminal in the police shot, and the come-hither look of the actor in the publicity image. These genres differ greatly, of course, but all involve the mechanical representation of a self for purposes of identification; willing or not, this self is subject to both alienation in the image and automatization in the process.[50] And yet despite the motto "Everybody should be a machine," Warhol did not simply celebrate mechanization and automatization. Often,

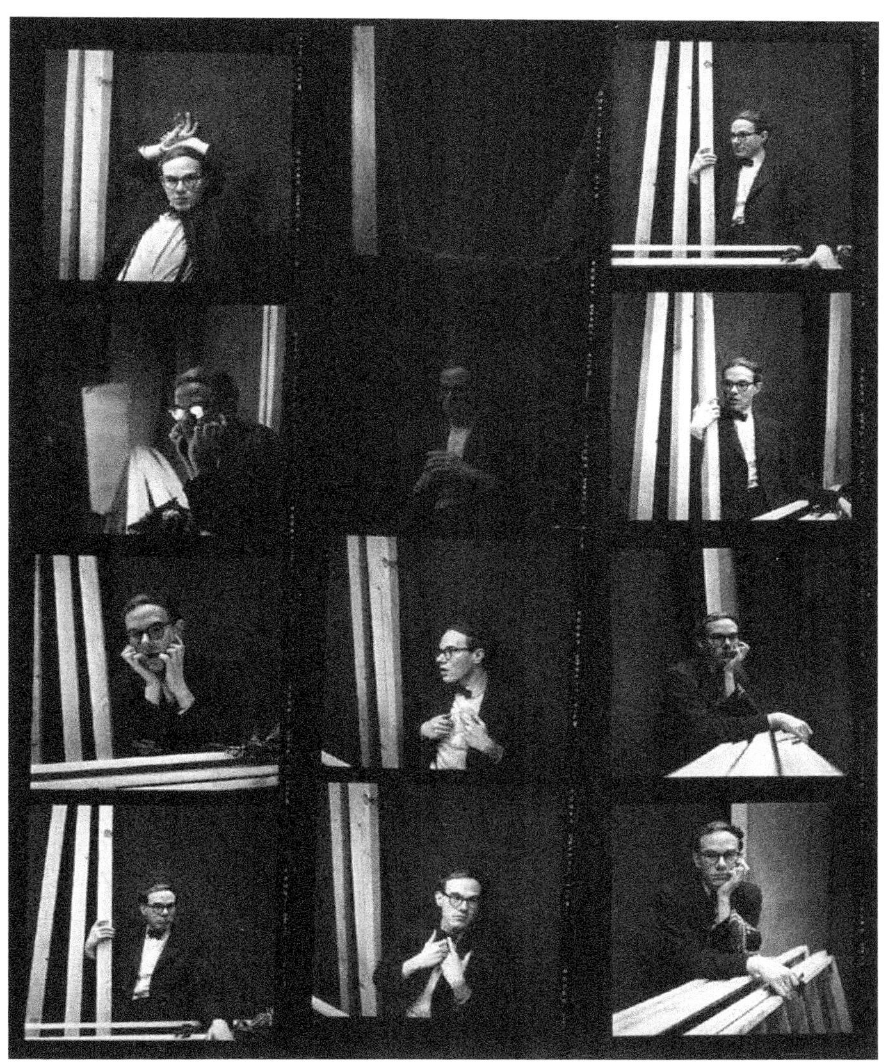

3.30 Otto Fenn, *Andy Warhol*, 1952–54. Black and white contact sheet, 10 × 8¼ in. © 2012 The Andy Warhol Foundation for the Visual Arts, Inc. / Artists Rights Society (ARS), New York.

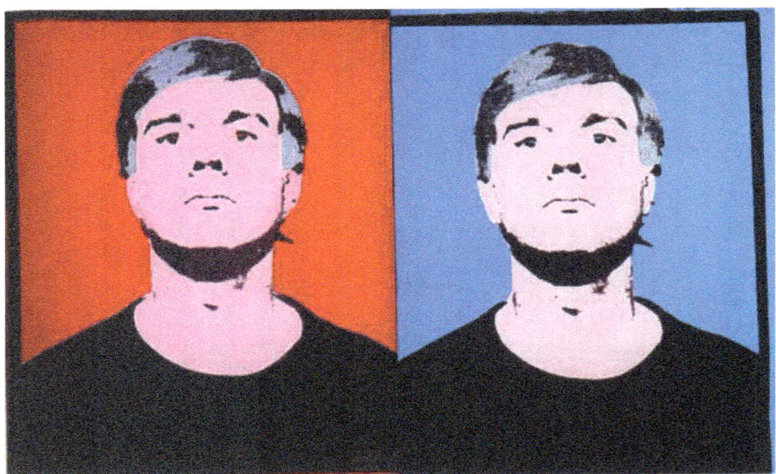

3.31 *Self-Portrait*, 1964. Silk-screen ink on synthetic polymer paint on canvas, two panels, each 20 × 16 in. © 2012 The Andy Warhol Foundation for the Visual Arts, Inc. / Artists Rights Society (ARS), New York.

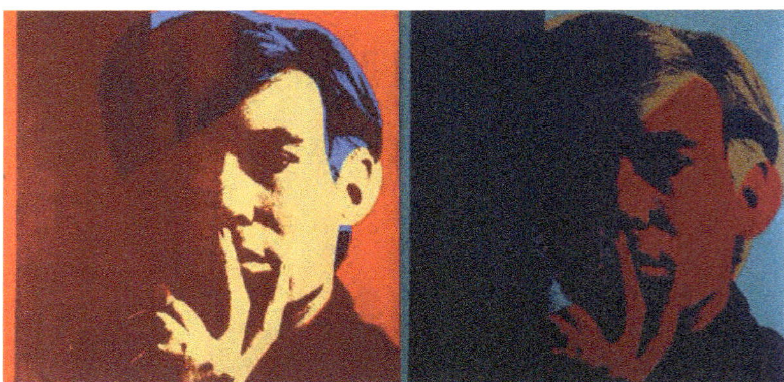

3.32 *Double Self-Portrait*, 1967. Silk-screen ink on synthetic polymer paint on canvas, two panels, each 72 × 72 in. © 2012 The Andy Warhol Foundation for the Visual Arts, Inc. / Artists Rights Society (ARS), New York.

he pointed to the effects of these operations indirectly, through the products that result from them, such as matchbooks, canned goods, dance diagrams, number paintings, and so on. In fact, his early Pop works all but resume the automatized actions that Walter Benjamin picked out as the most telling in industrial society. "Comfort isolates," Benjamin writes in his 1940 essay on Baudelaire; "on the other hand, it brings those enjoying it closer to mechanization":

> The invention of the match around the middle of the nineteenth century brought forth a number of innovations which have one thing in common: one abrupt movement of the hand triggers a process of many steps. This development is taking place in many areas. One case in point is the telephone, where the lifting of a receiver has taken the place of the steady movement that used to be required to crank the older models. Of the countless movements of switching, inserting, pressing, and the like, the "snapping" of the photographer has had the greatest consequences. A touch of the finger now sufficed to fix an event for an unlimited period of time. The camera gave the moment a posthumous shock, as it were. Haptic experiences of this kind were joined by optic ones, such as are supplied by the advertising pages of a newspaper or the traffic of a big city.[51]

Condensed in these automatized actions, according to Benjamin, are "shocks and collisions" that the modern subject has learned to parry or to absorb for its very survival. "Thus," Benjamin concludes, "technology has subjected the human sensorium to a complex kind of training."[52] This training is an important subtext in Warhol, and his reframing of select images of automatization can provide little insights into its long history.

Consider again his treatments of photo-booth pictures, mug shots, and publicity images: here Warhol reviews key ways in which particular subjects have parried "the 'snapping' of the photographer." Concentrated in the years 1963–66, the photo-booth pictures involve friends on a lark as well as sitters for portraits, a practice Warhol initiated with *Ethel Scull Thirty-Six Times* (1963; fig. 3.33). If, as Benjamin argues in "Little History of Photography" (1931), the long exposure required for early forms of photography allowed the sitter time enough to develop into an image, as it were, and thereby to convey a strong sense of an inward self, the unexpected click of

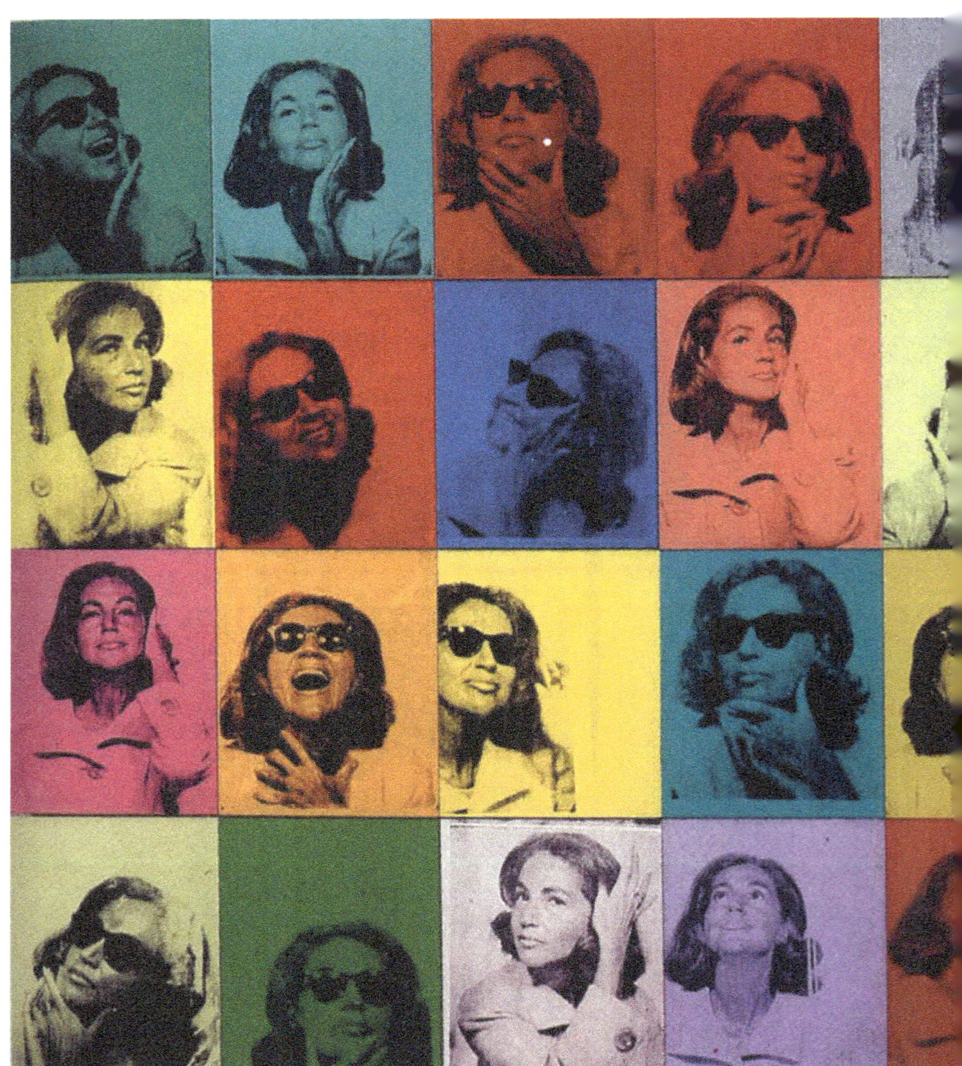

3.33 *Ethel Scull Thirty-Six Times*, 1963. Silk-screen ink on synthetic polymer paint on canvas, 36 panels, each 19⅞ × 15⅞ in. © 2012 The Andy Warhol Foundation for the Visual Arts, Inc. / Artists Rights Society (ARS), New York.

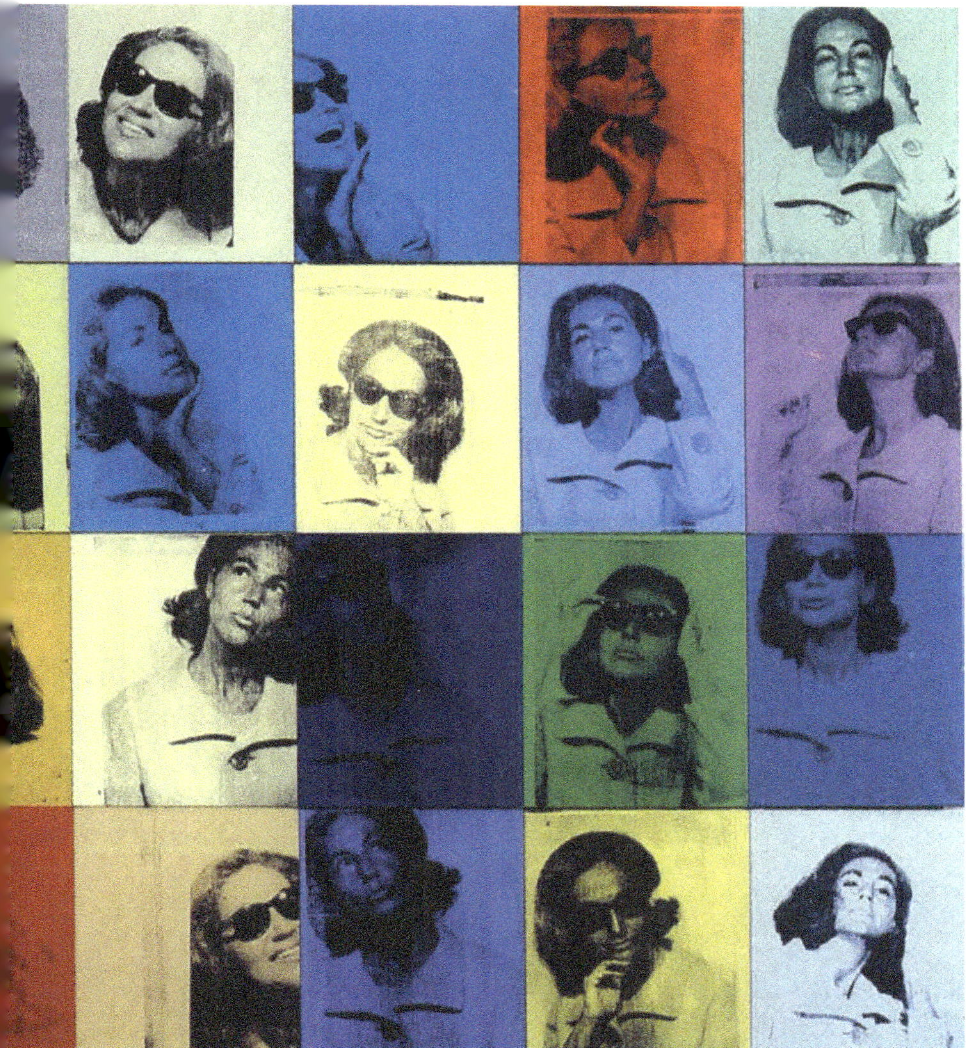

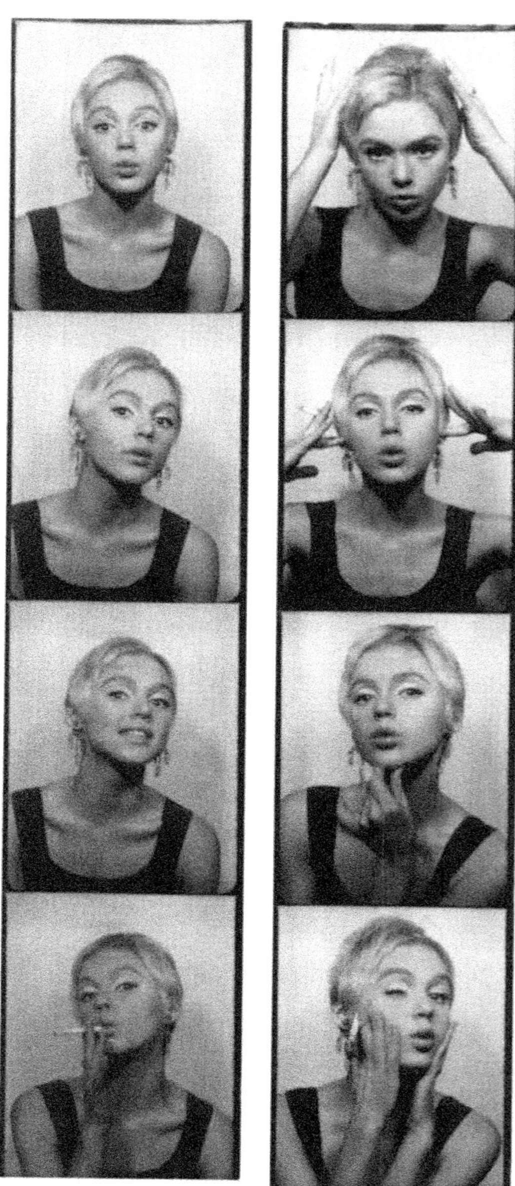

3.34 Photo-booth shots of Edie Sedgwick, ca. 1963. Two strips, each 7¾ × 1½ in. © 2012 The Andy Warhol Foundation for the Visual Arts, Inc. / Artists Rights Society (ARS), New York.

the snapshot produces much the opposite effect. With the additional pressure of its sudden flashes, the photo-booth in particular often surprises, even mortifies, its subjects, who are sometimes led, in a preemptive move, to mug for the camera (which usually produces only further humiliation once the photos appear). Sometimes, even when the sitter is an accomplished self-presenter like Edie, the mortification in such sudden mediation is evident (fig. 3.34). In short, Warhol reveals the photo booth to be a site not only of self-staging but also of subject testing—in effect, a "drill" that, in the Benjaminian sense of these terms, is not conducive to an "experience" that lives on as a memory, but is often corrosive of this building block of the traditional self.[53] And when the exposure to the camera is prolonged, as it is in the *Screen Tests*, the drill is extended, to the further detriment of such experience, memory, and identity.

If self-presentation is largely willing in the photo-booth picture, it is not so in the mug shot; its strict frontal and side views are compulsory, and identification approaches mortification as a matter of course. Yet sometimes this setup is resisted by the subject, and in *The Thirteen Most Wanted Men* (1964), Warhol favors shots in which the criminals attempt either to stare down the camera or to look so blank as to challenge its capacity to individualize them (fig. 3.35). Warhol seems to support this tacit resistance to the disciplinary regime of the mug shot in other ways too: not only does he choose dated material (his cases are from 1955 to 1961), but he sometimes strips it of salient information needed for positive identification (last names are not given, and some photos are blown up to the point of grainy obscurity).[54] Finally, as the art historian Richard Meyer has argued, Warhol cuts the explicit gaze of the state with a very different look, an implicit one of gay desire, in which the term "most wanted men" takes on a connotation that mocks the disinterested posture of officers of the law.[55]

By and large, criminals shun recognition, and are threatened if they become too iconic, whereas stars seek recognition, and are threatened if they are not iconic enough; in this regard, the early silk screens of celebrities appear as complements to *The Thirteen Most Wanted Men*. Yet sometimes with stars, too much visibility can also be problematic, and Warhol was drawn to celebrities at moments of public distress, as with Jackie Kennedy

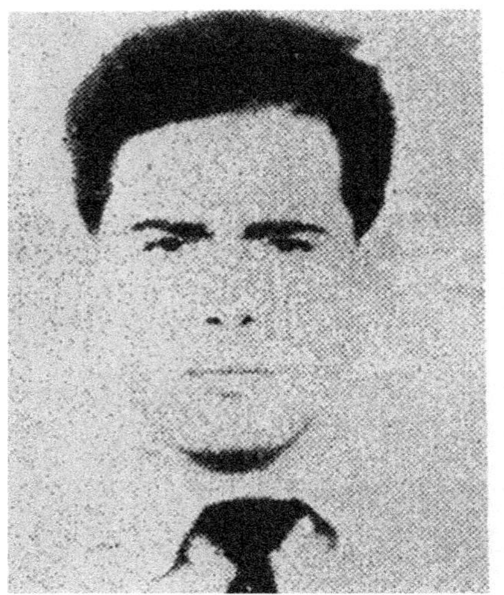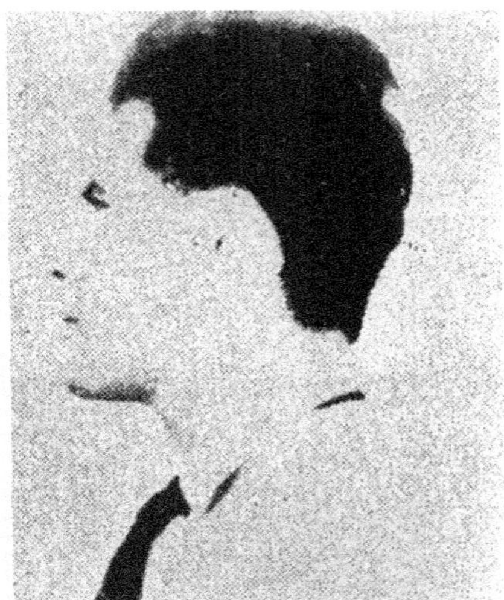

3.35 *The Thirteen Most Wanted Men (#13; Joseph F)*, 1964. Silk-screen ink on canvas, two panels, each 48 × 40 in. © 2012 The Andy Warhol Foundation for the Visual Arts, Inc. / Artists Rights Society (ARS), New York.

(whose blurred image seems to register her aggrieved life). Moreover, under the apparent ease of such figures as Marilyn Monroe and Elizabeth Taylor, one senses, in the silk screens, the actual strain of this visibility—the vicissitudes of producing, inhabiting, and sustaining an iconic image for a mass spectatorship. For his classic portraits of Marilyn, for example, Warhol selected a publicity image for the film *Niagara* from his own archive of more than one hundred stills of the star, and so redoubled her anxious own selectivity regarding her image.[56] And in his many representations of Liz, he followed her troubled path from fresh-faced ingénue in *National Velvet* to steamy contract player for MGM to stricken tabloid figure in *Cleopatra* and beyond, and so retraced her own uneven stewardship of her iconicity (figs. 3.36–3.38). Warhol also underscores the constructed nature of such images at the level of procedure: with his brash colors and thick lines often off-register, his portraits appear as blatant makeup, even extreme makeover, a cosmetic construction of disparate parts—lips, eyes, brows, hair (fig. 3.39).[57] Especially in silk screens involving multiple images (for example, *Natalie* [1962; fig. 3.40]), the making up of the subject vies with its breaking down, and often loses.

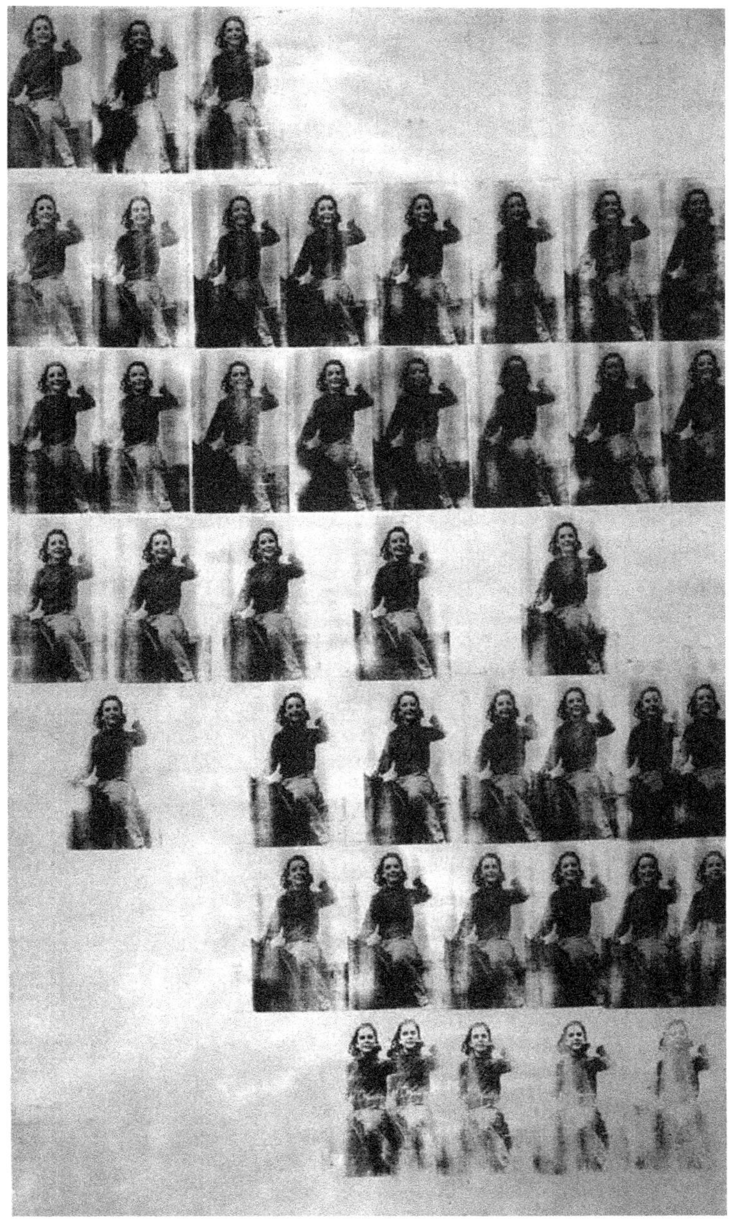

3.36 *National Velvet*, 1963. Silk-screen ink, silver paint, and pencil on linen, 136⅜ × 83½ in. © 2012 The Andy Warhol Foundation for the Visual Arts, Inc. / Artists Rights Society (ARS), New York.

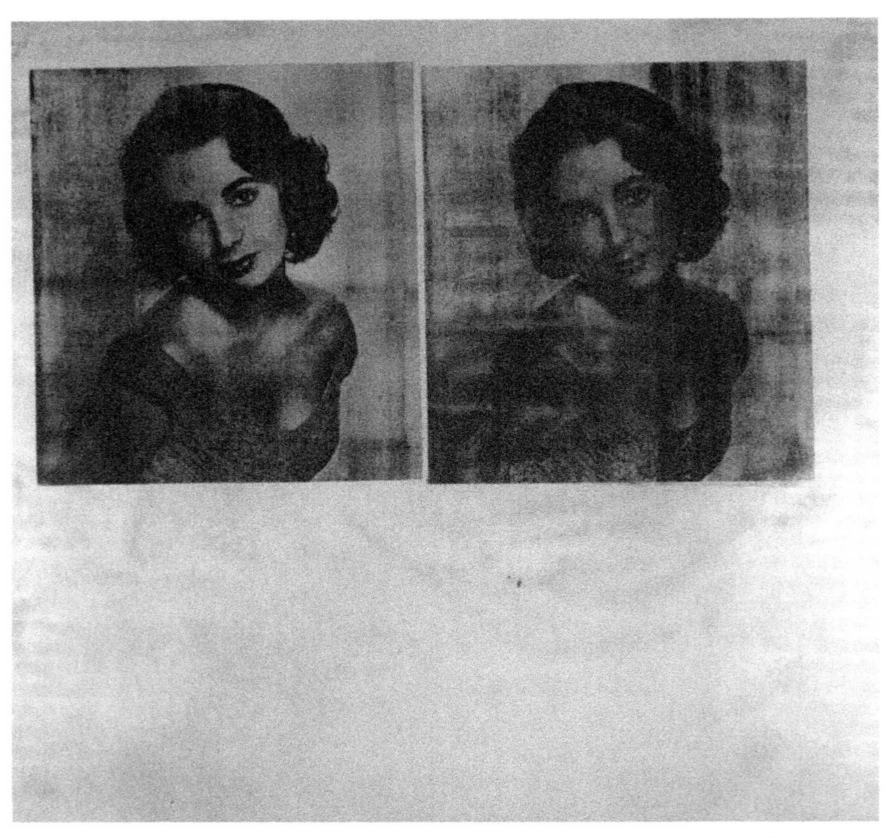

3.37 *Double Liz*, 1963. Silk-screen ink and silver paint on linen, 80 × 83 in. © 2012 The Andy Warhol Foundation for the Visual Arts, Inc. / Artists Rights Society (ARS), New York.

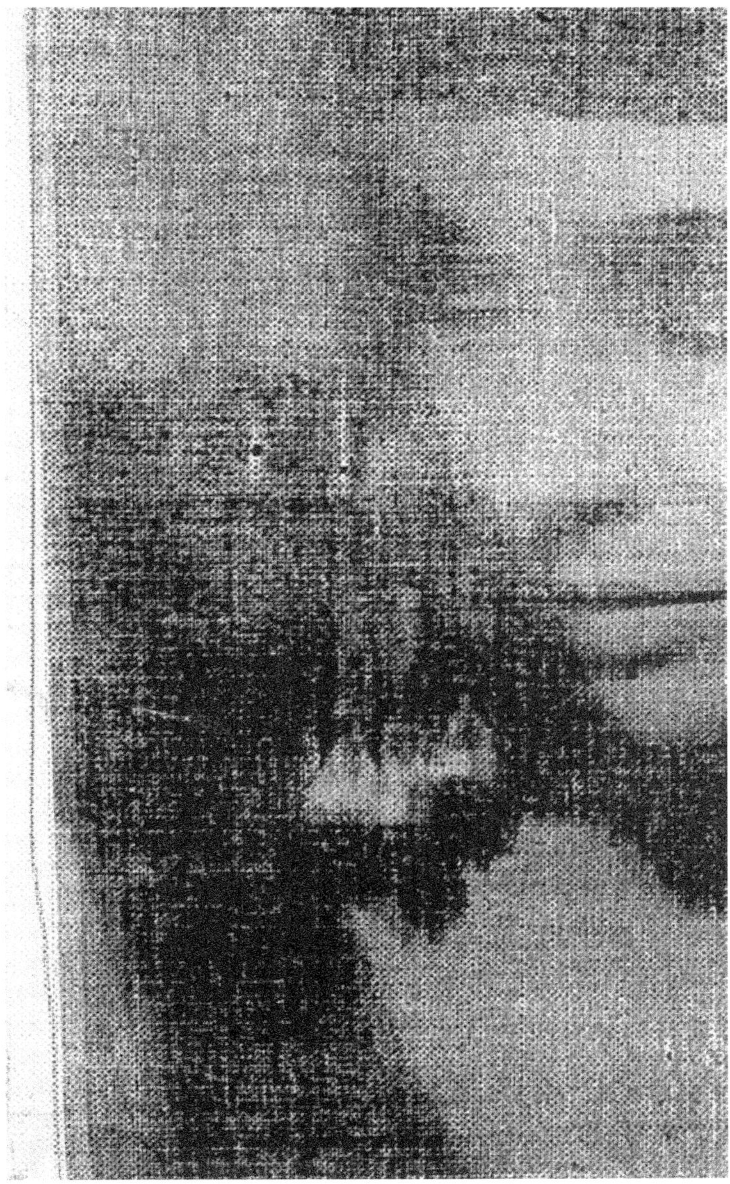

3.38 *Liz as Cleopatra*, 1963. Silk-screen ink and pencil on linen, 10 × 6 in. © 2012 The Andy Warhol Foundation for the Visual Arts, Inc. / Artists Rights Society (ARS), New York.

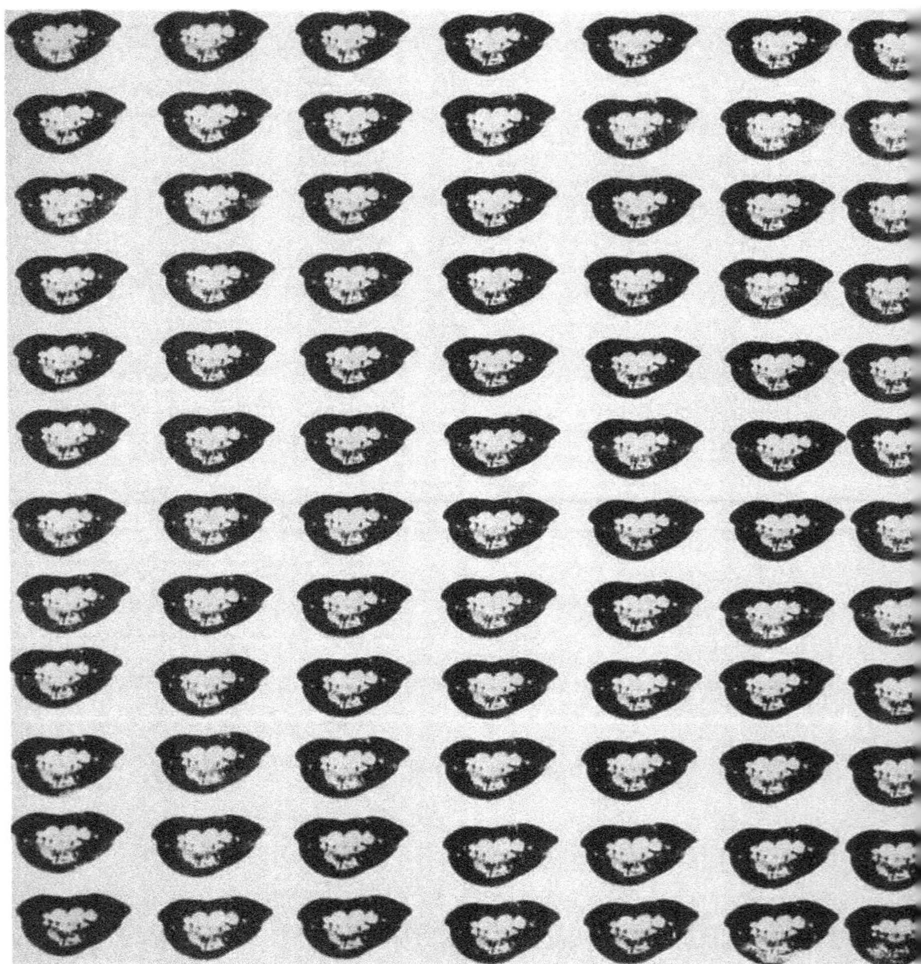

3.39 *Marilyn's Lips*, 1962. Acrylic, silk-screen ink, and pencil on linen, 82¾ × 82⅜ in. (left panel), 82¾ × 80¾ in. (right panel). © 2012 The Andy Warhol Foundation for the Visual Arts, Inc. / Artists Rights Society (ARS), New York.

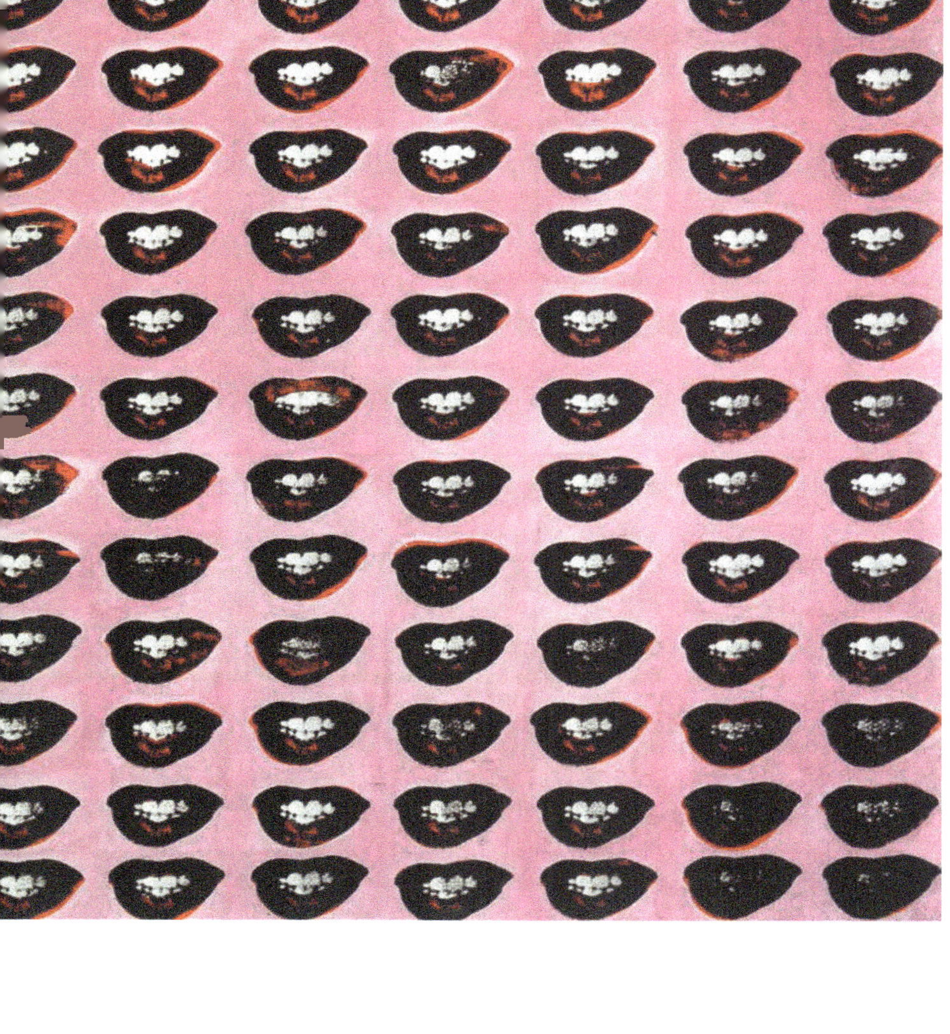

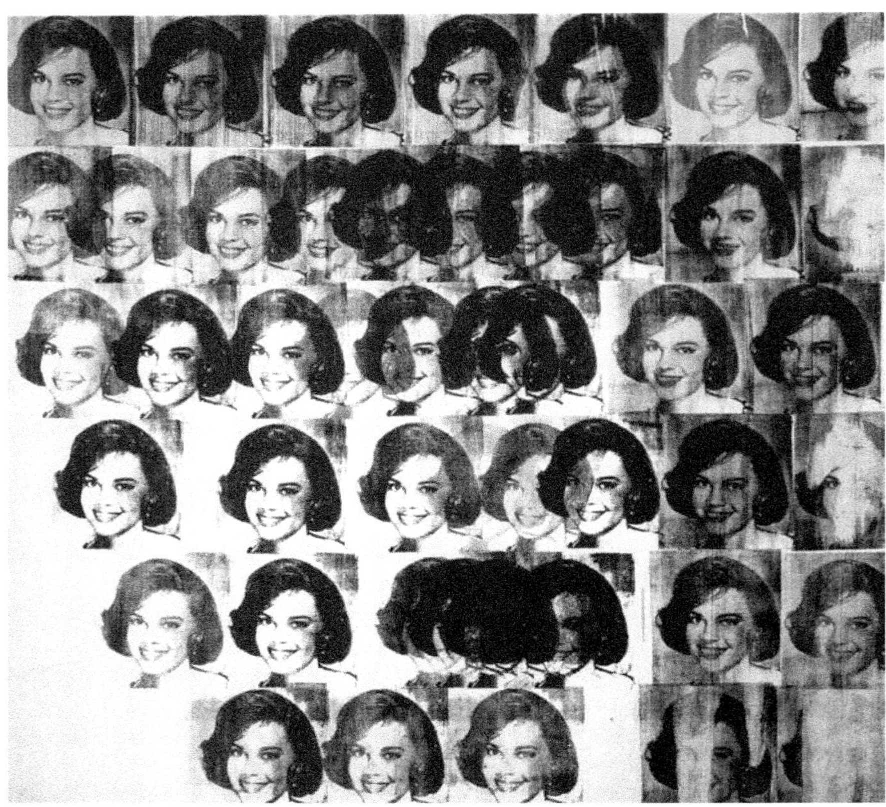

3.40 *Natalie*, 1962. Silk-screen ink on linen, 83 × 89⅛ in. © 2012 The Andy Warhol Foundation for the Visual Arts, Inc. / Artists Rights Society (ARS), New York.

A proposition can be extracted here, one that is historically specific to a society of spectacle but also possessed of a psychological validity that might extend beyond it. If, in the first instance, the ego is seen as a kind of image (according to psychoanalytic theory, our investment in our body images is the initial step in the formation of our egos), then the image might be understood as a kind of ego or ego prosthetic, a surface or screen where we project our identifications and idealizations.[58] Generally speaking, in a spectacle society, two models of the image dominate all others: the image as commodity and the image as celebrity (as the French sociologist Edgar Morin pointed out in the early days of Pop, these two are often condensed into one: "star-merchandise").[59] Of course, these images are offered up expressly for our projections, and this process drives spectacle society more than anything else. Now if it is true, as the critic Michael Warner has argued, that "the mass subject cannot have a body except the body it witnesses," this might suggest why Warhol evokes this subject primarily through commodities and celebrities—from products like Campbell's and Coke to stars and politicians like Marilyn and Mao, to all the cover people of *Interview* magazine.[60] As Warhol knew, the mass subject could also be evoked through another set of proxies, its objects of kitschy taste, as in his paintings of superbright flowers (1964) and his wallpaper of folksy cows (1966). Yet all is not perfect in this system. For example, the vicissitudes of the star in the making of an image for mass spectatorship might be compounded by the vicissitudes visited on this image by the fickle projections of the mass subject—our resentments, disappointments, and so on—for if the star lives by our projections, he or she dies by them too, as does any other product. "In the figures of Elvis, Liz, Michael, Oprah, Geraldo, Brando, and the like," Warner writes, "we witness and transact the bloating, slimming, wounding, and general humiliation of the public body. The bodies of these public figures are prostheses for our own mutant desirability."[61] Warhol was astute about this sadistic side of consumption (we "eat up" stars, he remarked in a 1966 interview), which is intimated in his distressed images of celebrities and commodities alike.[62]

This distressing is not removed from the drilling or testing of the subject mentioned above. "Another nature . . . speaks to the camera rather than to the eye," Benjamin asserts in "Little History of Photography," and in his treatment of the photo-booth pictures, the mug shots, and the publicity images, Warhol suggests that different natures also speak to different photographic genres and camera setups.[63] He was especially intrigued by the particular nature that speaks to the movie camera, which is a primary concern of his films; in fact, both the psychological vicissitudes of self-imaging and the technological training of the modern subject are most evident there, and nowhere more so than in his 472 known *Screen Tests*, produced between 1964 and 1967.

Made with a sixteen-millimeter Bolex camera on a tripod, each *Screen Test* is the given length of a hundred-foot roll of film, just under three

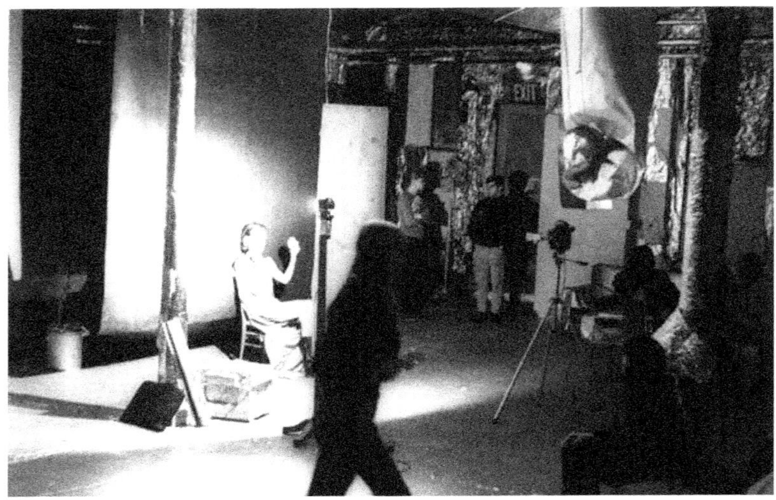

3.41 Ivy Nicholson prepares for her *Screen Test* at the Factory, 1966. Photograph by Billy Name. © 2012 The Andy Warhol Foundation for the Visual Arts, Inc. / Artists Rights Society (ARS), New York.

minutes in the shooting, and each was to follow these guidelines (which were often disobeyed): a stationary camera, with no zooming in or out, and a centered sitter, face forward, full in the frame, and as motionless as possible. Conceived as filmic portraits (they were initially called "still-ies"), the *Screen Tests* are, in effect, photo-booth pictures, mug shots, and publicity images rolled into one. And they are not screen tests at all—none was a proper audition for a scripted movie—but they are tests nonetheless. Indeed, without ulterior motive, they are pure tests of the capacity of the filmed subject to confront a camera, hold a pose, present an image, and sustain the performance for the duration of the shooting. Each sitter attempts to do so, moreover, not only without the armature of given character or the benefit of scripted direction, but also under the strain of enjoined immobility and in the midst of ambient distractions—the subjects are frequently teased, prompted or otherwise provoked by Factory onlookers, and sometimes they are abandoned by Warhol or whoever is nominally in charge of the filming.[64] In short, the sitter has no one truly to interact with, not even

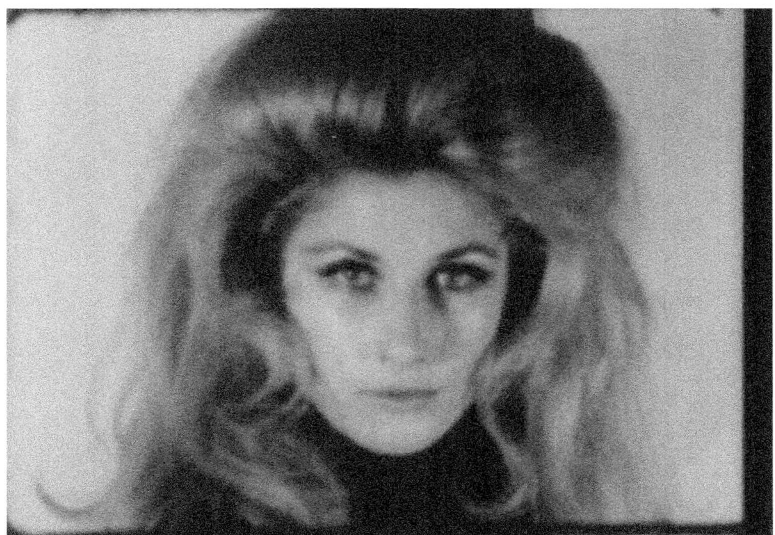

3.42 Frame from *Screen Test: Jane Holzer*, 1964. 16mm black and white film. © 2012 The Andy
      Warhol Foundation for the Visual Arts, Inc. / Artists Rights Society (ARS), New York, and The
      Andy Warhol Museum, Pittsburgh, PA, a museum of Carnegie Institute. All rights reserved.

in the guise of the camera, which, fixed in position, offers no reciprocity at
all. If there is a scenario here then, it is one of an unaided encounter with a
technological apparatus, in the blank face of which the lone subject is left to
project a self-image as best he or she can (fig. 3.41).

"Somehow we attract people who can turn themselves on in front of the
camera," Warhol once commented of his films. "In this sense, they're *really*
superstars. It's much harder, you know, to *be* your own script" (fig. 3.42).[65]
Yet many *Screen Tests* attest precisely to the difficulty of this turning on, this
self-scripting, and the sheer duress of filmic iconicity and coherent presence
becomes the principal subject.[66] Certainly there is distress at the level of the
image: often the lighting is inconsistent and the exposure uneven, and occasionally the image blanches altogether; also, as in the silk screens, flashes
and pops sometimes occur, and the camera jumps jerkily or zooms abruptly
at moments too. Yet there is more distress in the place of the subject, in its
encounter with the camera (fig. 3.43).[67] The lighting is frequently harsh

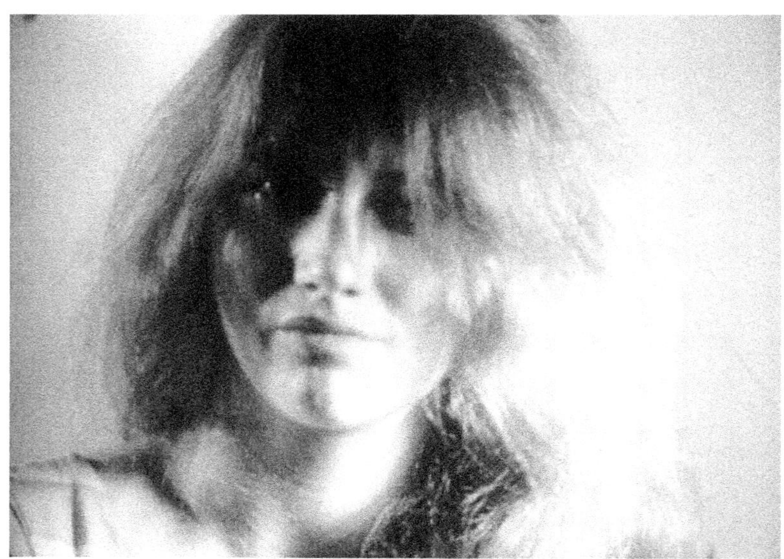

3.43 Frame from *Screen Test: Sally Kirkland*, 1964. 16mm black and white film. © 2012 The Andy Warhol Foundation for the Visual Arts, Inc. / Artists Rights Society (ARS), New York, and The Andy Warhol Museum, Pittsburgh, PA, a museum of Carnegie Institute. All rights reserved.

(especially on women), which causes some sitters to resort to sunglasses for protection. Others attempt to look away, as if the gaze of the camera might thus be averted, while still others try to stare the camera down, as in the mug shots, as if it might blink first—or as if such staring were the best way (the only way) to project and to hold a self-image at all, to keep it intact (the problem is that this staring is often so fixed that it becomes strained in its own way; fig. 3.44).[68] As in the photo-booth pictures, some testees resort to posing or mugging that, when histrionic, can appear defensive and, when aggressive, can seem desperate. In short, no matter how self-possessed the sitters might be (and a few were professional actors), many subjects of the *Screen Tests* are "stricken and exhausted" by the process.[69] For some sitters, the ordeal was primarily psychological: the *Screen Test*, the poet Ron Padgett commented, was like "doing an instant Rorschach on yourself."[70] For others, the strain was physiological as well as psychological, as if the

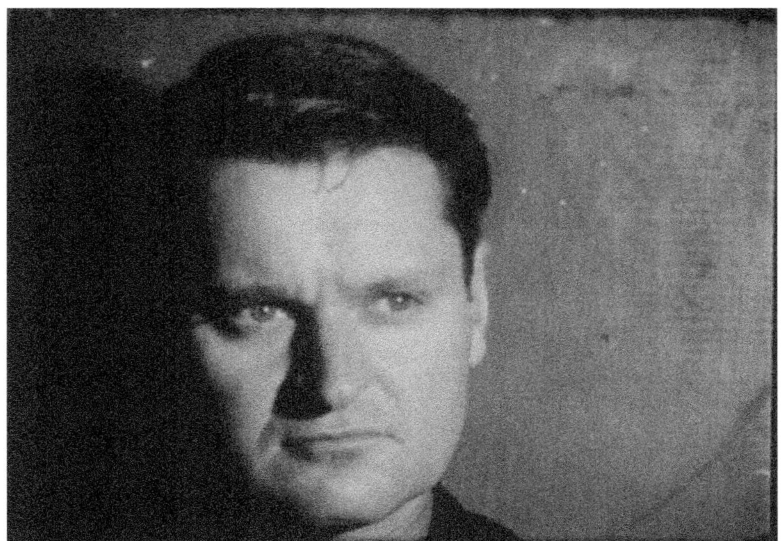

3.44 Frame from *Screen Test: John Ashbery*, 1966. 16mm black and white film. © 2012 The Andy Warhol Foundation for the Visual Arts, Inc. / Artists Rights Society (ARS), New York, and The Andy Warhol Museum, Pittsburgh, PA, a museum of Carnegie Institute. All rights reserved.

body image as such were under attack. "You sit staring at the camera," the actor Sally Kirkland remarked, "and after a while your face begins to disintegrate."[71] This is a severe testing indeed, and the distress seems to affect men as well as women, straight as well as gay (fig. 3.45).

"The film director occupies exactly the same position as the examiner in an aptitude test," Benjamin wrote in the mid-1930s; and this testing is more difficult, not less, when the director is removed or indifferent, as is the case with many *Screen Tests*.[72] And yet, Benjamin continues, the film actor, who "performs not in front of an audience but in front of an apparatus," is in a good position to pass the test, for he is trained to address the camera, to win it over, as it were, to the advantage of his or her performance. According to Benjamin, a primary interest in the movies of his time lay in this technical triumph: most "citydwellers, throughout the workday in offices and factories, have to relinquish their humanity in the face of an apparatus," he

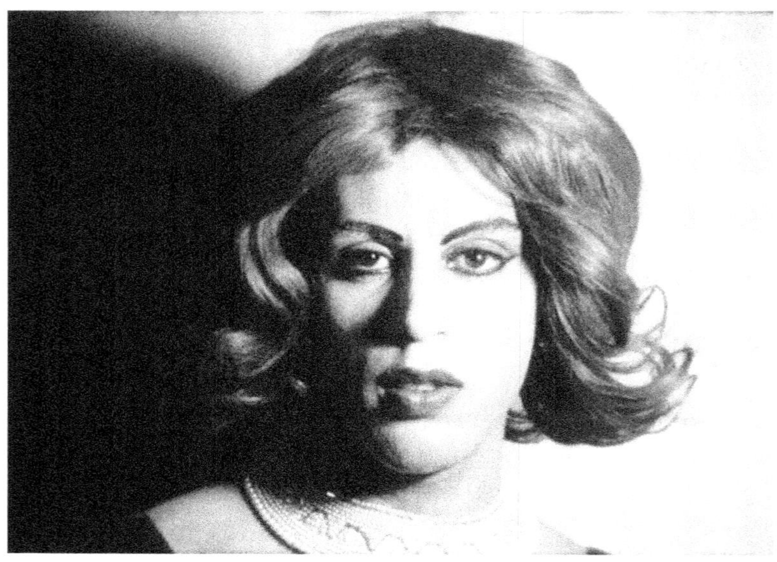

3.45 Frame from *Screen Test: Mario Montez*, 1965. 16mm black and white film. © 2012 The Andy Warhol Foundation for the Visual Arts, Inc. / Artists Rights Society (ARS), New York, and The Andy Warhol Museum, Pittsburgh, PA, a museum of Carnegie Institute. All rights reserved.

argues, yet "in the evening these same masses fill the cinemas to witness the film actor taking revenge on their behalf not only by asserting *his* humanity (or what appears to them as such) against the apparatus, but by placing that apparatus in the service of his triumph."[73] The situation of the *Screen Test*s is very different: such revenge might be attempted, but it is rarely achieved; the apparatus triumphs over the sitter far more often than the reverse; and there is no humanist redemption in the face of the camera.[74] And for the most part, the viewer has little choice but to associate, sadistically, with this machine vision or to identify, masochistically, with the filmed subject under its power; at times, the latter option seems almost the only common ground of "humanity" here. In fact, in Warholian cinema at large, to film a person often meant to provoke or to expose him or her, and to be filmed meant to parry this probing or to be laid bare by it.[75] As a result, the viewer cannot idealize the filmed person, as is usually the case with Hollywood cinema. One can only empathize, intermittently, with his or her travails before the relentless camera, that is, again, to empathize with the vicissitudes of the subject becoming an image—with wanting this condition too much, resisting it too much, or otherwise failing at it.

Warhol shot the *Screen Tests* in the sound-film speed of twenty-four frames a second, but wanted them to be projected at the silent-film speed of sixteen frames (after 1970, the industry standard became eighteen frames a second). The testing of the sitter seems more severe in the screening, then, since "each involuntary tremor or flutter of an eyelid [is revealed] in clinical slow motion."[76] It is also more severe for the viewer, since this speed of projection lengthens the duration of each test in our watching to four minutes. The *Screen Test*s are trials for us in another way, too, for if the sitter attempts to grapple with the camera, the viewer attempts to greet the sitter, yet here again, reciprocity is lacking. For even though the subjects seem positioned to be utterly present for us (there is no narrative to place them in a fictional elsewhere), we exist in a space-time that does not, cannot, communicate with theirs. Each *Screen Test* is thus literally a missed encounter.[77]

Technically, of course, this nonrelation is the basis of any experience of film, but it is made explicit here, and some of the poignancy of the *Screen Tests* arises from a sense—on both sides, so it sometimes seems—that this is not only a cinematic condition but also an existential one (this dark intuition trumps any intermittent sense of empathy). Gazed on by an absent other, both sitter and viewer attempt to return this gaze but cannot. As our awareness of this nonreciprocity sinks in, a gap seems to open in the otherwise seamless projection of the film, like a traumatic break that neither sitter nor viewer can quite live, let alone comprehend, and this missed encounter seems related to the one sometimes registered in the silk screens. In a sense, the *Screen Tests* give a face (many faces) to the disturbing automatisms probed there—though it is hard to say whether this face makes the automatisms appear more human or we humans more automatic.[78]

Doing an Instant Rorschach on Yourself

In all these ways, the *Screen Tests* are a rich instance of the Warholian distressing of image and subject alike, one that invites further inquiry. For example, they might also be associated with the protocols of the test in postwar America at large. As consumerism expanded during this period, there emerged an advocacy movement spearheaded by Ralph Nader, which came to the fore just after the early silk screens and during the *Screen Tests*. In 1965, Nader published his *Unsafe at Any Speed*, which questioned the safety of a wide range of American automobiles, and other books involving food and drug dangers, as well as air and water contaminants, soon followed. Some of the "Death and Disaster" images focus precisely on catastrophes stemming from products not properly regulated, on "test failures" such as teenagers killed in car wrecks before seat belts were required and housewives poisoned by tainted tuna before adequate controls were instituted. Again, this interest in testing and training runs throughout Warhol, early (as in the *Do It Yourself*s, *Dance Diagram*s, and *Screen Test*s) and late (the *Shadow*s, *Diamond Dust Shoes*, *Zeitgeist*s, *Camouflage*s, *Yarn*s, and *Gem*s are all tests of our vision). In fact, his *Rorschach* paintings (1984) play explicitly on the most famous of all perceptual-psychological tests—the ten inkblots published by the Swiss psychologist Hermann Rorschach in 1921.[79]

On the one hand, with his interest in the effects of automatization, the agon between actor and apparatus, and so on, Warhol looks back to the moment of industrial culture that Benjamin sought to understand. On the other hand, Warhol looks ahead to our moment of a capitalist society in which testing and training are pervasive. By his own account, he was intrigued by Factory associates who could "turn on" and be their "own script." Today, advanced capitalism requires such self-scripting from most of us—to project a self-image fitted for each new interview, to adapt a skill set for each new job, in effect, to be screen-tested on such improvised capabilities at every turn.[80] In the *Screen Test*s in particular, and at the Factory generally, people were treated as so much capital to be shaped and reshaped, and this flexibility is now demanded of most subjects in a neoliberal economy.[81] "Production thus not only creates an object for the subject," Marx writes in a celebrated line in the *Grundrisse* (1857–61), "but also a subject for the object," and this remains the case for our own mode of production.[82] In this respect, Warhol does not demonstrate the final dissolution of the subject, as some critics claim, so much as he explores its continual construction and deconstruction.[83]

Yet, finally, Warhol does not simply conform to this "new spirit of capitalism"; in fact, he might be understood to resist it, however obliquely, in two ways at least. First, although failure can be the outcome of any test, it often appears to be the purpose in Warhol. Can anyone—sitter or viewer—be said to pass his screen tests? Again, they speak instead to the sheer difficulty of coherent presence on the part of the sitter, and the viewer also seems to fail, unable as he or she is to rescue the sitter from this predicament. So, too, Warhol was committed to his own version of failure, and he excelled at it (another point in common with Duchamp): in quick succession in the 1960s, he apparently quit illustration, painting, film, and then art altogether—or rather, he seemed to give up each activity for the next (ending with "business art").

Second, Warhol not only distresses the image; at times he seems to distress the imaginary as such, that psychic space in which, according to Lacan, we misrecognize ourselves. It is in this space that ideology operates on us most effectively; in fact, in his influential account of ideology, Louis Althusser adapted the Lacanian definition of the imaginary to suggest how we misrecognize the social world at large in this way (in his famous formula, ideology proposes imaginary resolutions to real contradictions).[84] In some respects, this misrecognition occurs most perfectly in classic cinema, which some theorists describe as hypnotic and others as fetishistic. According to the first view, film places us in a condition of semiconscious suggestibility, while according to the second view, it allows us to deny the reality of the apparatus of the movie in order to believe the illusion of its story.[85] In his *Screen Tests*, Warhol breaks both hypnotic and fetishistic effects of this filmic capture. In his still work too, Warhol disturbs, more radically than any other Pop artist, the operations of the imaginary and the ideological.[86] In this light, Lichtenstein was right: he is an old-fashioned artist compared to Warhol, for like Hamilton, Lichtenstein remains a painter of modern life, whereas in Warhol, that modernity overwhelms painting, and the tableau tradition dedicated to the autonomous subject lies in ruins.

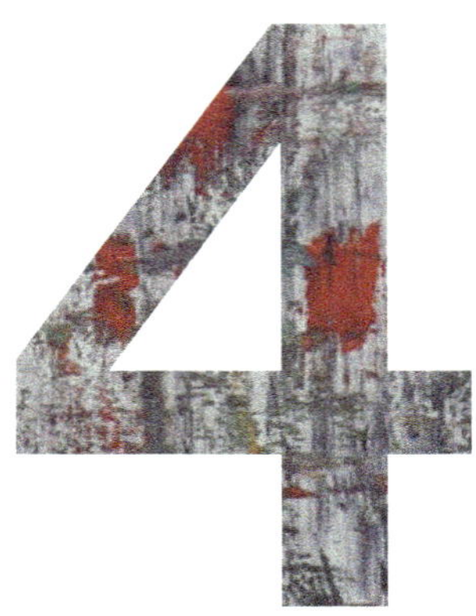

Gerhard Richter, or the Photogenic Image

"Andy Warhol is not so much an artist as a symptom of a cultural situation, created by that situation and used as a substitute for an artist," Gerhard Richter wrote in a personal note dated November 4, 1989, more than two years after Warhol died. "It is to his credit that he made no 'art'; that he touched none of the methods and themes that traditionally constrain other artists (thus sparing us the great mass of 'artistic' nonsense that we see in other people's pictures)."[1] However, in a 2002 conversation concerning his own work, Richter had this to say: "I owe something to Warhol. He legitimized the mechanical. He showed me how it is done . . . this modern way of letting details disappear, or at least he validated its possibilities" (Richter, *Writings, 1961–2007*, 414). The ambivalence voiced in these comments is telling. On the one hand, Richter acknowledges the anti-aesthetic position of Warhol as true to the changed status of fine art in postwar culture, a status registered in his "mechanical" technique, which Richter adapts in his own work (fig. 4.1). On the other hand, Richter sees Warhol as a "symptom" without sufficient distance from his "cultural situation." In this ambivalence, Richter effectively affirms the tradition of fine art and high painting, as Hamilton and

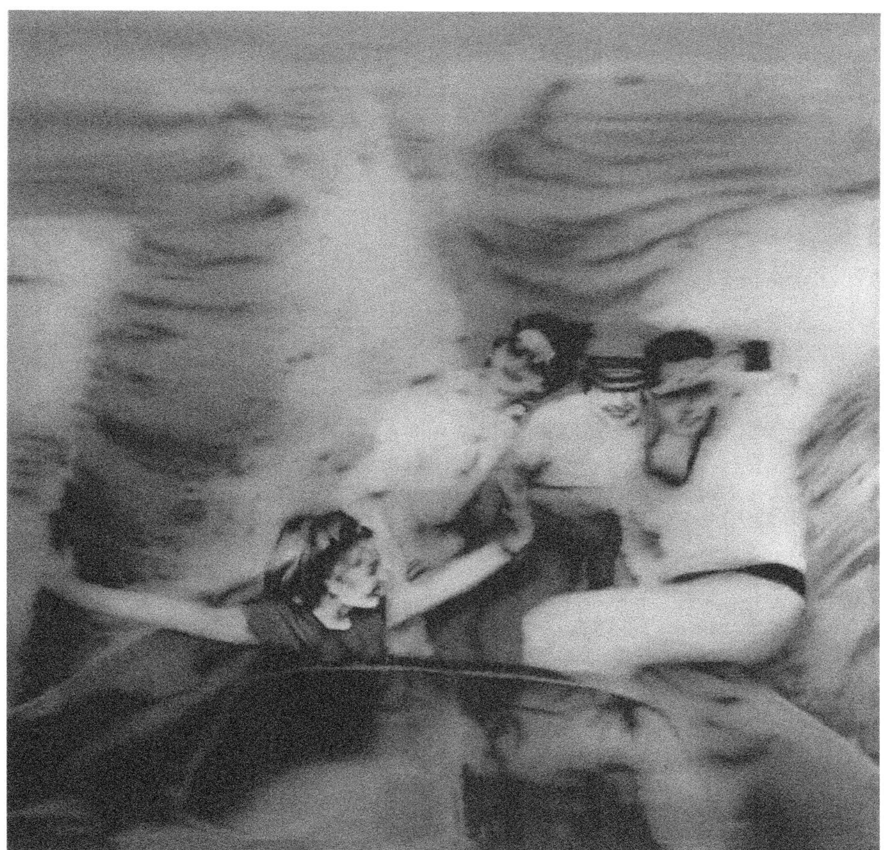

4.1 *Motor Boat*, 1965. Oil on canvas, 67 × 67 in.

Lichtenstein do, but suggests that it must also come to terms with "the modern way" indicated by Warhol—a way that brooks no "'artistic' nonsense."

Not restricted to painting, Richter has produced thousands of photographs, not to mention numerous installations and several sculptures. Yet even if we regard him strictly as a painter, his practice is complicated and capacious enough: it encompasses not only different modes of painting, from the representational to the abstract, but also diverse classes of images, from low culture to high art. As is well known, many of his early canvases are blurry renditions of banal photos of everyday life, such as newspaper images, magazine ads, family snaps, soft-porn shots, and aerial views of assorted cities, while many of his later canvases recall the old genres of academic painting also seen as if through a fuzzy optic: still lifes, landscapes, portraits, even history paintings. Thus Richter has ranged from low categories to high and back again—back again insofar as the high genres, his landscapes in particular, sometimes approach the low forms once more, such as the pretty postcard or the sentimental photo souvenir.

In this way, like Warhol, Richter has moved to desublimate painting; "I consider many amateur photographs better than the best Cézannes," he remarked in 1966 (43). At the same time, unlike Warhol, Richter has also strived to support its fragile autonomy: "In every respect, my work has more to do with traditional art than anything else," Richter commented in 1964, not long after the blurry paintings first appeared (22). (Indeed, his celebrated suite of images concerning the revolutionary Baader-Meinhof Gang, *October 18, 1977* [1988], nearly resurrects the academic genre of history painting, yet does so, tellingly, with subjects alien to the official ones: dead radicals who remain "unburied" in postwar Germany [fig. 4.2].)[2] His commitment to this aporia—the debasement of pictorial content on the one hand, the preservation of pictorial form on the other—renders his painting intensely ambiguous, skeptical of its traditional authority yet committed to this tradition nonetheless. In similar ways, Richter shows contrary allegiances to divergent lineages of art, both historical and avant-garde, with echoes of the romantic landscapes of Caspar David Friedrich as well as the conceptual provocations of Marcel Duchamp, the Color Field abstractions of Barnett Newman as well as the murky media images of Warhol. It is as though Richter wanted to run these diverse strands of practice together, to put the exalted pictorial formats of the "Northern Romantic Tradition" from Friedrich to Newman through the anti-aesthetic paces of the Duchampian (neo) avant-garde, the found image above all, to test the ideal of "beautiful semblance" in art foregrounded in the Romantic line with the fact of the commodification of art underscored by the (neo) avant-garde line (fig. 4.3).[3] In effect, Richter poses the question, can there be lyric painting after Warhol? Behind this question lies the more profound dilemma of lyric painting after Auschwitz, which he also ponders in his work.[4]

"All that I am trying to do in each picture," Richter has stated in his characteristic manner, at once modest and grand, "is to bring together the most disparate and mutually contradictory elements, alive and viable, in the greatest possible freedom" (187). His intermingling of apparent opposites—painting and photography, crafted facture and readymade image, abstraction and representation—is evident enough; the question is to what effects, and to what ends, is it performed. Do these opposites appear as antinomies that arrest his oeuvre in a static oscillation between different modes, or do they pose contradictions that Richter works through dialectically? Is his art one of simple eclecticism in the familiar manner of postmodern pastiche, or is it a complex rehearsal of pictorial styles that is deconstructive in spirit? Or does Richter suggest an alternative to these approaches, between or beyond them?[5]

Cuckoo's Eggs

In a 1986 dialogue with Benjamin Buchloh, his most engaged critic, Richter touches on these matters at several points. First, on the problem of pastiche, Buchloh comments: "Your work looks like a survey of the whole universe of twentieth-century panting presented in one vast, cynical retrospective." Richter replies: "Now that definitely is a misunderstanding. I see not cynicism or trickery or guile in any of this." Then, on the question of antinomies, Buchloh asks: "But aren't they [representation and abstraction] juxtaposed in order to show up the inadequacy, the bankruptcy, of both?" Richter responds: "Not bankruptcy, but always inadequacy" (174). Finally, on the role of deconstruction, Buchloh asserts: "You are making the spectacle of painting visible in its rhetoric, without practicing it." Richter parries: "And what would be the point of that? That's the last thing I'd want to do." Buchloh presses: "You don't see the abstract pictures . . . as kind of reflection on the history of painting? . . . They not only have a rhetorical quality but also a quality of reflection on what used to be possible." Richter meets him halfway: "That would apply rather to the landscapes and some

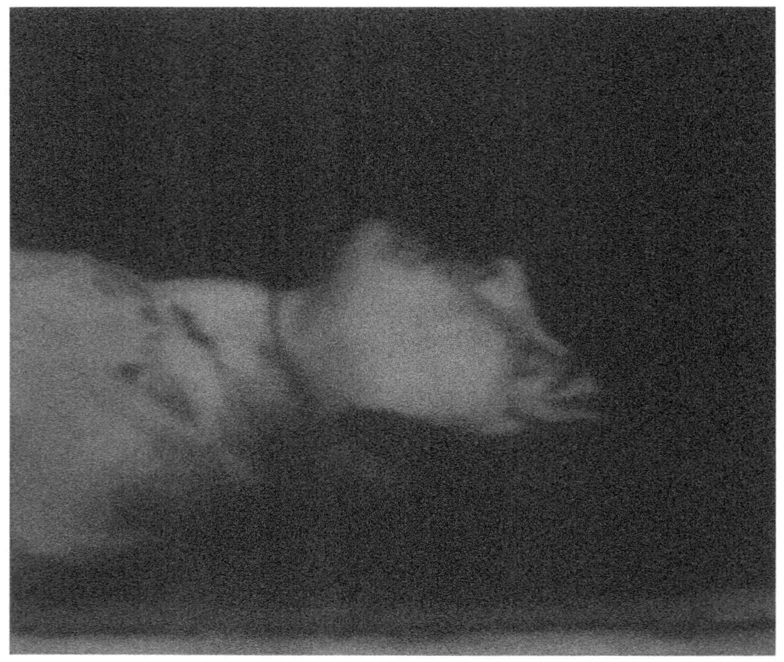

4.2 *Dead (October 18, 1977)*, 1988. Oil on canvas, 24½ × 24½ in.

of the photo paintings, which I've described on occasion as cuckoo's eggs, because people take them for something they aren't" (185).

There is cat-and-mousing here, to be sure, and certainly Richter in 1986 differs from Richter in the early 1960s, not to mention Richter in the present. In the early 1960s, he seemed to subscribe to a Warholian aesthetic of indifference: "I like everything that has no style: dictionaries, photographs, nature, myself and my paintings" is a repeated statement of this period (32). However, by 2002, the year of his retrospective initiated by the Museum of Modern Art, Richter spoke freely of "masterpieces," and he seemed content to be hailed as "Europe's greatest modern painter" in the *New York Times*.[6] In the interim, Richter tacked between these positions, at times insisting on the rupture produced by the Duchampian readymade, with Minimalism

4.3 *Davos S.*, 1981. Oil on canvas, 27½ × 39½ in.

deemed a "new alphabet for the art of the future," and at times deferring "to a vast, great, rich culture of painting—of art in general—which we have lost, but which places obligations on us" (129, 175). In the 1986 conversation, after a discussion of Fluxus, Minimalism, and Pop, Buchloh states, "You align your own painting with this anti-aesthetic impulse, and at the same time you maintain a pro-painting position. To me this seems to be one of the entirely typical contradictions out of which your work has essentially evolved." "Yes," Richter replies, "it is curious, but I don't actually find it contradictory. It's rather as if I were doing the same things by other means, means that are less spectacular and less advanced" (168).

How, then, are we to understand the bringing together of "the most disparate elements" in his art? The question bears not only on the apparent variety of his styles but also on the sheer abundance of his images. In 1962, Richter began to assemble his *Atlas*, which has since become a vast compendium of public representations and private photos, a fraction of which have served as the source of his paintings over the years (fig. 4.4). In 1989, he described the *Atlas* as "a deluge of images" with "no individual images left at all" (235), that is, as an archive whose great number of pictures relativizes the value of each one; and except for an early juxtaposition of concentration-camp and porn photos, *Atlas* contains very little in the way of significant montage (figs. 4.5 and 4.6). This proliferation of images can also relativize the position of the subject (both artist and viewer), and Buchloh has written of the Richter archive of photos as precisely "anomic" (etymologically, "without rule or law"), shot through with an arbitrariness that undercuts confidence in the images as bearers of truth or meaning.[7] "Ce n'est pas une image juste," Jean-Luc Godard remarked in his 1970 film *Vent d'est*; "c'est juste une image": throughout his early period, Richter seemed to participate in this critical relativization of both the referential value and the artistic merit of his representations. In 1973, for example, he spoke of the photograph as a "pure picture," "free of all the conventional criteria I had always associated with art: It had no style, no composition, no judgment" (59). Yet it is more accurate to say that Richter worked to *suspend* the alternative implied by Godard—to make "a just painting" that is also "just a painting," to produce images that are both motivated and arbitrary, composed and casual, "classical" and "Informel."[8] As Richter indicates, some of his paintings are "cuckoo's eggs," taken for what they are not, or are not fully.[9]

In this light, consider the Gray Paintings, which date from 1967 (fig. 4.7). Made with various kinds of strokes—tight and finicky in one painting, broad and meandering in another, somewhere in between in several others—they resemble any number of late-modernist monochromes that explore the material constituents and formal parameters of the medium; in this regard, they might be taken as attempts at "total" or "meta" painting, painting that is concerned with painting and nothing else. At the same time, the Gray Paintings appear to be in keeping with the asperity of Minimalist art, pledged to an emptying out of the medium, a zero degree of its

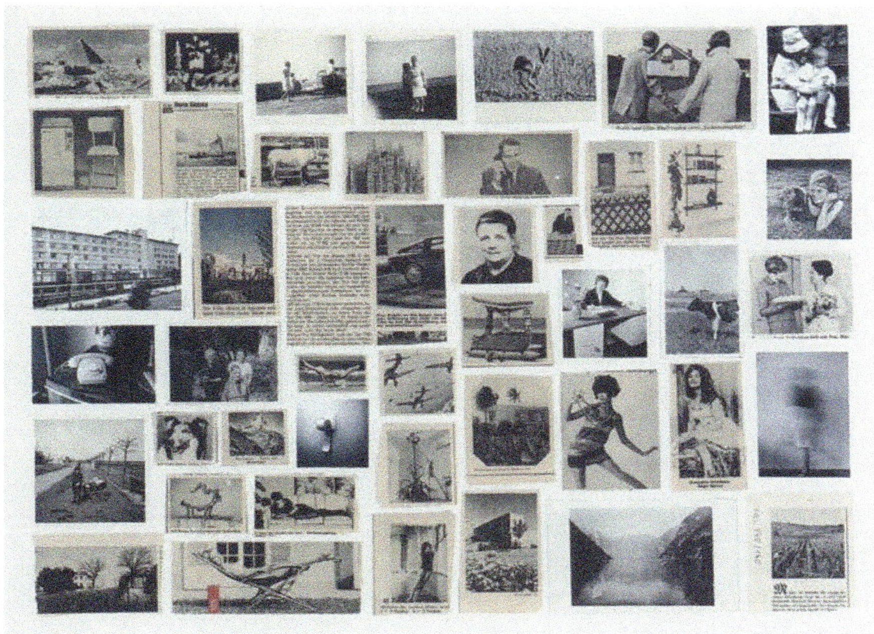

4.4 *Atlas: Panel 5*, 1962–66. Black-and-white and color clippings and photographs, 20⅜ × 26¼ in.

figurative and expressive capacities; in this respect, they might be understood as instances of "null" or even "anti" painting.

Or consider the Color Charts that recur from 1966 on (fig. 4.8). As sheer paint pushed to the point of mere readymade, these grids of color samples, some laboriously mixed, others simply given, also appear both full and empty, deductive and arbitrary, all painting and none at all. Moreover, as the Color Charts grow in size and complexity (from six rectangles to thousands), they become, as Richter once remarked, evermore "boundless," in the sense of potential, yet evermore "meaningless," in the sense of random (71). And there is a further ambiguity of beginnings and ends here. Like the Gray Paintings, the Color Charts might evoke the famous three panels produced by Aleksandr Rodchenko in 1921, *Pure Red, Pure Blue, Pure Yellow.* "This is the end of painting," Rodchenko later declared of these monochromes.

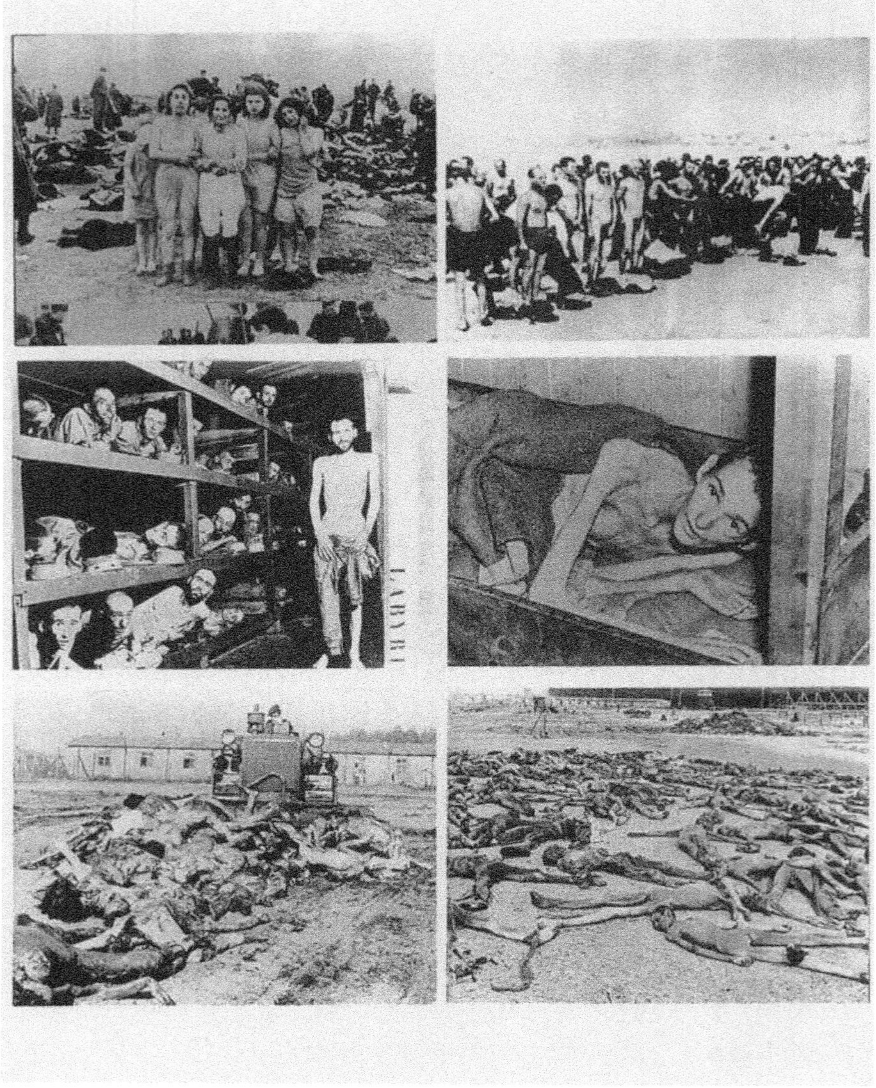

4.5 *Atlas: Panel 18*, 1967. Black-and-white clippings and photographs, 26¼ × 20⅜ in.

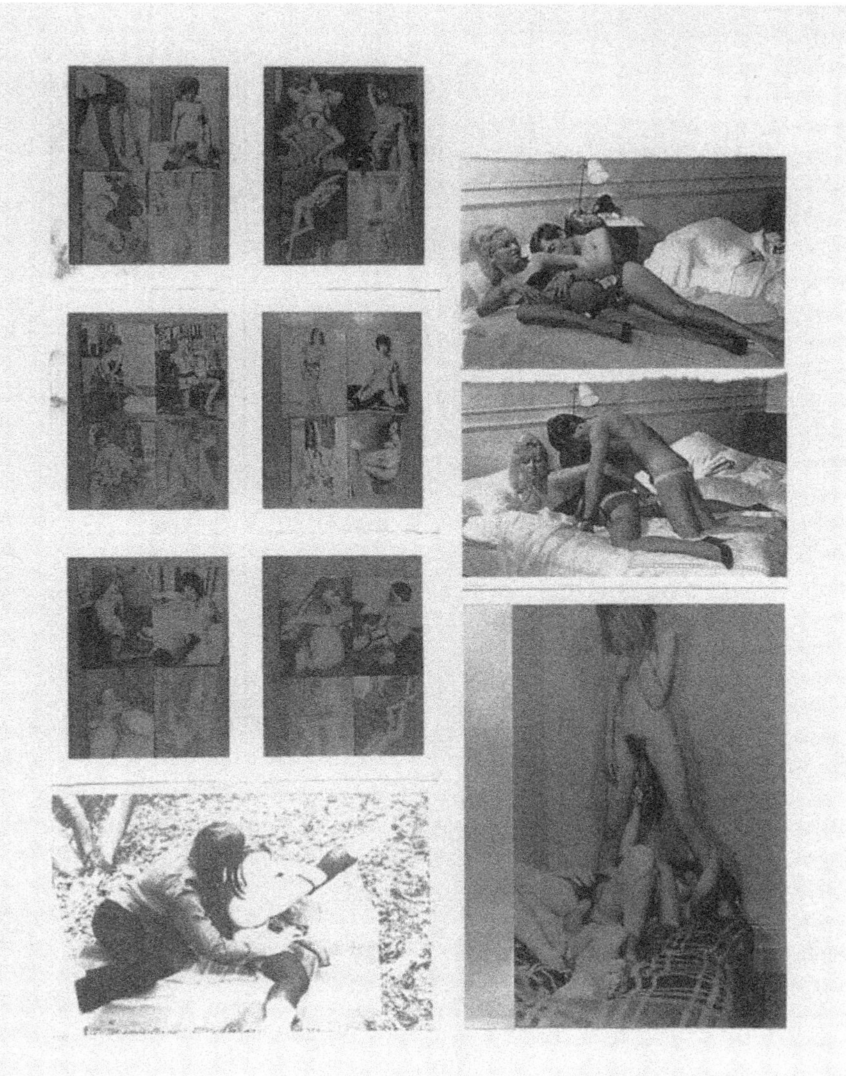

4.6 *Atlas: Panel 22*, 1967. Black-and-white clippings and photographs, 26¼ × 20⅜ in.

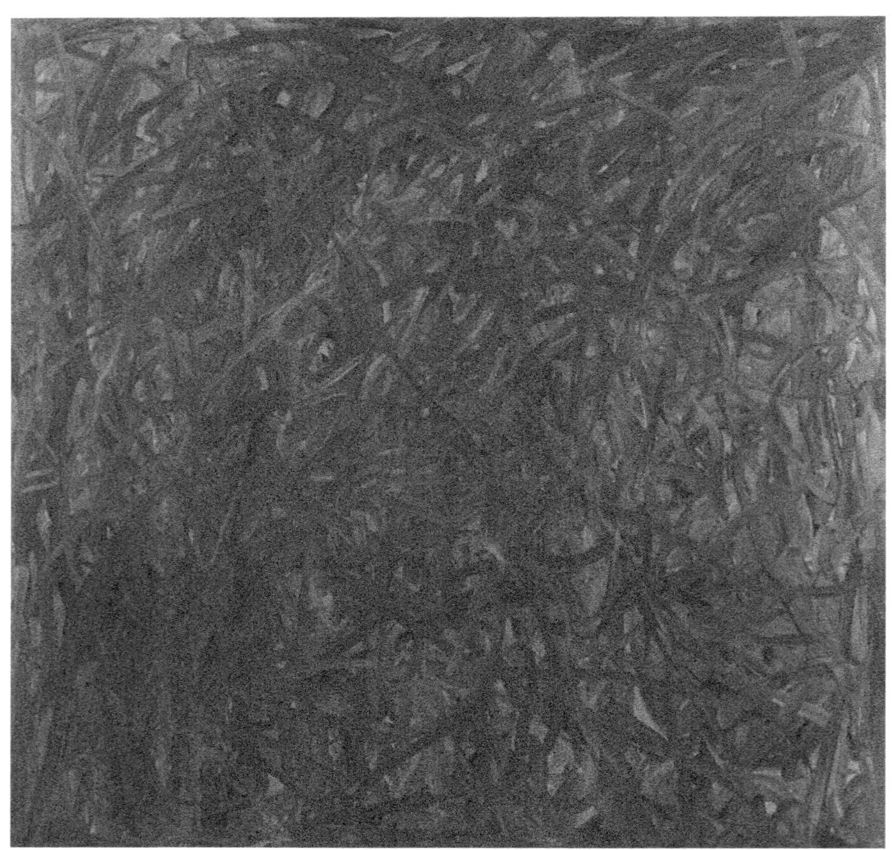

4.7 *Un-Painting (Gray)*, 1972. Oil on canvas, 78¾ × 78¾ in.

"There will be no more representation."[10] Yet such is the millenarian ambiguity of modernist forms like the monochrome that Rodchenko might also have advanced his panels as a new beginning of painting, as Kazimir Malevich had done with his first Suprematist abstractions. By the mid-1960s, however, the question of "the end of bourgeois painting" was hardly as momentous as it had been in the mid-1920s; after all, Richter, who grew up in East Germany, painted through the fall of the communist order, not during

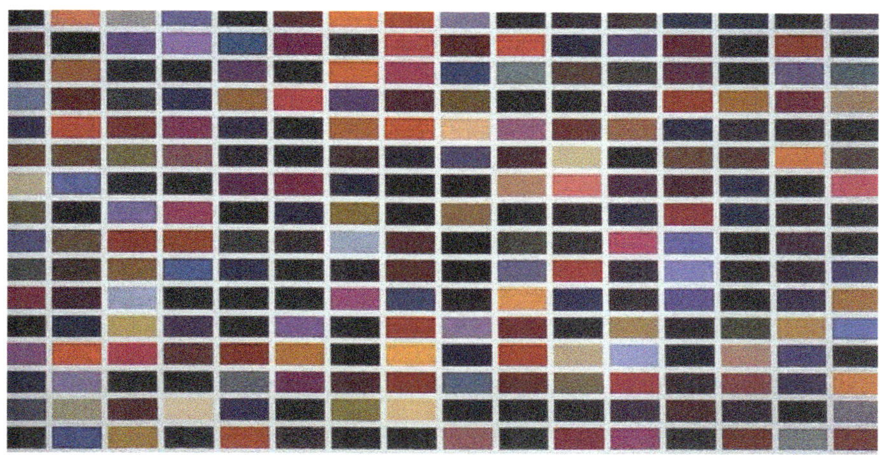

4.8 *256 Colors*, 1974. Oil on canvas, 87½ × 163 in.

its rise, as did the Russians. In any case, like the Gray Paintings, the Color Charts can be conscripted for either side of this old debate.

Or, finally, consider the gestural abstractions that Richter began in 1971, complex layers of different colors in various factures built up with assorted tools (figs. 4.9–4.11; since the late 1980s, he has also effected this palimpsest through aggressive scraping down). These paintings are worked, often exquisitely, to a point of formal suspension, which is not the same thing as pictorial resolution, for they, too, can seem almost arbitrary in composition. Stroke by stroke, the gestures are oddly self-canceling—again, both full and null, subjective and subjectless, like the marks of an Abstract Expressionist with Alzheimer's.[11] Richter once spoke of a "blind, random motor activity" (71), and a strange mechanicity, at once photographic and painterly, does govern the facture of his abstractions no less than of his representations. This (non)quality persists in his later paintings; it is pronounced, for example, in the *Silicate* series of 2003, which feature all-over patterns in blurred shades of black and white that appear at once molecular and mechanical, as if natural and technological worlds had combined in a new order of "needless and meaningless" design—an effect that is perhaps fitting for an age that Richter calls "technoanimalistic" (432) (fig. 4.12).[12]

So, too, each painting, even each series, can differ in an almost indifferent way; that is to say, they can appear somehow casual, almost interchangeable, even when they are highly wrought and quite distinctive. In this manner, Richter sometimes suggests the condition of the blasé, which the German sociologist Georg Simmel ascribed one hundred years ago to the metropolitan subjectivity of the capitalist marketplace. For Simmel, the gray-on-gray exchanges that dominate a money economy promote a blunted (*blasé*) sensibility, one characterized, on the one hand, by a sensitivity prompted by the superficial variety of the market environment and, on the other, by an indifference produced by the deeper homogeneity of the greater system.[13] With Richter, it is as though this paradoxical effect has come to penetrate the very artistic form, painting, that was once most dedicated to the articulation of difference—to the unique, the original, and the autonomous. "In the Gray pictures it's lack of differentiation, nothing, nil, the Beginning and the End," Richter wrote Buchloh in a 1977 letter; "in the Color Charts it's chance, anything is correct, or rather Form Is Nonsense; in the new Abstract Pictures it's arbitrariness, almost anything is possible. To me this arbitrariness has always seemed the central problem in both abstract and representational painting" (93). By various means, then, Richter performs this arbitrariness, yet in performing it, he also works to expose it, perhaps even to suspend it. He calls the latter effect "planned spontaneity" or "planned arbitrariness" (136, 162).[14]

A Lasting Trauma

The Duchampian term for planned arbitrariness is "canned chance."[15] John Cage elaborated this notion in postwar music, of course, and under his influence, many others experimented with it too, usually in order to shift the work away from the intentions of the composer or artist toward the circumstances of its listener or viewer—to render it more objective, open, and active.[16] Especially strong in the 1960s, this concern was evident in such de-skilling operations as the appropriation of media imagery in Pop

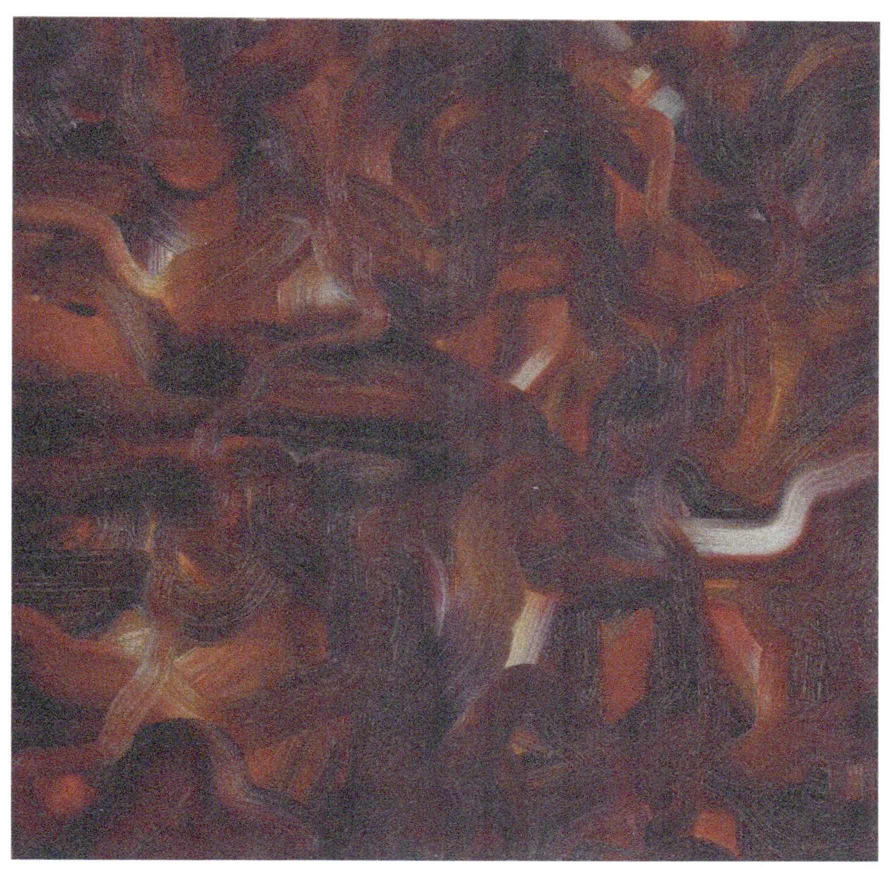

4.9 *Red-Blue-Yellow*, 1972. Oil on canvas, 59 × 59 in.

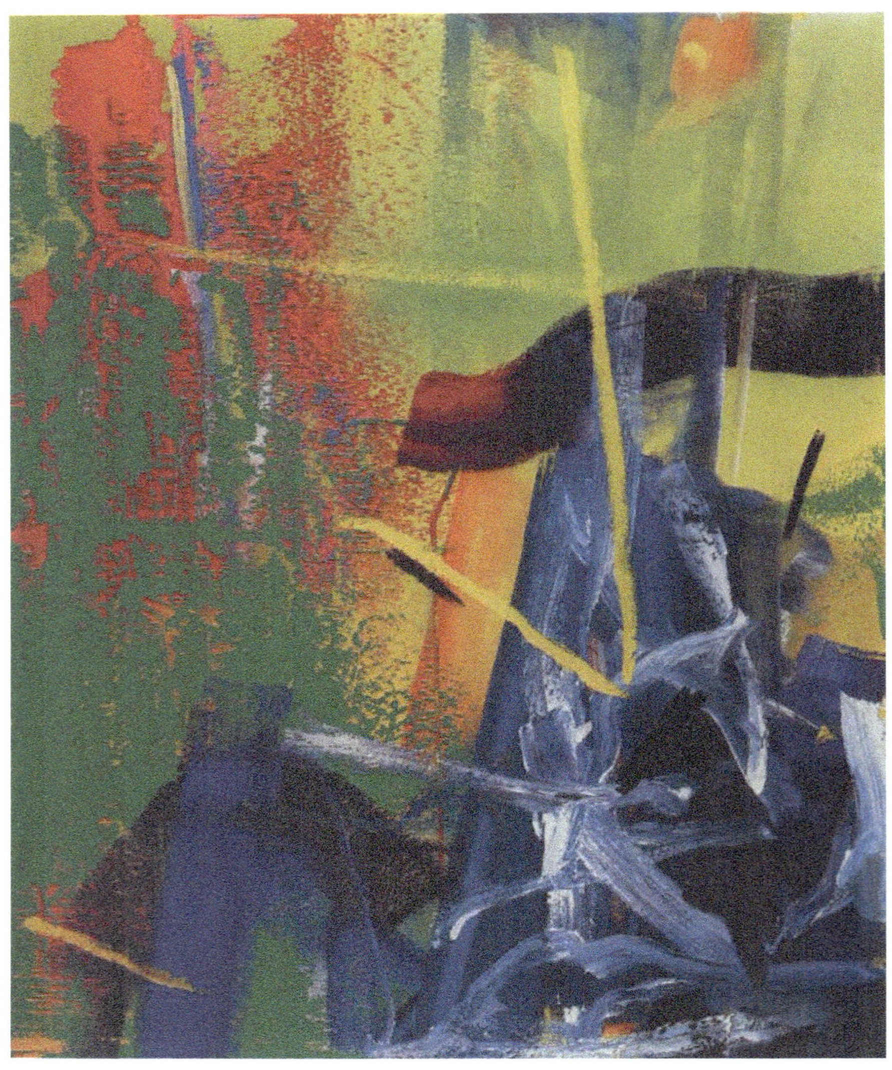

4.10 *Corn*, 1982. Oil on canvas, 98½ × 78¾ in.

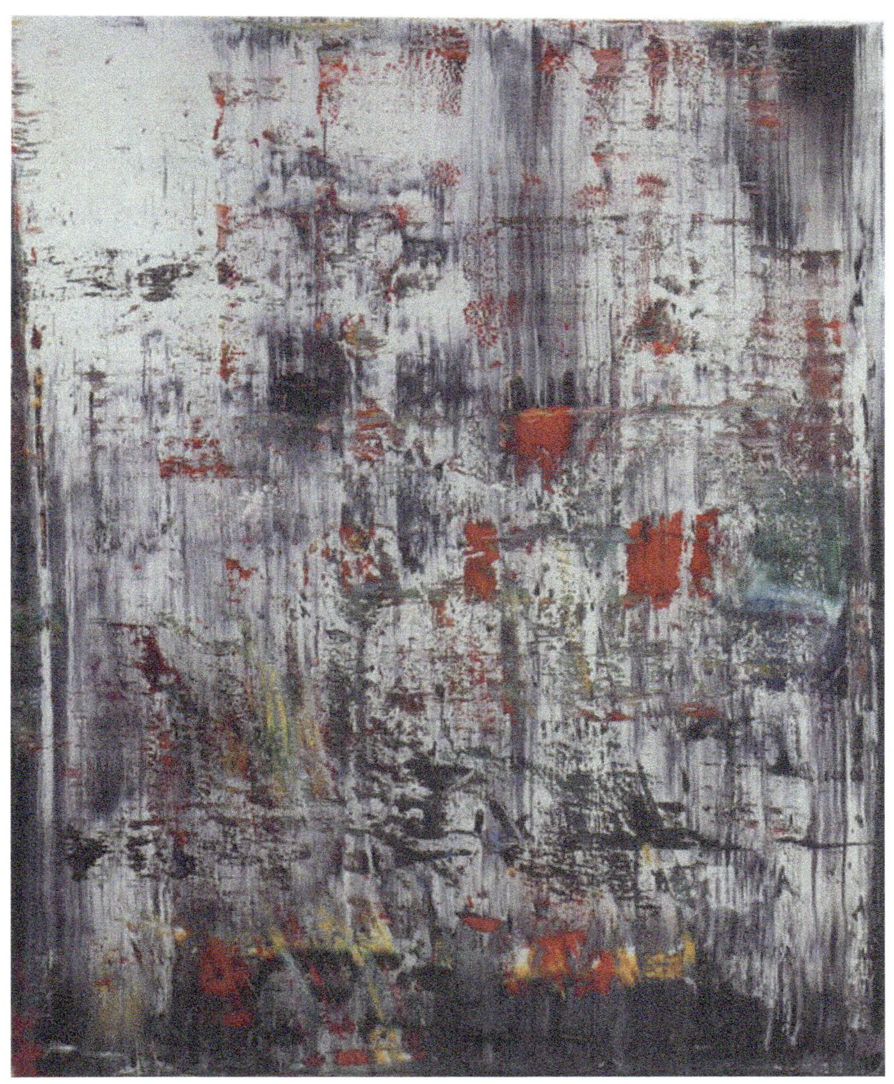

4.11 *Ice (2),* 1989. Oil on canvas, 80 × 63⅞ in.

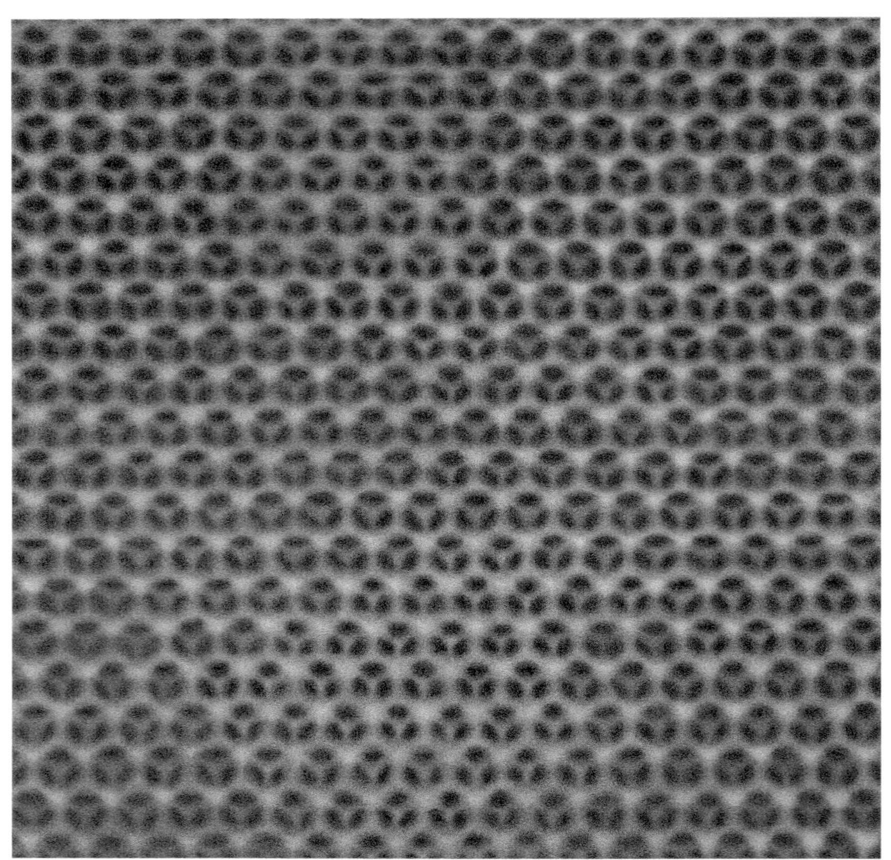

4.12 *Silicate (885-1)*, 2003. Oil on canvas, 114⅛ × 114⅛ in.

paintings and the use of industrial fabrication in Minimalist objects; a related move was the use of banal photographs, as in such photo books by Ed Ruscha as *Twentysix Gasoline Stations* (1963). Early on, Richter followed this line. "I hate the dazzlement of skill," he stated in 1964; painting from photos was "the most moronic and inartistic thing that anyone could do" (21; fig. 4.13). This is a tendentious statement from a virtuoso painter, but its aesthetic of indifference is more than a cool pose: the partial disconnection between work and self, effected by his photographic datum as much as by his quasi-mechanical facture, provides Richter with a desired defense, and we might speculate about why this protection is important to him.[17]

In the mid-1960s, Richter spoke of his encounter with photography in traumatic terms: "For a time I worked as a photographic laboratory assistant: the masses of photographs that passed through the bath of developer every day may well have caused a lasting trauma."[18] Although this seems overstated, it is not absurd; what, then, might the nature of this trauma be? It is not the old threat of the photographic usurpation of the representational function of painting as foretold by Baudelaire, Antoine Wiertz, and others. That is long since a historical given, and in part Richter challenges, even reverses, the triumphal teleology of this familiar story. Rather, for Richter, the trauma of photography seems to lie both in the sheer proliferation of its number ("the masses of photographs") and in its pervasive transformation of appearance (the passage "through the bath of developer"). As Buchloh has suggested, this reaction brings Richter closer to Siegfried Kracauer than to Baudelaire and others: "The world itself has taken on a 'photographic face,'" Kracauer wrote in his great 1927 essay on photography; "it can be photographed because it strives to be absorbed into the spatial continuum which yields to snapshots."[19] Like Warhol, Richter explores this "photographic face" of the modern world, its reconfiguration around such images and its conformity with them. "That the world devours them is a sign of the *fear of death*," Kracauer continues. "What the photographs by their accumulation attempt to banish is the recollection of death, which is part and parcel of every memory image."[20] Richter would seem to accept this Kracauerian opposition of photograph and "memory image," yet, intermittently, he also seeks to overcome it—to reveal the deathliness of

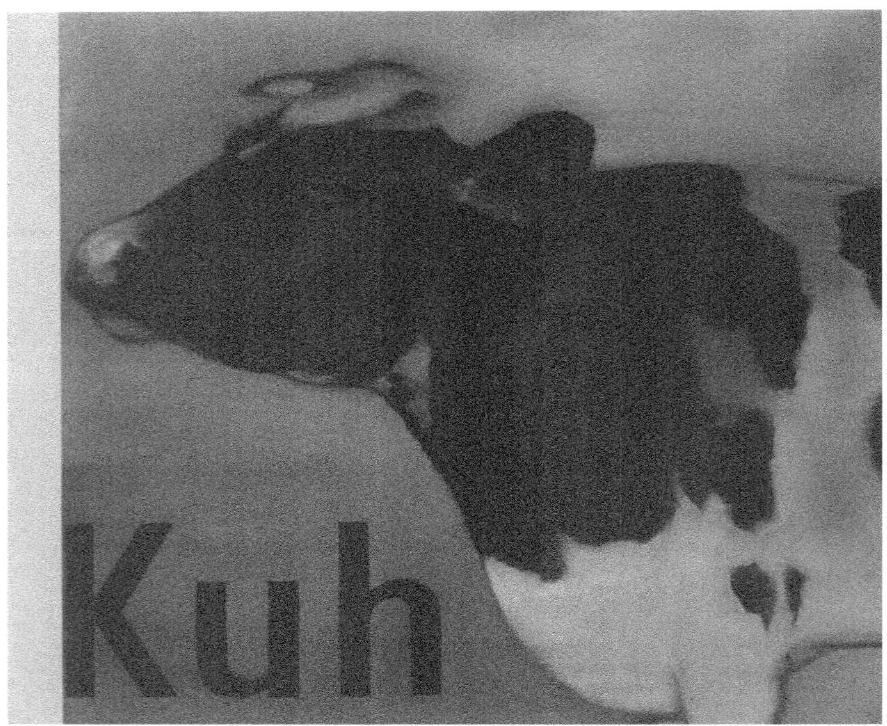

4.13 *Cow*, 1964. Oil on canvas, 51³⁄₁₆ × 59¹⁄₁₆ in.

this photographic face and to render the photograph mnemonic in painting, *as* painting (the latter aim is intimated in his intention "not [to] use [photography] as a means to painting but [to] use painting as a means to photography" [59]). The Baader-Meinhof suite of paintings is a powerful instance of this transformation of potentially anti-mnemonic photographs into potent memory images.

Richter sometimes employs the term "banality," and it is a notion that can gather some of our divergent concerns thus far, such as the recourse to de-skilling, the traumatic aspect of photography, and the protective potential of painting.[21] Certainly, Richter has long used banal subject matter.

What could be more banal, for example, than the everyday rolls of toilet paper he painted in 1965 (fig. 4.14)? Yet this banality is both obvious and too readily redeemed through his almost auratic rendering (especially in the soft version of the motif). More biting is the banality of the ornate chandelier he captured in *Flemish Crown* (1965; fig. 4.15), an exemplum not just of a homey thing but of petit bourgeois taste at its homeliest; or the banality of the humble turntable in *Record Player* (1988; fig. 4.16) in the Baader-Meinhof suite, a harmless appliance, but one viewed almost forensically from above, and now charged by our knowledge that it concealed the gun that killed Andreas Baader in prison.[22]

A further banality, at the level of address, also interests Richter: the traumatic banality that befalls a person made over into a photograph, a life congealed into an image. This transformation occurs in the existential flashing of the photographic shot—the shuttering of the camera that can produce a shuddering in the subject—an effect underscored by Roland Barthes in *Camera Lucida* (1980).[23] This little death can also occur in the automatic posing of the subject before the photographic apparatus, the voluntary assumption of a self-image, a personal stereotype, in order to conform to the photographic face of the world, to its photogenic expectations. The young fun seekers in *Motor Boat* (1965; fig. 4.1), for example, do indeed "strive to be absorbed into the spatial continuum which yields to snapshots," as do many subjects Richter has painted from family pictures.[24]

From the start of his mature work, Richter has captured this fashioning of subjects into stereotypes, and sometimes it has led him to travesty familiar figures in art history as well. For instance, his can-can *Ballet Dancers* (1966; fig. 4.17) and soft-porn *Bathers* (1967) are degraded descendants of the dancers and bathers of Edgar Degas and Paul Cézanne, and his striptease *Olympia* (1967; fig. 4.18) updates the prostitute of Manet in the context of a modern middle-class home. Yet this banality might also be a little facile in its very travesty; it is more effective when more everyday, as in his Warholian rendering of *Eight Student Nurses* (1966; fig. 4.19), the serial-murder victims who had already been shot serially in the yearbook that Richter used as his source.[25] This latter banality is most chilling in his picturing of *Three Sisters* (1965; fig. 4.20), who, set in matching dresses on

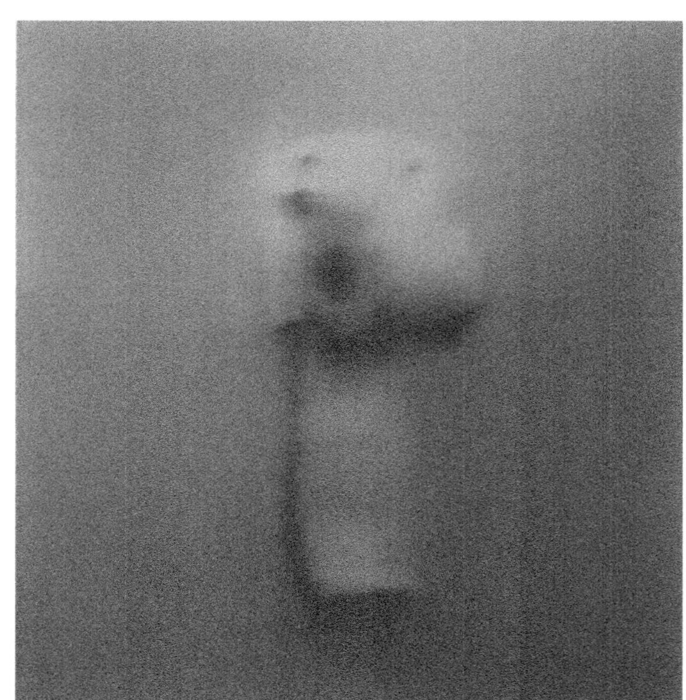

4.14 *Toilet Paper*,
1965. Oil on canvas,
27½ × 25⅝ in.

4.15 *Flemish Crown*,
1965. Oil on canvas,
35½ × 43¼ in.

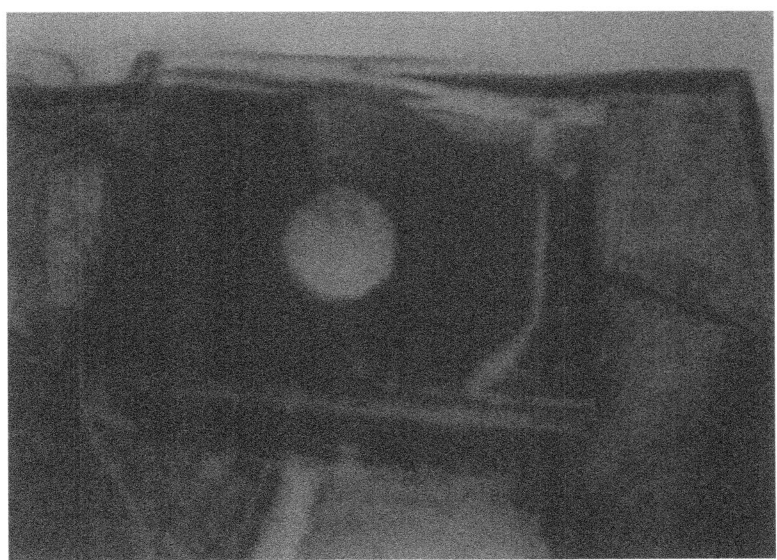

4.16 *Record Player*, 1988. Oil on canvas, 24⅝ × 32¾ in.

a family couch, appear as nearly cloned in self-presentation as they are in gene structure: here it is as if conformity to petit bourgeois expectation, to the cliché of the family photo, were the only way for these girls to attain social recognition at all.[26]

"It's all evasive action," Richter once remarked of the role of banality in his art (62). Apparently, the banal has a defensive function as well as a traumatic effect for Richter, and the same seems true of the photographic. Painting from photographs freed him from "conscious thinking," Richter wrote early on; it is "neutralized and therefore painless," he added later (30). It is as though Richter aimed to transform the photograph, a medium that concentrates a traumatic threat for him, into an apotropaic defense against this same threat. Certainly, the grays and the blurs in his painting, both of which register as photographic, can be muting, even taming, in effect.[27] Of course, the grays and the blurs also work in other, often opposite ways, and this ambiguity is key to the enigmatic nature of his work (as psychoanalysis

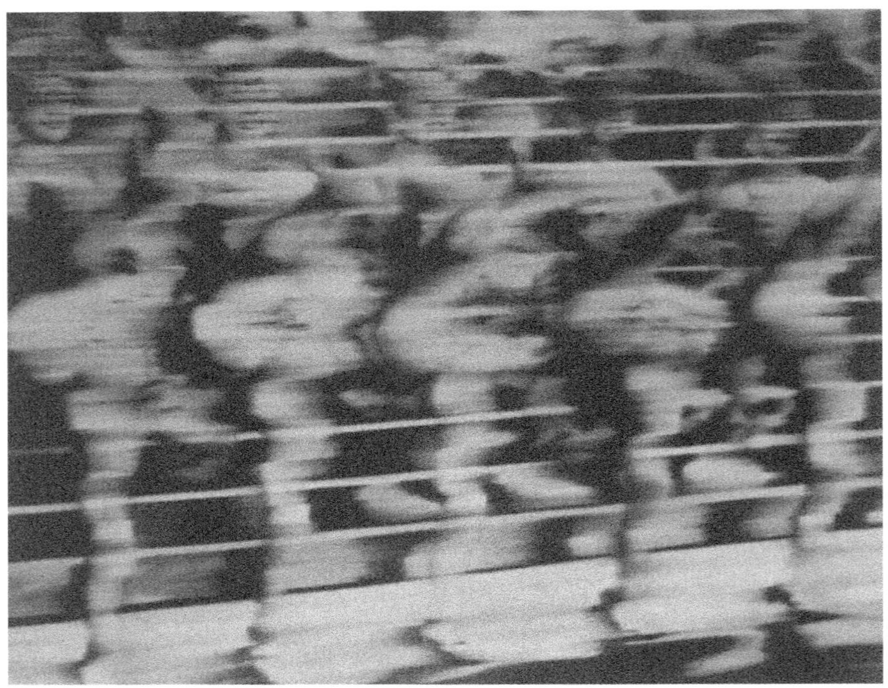

4.17 *Ballet Dancers*, 1966. Oil on canvas, 63 × 78¾ in.

has shown us, the enigmatic and the traumatic often implicate each other).[28] For example, the grays can be read as both the material actuality of pigment and the mediated virtuality of print. And the associations of the blurs are even more complex: they can evoke the speed of an object or the distraction of a viewer; a memory image or the fading away of the same; a lurid, even obscene scene or a screened, obscured one; and so on. And yet, however different, even contrary, these effects might appear, all are common aspects of the photographic face of the modern world. They suggest how our very sensorium, memory, and unconscious have become, at least in part, "photogenic," that is to say, not only affected by photography and film but also somehow adjusted to them—suited, even designed, to be photographed or filmed, created with such light in mind, along the lines suggested by

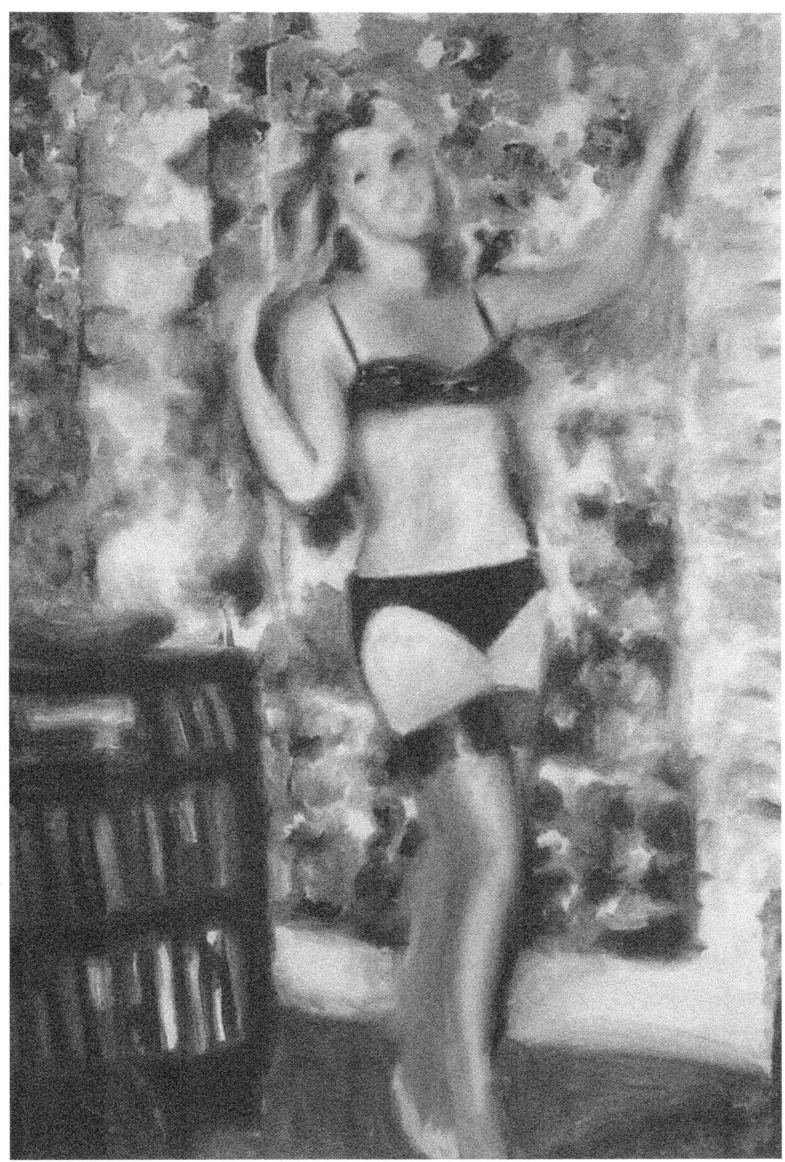

4.18 *Olympia*, 1967. Oil on canvas, 78¾ × 51¼ in.

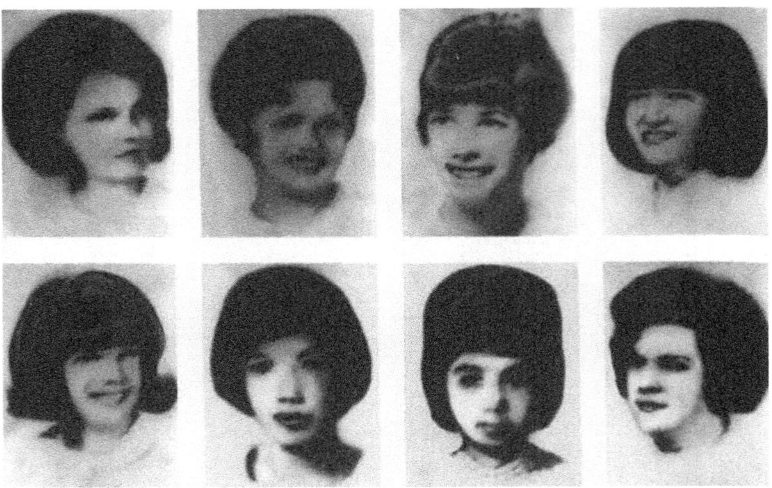

4.19 *Eight Student Nurses*, 1966. Oil on canvas, eight panels, each 36⅜ × 27½ in.

Kracauer in 1927.[29] This shift in appearance is a prime subject for Richter, and it produces a doubt that is epistemological, even ontological, one that his painting also strives to register: "My own relationship to reality," he remarked in 1971, "has a great deal to do with imprecision, uncertainty, transience, incompleteness" (60).[30]

The Richter blur might be the most evasive of his actions. Like his version of the banal, it can appear at once immediate and mediated, traumatic and protective, piercing and blasé.[31] In *Camera Lucida*, Barthes locates the traumatic point, or *punctum*, of a given photograph in a particular detail; in a Richter painting, on the other hand, the charge is as likely to emerge from a blur—a blur that can also serve as a buffer against this same trauma (in chapter 3, we encountered a similar double effect in Warhol silk screens). Among the most charged spots are his blurred details (oxymoron though that might be), such as the streaked eyes and blackened smiles of some of his early figures (fig. 4.21). "Something has to be shown and simultaneously not shown," Richter has said of his blur (in a way that also evokes Barthes), "in order perhaps to say something else again, a third thing" (272).[32] This

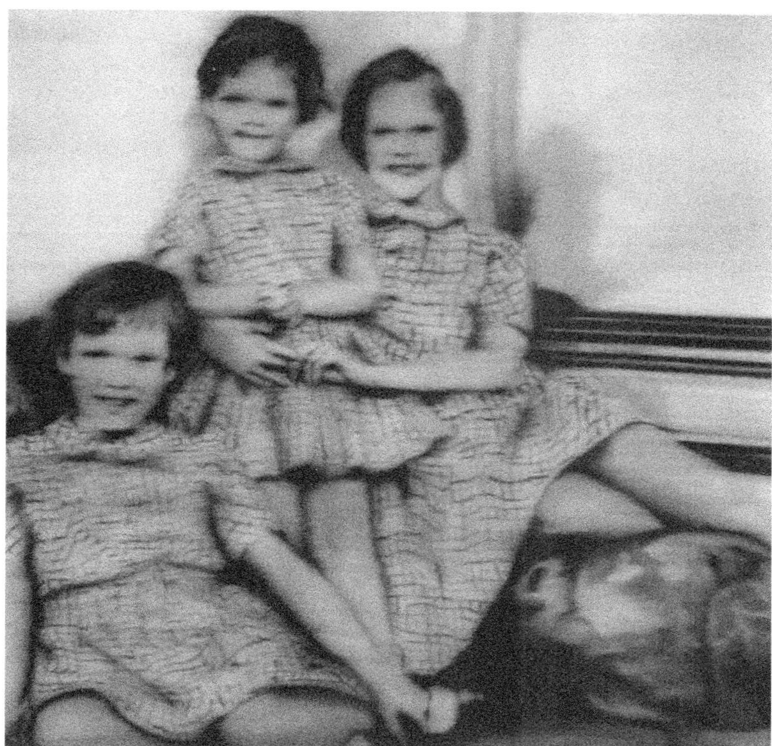

4.20 *Three Sisters*, 1965. Oil on canvas, 53 × 51¼ in.

statement conjures up a contradictory structure of recognition and disavowal, exposure and concealment, one that is familiar from psychoanalytic accounts not only of sexual fetishism but also of any screen memory, any protective displacement of a traumatic sight. The Freud texts on these subjects highlight charged spots or scenes of brilliance that, though bound up with traumatic sights, often serve to obscure them, and sometimes the Richter blur seems occlusive in this way too, when it possesses a paradoxical brightness. Similarly, the blur can evoke a psychic deformation of the visual field, one that "wilds" the image, and not just tames it, that intensifies our gaze, and not just sublimates it.[33] At moments, Richter almost specifies this

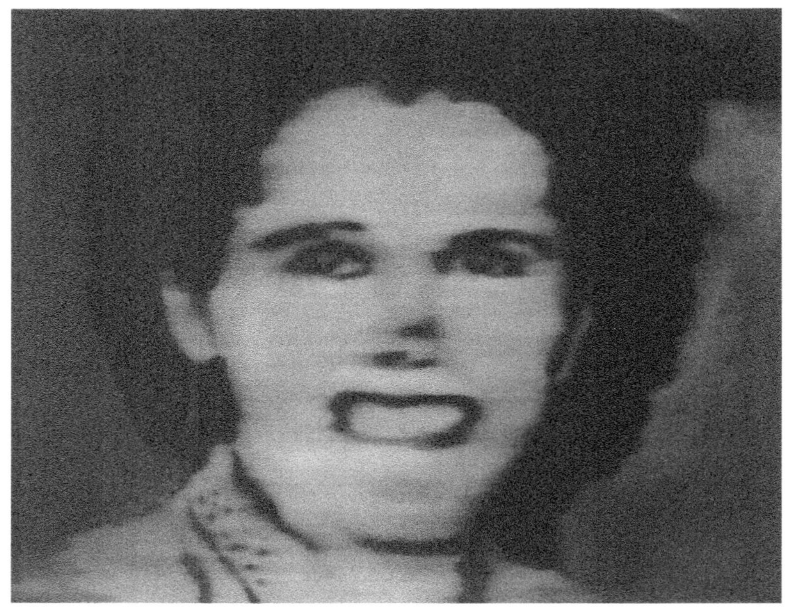

4.21 *Frau Marlow*, 1964. Oil on canvas, 30¼ × 37¾ in.

working over of the traumatic in his work and associates it with his relay between photography and painting. "The photograph provokes horror," he stated in 1989 (again with the Baader-Meinhof suite foremost in mind), "and the painting—with the same motif—something more like grief" (229). "Death and suffering" are "*the* theme" carried by the photograph, Richter added; and, implicitly, the painting treats this theme—treats it as one might a wound (227). If the picture remains too photographic, he insisted, it is "unendurable" (229); at the same time, if it does not register the traumatic somehow, it might not be effective.[34]

The Reflected Light of Semblance

"Illusion—or rather appearance, semblance—is the theme of my life," Richter also commented in 1989 (215). A central topos of German idealist philosophy and romantic poetics, "beautiful semblance" (*schön Schein*) is much discussed from Kant, Goethe, Schiller, Schelling, and Hegel through Nietzsche, Rilke, and Heidegger to Benjamin and Adorno; it could be, as Richter joked in the same 1989 note, "the theme of a speech welcoming freshmen to the Academy." But what counts as semblance is hardly academic. In the end, the oppositions that seem to govern his work—painting and photography, abstraction and representation—do not capture his distinctive variation on this celebrated topic, for, again, Richter undoes these binaries, or rather, he suggests how they are undone historically: how the postwar world to be painted arrives with a photographic, even photogenic, face, and how abstraction can be found in representation and vice versa. In any case, the question of semblance cuts across such categories, for semblance is not the resemblance produced in representation any more than it is the negation of this resemblance produced in abstraction. Semblance comprehends both modalities because it concerns the very consistency of appearance—it is what allows the world before us, natural or mediated, or natural *as* mediated, to cohere—and this concerns Richter above all else: "'Appearance,' that to me is a phenomenon" (405).

"All that is, seems, and is visible to us because we perceive it by the reflected light of semblance," Richter continued in the 1989 statement. "Nothing else is visible." In this sense, semblance is less appearance per se than our apprehension of appearance; it concerns human perception, embodiment, and agency—not as they are for all time but as they are altered by social change and technological transformation. Such semblance is at stake in photography, of course, but Richter sees an advantage in painting: "Painting concerns itself, as no other art does, exclusively with semblance (I include photography, of course)." Yet access to the semblance of the world is not given; according to Richter, the painter must "repeat" it or, more exactly, "fabricate" it. In his "Creative Credo," Paul Klee declared famously, "Art does not reproduce the visible; rather, it makes visible."[35] Richter would agree: the truly difficult task is to make the visible visible, that is, to capture "reflected light" as we experience it today, to make it "valid" (an early note reads: "The central problem in my painting is light" [35]).[36] "I would like to make it valid, make it visible," he remarked early on of the photograph, with "valid" here in the sense less of affirmation than of understanding (31).[37]

For Richter the photograph alone cannot deliver semblance because "the camera does not apprehend objects, it sees them" (32).[38] This is not to say that the photograph is not deeply implicated in contemporary appearance; on the contrary, it provides much of "the reflected light" of the modern world, and, again, it is this mediated light that Richter paints, with his artificial colors suspended in gelatinous layers, into many of his surfaces. Hence, his is less a critique of the society of the spectacle as such (he dismisses such critique, too quickly, as ideological) than a phenomenology of mediated appearance, of this *Schein*-ing of the modern world, of how it looks for us. The semblance that concerned Friedrich, say, was one of a nature still imbued with the light of God; its luminosity was still numinous. The semblance that concerns Richter is one of a "second nature" (to evoke again a salient term introduced nearly one hundred years ago by Georg Lukács), a culture-become-nature bathed in the glow of the media, a semblance permeated with photographic, televisual, and digital visualities, one that is photogenic in the sense developed above (figs. 4.22, 4.23).[39] "Photographs are almost nature" (228), Richter has commented, and many of his "natural" subjects are given as mediated, with colors variously faded (as in old snapshots), saturated (as in magazine ads), or entirely artificial (as in pixelated images); indeed, some of his subjects, as in the *Moonscapes* (1968; fig. 4.24), exist for us only as mediated.[40] A few early paintings also resemble images captured from television; in this respect, the blur can evoke the horizontal smear of television screens and video monitors, too. Moreover, as early as the 1970s, a few abstractions anticipated the bizarre dimensions of digital space, neither deep nor shallow but somehow both at once.

This pervasive mediation of the world is a central dilemma of lyric painting after Warhol.[41] Despite his avowed uninterest in "any critique of packaged culture or the consumer world" (138), Richter confronts the penetration of semblance by the commodity as a given of his historical moment. In "the consumer world," images and products are not easily held apart: the commodity has affected not only the structure of the sign but the nature of representation as well—a double transformation that Pop art in general explores.[42] Just as Minimalism often assumes the serial logic of industrial production ("one thing after another," in the familiar phrase of Donald Judd regarding his stacks of shelves and his rows of boxes), so Pop often reflects on the simulacral nature of the commodity-image—its status as a copy often loosened from any original (think, for example, of how the very seriality of such Warhol images as *Two Hundred Campbell's Soup Cans* detaches them from any referent in the world). Understood as a type of sign, the Pop simulacrum might be taken to undercut the referential claims of traditional representation no less than the metaphysical claims of modernist abstraction.[43] Yet Richter does not simply surrender painting to the simulacral order of our image world, as Warhol often does: sometimes, just as Richter wrests an auratic quality from banal reproductions, so too does he produce a piercing referentiality out of flimsy representations (again the turntable painting in the Baader-Meinhof suite comes to mind). In this way, more emphatically than his Pop peers, Richter insists on painting as a medium that can still reflect on the nature of semblance. Once more, Kracauer is pertinent here: "In order for history to present itself," he writes in his 1927 essay, "the mere surface coherence offered by photography must be destroyed."[44] Similarly for Richter, "the picture is the depiction, and painting is the technique for shattering it" (273), which is to suggest that the photograph delivers a resemblance (it merely "sees" objects) that the painting can—indeed must—open up so that semblance might be revealed ("apprehended").

"Illusion—or rather appearance, semblance": in the German tradition, *Schein* often slides in meaning between mere illusion and numinous appearance, and Richter conjures up the effects of both, the superficiality of the former as well as the aura of the latter. At the same time, he does not celebrate mere illusion, as his Pop colleagues often do, any more than he imagines that numinous appearance is still readily available to us: "We have lost the feeling of 'God's omnipresence in nature.' For us, everything is empty" (82). Here again, Richter follows his German predecessors, for whom (as Adorno once put it) the very "idea of art" is "to gain control of semblance, to determine it as semblance, as well as to negate it as unreal."[45] All three operations suggested by Adorno—control, definition, and negation of

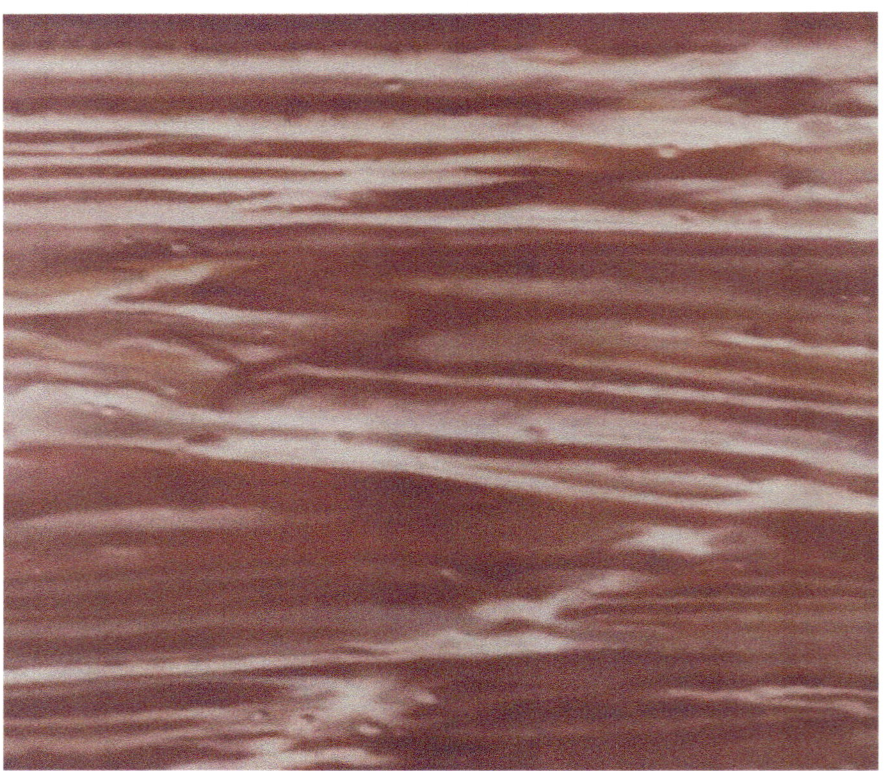

4.22 *Detail (Brown)*, 1970. Oil on canvas, 53¼ × 59 in.

appearance—are at work in Richter; yet what is left, then, of "beautiful semblance"? More than forty years ago, Clement Greenberg devised the phrase "homeless representation" to indicate the persistence of figurative traces in the abstract paintings of Willem de Kooning: "I mean by this," Greenberg wrote, "a plastic and descriptive painterliness that is applied to abstract ends, but which continues to suggest representational ones."[46] Perhaps in analogy, we might speak of "homeless semblance" in Richter. If so, it is a semblance that is homeless twice over: its numinous dimension has all but evaporated, and it does not seem rooted in the world—its mediated

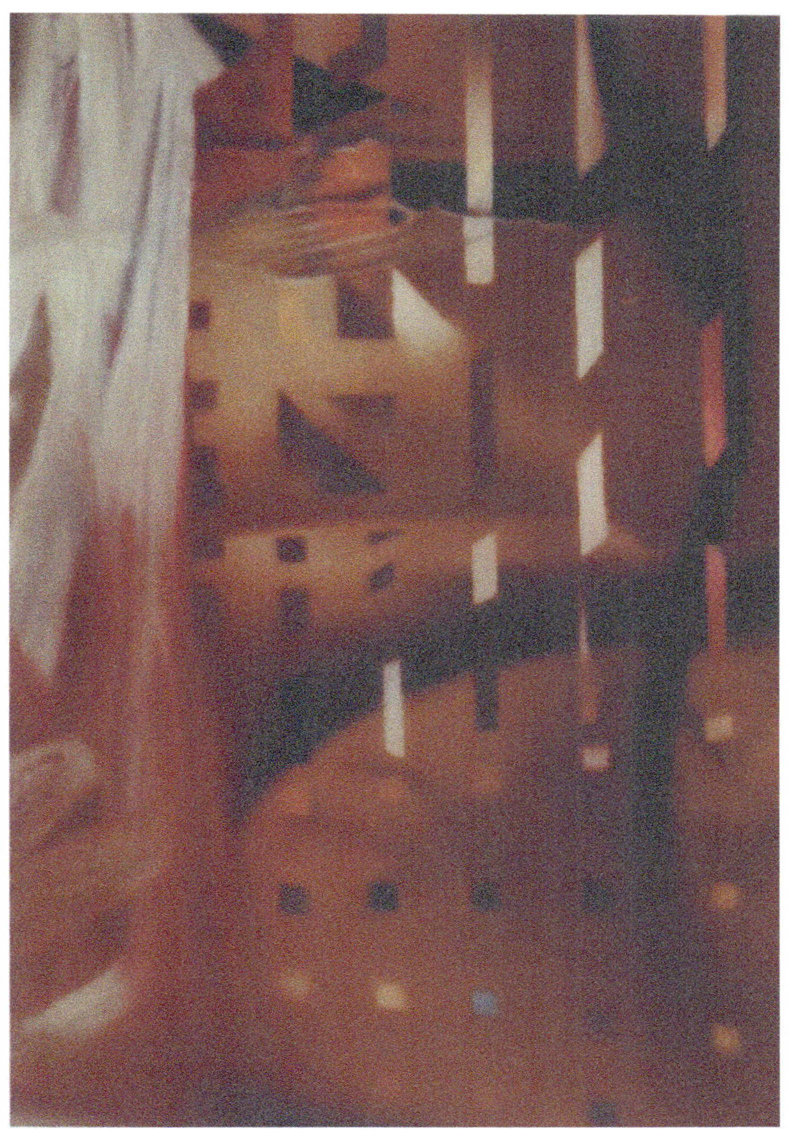

4.23 *Abstract Picture*, 1977. Oil on canvas, 118⅛ × 78¾ in.

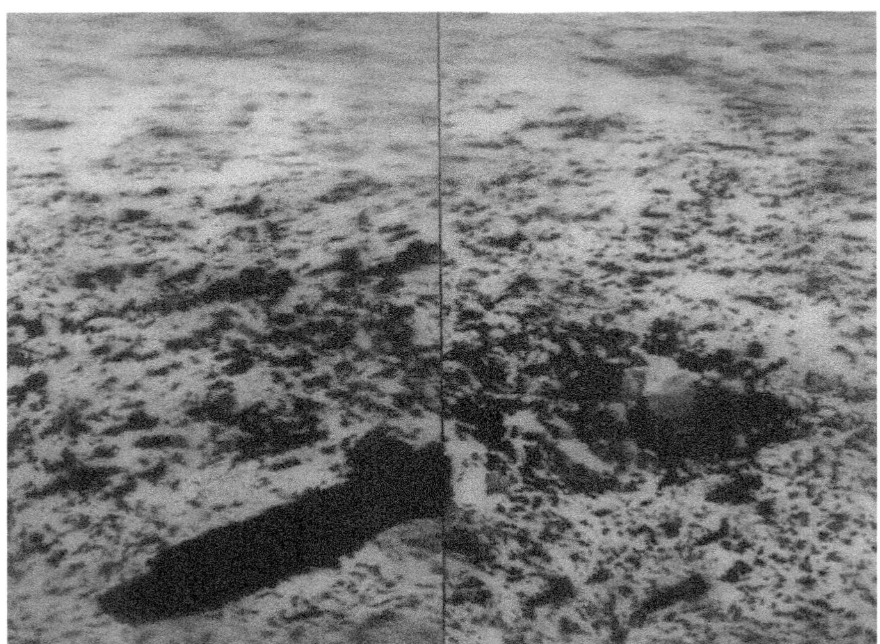

4.24 *Moonscape*, 1968. Oil on canvas, 78¾ × 102½ in.

dimension makes it mostly groundless. In this way do the shiny blurs in Richter reflect on the modern vicissitudes of *Schein*.

Traditionally, the aesthetic is placed on the side of reconciliation: in Kant, aesthetic judgment is asked to reconcile pure reason and practical reason, necessity and freedom, judgments of value and judgments of fact; in Schiller, the creative arts are asked to assuage the divisions caused by the technological arts ("art to heal art" is his famous phrase); in Stendhal, art is asked to offer beauty as "the promise of happiness" (the most famous aphorism of all); and so on. For some critics, such notions of the aesthetic are so many instances of ideological displacement: to focus such reconciliation in art, they argue, is to distract us from its possibilities elsewhere—in matters of social justice above all.[47] Yet Richter remains committed to the conciliatory ideal of the aesthetic. Asked in 2000, "Is there a message inherent in the beauty of your paintings?" he responded, "Not a message, but the hope that life can be beautiful" (354).[48] At the same time, with semblance altered by technological media, and beauty damaged by catastrophic events, he shows this ideal to be under enormous strain, to be, in short, an illusion of its own.[49] Richter delivers beauty, to be sure, but even from his own perspective, it is credible only when "wounded" somehow (129). This is a beauty no longer opposed to the sublime, for it is both sublimatory and desublimatory; it is a beauty that foregrounds its own inability to deliver reconciliation or promise happiness, a beauty that can offer only "a kind of tense cheeriness . . . with gritted teeth" (489). His art is impressive when implacable in this way, precisely when tense or gritted; when it is not, it can verge on sentimentality (as it does in some portraits of his wife Sabine and child Moritz from the mid-1990s [fig. 4.25]). But then Richter might risk this sentimentality in order to present the contemporary condition of semblance as in part specious, and of beauty as in part "hackneyed" (505).[50]

"Once obsessed [with painting], one ultimately carries it to the point of believing that one might change human beings through painting. But if one lacks this passionate commitment, there is nothing left to do. Then it is best to leave it alone. For basically painting is total idiocy" (70). Written in 1973, at a time when the death of painting was once again debated, this notorious statement does not affirm its end; rather, it casts painting in the register of agnosticism, of belief in lieu of institutional belief, of "moral action" outside any official code. Here Richter is not far from late modernists like Michael Fried who also look to painting as a reserve of value in a world stripped of the same, as a site of "binding," "hope," even "utopia" (121, 161).[51] Yet Richter is more sensitive than Fried and others to the difficulty, even (at times) the absurdity, of this conviction; for the most part, Richter possesses a lucid sense of the fragile predicament of contemporary painting in cultural history. Sometimes he is defiant about its conventions: "I am bourgeois enough to go on eating with a knife and fork, just as I paint in oil on canvas," Richter remarked in his 1986 conversation with Buchloh (177), and sometimes he is resigned to its "inadequacy," which he calls "the normal mess" (181). This persistent "skepticism that stands in for capacity" (200) is the other side of his "passionate commitment" to painting, and it is

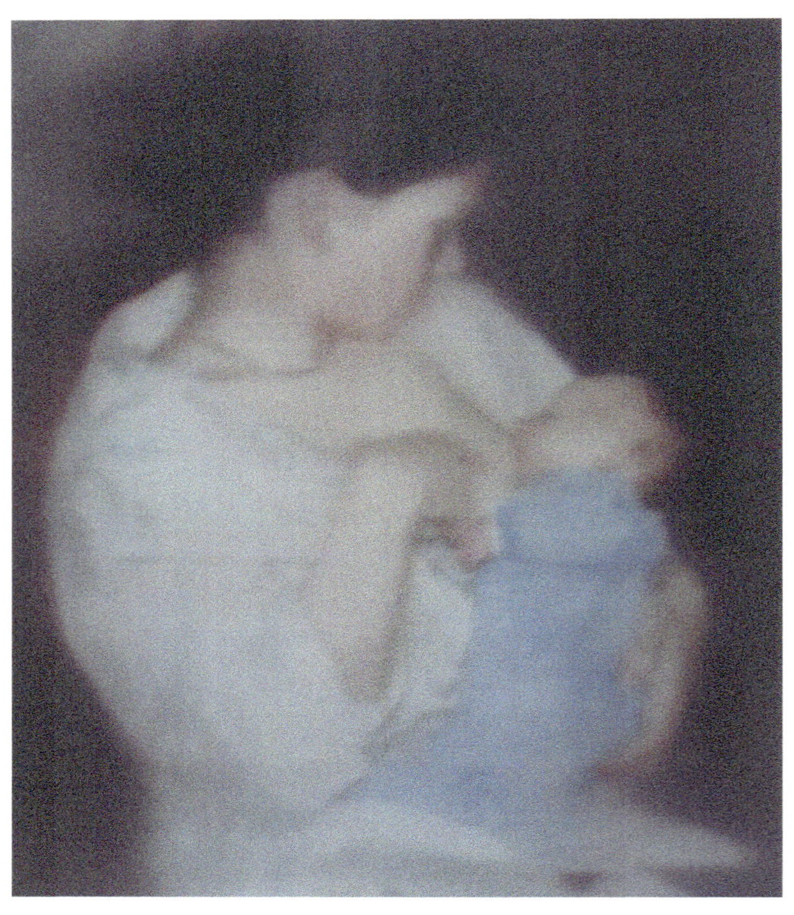

4.25 *S. with Child*, 1995. Oil on canvas, 24 × 20$\frac{1}{16}$ in.

this agnosticism that enables Richter to hew the aporetic line (the Adornian line) whereby to "liquidate" painting is also to affirm its "autonomy" (176).

This, then, is one response to our initial question about Richter: his painting is neither a progressive form of critical art nor a cynical kind of posthistorical pastiche. It does not resolve its contradictions so much as it performs them, and in this performance, it sometimes suspends them as well. This suspension can be viewed variously. Some might see it as a compromise formation, for which Richter is lavishly rewarded as "Europe's greatest modern painter" precisely because he lets us have it both ways (indeed many ways)—anti-aesthetic and pro-painting, avant-garde and traditional, banal and beautiful, indifferent and affective—in a quasi-schizoid pleasing of all parties.[52] Others might see this suspension as a holding open of artistic possibilities for the future, even as a staging of aesthetic contradictions that can produce a critical consciousness in the present. His own understanding selects parts of both these accounts: "All that I am trying to do in each picture is to bring together the most disparate and mutually contradictory elements, alive and viable, in the greatest possible freedom. No Paradises" (166).

My view is that Richter is neither dialectical nor deconstructive in approach or effect, but this is not to say that his work issues in static oscillation or simple eclecticism. If he aims to be neutral, it is a complex, not null, neutrality, one that might respond to a traumatic surfeit of invasive ideology in his life, a life spent successively under Nazi, communist, and capitalist regimes.[53] First there was his early experience of total war: "Seeing Dresden as an expanse of rubble, living amongst those ruins, changed my life," Richter had stated (355). Then there was the shock of his delayed discovery of the Holocaust, conveyed to him, significantly, via photography: "There, in that yard [of the Dresden Art Academy, which Richter attended from 1952 to 1956], I was first shown two books with photographs of the concentration camps and the horrors that had taken place there. I was in my early twenties. I'll never forget it" (469). At this time, too, Richter was subject to the lost-father complex experienced by "his entire generation": "Most of our fathers were away in the war for a long time, and they either didn't return or they came back shattered and broken—and as perpetrators" (442, 502).

More generally, he remains suspicious of the official ideologies of both communism and capitalism. Thus, as much as Richter insists on belief in the register of hope, he opposes belief in the guise of ideology, which he deems not only false but also destructive. This view crystallized as he labored on his suite concerning the Baader-Meinhof terrorists: "I think that we shouldn't have ideas, or Utopias, or ideologies," Richter remarked in 1989. "We don't need belief. Religion, Khomeini, Catholicism, Marxism: every belief is dangerous and wrong" (221).

This aversion to ideology seems a key motivation of his basic devices: the "no style" of the snapshot paintings, the blandness of the encyclopedia pictures ("which neutralize everything and all ideology" [421]), the evasive quality of the blurred images, the blasé indifference of the gray paintings, the arbitrary quality of the color charts, and so on (fig. 4.26). This pursuit of neutrality as a protection against ideology recalls the early Barthes of *Writing Degree Zero* (1953), but finally, Richter might be closer to the later Barthes of *The Neutral* (1977–78), for whom the neutral does not cancel meaning so much as "baffles" it. "I define the Neutral as that which outplays [*déjoue*] the paradigm," Barthes writes, with the linguistic understanding of "paradigm" in mind, defined here as "the opposition of two virtual terms from which, in speaking, I actualize one to produce meaning." "Or rather," Barthes continues, "I call Neutral everything that baffles the paradigm . . . Whence the idea of a structural creation that would defeat, annul, or contradict the implacable binarism of the paradigm by means of a third term."[54] It is this unstable structure, this third term, this enigmatic way through intolerable oppositions, that Richter seeks: "Something has to be shown and simultaneously not shown in order perhaps to say something else again, a third thing" (272). Again, one might dismiss this practice as a convenient convergence of positions, an aesthetic triangulation in keeping with the problematic "third ways" witnessed in Western politics over the last generation, but to dismiss it would be to indulge in the very cynicism that Richter resists. In the end, his importance might lie in his posing of such contradictory possibilities, in his tarrying in their intriguing difficulties.

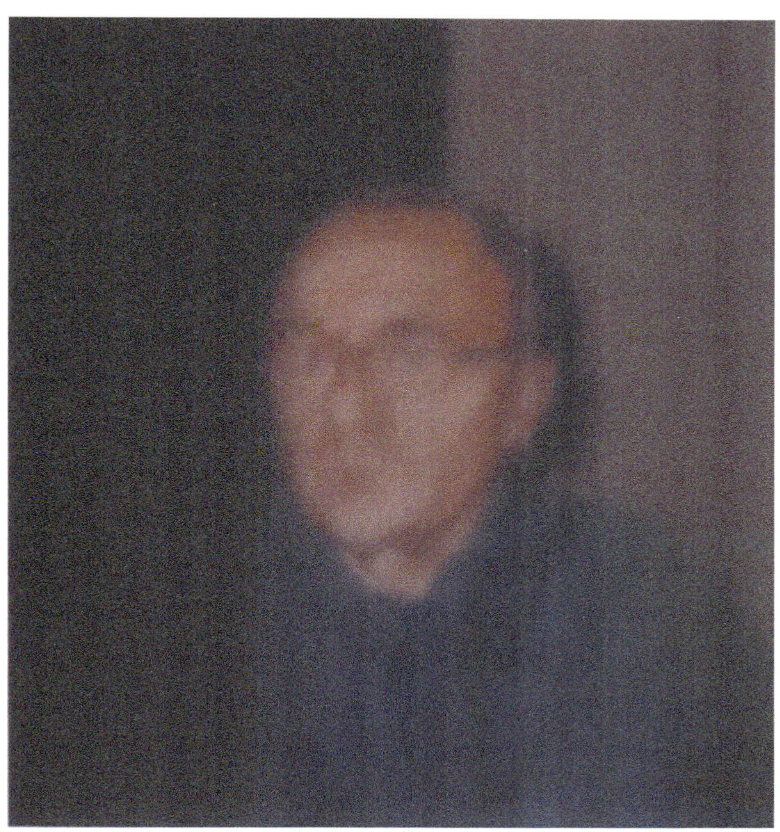

4.26 *Self-Portrait*, 1996. Oil on linen, 20⅛ × 18¼ in.

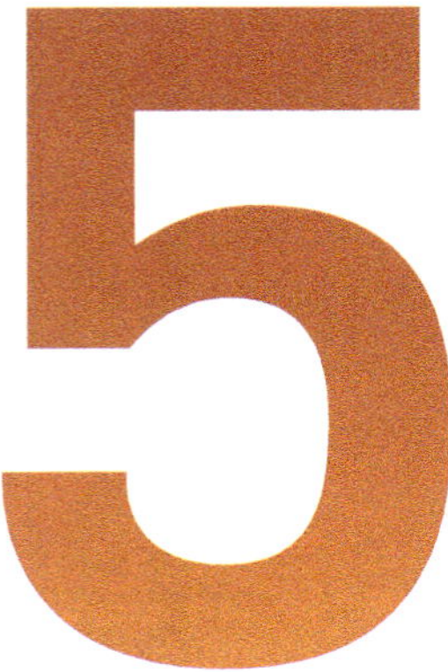

Ed Ruscha, or the Deadpan Image

According to Gerhard Richter, "there is a vast, great, rich culture of painting—of art in general—which we have lost, but which places obligations on us"; and clearly, he feels this loss and that responsibility, toiling under the burden of both. Ed Ruscha seems to feel neither. "My work has no connection to Europe," he remarked in 1990, and Ruscha appears to see little to develop in its tradition of the tableau.[1] At the same time, he has several points in common with Richter: like his contemporary, Ruscha is interested in the banal and the neutral; his painting also reflects on the changed nature of appearance in the postwar period; and he, too, has pursued these interests outside New York. In fact, his first move as an artist was in the opposite direction: born in Omaha in 1937, Ruscha left Oklahoma City in 1956 to attend the Chouinard Art Institute in Los Angeles, and he has remained there since.[2] Among other formative events, it was in LA that Ruscha discovered Jasper Johns, specifically *Flag* (1954–55) and *Target with Four Faces* (1955), in *Print Magazine* in 1957 (tellingly, this influence came to him through reproduction); that he saw the first Andy Warhol exhibition at the Ferus Gallery in summer 1962 (where the full array of single *Campbell's Soup Cans* was first exhibited); and that he attended the Marcel Duchamp retrospective at the Pasadena Museum of Art in fall 1963.

During his initial period in Los Angeles, Ruscha worked as a graphic artist, designing advertisements briefly, then magazines (including *Artforum* from 1965 to 1967). While other artists associated with Pop begin with fragments of print sources, Ruscha often adapts an entire graphic look, and some of his early paintings partake equally of abstraction and design as a result.[3] Consider his well-known *Annie* (1962; fig. 5.1), which consists of two broad rectangles of primary colors à la Color Field painting—yellow above, blue below, separated by a pale band with a line in India ink—with the name of the Little Orphan in her signature plump font painted in big red letters outlined in black on the yellow ground. Here Ruscha registers a convergence between abstract painting and commercial design as directly as any Pop artist, Warhol included.

Crucially, however, there is no such convergence in his procedure: "Abstract Expressionism collapsed the whole art process into one act," Ruscha remarked in 1982; "I wanted to break it into stages, which is what I do now" (Ruscha, *Leave Any Information at the Signal*, 228).[4] The methodical calculation of design work, apparent throughout his work, is especially evident in the photo books, which include *Twentysix Gasoline Stations* (1963; fig. 5.2), *Some Los Angeles Apartments* (1965), *Every Building on the Sunset Strip* (1966), *Thirtyfour Parking Lots* (1967), *Nine Swimming Pools and a Broken Glass* (1968), and *Real Estate Opportunities* (1970). At the same time, these books appear almost casual. "I don't even look at it as photography," Ruscha commented in 1972; "they're just images to fill a book" (49).[5] Although the subjects are hardly as random as he implies here (several books survey structures or spaces specific to LA), the presentation is as "neuter general" as possible: "They're a collection of 'facts' . . . a collection of 'readymades'" (40, 26). In these ways, the young Ruscha damped down his style and, through this very understatement ("it is not important who took the photos" [25]), came to produce a distinctive statement. A deadpanness—funny, desolate, usually both—is conveyed in these homely shots of solitary gas stations, the aerial images of empty parking lots, and so on; and the apparently arbitrary numbers (why exactly twenty-six stations, thirty-four lots, nine pools, etc.?) only add to the sense of blank absurdity or flat enigma.

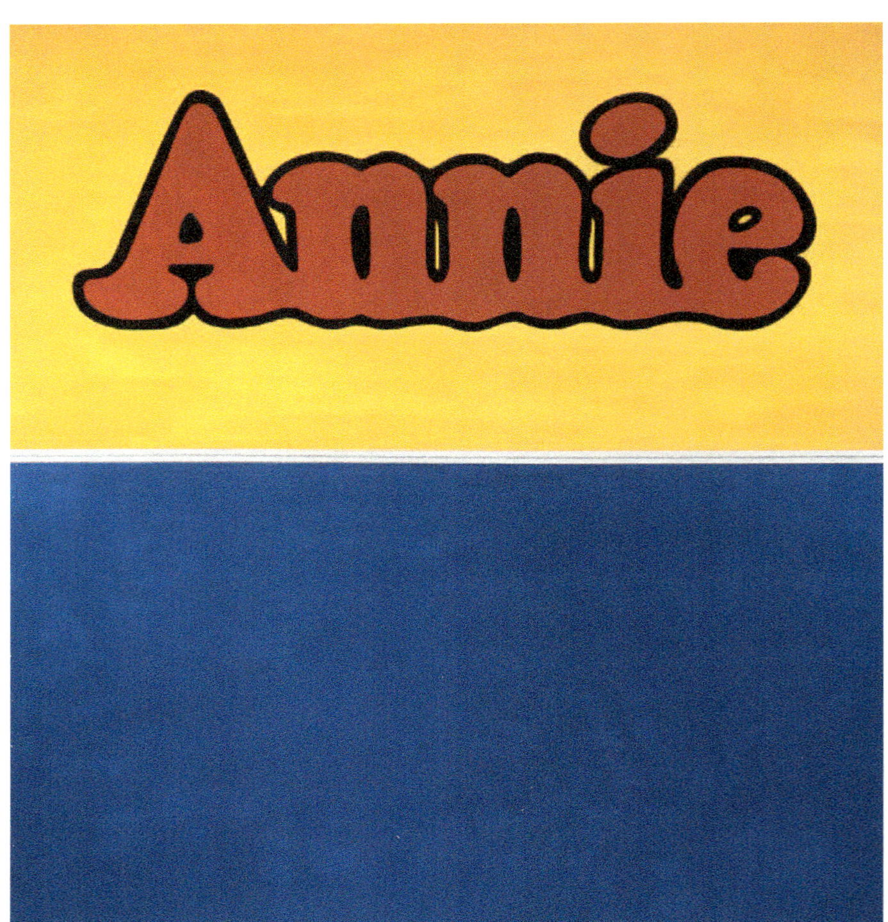

5.1 *Annie*, 1962. Oil on canvas, 72 × 67 in.

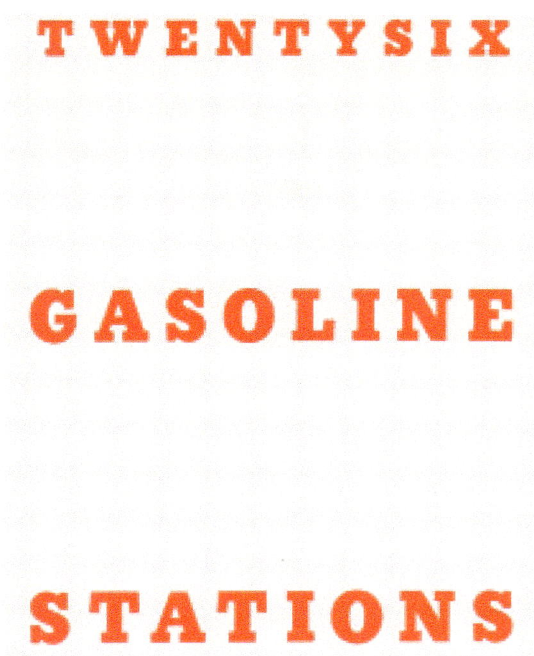

5.2 *Twentysix Gasoline Stations*, 1963. Cover of 48-page book with 26 photographs, 7 1/16 × 5 1/2 in.

"Huh?"

Ruscha speaks of this effect as "a kind of a 'Huh?'" and often it stems from his use of words, which, as in a "misspelled grocery sign," can appear both declarative, even obvious, and incorrect, even obscure, like so many "incomplete sputterings" or irksome puzzles (65, 91, 156). Several of his early word paintings evoke signals, the most direct of semiotic categories, which, as commands or warnings like stop signs, cannot afford to be ambiguous, yet that is how they frequently appear in Ruscha. What are we to make, for example, of a painting in which the word "electric" glows in yellow and red italics on a dark blue ground in a manner that attracts as much as alarms (fig. 5.3)? Whereas the workaday world requires clarity in such signs, Ruscha offers ambiguity, with effects that are often humorous, sometimes seductive, and occasionally (as in *Electric*) ominous.

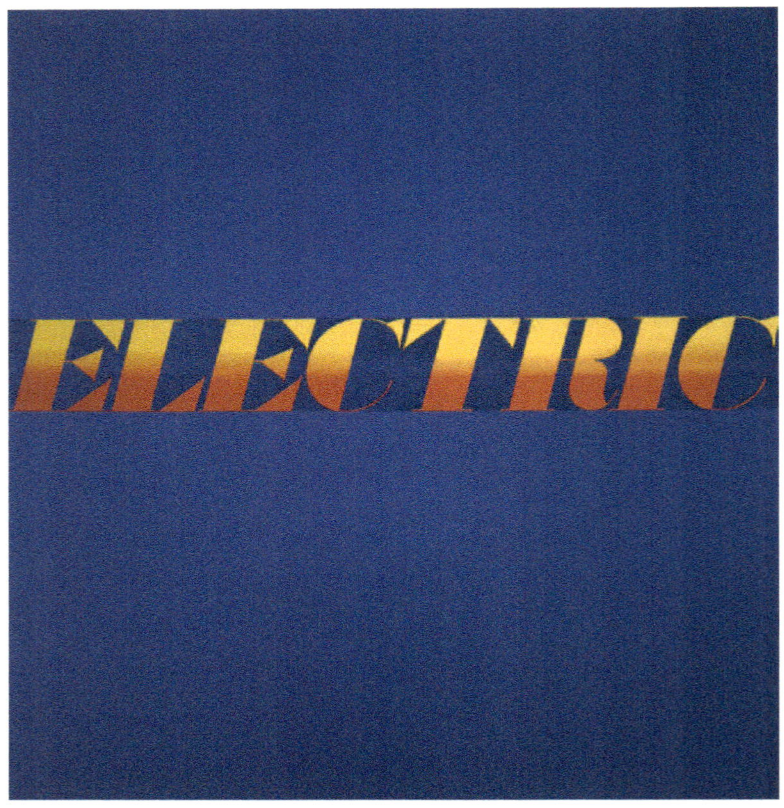

5.3 *Electric*, 1963. Oil on canvas, 72 × 67 in.

"No information can ever exist," Yve-Alain Bois writes in an important essay on the artist, "that does not have to rise above an ocean of noise," and Ruscha is adept at such disturbances in communication, with the result that his words can appear as suspended in meaning as they are in space.[6] "Words without thoughts never to heaven go": this familiar line from *Hamlet* recurs in Ruscha, and it might be taken as his motto, minus the possibility of arrival in heaven or any secure destination (certainly Claudius, who speaks the line in the play, does not end well). "Leave any information at the signal" is another quasi-standard phrase favored by Ruscha (the message on his

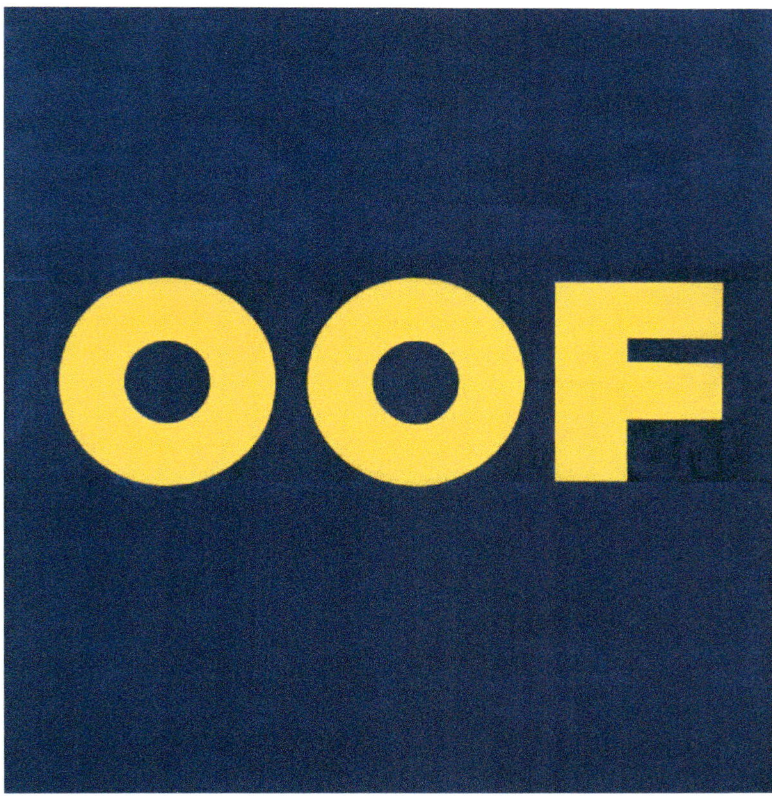

5.4 *Oof*, 1962–63. Oil on canvas, 72½ × 67 in.

answering machine, it is also the title of his 2002 collection of writings, notes, and interviews); despite its impersonal tone of mechanistic certainty, it, too, suggests the possibility of communication failure—and at any point in the message (transmitter, code, or receiver). Words, Ruscha implies again and again, are transparent neither to "thoughts" nor to "information."[7]

As is often noted, Ruscha was drawn early on to onomatopoeic words, such as "oof," "honk," and "smash," which aim to sound like what they signify (fig. 5.4). These terms are assumed to be more natural or motivated than other words, more grounded in the sounds of the world. But as linguists since Ferdinand de Saussure have acknowledged, this is not necessarily the case: such terms have a conventional dimension as well (not all humans say "oof" when punched), and Ruscha exploits this bit of arbitrariness to create another touch of ambiguity, another "huh?" effect ("huh" is such an utterance, too). How odd "oof" appears, for instance, when we encounter it, at human scale, painted in bright yellow sans-serif capitals on a deep blue ground, like a comic-book exclamation without the comic-book character to voice it. As Ruscha reframes such words for us, they become denaturalized or "de-automatized" before our eyes (these terms are rarely encountered in reading in any case, and some do not qualify as words at all).[8]

Ruscha produces a similar effect with apparent look-alikes, that is, with devices that seem to support visually what the words convey verbally. They appear frequently in paintings of 1964 such as *Damage*, in which the letters AG seem to burn with yellow and red flames, and *Scream* (fig. 5.5), in which the word, in black on a yellow ground, is shot through with diagonals that radiate from the S in a manner that suggests the force of a shout through a megaphone.[9] Of course, these are but signs for "flame" and "scream," coded figures that are deployed in comics and art alike (as we have seen, the sharing of such signs across these two domains is a familiar topos of Pop), and here, too, Ruscha invites us to see how odd they are. As Bois has stressed, Ruscha is no Cratylist—that is, he hardly believes that signs are grounded in the appearance of referents—and yet, as with his onomatopoeic words, he plays on our old belief in such worldly grounding, only then to disturb it, and in so doing to produce more "huh?"

In these ways, the redoublings of word and image in Ruscha render meaning less stable, not more. Over the years, this calculated ambiguity has led critics to associate him with Surrealist painters, René Magritte in particular, and though Ruscha is leery of the connection, there are points in common, such as the play with both trompe l'oeil illusion and word-image juxtaposition.[10] In a brilliant discussion of Magritte (first published in 1968), Michel Foucault focuses on the calligram, a figure in which the words of a text are arranged on a page in such a way as to image its principal motif or meaning (the best-known examples are *Calligrammes* [1918] by Guillaume Apollinaire). As Foucault explains, the calligram is designed "to

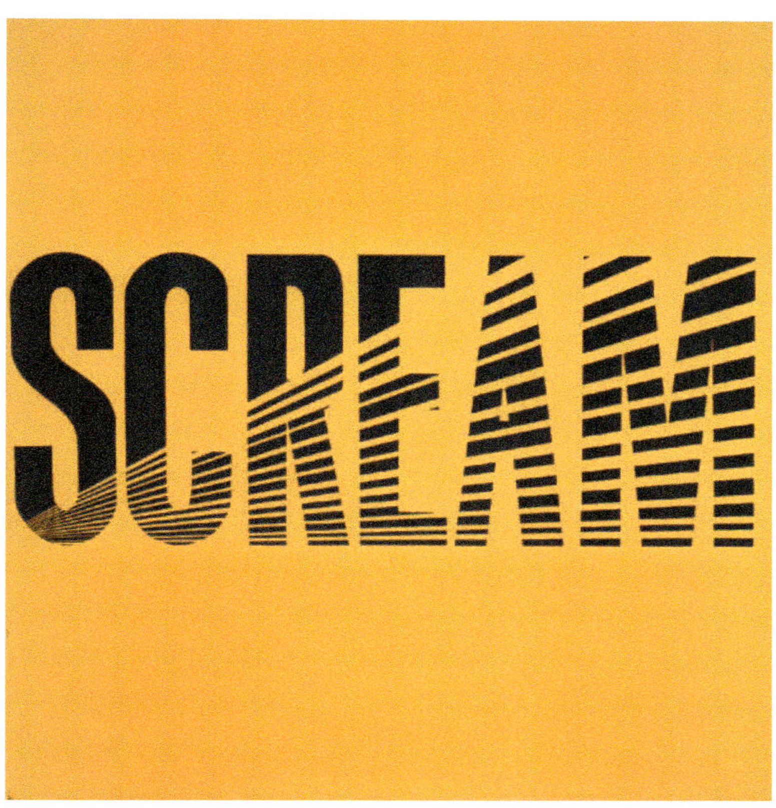

5.5 *Scream*, 1964. Oil on canvas, 71 × 67 in.

trap things in a double cipher": "It lodges statements in the space of a shape, and makes the text *say* what the drawing *represents*." Nevertheless, the differences between the visual and verbal orders persist: "The calligram never speaks and represents at the same moment. The very thing that is both seen and read is hushed in the vision, hidden in the reading."[11] In such celebrated works as *La Trahison des images (Ceci n'est pas une pipe)* (1926; fig. 5.6), then, Magritte plays on tensions already at work in the calligram and unravels its apparent redoubling of word by image from within: "Magritte reopens the trap the calligram has sprung on the thing it described," with the result that

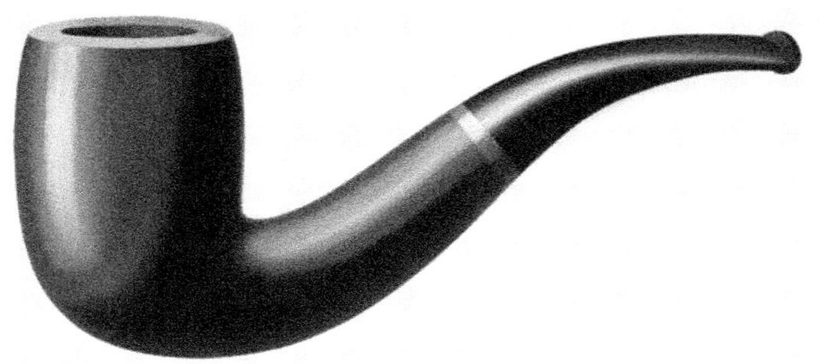

5.6 René Magritte, *La Trahison des images (Ceci n'est pas une pipe)*, 1929. Oil on canvas, 25⅜ × 37 in. © 2012 C. Herscovici, London / Artists Rights Society (ARS), New York.

the object "escapes" and the text and the image are "redistributed" in space, with little common ground between them.[12]

Although Ruscha rarely configures his texts calligrammatically, his word-image juxtapositions often perform a similar mischief: "I began to see the printed word," he once remarked, "and it took over from there" (151). Nevertheless, in his work, seeing is never quite congruent with reading. For example, various canvases of 1964 depict clamps attached to the first or last letter of the word "dimple" as if to perform this very dimpling (Ruscha did the same thing with other favorite terms like "boss" and "radio" [fig. 5.7]). Yet here again, redoubling produces ambiguity, for even as the word is depicted as if it were an object, it is the difference between the two that is underscored.[13] "A flip-flop between those two things" is his more accurate account of the word-image relationship in his art (282), and this odd

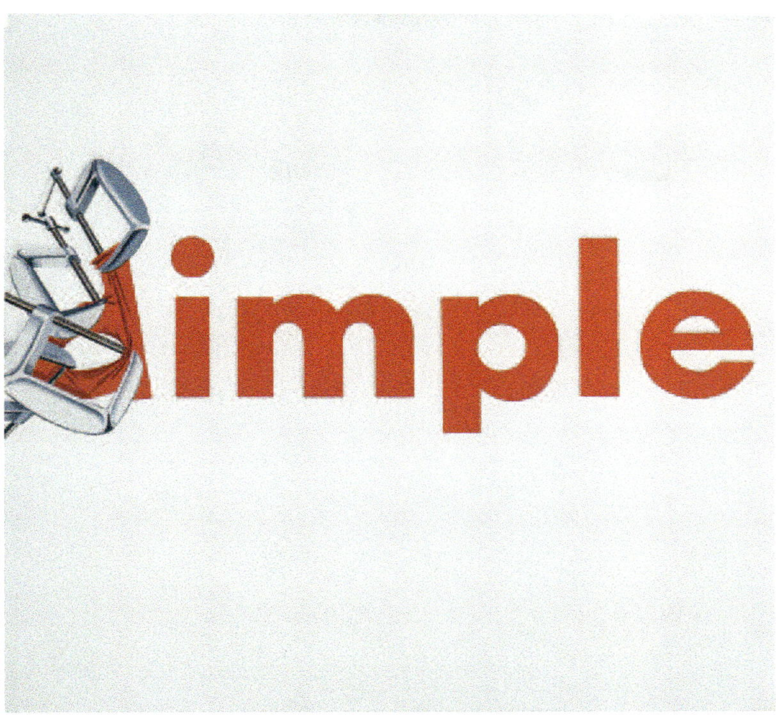

5.7 *Squeezing Dimple (red with four clamps)*, 1964. Oil on canvas, 28¼ × 29⅞ in.

elasticity is even closer to the case: "I like the idea of a word becoming a picture, almost leaving its body, then coming back and becoming a word again."[14] At the extreme, Ruscha acknowledges, "I see myself working with two things that don't even ask to understand each other" (302).[15] Typically, then, the ambiguity of the "huh?" effect, whether funny, enigmatic, or edgy, is produced through an unsettling of distinctions that structure meaning in art and beyond—such pairings as abstract painting and commercial design, casual presentation and methodical calculation, motivated marks and conventional signs. These are only a few of the distinctions that Ruscha puts, with apparent nonchalance, to the test.

Common Objects

His great interest in the "huh?" effect, Ruscha tells us, stems from his "deep respect for things that are odd, for things which cannot be explained" (305). This admiration for the odd thing, moreover, is bound up with an appreciation for the common thing—for vernacular words, images, and objects that, however familiar, either are odd or might be restored to our attention if made to appear so.[16] Early on, for instance, Ruscha painted some motifs "actual size," which is how they are often painted in folk art, that is, in a manner that, at least to our eyes, is at once common and odd. For example, in *Actual Size* (1962; fig. 5.8), a can of Spam, depicted at scale, seems to fly, replete with fiery afterburner, through the space below, while the word "Spam" appears in yellow capitals on dark blue in the space above. A common joke of the time—early astronauts were called "spam in a can"—thus issues in an odd painting, in large part because, as Ruscha remarks, "words exist in a world of no size" (231), and so his juxtaposition of the "actual size" of the can and the "no size" of the word renders the pictorial space of *Actual Size* very uncertain. How do the two spaces, with paint drips from the upper to the lower, relate to each other? Does the lower space, with its rocket can, suggest "outer space"? Does the upper space, with its brand name, indicate "commercial space"? In this case, the convergence of abstract painting and commercial design presents less a conflation of the two categories than a collision that defamiliarizes both.[17]

Ruscha invites us to consider the place of the common as an ambiguous term somewhere between the folk and the Pop. (In which category, for instance, do the images in *Twentysix Gasoline Stations* fall?)[18] Drawn to the common, he works to draw it out in turn, and from folk and Pop elements alike. Biographically, Ruscha is well positioned to do so: born and raised in the Midwest, often seen as the folk heart of the country, he migrated to Los Angeles, often taken to be its Pop capital, and he is fully aware of the "Okie" tradition in this passage. "In the early 1950s," Ruscha commented in 1985, "I was awakened by the photographs of Walker Evans and the movies of John Ford, especially *Grapes of Wrath* where the poor 'Okies' (mostly farmers whose land dried up) go to California with mattresses on

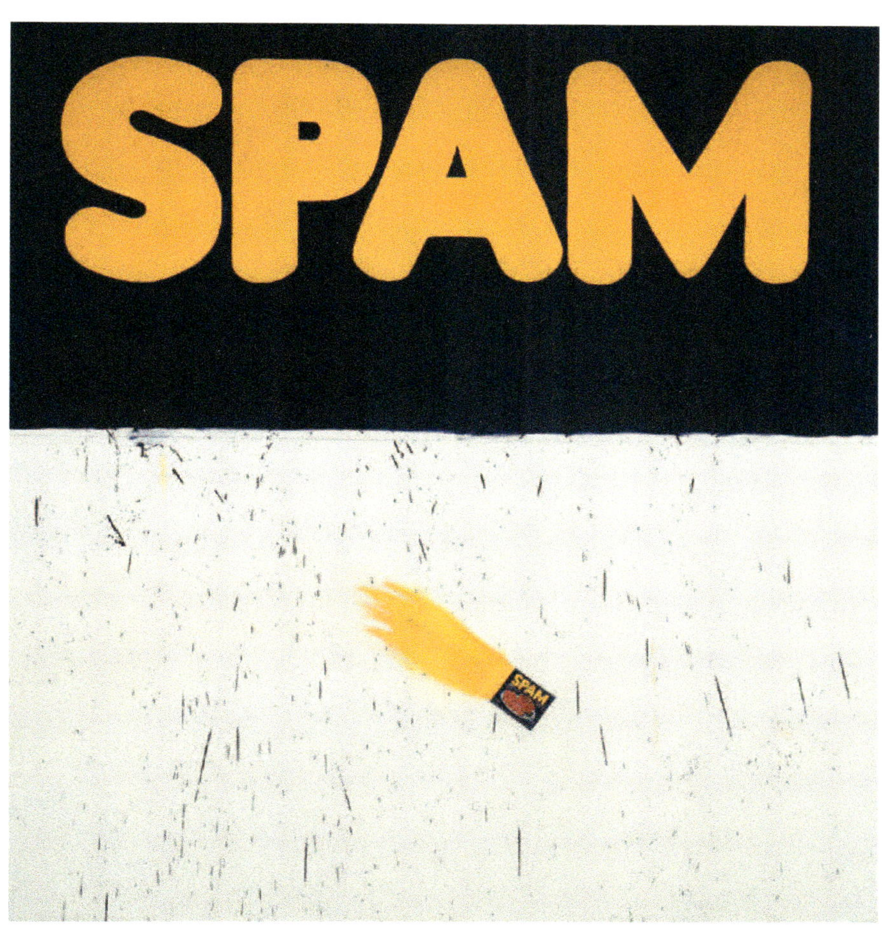

5.8 *Actual Size*, 1962. Oil on canvas, 72 × 67 in.

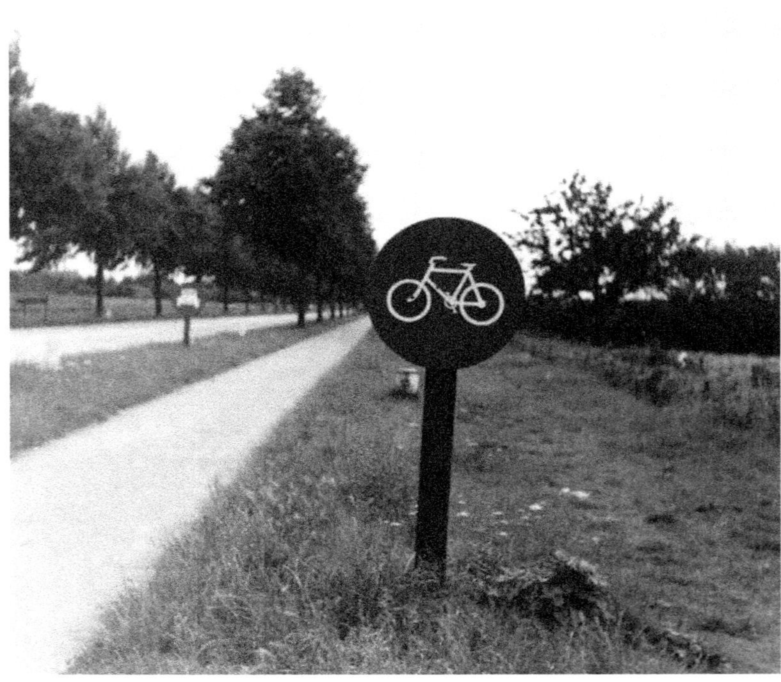

5.9 *Amsterdam*, 1961. Gelatin silver print, 5 × 4 in.

their cars rather than stay in Oklahoma and starve" (250). Here Ruscha presents folk experience as already mediated, and he looks back on his own "identity crisis" in "black-and-white cinematic" terms, too (250). Neverthe-less, he is not willing to let go of the folk: for example, some of his early photographs (especially the ones made on his European sojourn) focus on emblematic signs and structures that might qualify as folk (fig. 5.9); some of his early paintings allude to naïve signage, another attribute of folk art (a few include the names of southern towns visited on a 1952 hitchhiking

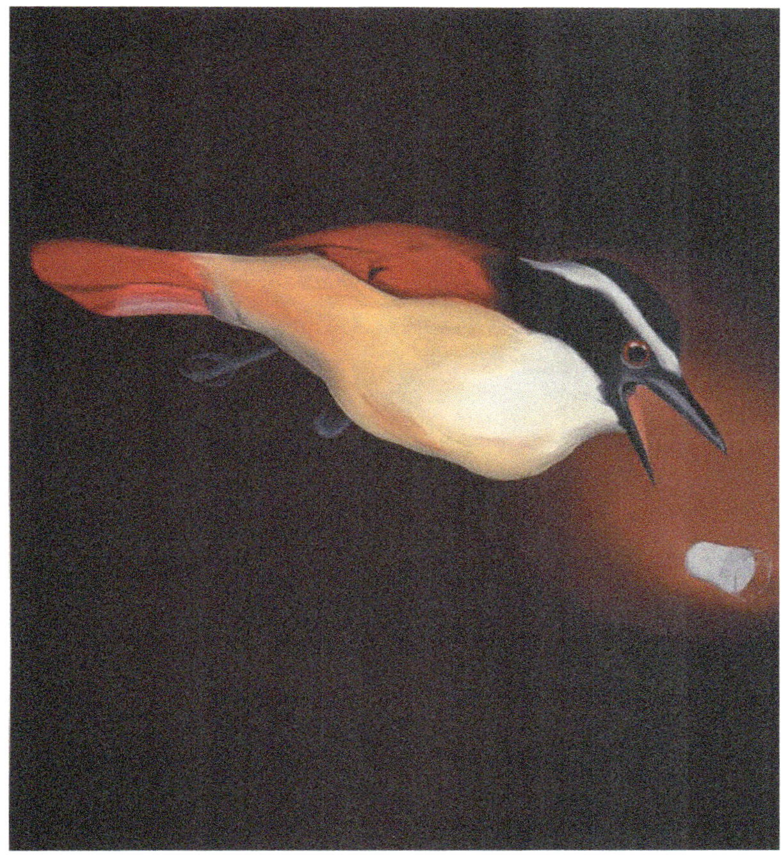

5.10 *Angry Because It's Plaster, Not Milk*, 1965. Oil on canvas, 55 × 48 in.

trip: Sweetwater, Dublin, Vicksburg); and his bird and fish paintings of the mid-1960s also play on folk painting, in this case of amateur naturalists and outdoorsmen, a country kind of kitsch art (fig. 5.10). This relation to the folk is not entirely ironic, for, again, Ruscha finds an element of the common there that he prizes.[19]

From the start, this concern with the common informed his attraction to both Duchamp and Johns. According to Ruscha, "Duchamp discovered common objects" as artistic material, and like Johns, Ruscha, too, has made them "the foreground central subject" of his work (330, 289).[20] He first did so at a time when, as in the moment of Duchamp, increased commodification altered the look not only of common objects but also of common words, images, colors, spaces—in short, the very nature of appearance.[21] In effect, Ruscha updated the device of the readymade in a way that addresses this condition, with particular attention to the branding of products, the reification of words, the abstraction of place, and the artificiality of color. His aim was not only to de-automatize our perception of these transformed things but also to wrest an element of the common from them. I will take up his transformation of products and words here, and that of place and color in the next section.

As attested by popular analyses like *The Hidden Persuaders* (1957) by Vance Packard and *Image: A Guide to Pseudo-Events* (1961) by Daniel Boorstin, the branding of products came into critical focus just as Ruscha began to emerge as an artist. In 1961, Ruscha produced a series of black-and-white photographs titled "Product Still Lifes," which present household commodities as iconic figures against blank grounds. He focused on products of cooking and cleaning like Spam, Sun-Maid Raisins, Oxydol Soap (fig. 5.11), Monarch Rubbing Compound, Wax Seal Car Polish, and Sherwin-Williams Turpentine, some of which appear in his paintings too; that is, he focused on tokens of the extensive industrialization of everyday life—of food, housework, and leisure—during this period.[22] As the series title announces, "still life" is shown to be governed by "product": the traditional offering of the former is literally subsumed by the commercial packaging of the latter, with ingredients reduced to words on labels (the only vestiges of food are the images of Spam and the grapes held by the Sun Maid on these labels).[23] And yet, in the very midst of this increased commodification, Ruscha detects a version of a common language: again, he presents the products more iconically than ironically, and the brands are indeed household names (the Sun Maid lives on, as does the "covering the earth" logo of Sherwin-Williams, and Spam is as colloquial a term as Kleenex, one given renewed life in e-mail lingo). In short, Ruscha captures a kind of folk Pop in emergence and features it in his early paintings too.[24]

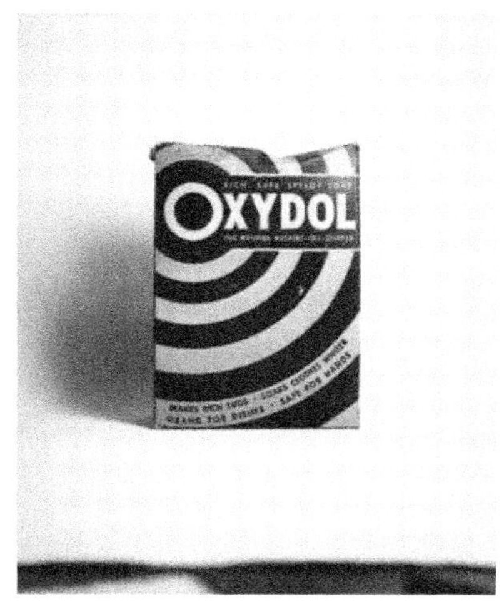
5.11 *Oxydol*, 1961.
Gelatin silver print, 13½ × 10 7⁄16 in.

The second category, the reification of words, is related to this first one. Just as Ruscha sometimes treats language as if it were an object (as in the aforementioned "dimple" paintings), he often addresses the hardening of words as clichés (a point of similarity with Roy Lichtenstein). The word paintings of the early 1960s tend to divide into three kinds of terms: sub-cultural argot like "boss" or "ace," bureaucratic lingo like "heavy industry" or "war surplus," and brand names like "Spam" or "Buick."[25] Such words are invented or inflected by various administrators of language—here, hip-sters, politicos, and admen respectively—with assorted goals of recognition and obfuscation; as these words circulate publicly, they signify differently, charged with meaning (or not) for various groups across the social spec-trum.[26] In some instances, Ruscha presents his chosen words in a way that pulls them back from the condition of one-dimensional cliché via ambiguity or oddity (the aforementioned *Electric* is just one example). "I have always operated on a kind of waste-retrieval method," he has remarked; "I retrieve and renew things that have been forgotten or wasted" (251). In other in-stances Ruscha presents his words as if to push them over, once and for all, into the status of administered stereotype. This effect is most emphatic in his celebrated treatment of two corporate emblems: 20th Century Fox, in *Large Trademark with Eight Spotlights* (1962; fig. 5.12), which announces its brand status in its very title (the spotlights underscore that the trademark is the primary star of the studio), and Standard Oil Company (fig. 5.13), in his various images of the Standard gas station, in which we reflect on a term of common value become an emblem of a multinational business.[27] In both sets of works, the logo is rendered as an architectural structure (the drafting lines in pencil are still apparent on the canvas) that projects diagonally toward us in a way that dominates the pictorial space: readymade image becomes environment and vice versa. In a sense, the logo is treated not only as a classical monument but also as a numinous utterance—the logo almost as *logos*—a formulation at once absurd and, given the power of entertainment and oil industries in the postwar period, almost plausible. This is commodity fetishism at the corporate level, and Ruscha was alert to its rise early on. Yet even here he focuses on the common element, referring to 20th Century Fox generically as "large trademark" and selecting, from all the oil companies available to him, the one named "standard."[28]

In 1913, apropos of the Duchampian "discovery" of the common object, Apollinaire speculated that an artist like Duchamp might help "reconcile Art and the People."[29] Fifty years later, in the same moment of increased commodification addressed by the young Ruscha, Warhol also considered the possibility of such reconciliation. Yet all Warhol could then envisage as a common culture was a capitalist equivalent of the Cold War image of communism in which "everybody looks alike and acts alike"—a condition that, in keeping with his strategy of mimetic exacerbation ("Everybody should be a machine"), he affirmed.[30] Ruscha is neither as hopeful as Apollinaire nor as cynical as Warhol; nonetheless, though his de-automatization of the degraded commonplace does not amount to much, politically speaking, it is also not nothing. The Italian Marxist Antonio Gramsci once defined "common sense" as "the folklore of philosophy," a mix in equal parts of superstition to be exposed and truth to be extracted.[31] Ruscha, too, is ambivalent about this folklore, concerned to disturb it as a self-evident sense on the one hand, yet also to recover it as a common language on the other. And in his work, for every impulse to mock, even to destroy, such "standards" and

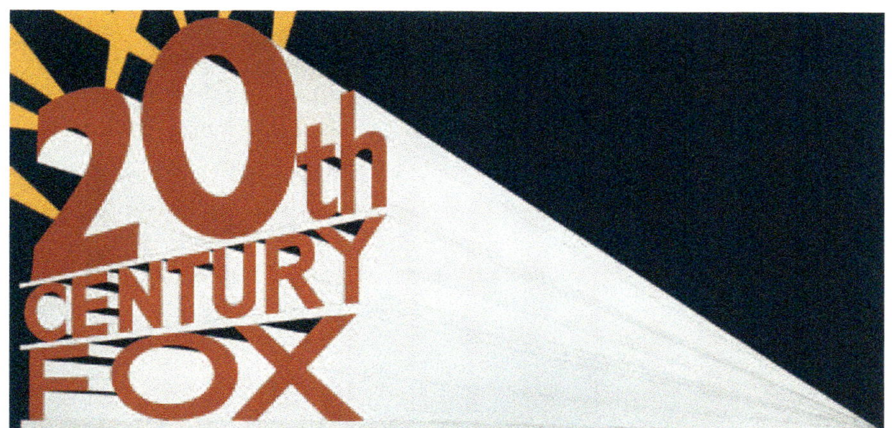

5.12 *Large Trademark with Eight Spotlights*, 1962. Oil on canvas, 67 × 132 in.

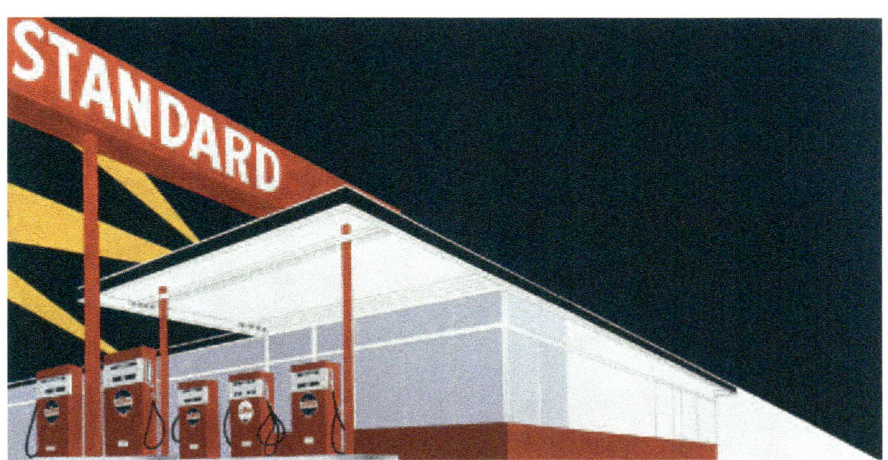

5.13 *Standard Station*, 1966. Oil on canvas, 20½ × 39 in.

"norms" (his images of the Standard station or Norm's diner in flames—or, for that matter, the Los Angeles County Museum of Art on fire—are not simply sight gags), there is a counterimpulse to reclaim the degraded commonplace as a shared vernacular. This is evident in some of the photo books, such as *Twentysix Gasoline Stations*, as well as in many of the word paintings, such as *Actual Size*.[32]

This concern with the common runs throughout Ruscha and illuminates his work in unexpected ways. Consider again the simple photographs in the early books: often described as de-skilled, some might equally be seen as amateur, which is another avatar of the common. Moreover, while the property in these photos is often private, its use is sometimes public, as with the gas stations and the parking lots. More centrally, the found language of his jokes, sayings, and clichés is held in common: since no one possesses this language, anyone can partake of it, and Ruscha exploits this commonality too. "This is the realm of the *commonplace*," Jean-Paul Sartre wrote in 1957. "And this fine word has several meanings; it refers, doubtless, to the most hackneyed of thoughts, but these thoughts had become the meeting-place of the community. Everyone finds himself in them and finds the others too. The commonplace is everyone's and it belongs to me; it belongs in me to everyone and it is the presence of everyone in me. It is, in essence, *generality*."[33] Ruscha makes of this commonplace his primary medium.

In the 1970s, Ruscha produced word paintings that declare shared ideals, as in *Mercy, Truth, Duty*, and *Hope* (all 1972; fig. 5.14), as well as ones that announce collective categories, as in *We Humans* (1974), *Days of the Week, Anybody's Destiny* (both 1979), and *The Future* (1981); a related commonality applies to later paintings that name such entities as decades, states, and countries—though all these proclamations also remain characteristically enigmatic. Finally, the mountains, earth, and constellations Ruscha has painted more recently are common in another sense, that is, as clichés or "ideas of ideas of ideas" of such things (fig. 5.15).[34] Moreover, some of these images evoke the contested terrain of "the commons"—that is, unregulated resources that, like air, are open to use by all of us (at least in principle)—while others suggest the ancient category of *res nullius*, "the things of no one" that, like mountains, are also, potentially, things for everyone.[35]

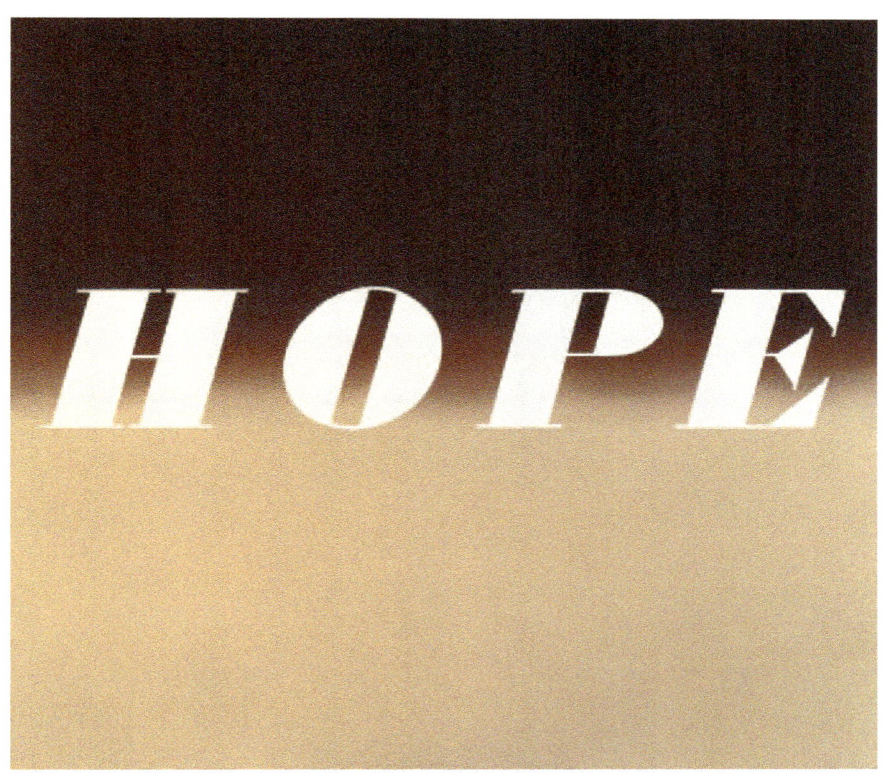

5.14 *Hope*, 1972. Oil on canvas, 54 × 60 in.

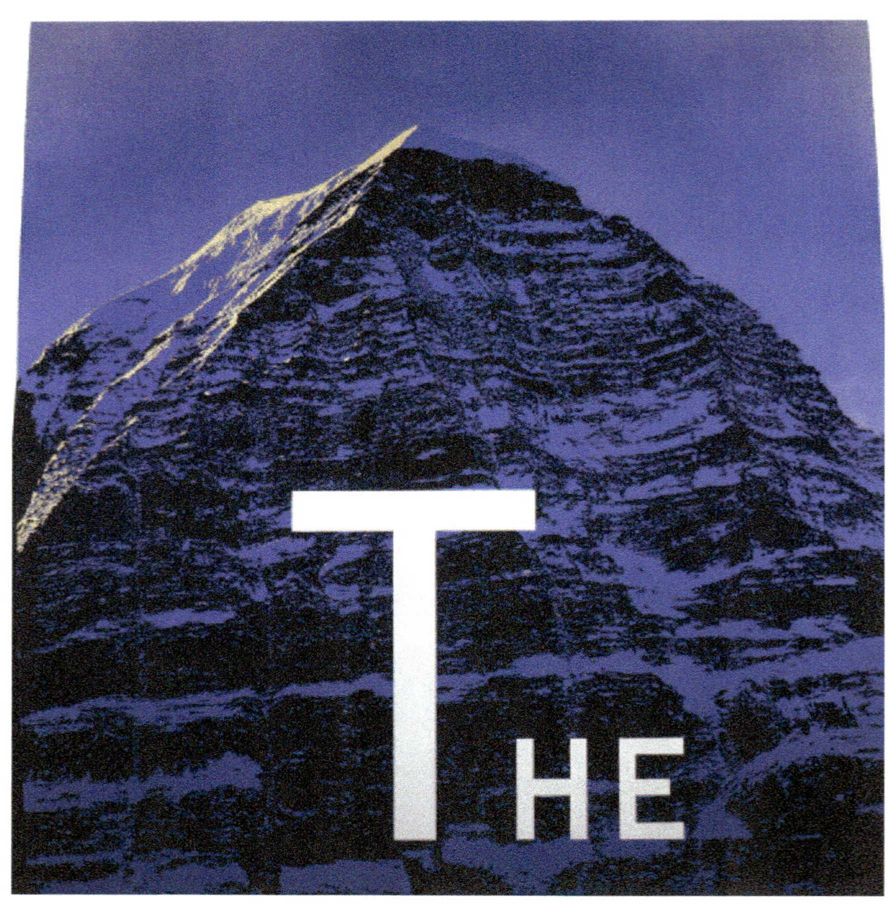

5.15 *The Mountain*, 1998. Acrylic on shaped canvas, 76 × 72 in.

Celluloid Gloss

In all these ways, Ruscha points to forms of possible commonality even within a condition of pervasive commodification. He hardly plays down this condition (on the contrary), yet there is a doubleness here too that he exploits. On the one hand, commodification can drain or deaden words, images, objects, and spaces, and Ruscha often presents them in this wasted state. Consider the abstraction of place mentioned above: sometimes he renders land as so much property, as in the bland photos of *Some Los Angeles Apartments* that resemble rental listings, or the stark photos of *Real Estate Opportunities*, an ironic title for the mostly derelict lots pictured here (fig. 5.16). Of course, land has appeared as property in landscape painting at least since Thomas Gainsborough, but frequently Ruscha represents it as real estate *tout court*: in *Every Building on the Sunset Strip*, for instance, it is gridded and numbered as such, and the title of each LA apartment or real-estate "opportunity" is its address.[36] Moreover, subsequent works such as the "Metroplots" from the late 1990s (fig. 5.17) carry this logic to an extreme; the title alone evokes a world given over to subdivision. Here the Greater LA cityscape appears in oblique aerial views (a perspective sometimes favored by Ruscha), yet there is nothing left to see except gray abstractions, inscribed with only a few faint lines and street names, suggesting a catastrophic condition in which the most schematic of maps is traced on the most flattened of spaces (the absence of people in the photo books—a nonquality that intrigued Warhol—becomes absolute here). This, too, is a commons, but it is a vacated one.[37]

On the other hand, commodification can also charge or animate words, images, objects, and spaces, and Ruscha sometimes underscores this paradoxical animation as well.[38] Again, he often presents logos like 20th Century Fox and Standard keyed up, in grand scale and inverse perspective, like special effects, as if they were the truly dominant features of the landscape, indeed the only public figures or historical agents left to portray—and sometimes this seems to be the case, especially in LA, where the famous Hollywood sign, another recurrent presence in his work, has long presided over the city like a genius loci—and Ruscha lends auratic power to this

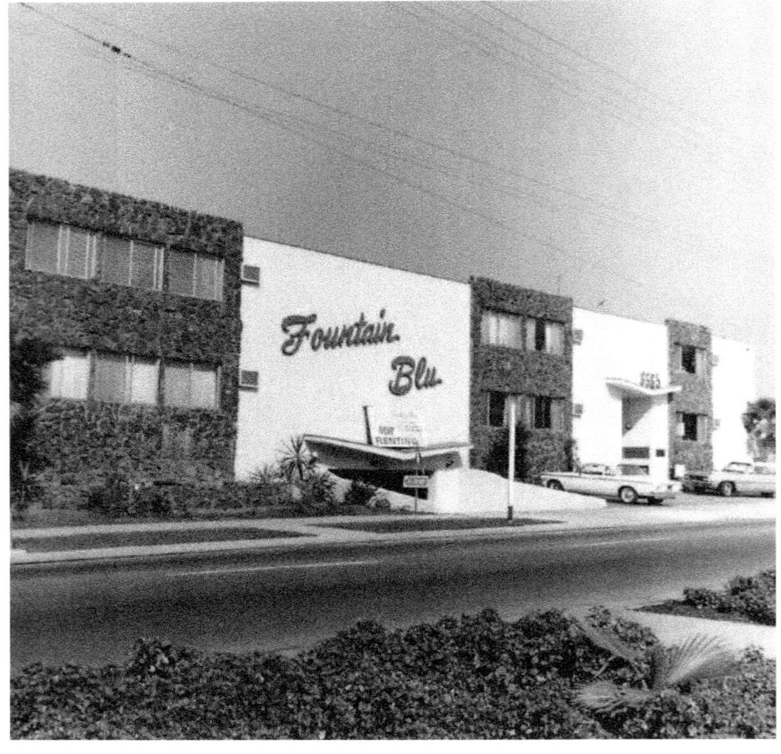

5.16 *6565 Fountain Ave.*, 1965. From *Some Los Angeles Apartments*. Gelatin silver print,
4¾ × 4¾ in.

wobbly structure (fig. 5.18). More generally, he appears to regard his words not just as pictures but almost as personages, and early on, he sized many of his word paintings to support this effect ("They seemed like friendly characters to me," he once remarked of his preferred six-foot-high format [159]). Moreover, as if to offset his stark abstraction of place, Ruscha tends toward a marked artificiality of color: though his heightened pastels are very different from the bold primaries of Lichtenstein, say, they are just as unnaturally animate: whereas Lichtenstein calls up comic-book melo-drama, Ruscha evokes the druggy atmospherics of science-fiction space (fig. 5.19).

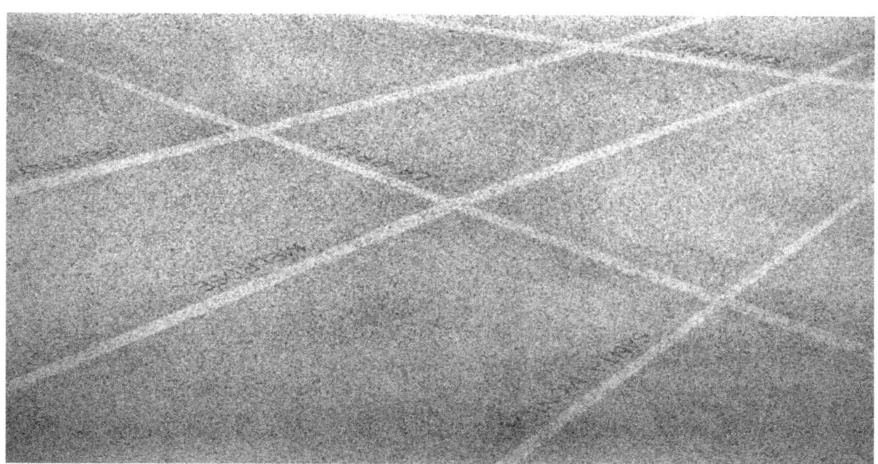

5.17 *Santa Monica, Melrose, La Brea, Fairfax*, 1998. Acrylic on canvas, 60 × 112 in.

Ruscha also points to the odd animation of commodified entities in his notion of "hot words." "Words have temperatures to me," he commented in 1973. "When they reach a certain point and become hot words, then they appeal to me" (57). In this same remark, Ruscha speaks of words that "boil" and even "boil apart," and often he evokes this "hot" condition through colors and space that appear liquid or gaseous or somewhere in between (as in his series of "liquid words" of the late 1960s, rendered precisely as if fluid, as well as his series of stained works, also begun in the late 1960s and made with nonart substances like beer or gasoline that were once literally fluid). In effect, what Ruscha intimates is a contemporary state of reification in which the commodity-form has spread through other categories—words, colors, and spaces—in a way that does not harden and fragment them, as in the classic account of reification presented by Georg Lukács in 1923, so much as it renders the world of appearance liquid or light.[39] Like Richard Hamilton before him, Ruscha evokes a reification that has come to resemble its nominal opposite—liquefaction, even rarefaction—a world less of disjunctive things than of de-differentiated effects, a world that appears medicated. This is announced, for example, in the title of *Three Darvons and Two Valiums* (1975), but its colors also convey this stoned state.

5.18 *Hollywood*, 1968. Eight-color silk screen, 17½ × 44½ in.

In this way, the paradoxical conjunction of the charged and the drained in Ruscha speaks to the characteristic structure of feeling in his work. "Deadpan" is the term often used to convey this affect or lack thereof (this, too, is ambiguous), usually without further comment. An American word that the *OED* dates to 1928, "deadpan" is defined as "expressionless" or "impassive," yet it signifies a kind of expression nonetheless: "to deadpan" is to convey a funny thing in a straight way—an irony that is everywhere in Ruscha—and to do so with a look as blank or blunted as a pan. (Buster Keaton is often mentioned in dictionary examples; tellingly, in his films he often plays stoic victims of industrial modernity.) "Deadpan," then, is close to *blasé* (French for "blunted"), a state of mind that, as noted in chapter 4, Georg Simmel associated with big-city life of a century ago. In this influential analysis, Simmel, a teacher of Lukács, saw the "matter-of-fact attitude" of "the metropolitan type" as a defense against "the intensification of

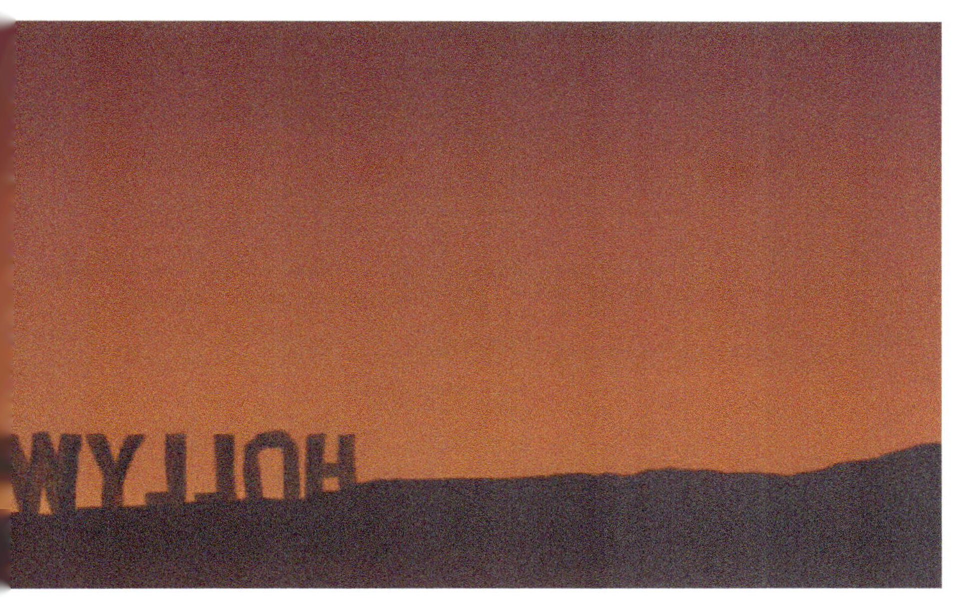

nervous stimulation" in the modern megalopolis—"an inconsiderate hardness" that "consists in "the blunting of discrimination."[40] However, according to Simmel, this blasé disposition is only a superficial shield, for at the same time, metropolitan life, with its pervasive marketplace, also demands an opposite response—the refinement of discrimination, the judgment of value, the determination of difference. In effect, then, the blasé attitude of the metropolitan type protects a sharpened "intellectuality," that is, a mind equipped to make the rapid calculations required for success, even survival, in the "money economy" of the big city.[41] Might it be that just as Ruscha points to a contemporary transformation in reification, he does the same for the blasé attitude? The deadpan aspect of his work is more than blasé in the Simmelian sense, for it evokes a world that is both "colorless" and "lurid," "indifferent" and "differentiated," precisely blunted and refined, and at times it induces this double effect in its viewers as well. Consider

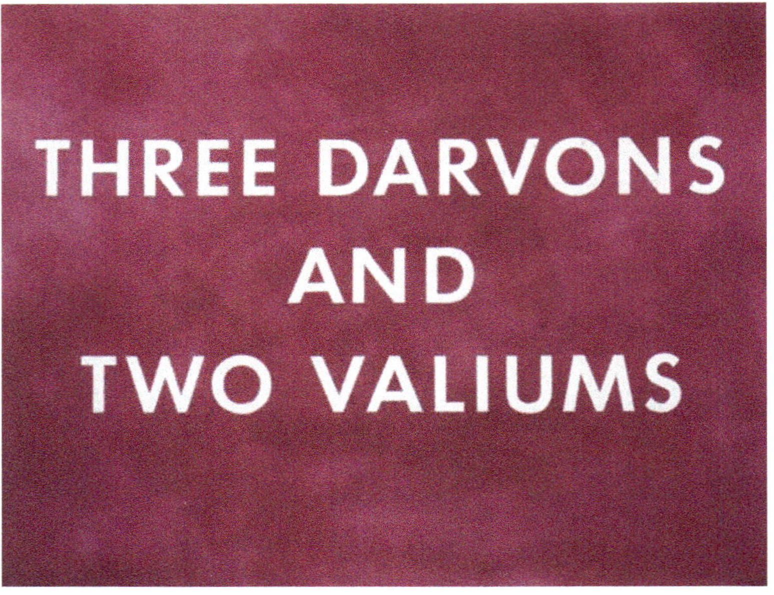

5.19 *Three Darvons and Two Valiums*, 1975. Pastel on paper, 22½ × 28⅝ in.

again the narcotic space, at once anesthetic and subtle, of *Three Darvons and Two Valiums*, or this undated studio note: "It's the little things that matter," Ruscha writes. "I believe an innocuous piece of industrial design can shape your attitudes of the world. In my case that could be the gearshift knob from a 1950 Ford sedan" (400).[42]

Again, Ruscha tests these distinctions in a manner that allows us to reflect on important transformations in modern experience; in this way he, too, might be considered "a painter of modern life." A century ago, critics like Simmel, Lukács, and Walter Benjamin concentrated on the abrupt exchanges that occur in dense metropolises like Berlin and Paris, and so foregrounded the intensity of urban shock; Ruscha operates in a different terrain, the diffuse autotopia of Los Angeles, and explores a different sensorium, the anesthetics of LA cool. Nonetheless, there are connections to be made. For instance, Benjamin tied some of his reflections on distraction in metropolitan culture to the reception of architecture and film: "Architecture has always offered the prototype of an artwork that is received in a state of distraction," he wrote in "The Work of Art in the Age of Its Technological Reproducibility" (1936), while "reception in distraction finds in film its true training ground."[43] Architecture and film also figure in Ruscha, and not only as subject matter but also as structures that inform the format of his paintings. After reification and the blasé attitude, then, distraction is a third theme in the discourse on modernity that Ruscha addresses.

"Los Angeles to me is like a series of storefront planes that are all vertical from the street," Ruscha has commented, "and there's almost like nothing behind the facades"; it is "the ultimate cardboard cut-out town" (223, 244).[44] Recognition of this flat frontality makes his otherwise odd photo books like *Every Building on the Sunset Strip* appear as perfectly appropriate ways to present his material. Along with storefronts and apartment façades, his LA is also a city of billboards, and in part Ruscha has modeled his painting on these large panels with giant words suspended in urban space (he has occasionally depicted billboards as well). Like a painting, Ruscha comments, a billboard consists of "paint on a lifted-up surface," and it, too, is "a backdrop for the drama that happens," a description that also conveys the theatrical spatiality of much of his work (165, 265).[45]

As other critics have noted, this focus on storefronts and billboards implies an automotive point of view. The car is "a missing link in the [photo] books," the critic Henri Man Barense remarks, "the conduit between the pools, apartments, and, of course, the parking lots and gas stations," not to mention the Sunset Strip (213). The car is also the unseen vehicle of the LA paintings that depict various signs at different scales amid broad horizons and vast skies. "I think of your work," the curator Bernard Blistène comments to Ruscha, "as a huge field in which you drive—and of the canvas as a kind of windshield" (304). Along with the billboard, Ruscha revises the old window model of painting in terms of the windshield. Both structures have informed the proportions of his paintings since the 1970s, which often favor the horizontal axis, sometimes in the extreme. (For example, *The Back of Hollywood* [1976–77], a painting three times wide as tall, combines references to both structures: an actual billboard commission, it presents the back of the famous sign, whose letters read correctly if ones imagines them in a rearview mirror.) Like billboards and windshields, Ruscha paintings often set the world in airy suspension, with the viewer placed in a mixed state of attention and distraction.[46]

"A huge field in which you drive": more than most cities, Los Angeles is a horizontal expanse across which one moves from horizon to horizon. "It's the idea of things running horizontally and trying to take off," Ruscha remarks. "The scale and the motion both take part in it" (161).[47] Both illusions of scale and motion implicate the cinema too: at times, like the spectator of a film, the viewer of a Ruscha painting has the impression of movement into and through space. Ruscha has long evoked the "celluloid gloss" of cinema as well (277). The spatiality of film is at once deep and superficial, illusionist and flat: in the movies, space is surface and vice versa, and titles and credits appear suspended in this surface-space (Ruscha replicates this condition, for example, in his different versions of the cinematic "The End," with flat letters, celluloid streaks, and airy space [fig. 5.20]).[48] This is simply to say that classic film is projected light on a flat surface that creates the illusion of space, yet it is a space that seems not only to invite us in but also, at times, to project toward us, and Ruscha captures this double effect too. In *Large Trademark with Eight Spotlights*, for instance, the yellow spotlights seem to originate in the distance, cut diagonally across the deep space toward us, and arrive on the picture plane as though on a movie screen: the lights align with its surface, around the 20th Century Fox emblem, which also appear to be projected. Here pictorial light and space seem subsumed by the cinematic versions of these qualities.

The cinematic aspect of his work is also registered in its proportions. When Ruscha speaks of the influence of the movies, he stresses "the panoramic-ness of the wide screen": "Most of my proportions are affected by the concept of the panorama" (291, 308). Committed to the "horizontal mode" of landscape, Ruscha returns this traditional genre of painting to us, yet here it is transformed by Panavision scale and Cinerama spectacle. In his later paintings, this "trans-panavision" (426) summons up vast dimensions and brilliant sunsets that often convey a "deeply Californian version of infinity."[49] "Close your eyes and what does it mean, visually?" Ruscha

5.20 *The End*, 1991. Acrylic on canvas, 70 × 112 in.

asks of this Hollywood sublime; "it means a way of light" (221). Such light is at once true and illusory, the stuff of Hollywood dreams: "If you look at the 20th Century Fox, you get this feeling of concrete immortality" (221). In this regard, Ruscha might not be as removed from the European tradition, that "vast, great, rich culture of painting" lamented by Richter, as he once thought. This is not to say that "the Northern Romantic Tradition" extends to the Los Angeles Basin, but it is to suggest that Ruscha remains in contact with landscape painting, especially of the American West, and that his Hollywood sublime figures in its legacy, which, like Hamilton and Richter, he shows to have been altered by cinema, advertising, and media culture in general.

The End

Notwithstanding "this feeling of concrete immortality," the weather of the work changed in the mid to late 1980s; whereas Ruscha had once painted his words liquid hot and his skies toxic brilliant, both took on a foggy chill, and almost everything became nocturnal. As he moved to new motifs like old film frames and handless clock faces, the sense of time shifted too, as if his subjects had receded not only into the dark but also into the past, often eerily so (fig. 5.21). In large part, this effect is due to his dominant technique of the last two decades, the silhouette, which Ruscha associates with "things that are immediately recognizable," like icons and logos (275). In a way like the blur in Richter, the silhouette in Ruscha conveys two opposite things at once: a powerful collective symbol, a shared memory image, and the fading away of these trusted things. Thus, the darkening seems cultural too, as though, not long after Ronald Reagan had declared "morning again in America," Ruscha countered with an evening world: in the paintings of this period, we sense not "a shining city on a hill," but the twilight of American gods.

The vaunted exceptionalism of the United States—its democratic dream, its eternal future—was long staked on its western frontier, but in a cycle of paintings that stretch into the mid-1990s, Ruscha displays such tokens as silhouetted teepees, buffalos, and wagon trains headed for night, with the implication, already at work in some westerns, that the West is largely a fiction and that it is bound to end soon anyway (fig. 5.22). And this fading to black is not limited to western subjects: everyday objects are also darkened or become distorted (for example, a coffee cup that looks burned into its linen support, clock faces skewed as if anamorphically), and American symbols become shapeless or worn (for example, a silhouette of Shirley Temple that borders on a blob, a profile of Thomas Jefferson that appears charred). This slow fade is perhaps most poignant in a 1996 painting of a lone post of a twilit porch (fig. 5.23): a staple shot in westerns (it could come from *The Searchers*, say), this picture appears in the midst of similar paintings of solitary Ionic and Doric columns as if to suggest that even as this post appears almost as classic as these columns, it seems almost as distant too—less a defiant marker, then, than a fragile relic.

This change in mood has also affected how Ruscha evokes the commons, as in his powerful silhouettes of lone coyotes and crows—creatures that, in Native American lore, are "tricksters," that is, in-between beings, at home

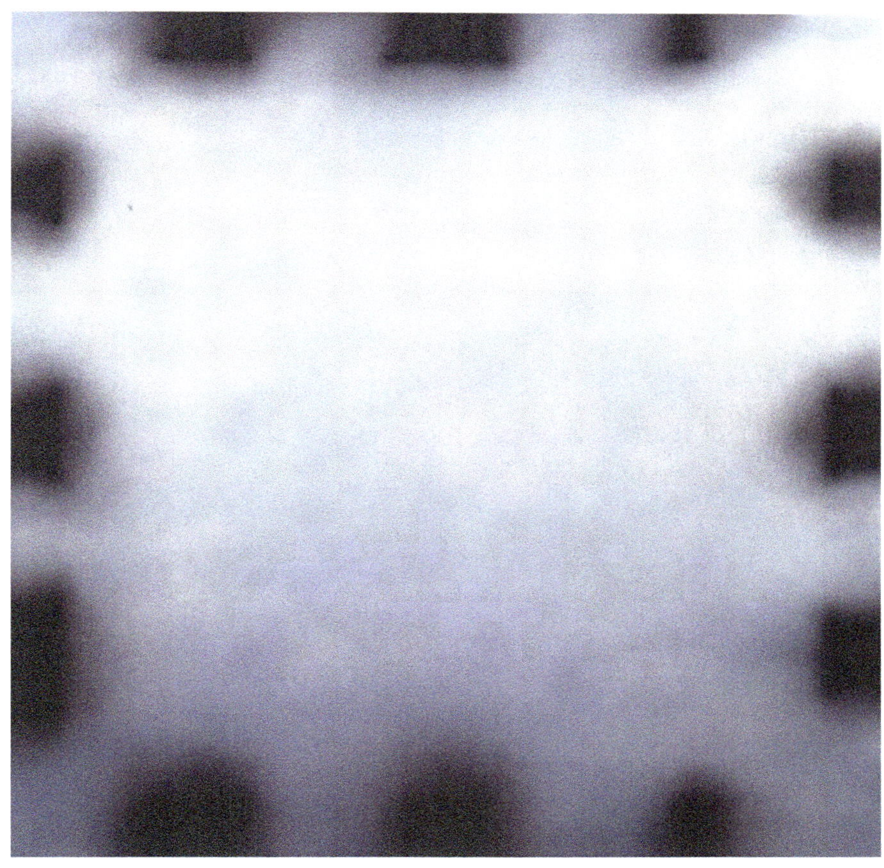

5.21 *Chrysler New Yorker*, 1994. Acrylic on canvas, 64 × 64 in.

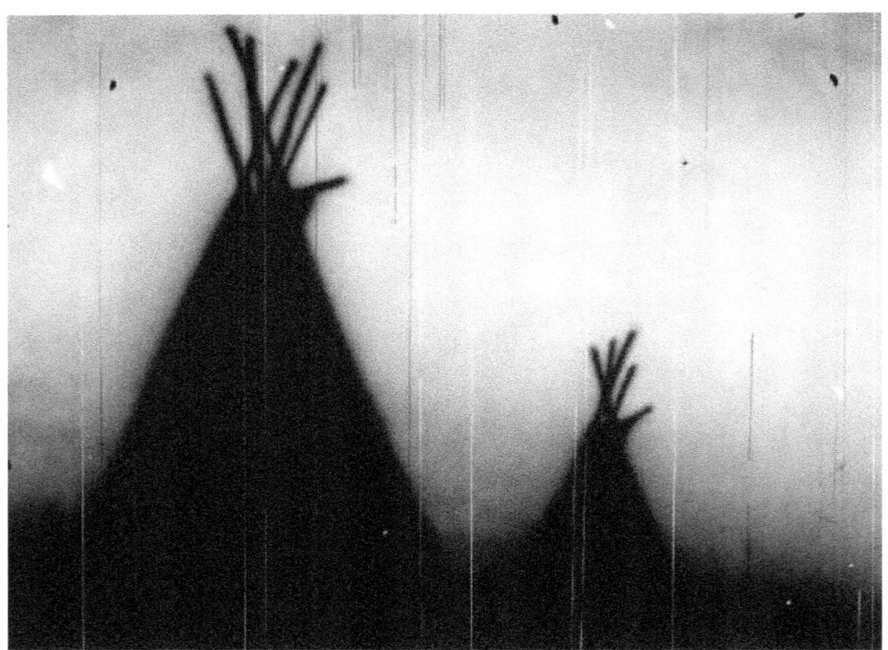

5.22 *Western*, 1991. Acrylic on canvas, 72 × 96 in.

everywhere and nowhere (fig. 5.24).[50] And then there is his recurrent motif of a ghost ship under full sail (fig. 5.25). This black barque calls to mind the great Kafka story about the Hunter Gracchus, who, neither alive nor dead, is doomed to wander from port to port in a purgatorial state: "Nobody knows of me, and if anyone knew he would not know where I could be found, and if he knew where I could be found, he would not how to deal with me, he would not know how to help me."[51] The spiritual America that Ruscha has limned over the last fifty years stretches from that hopeful Okie headed west on Route 66 in 1956 to these contemporary intimations of the lost Gracchus.

Even in the years when Ruscha evoked a "deeply Californian version of infinity," his pictorial space often appears thin and fragile, and sometimes there is a hint of catastrophe or "crash" in these pictures, too (214).[52] Like

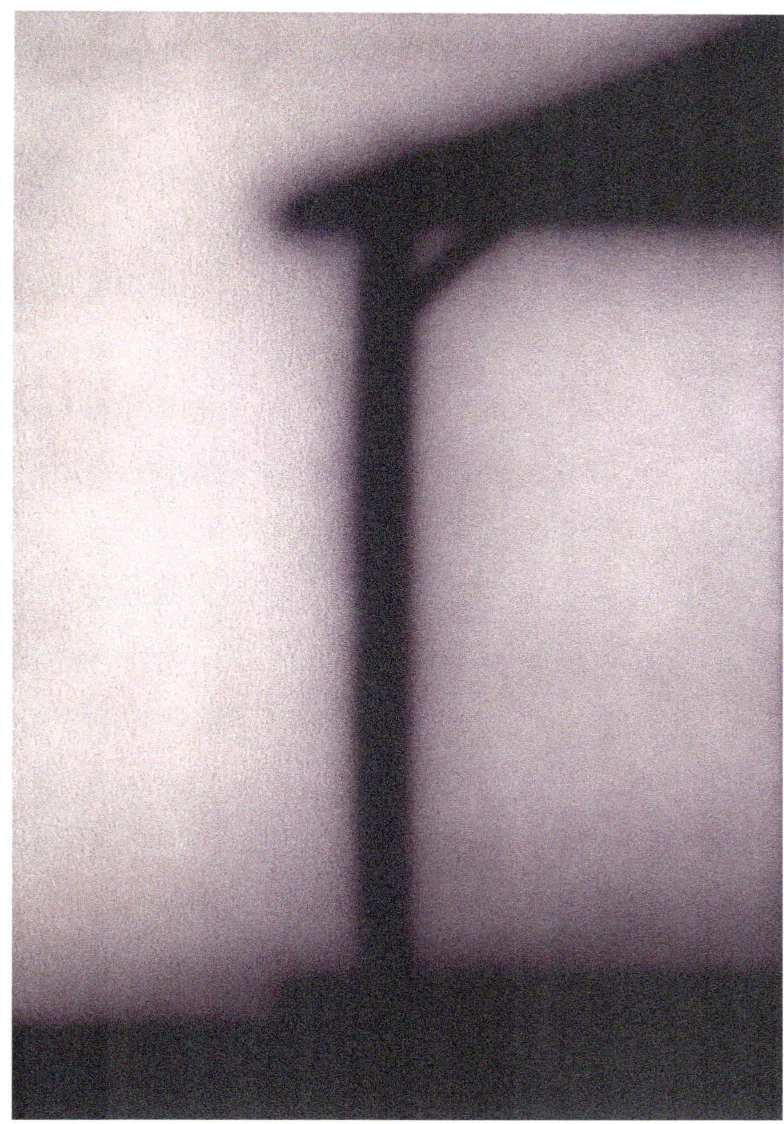

5.23 *Porch*, 1996. Acrylic on canvas, 36 × 24 in.

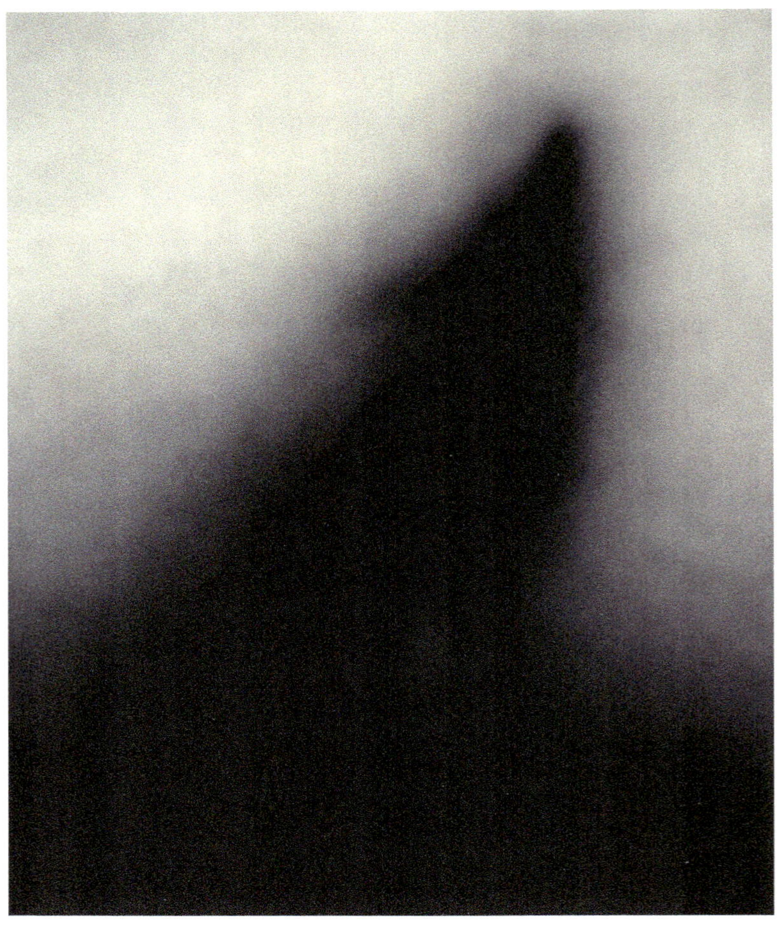

5.24 *Howl*, 1986. Acrylic on canvas, 78 × 64 in.

Nathanael West and Joan Didion, then, Ruscha intimates that Los Angeles is a mirage and California a myth—a façade about to crumble into the desert, a set about to liquefy into the sea (at least one of his stretch sunsets contains the phrase "eternal amnesia" in small print at the bottom).[53] More recently, Ruscha has suggested that the American empire at large might have run its course. In 1836, the British-born American Thomas Cole completed

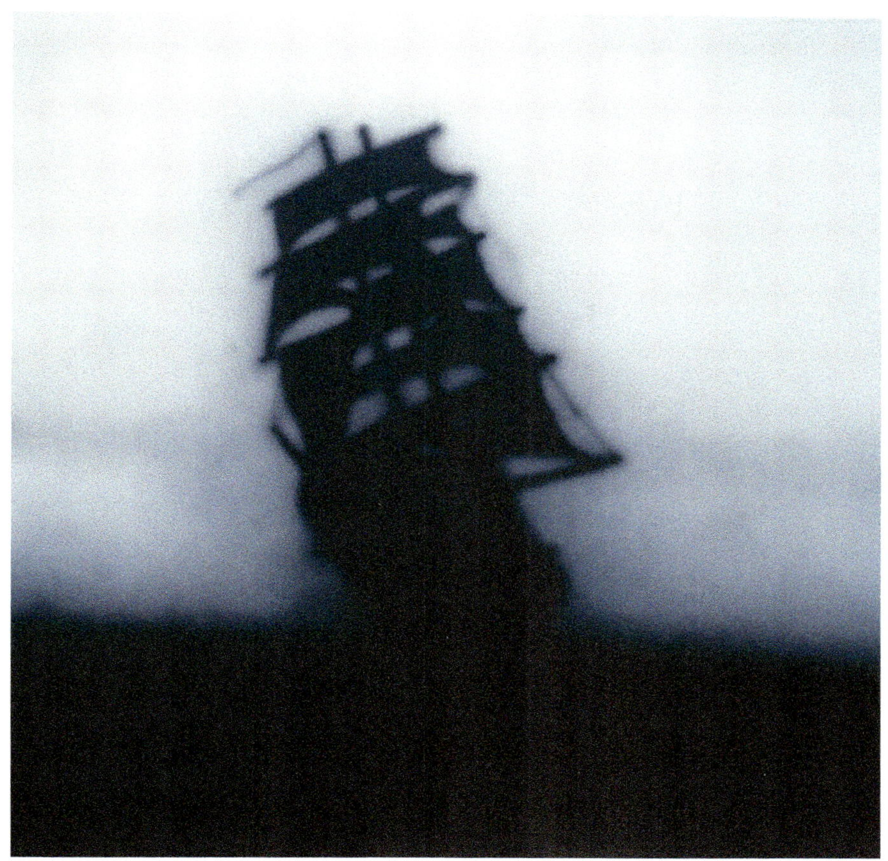

5.25 *Untitled*, 1986. Oil and enamel on canvas, 64 × 64 in.

a celebrated cycle of five paintings titled *The Course of Empire*, which il-
lustrates the life of an imagined nation from savage beginnings, through
pastoral peace and classical perfection, to war and violence, and finally to a
ruinous landscape in which nature has reclaimed all. Ruscha borrowed this
title for his own allegorical cycle of ten paintings, five done in black and
white from 1992 and five in color from 2002–5 (figs. 5.26, 5.27). Each

earlier picture conjures up a "blue collar" warehouse or retail store in the LA area in the schematic manner of a draftsman, and each is paired with a later picture of the same structure as it might be transformed by time.[54] Some enterprises appear to have thrived or changed hands (one front includes fictional Asian script), but most have fallen into disuse (the top of a telephone booth in the first set of paintings reminds us of a time when public amenities still existed). If the United States is still an empire, Ruscha implies, it is so only as a façade; its landscape is a new *terrain vague* dotted with "boxes with names on them" (as he puts it) under skies that look disturbed; and however much it might have boomed in the first Pop age, its future in the new network of global capital appears bleak. Of course, "the end of American empire" has become a cliché in its own right; yet rather than treat the topic sentimentally, Ruscha faces it, as one might expect, deadpan. Here we are a long way from that heady dream of American culture that drove the first manifestations of Pop in Britain; that initial thrill in postwar media and technology is also long gone.

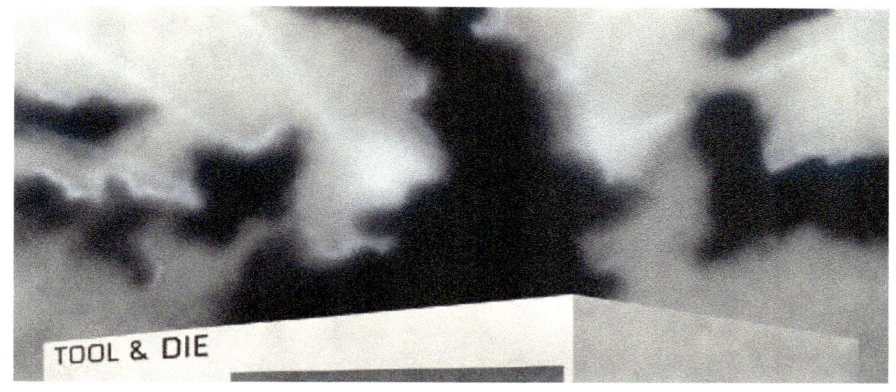

5.26 *Blue Collar Tool & Die*, 1992. Acrylic on canvas, 52 × 116 in.

5.27 *The Old Tool & Die Building*, 2004. Acrylic on canvas, 52 × 116 in.

Pop Test

There is a plan for a book, and then there is the book that is written: sometimes an author is surprised by his own insistences, which could be called symptomatic if they had not become a little more conscious in the writing. (That is one reason to write, at least for me: to see what my thinking might produce without my quite knowing it.) I want to conclude with a few words about some of these insistences here.

One prompt of this book was to puzzle over the political valence of Pop art, to ask in particular whether it is ever critical of popular culture or always complicit with it. However, it soon became clear that this question could not be posed as an either-or, that most of my artists aim for "an ironism of affirmation" that baffles positions pro and con alike. Some critics see this baffling as a move to have it both ways, to satisfy the interests of high and low cultures at once. With the same skepticism, they also regard the anti-ideological position of Richter, say, or the deadpan posture of Ruscha as tantamount to political indifference, and the exploration of photogenic semblance by the former or of celluloid gloss by the latter as a repackaging of spectacle in the guise of art. This is not my view, but it has its points to score, and I have not tried to argue them all down. That said, such criticism does miss the element of protection that these artists seek in this aesthetic of the neutral; more significantly, it overlooks the political limitations of Pop, which are structural to its position not only in a commercial art world but also in a class society whose divisions it sometimes obscures and sometimes exposes. Here the very ambivalence of Pop toward high and low cultures becomes double: often, rather than having it both ways, Pop values the two cultures even as it is also injects a modicum of doubt into our relations to each. At times, I want to insist, Pop highlights cultural contradictions in ways that do produce critical consciousness.

I have privileged moments of criticality in this art, and as a consequence, I have played down its sheer delight in popular culture. Yet this delight is only intermittent, and though it has a politics of its own, it is a lite politics, one that, in the long aftermath of Pop, now seems played out (especially in the work of such Warholian avatars as Jeff Koons, Damien Hirst, and Takashi Murakami). The politics in Pop I have stressed is pitched differently, centered on its commitment to what is held in common, including our shared image world understood (perhaps perversely) as a newfangled commons. To be sure, this commonality is often degraded, and this "Commonism" is often problematic. Certainly, it is rarely utopian; in fact, if we take Warhol or Ruscha as our guide, it is more dystopian than not.

This Commonism is one insistence I did not anticipate; another is a feeling-tone that it sometimes betrays, one rarely noted, and that is the desperation of Pop, which is the underside of its delight. Recall the initial call from the Smithsons to "get the measure" of new media in order to "match" them somehow, followed by this warning from Hamilton: "If the artist is not to lose much of his ancient purpose he may have to plunder the popular arts to recover the imagery which is his rightful inheritance." Born and bred in new media and popular culture, the Americans might be more expert on this front, but they, too, were challenged by this matching up (for his first viewers, Lichtenstein appeared overwhelmed by his mass sources, as did Warhol, though he hardly seemed to care). At times, my artists were also made anxious by the opposite term—by high art, the tableau tradition, the "ancient purpose" of the artist. For the most part, they deployed painting strategically, as a meta-medium with distance enough from new media and popular culture "to get the measure" of both, but some also sought, without irony, to be counted as great painters in their own right (Richter certainly, Hamilton and Lichtenstein probably, Ruscha perhaps). This leads to another double bind that made them desperate at times: to be positioned at once as early explorers of the first Pop Age and as latecomers in the Baudelairean tradition of modern painting, maybe the last in that great line. Finally, sometimes, too, there is desperation in the very deadpan of Pop, in the extremity of its willed impersonality, as well as in its very ambivalence, the aforementioned doubleness regarding high and low that likely runs back to its conflicted position politically. "I would be happy not only as a victim," Baudelaire once wrote; "it would not displease me to play the hangman as well." Warhol or Hamilton or Richter might have confessed to the same crime, if not in the same idiom.[1]

I have highlighted two strategies in Pop that can also appear desperate. Although my artists reiterate clichéd images of popular culture, they do so, as often as not, in order to de-reify them—either by defamiliarizing and so de-automatizing these clichés (the Ruscha way) or by exacerbating and so exploding them (the Lichtenstein way). This is another insistence I had not fully expected, and it points to a further one. From the start, many critics have viewed practitioners of Pop as dupes of the media, its zombies in art; in my view, on the contrary, the artists in question are not only its canny experts but also its dialectical theorists. Each, I have argued, produced a dis-tinctive version of the artistic image as a mimetic probe into a given matrix of cultural languages, both high and low—a probe that, far from facile, is complex in its making and viewing alike.

This complexity points to a final insistence. If these artists are tested, so are they testing. They test not only the tableau tradition, and its criteria for pictorial composition and its ends of subjective composure, but also popular culture and its refashioning of the postwar subject as *homo imago* with a new cultural literacy to learn, even a new symbolic order to negoti-ate. There is an intrinsic strain in the subject understood as an image (and vice versa), and my Pop artists pressure these vexed relations further. As we have seen, they are concerned, too, to explore the training and testing of the postwar subject by different technologies—photographic, cinematic, televisual, and other. In doing so, they also reflect on a test society on the rise—from the military-entertainment complex parodied by Lichtenstein to the neoliberal factory at large weirdly anticipated by Warhol. Perhaps the last word about painting and subjectivity in the first Pop Age should be his, from a book published just two years before his death, *America* (1985): "I always thought I'd like my own tombstone to be blank. No epitaph, and no name. Well, actually, I'd like it to say 'figment.'"

NOTES

Homo Imago

1. Hamilton removed the window of the van in the original photo through retouching; however, in the final version (the only one on board) he reconstructed it as a plywood frame with sliding glass panes. This play with design elements is typical of Hamilton, who also likes to explore different effects with different mediums (*Swingeing London 67* appears in the form of prints, too).

2. The judge is quoted in Richard Morphet, ed., *Richard Hamilton* (London: Tate Gallery, 1992), 166. At the time, Fraser was both friend and dealer to Hamilton, who also indicates here how, in London as in New York, art world and celebrity culture were already intertwined.

3. See in particular Russell Ferguson, ed., *Hand-Painted Pop: American Art in Transition 1955–62* (Los Angeles: LAMOCA/Rizzoli, 1993). I discuss these connections in chapters 1 and 2. Throughout this book, I use "Pop" to refer to Pop art and "pop" to refer to pop culture.

4. Hamilton has in mind Warhol above all here. Of course, by this time collage had long been recuperated as a device of advertising.

5. There is a vast literature on the tableau, but Denis Diderot captured its essence in his essay "Composition" for the *Encyclopédie* (1751–72):

> A well-composed picture [*tableau*] is a whole contained under a single point of view, in which the parts work together to one end and form by their mutual correspondence a unity as real as that of the members of the body of an animal; so that a piece of painting made up of a large number of figures thrown at random on to the canvas, with neither proportion, intelligence nor unity, no more deserves to be called a *true composition* than scattered studies of legs, nose and eyes on the same cartoon deserve to called a *portrait* or even a *human figure*. (Quoted in Roland Barthes, "Diderot, Eisenstein, Brecht," in *Image-Music-Text*, trans. Stephen Heath [New York: Hill and Wang, 1977], 71)

Also in this period of the Enlightenment, Gotthold Lessing presented his opposition between the spatial and the temporal arts, which affirmed the unity Diderot prescribed for painting, with this added proviso: "Painting can use only a single moment of an action in its coexisting compositions and must therefore choose the one which is most pregnant [*trächtig*] and from which the preceding and succeeding actions are most easily comprehensible" (*Laocoön* [1766], trans. Edward Allen McCormick [Indianapolis: Bobbs-Merrill, 1962], 79 (translation slightly modified). Two hundred years later, Clement Greenberg updated these neoclassical definitions in his account of "modernist painting," with stress on a "single moment" of reception as well: "Ideally the whole of a picture should be taken in at a glance; its unity should be immediately evident, and the supreme quality of a picture, the highest measure of its power to move and control the visual imagination, should reside in its unity. And this is something to be grasped only in an indivisible instant of time" ("The Case for Abstract Art" [1959], in John O'Brian, ed., *Clement Greenberg: The Collected Essays and Criticism, Volume 4* [Chicago: University of Chicago Press, 1993], 80). This was a reactive position, for a decade earlier, Greenberg had acknowledged "the crisis of the easel picture" in his 1948 essay of that title (in John O'Brian, ed., *Clement Greenberg: The Collected Essays and Criticism, Volume 2* [Chicago: University of Chicago Press, 1986]). The tableau had already been contested by the Russian Constructivists (and others) as the epitome of the bourgeois tradition of painting. I return to the Pop disturbance of the tableau often in this book; for example, in chapter 1, I suggest that this disturbance might be less an opposition than a deconstruction whereby Pop intensifies the response of the implied viewer of the modernist tableau to the point that its desired "presentness" flips into its dreaded opposite. For a magisterial account of the importance of the tableau for Diderot and his contemporaries, see Michael Fried, *Absorption and Theatricality: Painting and Beholder in the Age of Diderot* (Berkeley and Los Angeles: University of California Press, 1980), 71–105. Fried returns to the subject, again impressively, in *Manet's Modernism* (Chicago: University of Chicago Press, 1996), 267–80.

6. Charles Baudelaire, "The Painter of Modern Life" (1863), in *The Painter of Modern Life, and Other Essays*, trans. and ed., Jonathan Mayne (London: Phaidon, 1964), 12. In this celebrated essay, some of which is anticipated in his "Salon of 1846," Baudelaire called for a shift in subject matter—already begun in the practice of Édouard Manet and others—away from the elevated themes of myth and history toward the everyday activities of urban life, especially of middle-class leisure. Such a shift in content implied a shift in form, even in medium, too; for example, to capture the mobility of bourgeois types on the town, Baudelaire speculated, the sketch might be more useful than other means (the exemplar in the essay is not Manet but Constantin Guys, who was then known for his quick studies of Parisian life). In fact, what better vehicle to convey "the ephemeral, the fugitive, the contingent," key qualities of "the kaleidoscope" of metropolitan life according to Baudelaire, than the photograph? Yet the poet remained suspicious of the new medium, in part because he did not see its potential for imaginative invention (which was soon to be the received opinion about photography), in part because he did not deem it suited to "the other half" of his mandate for art, which was to extract "the eternal and the immutable" from this protean modernity. This other half was still the province of painting, and so painting—though pressured, to be sure, by attributes already associated with the photographic—remained the essential medium.

7. Leo Steinberg quoted in Peter Selz, ed., "A Symposium on Pop Art," *Arts* (April 1963), 35–35, reprinted in Stephen Henry Madoff, ed., *Pop Art: A Critical History* (Berkeley and Los Angeles: University of California Press, 1997), 72. Besides Steinberg and Selz, the symposium included Henry Geldzahler, Hilton Kramer, Dore Ashton, and Stanley Kunitz. I say more about the early reception of Pop in chapter 2.

8. See Madoff, *Pop Art*, for a representative sampling of this hostile reception.

9. I refer to the relevant essays in Leo Steinberg, *Other Criteria: Confrontations with Twentieth-Century Art* (Oxford: Oxford University Press, 1972); these quotations are on page 88. It is for this reason that I often quote my five artists (each is also linguistically inventive in his own way).

10. Brian O'Doherty, "Doubtful but Definite Triumph of the Banal," *New York Times*, October 27, 1963. David Deitcher develops the notion in "The

Unsentimental Education: The Professionalization of the American Artist," in Ferguson, *Hand-Painted Pop*.

11. The concept of the simulacrum was revived at this moment, sometimes with Pop in mind, by such theorists as Michel Foucault, Gilles Deleuze, and Jean Baudrillard. I elaborate on this point in chapters 3 and 4.

12. Richard Hamilton, *Collected Words, 1953–1982* (London: Thames and Hudson, 1982), 78.

13. Quoted in Gretchen Berg, "Andy: My True Story," *Los Angeles Free Press*, March 17, 1963.

14. There were other instances of this antisubjective impulse at the time, such as the *nouveau roman* of Alain Robbe-Grillet and the early criticism of Roland Barthes, but they saw the neutral as a way to avoid the ideological, which concerns a different (European) problematic, involving Cold War politics rather than consumer-society sensibility. I return to this topic in chapter 4.

15. Pop also registers the historical, as such authors as Thomas Crow, Anne Wagner, and Michael Lobel have demonstrated.

16. In *Other Criteria*, Steinberg associates the subject-effect of a Rauschenberg with schizophrenia and that of a Johns with sufferance; here again, Pop tends to combine these two effects and so to differ from both. Such paradoxes were also active elsewhere at this time: for example, while some writers delighted in a delirium of interpretation (e.g., Thomas Pynchon, Philip K. Dick, William Burroughs, William Gaddis), others argued "against interpretation" (e.g., Susan Sontag).

17. Jacques Lacan, *The Seminar of Jacques Lacan; Book II: The Ego in Freud's Theory and in the Technique of Psychoanalysis, 1954–1955*, ed. Jacques-Alain Miller, trans. Sylvana Tomaselli (New York: Norton, 1988), 36. Here Lacan develops the paper "On Narcissism" (1914), in which Freud argues that the ego first emerges out of libidinal investment in the image of the body. Regarding the ego as "an imaginary function," consider this remark by Warhol: "I usually accept people on the basis of their self-images, because their self-images have more to do with the way they think than their objective-images do" (*The Philosophy of Andy Warhol* [New York: Harcourt Brace Jovanovich, 1975], 69).

18. "Aggressivity is the correlative tendency of a mode of identification that we call narcissistic," Lacan writes in "Aggressivity in Psychoanalysis" (1948), the companion piece to his famous paper "The Mirror Stage as Formative of the Function of the I" (1936/49). See *Écrits*, trans. Alan Sheridan (New York: Norton, 1977), 16.

19. This tension between the iconic and the evanescent is replayed in accounts of the Pop subject, especially as it appears in Warhol. For example, on the one side

is Barthes (among others): "Marilyn, Liz, Elvis, Troy Donahue are not presented, strictly speaking, according to their contingency, but according to their eternal identity: they have an 'eidos,' which it is the task of Pop art to represent." On the other side is Benjamin Buchloh (among others), for whom Warhol offers consumers a chance "to celebrate their proper status of having been erased as subjects." In my view these two poles must be held together to the same extent that they are in the art. See Barthes, "That Old Thing, Art" (1980), in *The Responsibility of Forms*, trans. Richard Howard [Berkeley and Los Angeles: University of California Press, 1991], 205; and Buchloh, "Andy Warhol's One-Dimensional Art," in Kynaston McShine, ed., *Andy Warhol: A Retrospective* (New York: MoMA, 1989), 57. On Warhol as "figment," see chapter 3.

20. As a token of *homo imago, Elvis* updates, for the consumer age, not only the Vitruvian man of classical proportions but also the Muybridgean man of industrial discipline. Implicit here again is a new sense of the ego as projected—i.e., a new sense of identification understood almost cinematically as a projection of an idealized image. (In this light, Ray Johnson was right to title one of his collaged images of Elvis *Oedipus* [1955].)

21. Walter Benjamin, "Little History of Photography," in Michael Jennings, Howard Eiland, and Gary Smith, eds., *Selected Writings*, vol. 2, *1927–1934* (Cambridge, Mass.: Harvard University Press, 1999), 510. It would be like Warhol to play on the "flaming" homoeroticism of Elvis that is inadvertently implied by the movie title *Flaming Star*.

22. See F. R. Leavis, *The Great Tradition* (Garden City, N.Y.: Doubleday, 1954), and John McHale, "Plastic Parthenon," *Dot zero* (Spring 1967). As we will see in chapter 1, this new sense of self-fashioning, which Hamilton announces in a work like *Just what is it that makes today's homes so different, so appealing?* is a leitmotif of IG discourse, especially in the writing of Lawrence Alloway and Reyner Banham. "American films and magazines were the only live culture we knew as kids," Banham remarked of his IG associates. "We returned to Pop in the early fifties like Behans going to Dublin or Thomases to Llaregub, back to our native literature, our native arts" ("Who Is This Pop?" *Motif*, no. 10 [Winter 1962–63], 13). On the other hand, American critics on the Left and the Right tended to disparage this development, with notions like "masscult" and "midcult" and "guys-and-dolls lumpenbourgeoisie" (Dwight MacDonald in *Against the Grain: Essays on Mass Culture* [1962] and Tom Wolfe in *Kandy-Kolored Tangerine-Flake Streamline Baby* [1965], respectively). I should add that it is primarily for its own testing of the postwar training and testing of the subject that Pop remains for me an avant-garde.

23. Roy Lichtenstein quoted in Gene Swenson, "What Is Pop Art? Part I," *Art News* (November 1963), reprinted in Madoff, *Pop Art*, 108.

24. Hamilton, *Collected Words*, 136. Here I think especially of his *My Marilyn* (1965), which is discussed in chapter 1. With its suggestion of a *homo imago* in postwar art and culture, this book can be read in conjunction with my previous book, *Prosthetic Gods* (Cambridge, Mass.: MIT Press, 2004), which focuses on fantasies of the primitive and the machinic in prewar art and culture.

25. See Immanuel Kant, *The Critique of Judgment* (1790), and G.W.F. Hegel, *Aesthetics* (c. 1820–26).

26. Hamilton, *Collected Words*, 35.

27. Charles Baudelaire, *Correspondance* (Paris: Gallimard, 1973), 2:497. The conservative critic Hilton Kramer once placed Rauschenberg and Johns in "the decadent periphery of bourgeois taste" ("Month in Review," *Arts*, February 1959, 48–50). I take this put-down as praise, for it was in such decay that Pop art flourished.

28. "Commercial art is not our art," Lichtenstein commented in 1964; "it is our subject matter and in that sense it is nature." In a similar vein, Richter remarked in 1989, "Photographs are almost nature." See Lichtenstein in Ellen H. Johnson, ed., *American Artists on Art from 1940 to 1980* (New York: Harper and Row, 1982), 103; and Richter, *Writings, 1961–2007*, ed. Dietmar Elger and Hans Ulrich Obrist (New York: DAP, 2009), 228. Georg Lukács elaborated the concept of "second nature" (to which I return often) in *The Theory of the Novel* (1916; trans. Anna Bostock [Cambridge, Mass.: MIT Press, 1971]) and, in explicitly Marxist terms, in *History and Class Consciousness* (1923; trans. Rodney Livingstone [Cambridge, Mass.: MIT Press, 1971]), where the concept of reification is also presented.

29. In the mid-1950s, for example, Roland Barthes wrote, "The world *can* be plasticized, and even life itself" (*Mythologies*, trans. Annette Lavers [New York: Hill and Wang, 1975], 99). James Rosenquist intimated this shift in reification in *Reification* (1961), a bright orange, red, and yellow painting with white electric lights that spell out, in truncated fashion (and with some missing bulbs), the first three letters of the title. "Today," Walter Benjamin wrote in the mid-1920s, "the most real, mercantile gaze into the heart of things is the advertisement. It tears down the stage upon which contemplation moved, and all but hits us between the eyes with things as a car, growing to gigantic proportions, careens at us out of a film screen . . . What, in the end, makes advertisements so superior to criticism? Not what the moving red neon says—but the fiery pool reflecting it in the asphalt" ("One-Way Street," in Michael Jennings and Marcus Bullock, eds., *Selected Writings*, vol. 1, *1913–1926* [Cambridge, Mass.: Harvard University Press, 1996], 476).

30. Aspects of Pop, such as this super-fetishism, warrant interpretive methods, such as the Freudian and the Marxian, that are often seen as conflicting. To take a related example, Pop speaks to a spectacular world of imagistic surfaces, even as it also speaks to a human subject not altogether bereft of psychological depth, and so calls out for both Situationist and psychoanalytical accounts, accounts that otherwise dispute each other. In such cases, the theory must adapt to the art, not vice versa. (I explicate semiotic fetishism in chapter 1.)

31. This is a major insight of T. J. Clark and Thomas Crow, among others. See, e.g., Clark, *The Painting of Modern Life: Paris in the Art of Manet and His Followers* (New York: Knopf, 1985), and Crow, "Modernism and Mass Culture in the Visual Arts" (1983), in *Modern Art in the Common Culture* (New Haven, Conn.: Yale University Press, 1996).

32. Such historicization is the default mode of most art history today, whereas I am interested in a different historicity—that of the concepts developed in the work of art. For an account of this practice, see Giorgio Agamben, "What is a Paradigm?" in *The Signature of All Things: On Method*, trans. Luce D'Isanto (New York: Zone, 2009). For a critique of its application in modernist studies, see Caroline Jones, "The Modernist Paradigm: The Artworld and Thomas Kuhn," *Critical Inquiry* 26, no. 3 (Spring 2000).

33. Reyner Banham, *Theory and Design in the First Machine Age* (London: Architectural Press, 1960).

34. Such questions invite a parallactic view, and though I am as suspicious of *grands récits* as the next postmodernist, this skepticism has become doxa in its own right, and period fictions like "the first Pop Age" can be useful. On parallactic views, see my "Whatever Happened to Postmodernism," in *The Return of the Real* (Cambridge, Mass.: MIT Press, 1996); on period fictions, see my "Museum Tales of Twentieth-Century Art," in Elizabeth Cropper, ed., *Dialogues in Art History, from Mesopotamian to Modern: Readings for a New Century* (Washington: National Gallery of Art, 2009).

Certainly Warhol was the dominant precedent for artists in my New York milieu in the 1980s and 1990s, but this is not likely to be the case today. It is not clear, moreover, that art is still made or received in such genealogical terms. A further note of personal parallax: born in 1955 a month after Disneyland opened in July, in the same year Rauschenberg produced *Bed* and Johns produced *Target with Plaster Casts*, I am a creature of the first Pop Age in both its optimistic and its catastrophic guises—the utopia of world's fairs cut with the actuality of Kennedy assassinations, say, or images of the Apollo mission montaged with scenes of the Vietnam War.

During this time, a child, schooled in the wonders of medical technology and in the terrors of nuclear threat alike, could believe such opposite things as "I will live forever and I will die tomorrow." Perhaps it is this antinomical formation that prepared me to see Pop as double, both transformative and deathly.

35. For example, might Pop artists have missed the key shift in postwar regimes of control—a shift marked less by the spectacle of media images (as the Situationists believed) than by the administration of "biopower" (as Foucault came to argue)? But it also might be that spectacle and biopower are not as contradictory in practice as they are in theory, and that Pop also reflects on the latter, if not as explicitly as it does on the former.

36. For an early critique of Pop on this score, see Laura Mulvey, "Fears, Fantasies and the Male Unconscious, or 'You Don't Know What is Happening, Do You, Mr Jones?'" in *Spare Rib* (1973), reprinted in Mulvey, *Visual and Other Pleasures* (Bloomington: Indiana University Press, 1989). Also see Cecile Whiting, *A Taste for Pop: Pop Art, Gender and Consumer Culture* (Cambridge: Cambridge University Press, 1997), and "Seductive Subversion: Women Pop Artists 1958–1968," a 2010 show curated by Sid Sachs at the University of the Arts in Philadelphia, which was billed as "the first major exhibition of female Pop artists." There is, however, a distinct queering of art in Pop, most evidently with Warhol; this key topic has been well treated by Douglas Crimp, David Deitcher, Jonathan Flatley, Jonathan Katz, Richard Meyer, Kenneth Silver, and Jonathan Weinberg.

37. See, for example, Kobena Mercer, ed., *Pop Art and Vernacular Cultures* (Cambridge, Mass.: MIT Press, 2007).

38. These include, among others, Öyvind Fahlström, Sigmar Polke, and James Rosenquist; the first is the subject of a recent monograph by Michael Lobel, and the other two are not well served under the Pop rubric alone. I also see Pop developments in Britain and in France as subjects distinct from mine. All of this is to state the obvious: this book is not a comprehensive study of my five artists, let alone a general survey of Pop art.

1 Richard Hamilton, or the Tabular Image

1. Alison and Peter Smithson, "But Today We Collect Ads," *Ark*, no. 18 (November 1956), 50.

2. Ibid., 52. On modern architecture and mass media, see Beatriz Colomina, *Privacy and Publicity* (Cambridge, Mass.: MIT Press, 1994). A crucial resource on the IG remains David Robbins, ed., *The Independent Group: Postwar Britain and the Aesthetics of Plenty* (Cambridge, Mass.: MIT Press, 1990).

3. Smithson and Smithson, "Today We Collect Ads," 52.

4. Paolozzi found the word "bunk" in a Charles Atlas advertisement, which he later adapted in a collage. It is American slang, short for "bunkum," which is defined in the *Oxford English Dictionary* as "nonsense" or "ostentatious talking" (it was first used to describe the speeches of a congressman). But what exactly does Paolozzi label as "bunk" here—his popular sources or his own collages? Perhaps it is both, and we are invited to take neither mass culture nor its artistic elaboration too seriously—to *de*bunk both, in fact. Yet Paolozzi was likely familiar with another association, the famous saying of Henry Ford that "history is bunk." Especially in his caustic collages of *Time* magazine covers in the late 1940s and early 1950s, Paolozzi was inclined to agree. A reversal might be suggested here as well: not only that history is bunk, but that bunk possesses a history, too, or, more precisely, that it provides another way into history—bunk as a form of "nonsense" that might be used to debunk history as a form of "ostentatious talking." Hamilton is close in spirit to this proposition.

5. Banham, *First Machine Age*, 11.

6. Reyner Banham, "Machine Aesthetic," *Architectural Review* 117 (April 1955), 225.

7. Reyner Banham, "Vehicles of Desire," *Art*, no. 1 (1 September 1955), 3. Also see the excellent studies by Nigel Whiteley, *Reyner Banham: Historian of the Immediate Future* (Cambridge, Mass.: MIT Press, 2002), and Anthony Vidler, *Histories of the Immediate Present: Inventing Architectural Modernism* (Cambridge, Mass.: MIT Press, 2008).

8. See note 21 to the Introduction.

9. Banham, "Vehicles of Desire," 3. Soon enough, this aesthetic led Banham to celebrate the "plug-in" architecture of Cedric Price and Archigram.

10. Banham, "Design by Choice," *Architectural Review* 130 (July 1961), 44. Whiteley is instructive on this point.

11. For example, in 1963, in a revision of a phrase in James Joyce, Hamilton dubbed Westinghouse, Hoover, Singer, and General Electric "the grand new artificers." See Hamilton, *Collected Words*, 49; hereafter in the chapter, page numbers in the text refer to this volume.

12. Here again Hamilton was close to Banham, who wrote the entries for "Machine, Man & Motion." In 1960, for example, Hamilton asked, "Have we not now

reached a stage in the industrial era when appreciation, gratitude, and even affection are not out of place in our feelings for the products of the machine age?" (*Collected Words*, 153). But there were also differences between the two. For instance, in a review of *Theory and Design*, also in 1960, Hamilton suggested that Banham privileged Futurism too much (166).

13. According to Hamilton, the fundamental posture of the IG was "non-Aristotelian" (*Collected Words*, 78), neither critical nor celebratory, but at once analytical and playful—a neutrality that he also associates with Duchamp. As with Duchamp, this attitude led Hamilton, in his writing as well as his art, to delight in paradox more than to work through contradiction.

As for the critical literature on Hamilton, Richard Morphet paved the way with his 1970 and 1992 Tate Gallery catalogues. I have benefited from the texts in these and other publications, especially the extensive writings of Sarat Maharaj. Also see the texts by Julian Meyers and William Kaizen in *October* 94 (Fall 2000), a special issue devoted to the IG, and the texts in Hal Foster, with Alex Bacon, eds., *Richard Hamilton* (Cambridge, Mass.: MIT Press, 2010).

14. In the "This is Tomorrow" catalogue, Hamilton privileges the other term: "What is needed is not a definition of meaningful imagery, but the development of our perceptive potentialities to accept and utilize the continual enrichment of visual material" (*Collected Words*, 31). This concern with perception runs throughout the work, and it distinguishes Hamilton from Pop artists focused primarily on imagery.

15. For an exhaustive iconographic account of *Just what is it . . .?* see John-Paul Stonard, "Pop in the Age of Boom: Richard Hamilton's 'Just what is it that makes today's homes so attractive, so appealing?'" *Burlington Magazine* (September 2007). As Stonard demonstrates, the template of the collage is provided by an Armstrong Floors advertisement in the June 1955 issue of the *Ladies' Home Journal*.

16. In this letter, Hamilton offers his celebrated definition of Pop art (again, in the sense of popular; Pop art as we know it now did not yet exist): "Pop Art is: Popular (designed for a mass audience), Expendable (easily forgotten), Low cost, Mass produced, Young (aimed at youth), Witty, Sexy, Gimmicky, Glamorous, Big business)" (*Collected Words*, 28). In 1960, he reiterated some of these characteristics and added others—"glamour, overt sincerity, wit, direct appeal, professionalism, novelty, an ability to co-exist with an existing pattern of style, and, lastly, expendability" (155). The 1957 letter went unanswered—though Peter Smithson later claimed he never received it. See Beatriz Colomina, "Friends of the Future: A Conversation with Peter Smithson," *October* 94 (Fall 2000).

17. Below I mention a few paintings produced after this date that qualify as tabular pictures, but a full account of these and subsequent works must await another occasion.

18. Hamilton also acknowledges a Futurist connection here: *Hommage à Chrysler Corp.* carries "a faint echo of the 'Winged Victory of Samothrace'" (*Collected Words*, 32), another allusion to "The Founding and Manifesto of Futurism" (1909). Incidentally, the fascination with automobile styling is echoed in American Pop—Claes Oldenburg being obsessed with the 1934 Chrysler Airflow, for example, or Ed Ruscha with car customizing in Los Angeles.

19. The "corp" of the title suggests not only "body" but also "corporation," and perhaps, faintly, "corpse" as well (the notion that homage might be paid to a corporation is only somewhat less absurd today than it was in 1957). A juxtaposition of the organic and the mechanical runs throughout Hamilton. For example, "Man, Machine & Motion" followed "Growth and Form," and it was informed not only by D'Arcy Wentworth Thompson but also by Siegfried Giedion (*Mechanization Takes Command* appeared in 1948); references to Dada and Surrealism are matched by allusions to Futurism and the Bauhaus; and so on. In effect, Hamilton holds together the modernist strands that Alfred H. Barr, Jr., pulled apart in his famous diagram of "non-geometrical" and "geometrical" styles in his 1936 show "Cubism and Abstract Art" at the Museum of Modern Art.

20. Although the Duchampian readymade bears on commodity fetishism, and the Surrealist found object on sexual fetishism, sometimes they converge, and by the moment of Pop, they were commingled. For more on this distinction, see my *Compulsive Beauty* (Cambridge, Mass.: MIT Press, 1993); also see Helen Molesworth, ed., *Part Object Part Sculpture* (Columbus, Ohio: Wexner Center for the Arts, 2005).

Hamilton follows Paolozzi in this super-fetishism. See, for example, the collage *Real Gold* (dated 1950), in which Paolozzi combines a magazine cover of a bikinied sexpot with an advertisement for "Real Gold" lemon juice—yet he is more Dadaist in his pictorial disruptions than Hamilton.

21. See Sigmund Freud, *Three Essays on the Theory of Sexuality* (1905).

22. Walter Benjamin, "Paris, the Capital of the Nineteenth Century" (1935), in *The Arcades Project* (Cambridge, Mass.: Harvard University Press, 1999), 8. Hamilton suggests the inverse as well, that is, the inorganic appeal of the sexual, which is also to suggest the destructive drive of the sexual. Again, pronounced in the early collages of Paolozzi (e.g., *Yours Till the Boys Come Home*, c. 1951), not to mention

the early novels of J. G. Ballard (e.g., *Crash* [1968]), it is muted by comparison in Hamilton.

23. See Leo Steinberg, "'The Algerian Women' and Picasso at Large," in *Other Criteria*.

24. Not only are all things subject to fetishization here, but so too is space; it also appears fragmented and reified, even partially dissolved, as Marx and Engels could only imagine in *The Communist Manifesto* ("all that is solid melts into air"). Moreover, in this partial dissolution, space seems to attest to a disavowal that, for Freud, is fundamental to fetishization, which, in his account, is not only a fixing of vision but also a form of not-seeing, a blankness. In short, Hamilton registers here a psychosocial "doubt" about postwar vision.

25. Michel Foucault, "Fantasia of the Library" (1967), in *Language, Counter-Memory, Practice* (Ithaca: Cornell University Press, 1977), 92. Benjamin alludes to "exhibition value" in "The Work of Art in the Age of Its Technological Reproducibility" (1935–36), and to "consumption value" in other notes; see Walter Benjamin, *Selected Writings*, vol. 3, *1935–1938* (Cambridge, Mass.: Harvard University Press, 2002), 101–33.

26. This bodiliness recurs often in Hamilton; see, for example, the landscape and flower paintings of the early 1970s.

27. The tabular picture as a fitting together of parts is appropriate for an artist who worked as a draftsman in tool production during World War II. (Hamilton once referred to Duchamp as a "tinkerer" [*Collected Words*, 219]; he is one as well.) This suggests a connection to Fernand Léger, yet Hamilton does not "machine" his paintings as neatly as Léger did; they are retouched as ads are. Richard Morphet sees an "Arcimboldesque principle" in this composition by subtraction and addition, but sometimes (as in *Portrait of Hugh Gaitskell as a Famous Monster of Filmland* [1964]) it is closer to a Frankensteinian grafting of dead parts. See Morphet, *Richard Hamilton* (London: Tate Gallery, 1970), 23.

28. Hamilton remarks of this bumper: "One passage, for example, runs from a prim emulation of in-focus photographed gloss to out-of-focus gloss to an artist's representation of chrome to an ad-man's sign meaning 'chrome'" (*Collected Words*, 31).

29. This is also how Leo Bersani rethinks sublimation in *The Freudian Body: Psychoanalysis and Art* (New York: Columbia University Press, 1986) and other texts. Freud touches on sublimation from *Three Essays on the Theory of Sexuality* (1905) through *Civilization and Its Discontents* (1930), but it remains undertheorized in his work.

30. Marcel Duchamp, *The Essential Writings of Marcel Duchamp*, ed. Michel Sanouillet and Elmer Peterson (London: Thames and Hudson, 1975): "When one undergoes the examination of the shop window, one also pronounces one's own sentence. In fact, one's choice is 'round trip' . . . No obstinacy, ad absurdum, of hiding the coition through a glass pane with one or many objects of the shop window. The penalty consists in cutting the pane and in feeling regret as soon as possession is consummated. QED" (74).

Hamilton replicated other elements of the *Large Glass*, too, such as *The Glider* (1913–15), and wrote several texts on Duchamp as well (reprinted in *Collected Words*). The Duchampian definition of the picture as "an apparition of an appearance" is also suggestive vis-à-vis the tabular picture (*Collected Words*, 230).

31. This crucial insight was soon shared by Roy Lichtenstein, who (as we will see in chapter 2) shows us a modernism mediated through the comics and vice versa. Hamilton wrote a fine text on Lichtenstein in *Studio International* (January 1968), which is reprinted in *Collected Words*.

32. The term originated with Duchamp, and it was developed importantly by Michel Carrouges in *Les machines célibataires* (Paris: Arcanes, 1954) and by Gilles Deleuze and Felix Guattari in *Anti-Oedipus*, trans. Robert Hurley, Mark Seem, and Helen R. Lane (New York: Viking, 1977). In 1934, André Breton described the *Large Glass* as "a mechanistic, cynical interpretation of the phenomenon of love," but the interpretation in Hamilton is not so mechanistic and cynical. See Breton, *Surrealism and Painting*, trans. Simon Watson Taylor (London: Macdonald and Company, 1972), 94. With others in the IG, Hamilton also read *The Mechanical Bride: Folklore of the Industrial Man* (1951), in which Marshall McLuhan analyzes, in a semi-Freudian manner, ads, cartoons, pulp fiction, and the like of the early postwar period.

33. In 1959, Hamilton gave a lecture titled "Glorious Technicolor, Breathtaking Cinema-Scope and Stereophonic Sound"—a line from a song in a Hollywood musical of the time—with the support of pop music, slides, and an early version of a Polaroid camera. In his own words, it was an "account of entertainment technology in the '50s (*Collected Words*, 128) focusing on new developments in photography (e.g., the Polaroid), cinema (e.g., Cinerama), television (e.g., color), stereophonic sound, and printing techniques. The text is precise, enthusiastic, and technophilic, as befits an artist involved in the design, early on, of tools and machines and, later, of a stereo and a computer.

34. Studies suggest that the commingling of forms came early, and the appearance of the UN windshield and the Sophia lips late. Barely implicit here is the

notion (Warholian before Warhol) that, in this postwar regime, stars are equal to politicians in power, maybe even above them.

35. Hamilton proposed a "delirious New York" twenty years before Rem Koolhaas coined the term (and five years before Hamilton first visited the city). He anticipated the dialectic of Corbusierian principles (as ghosted in the UN building) and Surrealist principles (evoked via Bellmer) that is central to "Manhattanism," according to Koolhaas. For Koolhaas, too, Manhattan is "lush" in the double sense of the word exploited by Hamilton—luxuriant and intoxicated. See Rem Koolhaas, *Delirious New York* (New York: Rizzoli, 1978). From 1968 to 1972, Koolhaas studied at the Architectural Association in London, where among his teachers was Peter Cook, a member of Archigram, whose Pop vision of the city was influenced by Hamilton as well as by Banham. See "Image Building" in my *The Art-Architecture Complex* (London: Verso, 2011).

36. There is also a different kind of blossoming of the Bride in *Lush situation*: "To her rear," Hamilton writes of Sophia, "is left the stain of a prolonged breathy fart, the compounded exhaust of 300 brake horses" (*Collected Words*, 49). Again bodiliness is reasserted even as it seems diffused.

37. Roland Barthes, *Mythologies* (1957), trans. Annette Lavers (New York: Hill and Wang, 1972), 99. There are other parallels between the tabular pictures and *Mythologies*. However, Barthes is Brechtian in his analysis, working to expose bourgeois culture parading as nature through demystification, while Hamilton is "non-Aristotelian," working to exacerbate commercial culture through an "ironism of affirmation."

38. I return to this Pop reflection on postwar reification in chapter 5. On the Futurist dream of inorganic vitality, see the title essay in my *Prosthetic Gods* (Cambridge, Mass.: MIT Press, 2004).

39. See Jacques Lacan, "The Agency of the Letter in the Unconscious, or Reason Since Freud" (1957), in *Écrits*. The paintings from the early 1950s (e.g., *Trainsition III* and *Trainsition IV*, 1954) are explicitly concerned with the perceptual changes produced by movement (in these cases, of a subject on a train), and they often contain dots, arrows, and plus signs to locate focus and to track motion. One such plus sign remains in *Hommage*, and most of the tabular pictures include diagrammatic dots.

40. See Baudelaire, "Painter of Modern Life."

41. "I was fascinated by 'white goods' as they were called, washing machines and dishwashers and refrigerators, not simply the objects in themselves as designed objects,

but also in the ways in which they were presented to the audience" (Richard Hamilton, "In Conversation with Michael Craig-Martin," in Adrian Searle, ed., *Talking Art* [London: ICA Documents #12, 1993], 73, reprinted in Foster, *Richard Hamilton*).

42. In 1969, Hamilton painted the apron pink, since pentimenti had begun to show.

43. As in *Hommage* and *Lush situation*, a fetishistic displacement of energy is evident here: the products are as present as the woman and perhaps more real than she. Once again, in its fragmentation and reification, capitalist space is presented as both full and empty.

44. Although the assumed viewer is male, there is here, as in some other Hamilton images, the possibility of female desire as well as female identification. For the sardine-can anecdote, see Jacques Lacan, *The Four Fundamental Concepts of Psychoanalysis* (1973), trans. Alan Sheridan (New York: Norton, 1981). For *Etant donnés*, see Jean-François Lyotard, *Les TRANSformateurs Duchamp* (Paris: Galilée, 1977), as well as Rosalind E. Krauss, *The Optical Unconscious* (Cambridge, Mass.: MIT Press, 1993), 95–146. Hamilton tells me that, despite his intimacy with Duchamp, he did not have prior knowledge of *Etant donnés*.

45. This machine is also both connective and disconnected, like the Bachelor Machine as understood by Deleuze and Guattari in *Anti-Oedipus*.

46. This breakdown between private and public is a key topos of Pop art, explored especially by Warhol. Like Warhol, Hamilton sometimes suggests an indirect kind of history painting (for this facet of his work, see my "Citizen Hamilton," *Artforum* [Summer 2008], reprinted in Foster, *Richard Hamilton*). The kitchen debate occurred at the opening of the American National Exhibition in Moscow, for which a model house, furnished with consumer appliances such as a refrigerator, was constructed. Nixon concentrated the feisty conversation on the merits of these devices, that is, of the economic system that could provide them, while Khrushchev intimated that they were bourgeois luxuries. For "domesticity at war," see the book of that title by Beatriz Colomina (Barcelona: Actar, 2006).

47. Marshall McLuhan, *Understanding Media: The Extensions of Man* (New York: McGraw-Hill, 1964). For Hamilton, too, the medium is the message, and media are understood as extensions of the human sensorium. He also explored human adaptation to technology as early as his 1955 exhibition, "Man, Machine & Motion."

48. I develop this notion of mimetic excess or exacerbation in chapter 2.

49. The title of the painting looks back to the lecture "Glorious Technicolor, Breathtaking Cinema-Scope and Stereophonic Sound," cited in note 33. Here the

trope of the environment as movie (theater), implicit in *Hers is a lush situation*, is all but explicit.

50. Hamilton quoted in *Architectural Design* (November 1961), 497; this issue was devoted to the Congress.

51. Ibid.

52. These experiments with phloo anticipated his interest, already present in the mid-1960s, in electronic images and his use, in the late 1980s, of Paintbox software.

53. Reyner Banham, text in *Man, Machine & Motion* (Newcastle-upon-Tyne: Hatton Gallery, 1955), 14. In a contemporaneous essay on the Citroën DS 19, Barthes writes: "Until now, the ultimate in cars belonged rather to the bestiary of power; here it becomes . . . more attuned to the sublimation of the utensil which one also finds in the design of contemporary household equipment . . . All this signifies a kind of control exercised over motion, which is henceforth conceived as comfort rather than performance. One is obviously turning from an alchemy of speed to a relish in driving" (*Mythologies*, 89). Hamilton used a large photo of a DS in his 1958 scheme for a living-exhibiting room *Gallery for a Collector of Brutalist and Tachiste Art.*

54. Compare, for example, Sophia Loren in *Hers is a lush situation* to John Glenn in *Towards a definitive statement . . . (d)*. A few years before, again in *Mythologies*, Barthes speculated on the new figure of "the jet-man" in a manner apposite here: "The jet-man," he concludes, "is a reified man, as if even today we could conceive the heavens only as populated with semi-objects" (73).

55. Baudelaire, *Painter of Modern Life*, 4.

56. Ibid., 13, 5, 12. Hamilton is almost explicit about his Baudelairean affinity here: "I would like to think of my purpose as a search for what is epic in everyday objects and everyday attitudes," he wrote in 1962. "Irony has no place in it except in so far as irony is part of the ad man's repertoire" (*Collected Words*, 37). His definition of Pop in his letter to the Smithsons highlights the expendable, yet in his view, only Warhol met that criterion, and only in a few projects.

57. Try as he might, Hamilton could not banish irony altogether: "Any one of a whole range of hard, handsome, mature heroes like Glenn, Titov [*sic*], Kennedy, Cary Grant, can match the deeds of Theseus and look as good, men's wearwise" (*Collected Words*, 50).

58. In the poster version of *Swingeing London*, Hamilton montages various clippings about the event in a way that makes explicit this visual-verbal hybrid.

59. As the showroom in Hamilton displaces the shop window in Duchamp, so now the Web mall displaces the showroom. On this info-image hybrid, see T. J.

Clark, "Modernism, Postmodernism, and Steam," *October* 100 (Winter 2002). Technologically speaking, "tabular picture" was, in its own time of new media, an anachronistic, even archaic term (but then, so was "flatbed picture").

60. "It's an old obsession of mine to see conventions mix," Hamilton remarked in 1969. "I like the difference between a diagram and a photograph and a mark which is simply sensuous paint, even the addition of real, or simulations of real, objects. These relationships multiply the levels of meaning and ways of reading" (*Collected Words*, 65). Most of the tabular pictures contain diagrams of movement, but the diagrammatic might be understood to control the other modes of representation in evidence, too. This might be another lesson learned from Duchamp, from the *Green Box* and the *Large Glass* in particular. Hamilton also featured diagrams in his teaching (see *Collected Words*, 169–70). On the diagram in Duchamp, see David Joselit, "Dada's Diagrams," in Leah Dickerman, ed., *The Dada Seminars* (Washington: National Gallery of Art, 2005).

61. See "Passion of the Sign" in my *Return of the Real*.

62. Like his paintings, his texts are also collaged, revised, and reused. In fact, like Banham, Hamilton produces a distinctive kind of Pop prose. In some respects, this prose anticipates the "gonzo journalism" of Hunter S. Thompson, Tom Wolfe, and others, but it has more to do with the rambunctious mix and match of images and ideas in the IG—a lingo that is mimetic of a pop world of brash conjunctions, of a consumerscape that is often "clip-on" and "plug-in" in appearance.

63. Hamilton writes of "a willful acceptance of pastiche as a keystone of the approach—anything which moves the mind through the visual senses is as grist to the mill but the mill must not grind so small that the ingredients lose their flavour in the whole" (*Collected Words*, 31).

64. As William Turnbull recalled in 1983: "Magazines were an incredible way of randomizing one's thinking (one thing the Independent Group was interested in was breaking down logical thinking)—food on one page, pyramids in the desert on the next, a good-looking girl on the next; they were like collages" (in Robbins, *Independent Group*, 21).

65. Steinberg, "Other Criteria," in *Other Criteria*. There Steinberg defines this pictorial paradigm as a "flat documentary surface that tabulates information" (88); I return to this paradigm in chapter 2. Hamilton experiments with different orientations only rarely, such as in *Towards a definitive statement . . . (d)* featuring John Glenn, which he describes as a "null gravity picture" that "may be hung in any orientation" (46).

66. This is a term advanced by Lawrence Alloway in "The Long Front of Culture" (*Cambridge Opinion*, no. 17, 1959) and adopted by Hamilton.

67. The tabular picture is more screen than "dump, reservoir, switching center," the analogies Steinberg offers for the flatbed picture ("Other Criteria," 88). In some ways, Hamilton is closer to Johns—to his model of painting as a surface of impression or inscription (they also share a devotion to Duchamp). Yet in terms of signification and affect, Johns is allegorical, negational, deadpan, even morbid, in ways that Hamilton is not.

68. See Walter Benjamin, "One-Way Street" (1928), in *Selected Writings*, vol. 1, 456 (the essay was written c. 1923–25). Benjamin writes here of script: "If centuries ago it began gradually to lie down, passing from the upright inscription to the manuscript resting on sloping desks before finally taking itself to bed in the printed book, it now begins just as slowly to rise again from the ground. The newspaper is read more in the vertical than in the horizontal plane, while film and advertisement force the printed word entirely into the dictatorial perpendicular." Hamilton would not describe it so negatively (his term is "persuading image," more on which below). I recall this formulation here also to complicate the overvaluation, in much contemporary art and criticism, of the horizontal and the base—as if they could somehow overwhelm the dictatorial perpendicular on their own.

69. Brian O'Doherty, *American Masters: The Voice and the Myth* (New York: Random House, 1974), 198. Also see Branden Joseph, *Random Order: Robert Rauschenberg and the Neo Avant-Garde* (Cambridge, Mass.: MIT Press, 2003).

70. Pop artists emerged in the United States only after the key tabular pictures were produced (again, they were not shown until 1964). Hamilton first visited the United States, in the company of Duchamp, in October 1963, at which time he met Warhol, Lichtenstein, Oldenburg, and James Rosenquist, among others. "[My] immersion into American Pop was sudden," he said, "and I thought that there was something quite alien in the way I'd been approaching these problems. It seemed as though I'd been doing everything in a very analytical, prissy way . . . I couldn't refrain from making a lyrical little passage somewhere. I thought these guys don't care!" (Hamilton, "Conversation with Michael Craig-Martin," 76).

71. See Benjamin H. D. Buchloh, "Gerhard Richter's *Atlas*: The Anomic Archive," *October* 88 (Spring 1999), and chapter 4 below.

72. See László Moholy-Nagy, "Photography is Creation with Light," in Krisztina Passuth, *Moholy-Nagy* (London: Thames and Hudson, 1985), 302–5, and Benjamin, "Little History of Photography," 527.

73. On this shift in the canon from an IG perspective, see John McHale, "The Plastic Parthenon," *Dot zero* (Spring 1967). The recent "canon wars" in the academy

only obscured the fact that the operative canon today consists, in this way, of television shows, blockbuster movies, sports statistics, celebrity scandals, viral events on YouTube, and so on.

74. The media optimism of Moholy-Nagy and Benjamin is moderated here, yet Hamilton is more optimistic than others associated with Pop. However, his work shifted to political critique during the Thatcher era, with paintings of the 1980s such as *The Citizen*, *The Subject*, and *The State* focused on the Troubles in Northern Ireland. At this point, "non-Aristotelian neutrality," let alone the "ironism of affirmation," was less pertinent.

75. At the same time, Hamilton expands the sense of "the human figure" (or depicts it thus expanded in capitalist imagery), which, as we have seen, might be found in the curve of a car bumper.

76. The essay echoes an influential text by the sociologist Vance Packard, *The Hidden Persuaders* (1957). Yet in Hamilton, these persuaders are not so hidden: he has some of the skepticism but little of the paranoia of such accounts.

77. On consumerist interpellation in recent years, see my *Design and Crime (and Other Diatribes)* (London: Verso, 2002).

78. It was part of her contract with photographers that Monroe could vet their images. After her death, some photographers, such as George Barris and Bert Stern, published parts of their shoots.

79. I return to the difficulties of such iconicity in chapter 3. There are other representations of Monroe to mention here, such as the extraordinary Bruce Conner film *Marilyn Times Five* (1968–73).

80. On semiotic fetishism, see Jean Baudrillard, *For a Critique of the Political Economy of the Sign* (St. Louis: Telos Press, 1973). In the "fetishism of the signifier," Baudrillard writes, "the subject is trapped in the factitous, differential, encoded, systematized aspect of the object. It is not the passion (whether of objects or subjects) for substances that speaks in fetishism, it is the *passion for the code*, which, by governing both objects and subjects, and by subordinating them to itself, delivers them up to abstract manipulation" (92).

81. In a sense, Hamilton plays on the disjunction between "the realist *morceau* and the artistic *tableau*," which was so problematic to the generation of Manet, according to Fried in *Manet's Modernism*.

"The scanned image is replacing the screened look in many fields today," Hamilton remarked in 1963, thus distinguishing between electronic and print images (*Collected Words*, 50). On the one hand, "screening, the older process of rendering multi-toned visual information into useable components for reproduction purposes, utilizes a device which produces a grid of small black dots varying in size dependent on the values of light and dark in the subject." On the other hand, "scanning break[s] down visual information into simple variations of intensity of a point of light which passes across and down the image in a series of parallel lines" (52). Yet, Hamilton acknowledges, many images are a mix of the two: "So much of what we look at is sieved and screened and scanned in the process of conversion to another dimensionality" (251–52). And this mixing has implications for our reception of these images, which differs from our contemplation of the tableau: "The [print] image is seen all at once but broken down into units" (52), whereas the electronic image is scanned as much as seen.

82. See Gilles Deleuze and Felix Guattari, *Kafka: Toward a Minor Literature,* trans. Dana Polan (Minneapolis: University of Minnesota Press, 1986).

83. "The interesting thing for me about painting is that it is static," Hamilton commented in 1968. "I like the fact that [it] presents a moment of time. [It] . . . has to project very forcibly a significant instant in the ideas of the artist . . . Informing existence in a visual experience . . . can be an epiphany" (Hamilton, in conversation with Christopher Finch and James Scott concerning their 1968 film on his work, as quoted from a transcript by Morphet, *Richard Hamilton* [1970], 14). Here is Hamilton again thirty-five years later: "The dictionary defines the word 'epiphany' as 'a manifestation or appearance of some divine or superhuman being.' Joyce uses a broader and far more beautiful description of the experience he called an epiphany: it was the revelation of the whatness of a thing; the moment in which 'the soul of the commonest . . . object seems to us radiant.' Some thing, or some experience, could bring about this instant of understanding" (See Hamilton, *Products* [London: Gagosian Gallery, 2003, unpaginated]). A very different example for Hamilton is the *Arnolfini Marriage* by Jan van Eyck. "It is an epiphany," Hamilton wrote in 1978, "a crystallization of thought that gives us an instant awareness of life's meaning. No other art has this capacity to be entirely there, totally existent like a phenomenon of nature" (264).

The model of the ideal subject-effect of the modernist painting is derived from the disinterested contemplation espoused by Kant in his *Critique of Judgment* (1790). Greenberg articulates it in "The Case for Abstract Art" (1959) in terms most relevant here:

> Ideally the whole of a picture should be taken in at a glance; its unity should
> be immediately evident, and the supreme quality of a picture, the highest measure of its power to move and control the visual imagination, should reside in

its unity. And this is something to be grasped only in an indivisible instant of time . . . It's all there at once, like a sudden revelation. This 'at-onceness' an abstract picture usually drives homes to us with greater singleness and clarity than a representational painting does. And to apprehend this 'at-onceness' demands a freedom of mind and untrammeledness of eye that constitute 'at-onceness' in their own right. Those who have grown capable of experiencing this know what I mean. You are summoned and gathered into one point in the continuum of duration . . . You become all attention, which means that you become, for the moment, selfless and in a sense entirely identified with the object of your attention. (*Collected Essays, Volume 4*, 80–81)

This model was developed by Fried in such texts as "Three American Painters: Kenneth Noland, Jules Olitski, Frank Stella" (1965) and "Art and Objecthood" (1967), which concludes with his famous formulation "Presentness is grace." See Fried, *Art and Objecthood* (Chicago: University of Chicago Press, 1998). The opposition between instantaneity and duration is an old one in aesthetics, bearing as it does on distinctions between spatial and temporal, or visual and verbal, arts from Lessing to Fried. As intimated in note 81, this opposition is put under further strain by the general mixing of screened and scanned images in Hamilton and in visual culture at large.

84. To continue the quotation from *Products* cited in the previous note: "Some thing, or some experience, could bring about this instant of understanding. I sometimes wonder if a sudden epiphany hit Marcel Duchamp when he picked up a bicycle wheel and put it through a hole in the top of a kitchen stool in 1913. I experienced such a moment of understanding when I encountered a large button in a seedy gift shop in Pacific Ocean Park, Venice, California, with the words 'SLIP IT TO ME' blatantly displayed across it. The greatly enlarged version of the badge which I characterized as a work of art was entitled *Epiphany*'."

85. In a further critique along these lines, Rosalind Krauss argues that the opposition between late-modernist abstraction and Pop painting collapses here: "The phenomenological goals of the two map onto one another . . . that goal [being] to produce the illusion in the viewer that he is not there—an illusion that is set up in reciprocity with the status of the work as mirage" ("Theories of Art after Minimalism and Pop," in Hal Foster, ed., *Discussions in Contemporary Culture* [Seattle: Bay Press, 1987], 61).

86. See Fried, "Three American Painters": "While modernist painting has increasingly divorced itself from the concerns of the society in which it precariously

flourishes, the actual dialectic by which it is made has taken on more and more of the denseness, structure, and complexity of moral experience—that is, of life itself, but life lived as few are inclined to live it: in a state of continuous intellectual and moral alertness (219). Again, for a critique of this position, see Krauss as cited in note 85.

87. As Richard Morphet comments: "To many in those years, works which today seem almost classically unified and which fit with obvious authority into the mainstream of art, did not look like *art* at all" (*Richard Hamilton* [1970], 7).

88. Baudelaire, *Correspondance*, 2:497.

2 Roy Lichtenstein, or the Cliché Image

1. Hamilton, *Collected Words*, 252, 254.

2. Ibid., 250, 251. "I'm never drawing the object itself," Lichtenstein remarked in a 1962 interview. "I'm only drawing a depiction of the object—a kind of crystallized symbol of it" (cited in Jack Cowart, ed., *Roy Lichtenstein: Beginning to End* [Madrid: Fundacíon Juan March, 2007], 119.

3. Obviously Robert Rauschenberg and Jasper Johns were influential in this regard as well. Also in the Rutgers ambit as teachers, students, or neighbors were Geoffrey Hendricks, George Segal, George Brecht, Dick Higgins, Alison Knowles, Robert Whitman, and Lucas Samaras, among others. For this context, see Joan Marter, ed., *Off Limits: Rutgers University and the Avant-Garde, 1957–1963* (Newark: Newark Art Museum, 1999).

4. A few months earlier, Andy Warhol had also turned to motifs drawn from comic strips and product ads, yet he veered away, at least from the comics, upon meeting Lichtenstein in October 1961. This is a place to acknowledge two fine studies of Lichtenstein that have influenced my own thinking: Michael Lobel, *Image Duplicator: Roy Lichtenstein and the Emergence of Pop Art* (New Haven, Conn.: Yale University Press, 2002), and Graham Bader, *Hall of Mirrors: Roy Lichtenstein and the Face of Painting in the 1960s* (Cambridge, Mass.: MIT Press, 2010).

5. The 1962 show included *Turkey, Washing Machine, The Refrigerator, The Engagement Ring, The Kiss, The Grip,* and *Blam*. Early instances of the "banal" epithet are to be found in Dorothy Gees Sackler, "Folklore of the Banal," *Art in America* (Winter 1962), and Brian O'Doherty, "Doubtful but Definite Triumph of the

Banal," *New York Times*, October 27, 1963. "Banality" was a lightning-rod term of the time; witness the great controversy sparked by Hannah Arendt with her thesis of "the banality of evil" in *Eichmann in Jerusalem* (1963). Yet it was not pejorative for some Pop artists; Lichtenstein used it, as did Gerhard Richter (see chapter 4).

6. The Pop repudiation of the Abstract Expressionists is often overstated; in fact most Pop artists, Lichtenstein included, deferred to them even as they sought to move beyond them.

7. His attention to precedents and his practice in studio might also be considered "classical"; see Kevin Hatch, "Roy Lichtenstein: Wit, Invention, and the Afterlife of Pop," in Hal Foster, ed., *Pop at Princeton* (Princeton: Princeton University Art Museum, 2007).

8. Erle Loran, "Cézanne and Lichtenstein: Problems of 'Transformation,'" *Artforum* (September 1963), and "Pop Artists or Copy Cats?" *Art News* (September 1963). Not coincidentally, when Duchamp presented his urinal forty-five years before, he was charged with similar crimes—not copying and banality but plagiarism and obscenity.

9. Lichtenstein describes his process in John Coplans, "Talking with Roy Lichtenstein," *Artforum* (May 1967), reprinted in Madoff, *Pop*, 198–202. For other discussions of his technique, see Diane Waldman, *Roy Lichtenstein* (New York: Guggenheim Museum, 1993), 53–57, and Cowart, *Lichtenstein: Beginning to End*, 34–37. Lichtenstein used some oils (e.g., for his dots) but preferred Magna acrylic for its clean look. His procedure changed a little over time (initially, his dots were made with a dog brush dipped in paint, not stenciled; he began to use a slide projector in fall 1963; etc.)

10. On the other hand, masters of Abstract Expressionist gesture such as Willem de Kooning and Franz Kline sometimes used opaque projectors too. Lichtenstein was cued to the device by a remark made by Kline.

11. Unlike Hamilton, Lichtenstein never used an actual photograph or print as a support. Brian O'Doherty introduced the term "handmade readymade" in "Doubtful but Definite Triumph of the Banal," and David Deitcher developed the notion in "Unsentimental Education"; Lobel is also very good on the subject in *Image Duplicator*. The device of the painted Benday dot was quickly adapted by other artists soon to be associated with Pop—e.g., Gerald Laing, Alain Jacquet, and Sigmar Polke.

12. Lichtenstein in Swenson, "What Is Pop Art?" in Madoff, *Pop Art*, 108. In a similar fashion, Lichtenstein remarked to John Coplans in 1967: "I don't draw a

picture in order to reproduce it—I do it in order to recompose it. Nor am I trying to change it as much as possible. I try to make the minimum amount of change" ("Talking with Lichtenstein," 198). I return to this remark, another staple in the Lichtenstein literature, below.

13. Donald Judd, "In the Galleries," *Arts Magazine* (April 1962), reprinted in Judd, *Complete Writings, 1959–1975* (Halifax: Press of the Nova Scotia College of Art and Design, 1975), 48. This assessment holds true for both types of his initial Pop painting, whether focused, as Lichtenstein remarked, on "one thing isolated," as in *Golf Ball* (1962), or on "the whole arrangement," as in *Popeye* (1961); see John Jones, "Tape-recorded Interview with Roy Lichtenstein, October 5, 1965, 10:00 A.M.," in Graham Bader, ed., *Roy Lichtenstein* (Cambridge, Mass.: MIT Press, 2009), 26. "It's funny, incidentally," Judd added in an *Arts* review of the next show, in 1963, "that the best composition in years, in the word's ordinary sense, is seen only as a copy" (*Complete Writings*, 101).

14. Lichtenstein quoted in Bruce Glaser, "Oldenburg, Lichtenstein, Warhol: A Discussion," *Artforum* (February 1966), reprinted in Madoff, *Pop Art*, 143; Lichtenstein quoted in "Eight Statements," *Art in America* (July–August 1975), reprinted in Bader, *Roy Lichtenstein*, 54. Why does Lichtenstein include Oldenburg in this tradition? Perhaps he saw his work as essentially pictorial.

15. In many instances, Lichtenstein chose images from the comics based on the Lessing criterion of the "the pregnant moment": "It's the ones that sum up the idea that I like the best," he told John Jones ("Interview with Lichtenstein," 25). Lichtenstein also tended to reduce the temporality of his narrative subject in the interests of the instantaneity of his visual impact.

16. Brian O'Doherty coined the first phrase in *American Masters*, 198; Leo Steinberg coined the second in "Other Criteria," 84. The gaze in Lichtenstein also differs from the saccadic gaze prompted by Hamilton, as discussed in chapter 1.

17. Steinberg, *Other Criteria*, 88. This is true even (or especially) when Lichtenstein adopts the window and the mirror as motifs. "My use of evenly repeated dots and diagonal lines and uninflected color areas suggest that my work is *right where it is*, right on the canvas, definitely not *a window into the world*. Also, the dots and diagonal and unmodulated color suggests that my sources are two-dimensional" (Roy Lichtenstein, "About Art," unpublished 1995 paper, extracted in Cowart, *Lichtenstein: Beginning to End*, 128). We tend to read pictorial images in two ways, Walter Benjamin speculated in a short note of 1917, either as representational figures, if they appear in a vertical format (as in most paintings with a visual field

oriented so that we can enter it imaginatively), or as symbolic signs, if they appear in a horizontal format (as in many mosaics). Lichtenstein worked in both modes, representational-figurative and symbolic-semiotic, and often combined the two. See Walter Benjamin, "Painting and the Graphic Arts," in *Selected Writings*, vol. 1.

18. Alan Solomon, "Conversation with Lichtenstein," *Fantazaria* (July–August 1966), reprinted in Johns Coplans, ed., *Roy Lichtenstein* (New York: Praeger, 1972), 68.

19. See Steinberg, "Jasper Johns: The First Seven Years of His Art," in *Other Criteria*. Nonetheless, the painterliness of Johns, however muted, makes his work easier to assimilate to modernist painting.

20. Judd, *Complete Writings*, 48.

21. In 1988, Lichtenstein produced paintings directly modeled on the plus-and-minus Mondrians in question.

22. See Ernst Gombrich, *Art and Illusion* (Princeton, N.J.: Princeton University Press, 1960). Lobel discusses his possible influence on Lichtenstein in *Image Duplicator*, 113–17. Certainly, Gombrich would have supported his interest in cartoons, ads, and comics in particular, and in devices of illusion and questions of conventionality in general. Both men saw representation as a code, to be sure, but for Gombrich, its schema were corrected by observation of nature—such is the principal "story of art" since "the Greek revolution" for him—whereas for Lichtenstein, there is no such march to verisimilitude—the only nature in his work is the "second nature" of the commodity-image world. On the other hand, Lichtenstein shows little of the criticality vis-à-vis nature (first or second) that one finds in Roland Barthes, who also began to investigate representation as a code in the late 1950s and early 1960s.

23. Lichtenstein: "This tension between apparent object-directed products and actual ground-directed processes is an important strength of Pop Art" (quoted in Swenson, "What Is Pop Art?" in Madoff, *Pop Art*, 108).

24. In other paintings, Lichtenstein liked to underscore the force of this blow with the onomatopoeic terms of the comics: his punches go "pow," his guns "blam."

25. See note 83 in chapter 1.

26. Solomon, "Conversation with Lichtenstein," 67. Lichtenstein attributes this response to "the lack of sensibility, the lack of refinement," in consumerist culture at large, more on which below.

27. See chapter 1 for this debate, to which I return below. This disturbance of modernist painting from within might have been more effective than attacks from without, i.e., through an outright embrace of temporal events or theatrical experiences.

28. Swenson, "What Is Pop Art?" in Madoff, *Pop Art*, 108. In the recent literature, the connection to Sherman is discussed by Deitcher, Lobel, and Bader as well as by Bonnie Clearwater in her *Roy Lichtenstein Inside/Outside* (North Miami: Museum of Contemporary Art, 2001).

29. See Hoyt L. Sherman, *Drawing by Seeing: A New Development in the Teaching of the Visual Arts through the Training of Perception* (New York: Hayden and Eldredge, 1947). Lichtenstein used this and similar terms. He also sought to create his own flash lab as an instructor at Oswego and at Rutgers.

30. Deitcher, "Unsentimental Education," 102. Here again we see the difference from the gaze solicited in Hamilton.

31. Bader is especially good on this point.

32. Hamilton, *Collected Words*, 252, 254. This was indeed the case; for example, Lichtenstein first encountered Abstract Expressionist painting in art publications.

33. Jones, "Interview with Lichtenstein," 22. In the same conversation, Lichtenstein describes his parody as "a misconstrued picture of a picture" (22). "A Picasso has become a kind of popular object," Lichtenstein remarked in 1967; "one has the feeling there should be a reproduction of Picasso in every home" (Coplans, "Talking with Lichtenstein," 201). His parodies of other modernist masters, such as Mondrian, Matisse, Miró, and Léger, suggest much the same status of cliché, more on which below.

34. It might be argued that Neo-Impressionist divisionism, with which Lichtenstein aligns his own work, had already made this point. There was a hardening of line and color in Picasso, too, as early as 1915, and certainly in his Synthetic Cubist work, which Lichtenstein once described as "a picture of a collage" (in David Sylvester, *Interviews with American Artists* [New Haven, Conn.: Yale University Press, 2001], 233). In *The Picasso Papers* (New York: Farrar, Straus and Giroux, 1998), Rosalind Krauss argues that this hardening is a symptomatic reaction to the penetration of photography into art practice around Picasso at this time. On the quasi-mechanical aspect in Monet, see Robert L. Herbert, "Method and Meaning in Monet," *Art in America* (September 1979).

35. The "Explosions" emerged at a moment when shape, as a shared property of painting and sculpture, was much disputed and when some artworks became difficult to distinguish from mere objects (I adopt the terms of the celebrated essay by Michael Fried, "Art and Objecthood"). Here Lichtenstein confounds these oppositions: the "Explosions" offer shapes that are neither painting nor sculpture, and though they defeat objecthood, it is not obvious that they do so in the name of art, so insistent is their connection to comic-book signs. Also relevant here are

his still lifes (from the 1970s), a pictorial genre rendered in object form, as well as his brushstrokes (many from the early 1980s on), the most painterly of elements turned into upright figures, the most sculptural of genres. Even his schematic houses (from the mid-1990s on) exist in a no-man's-land between the virtual and the actual, and his painted enamel plaques and layered planes with perforated screens are also hybrid forms. Some present a single profile (a few are quite flat, only as thick as the steel armature), and most favor a single point of view (a few are legible only *en face* or in perspective). Both attributes are essential to the effect of a semi–trompe l'oeil sculpture, for more on which see my "Pop Pygmalion," in Bader, *Roy Lichtenstein.*

36. Jones, "Interview with Roy Lichtenstein," 18; Solomon, "Conversation with Lichtenstein," 67. In a sense, Lichtenstein anticipated here the important account of the economist Ernest Mandel: "Far from representing a 'post-industrial society,' late capitalism thus constitutes *generalized universal industrialization* for the first time in history. Mechanization, standardization, over-specialization, and parcellization of labour, which in the past determined only the realm of commodity production in actual industry, now penetrate into all sectors of social life" (*Late Capital* [London: Verso, 1978], 387).

37. In chapter 3, however, I argue that Warhol did not simply celebrate these effects either.

38. Solomon, "Conversation with Lichtenstein," 66, 67; Swenson, "What Is Pop Art?" in Madoff, *Pop Art,* 107.

39. This strategy runs deep in the history of the avant-garde: "Art is modern art through mimesis of the hardened and alienated," Theodor Adorno wrote in 1970. "Baudelaire neither railed against nor portrayed reification; he protested against it in the experience of its archetypes" (*Aesthetic Theory,* trans. Robert Hullot-Kentor [Minneapolis: University of Minnesota Press, 1997], 21). Here Adorno draws on Benjamin: "The unique importance of Baudelaire resides in his being the first and the most unflinching to have taken the measure of the self-estranged human being, in the double sense of acknowledging this being and fortifying it with armor against the reified world" (*Arcades Project,* 322). On this strategy, see my "Dada Mime," *October* 105 (Summer 2003).

40. Solomon, "Conversation with Lichtenstein," 85; Coplans, "Talking with Lichtenstein," 199; Waldman, *Roy Lichtenstein,* 26. In 1966, Lichtenstein produced several landscapes and seascapes involving Plexiglas, metal, motors, lamps, and a shimmery plastic called Rowlux.

41. John Coplans, "Interview: Roy Lichtenstein," in Coplans, *Roy Lichten-stein,* and reprinted in Bader, *Roy Lichtenstein,* 33. On this series, also see Lawrence

Alloway, "Roy Lichtenstein's Period Style: From the Thirties to the Sixties and Back," *Arts Magazine* (September–October 1967), reprinted in Coplans, *Roy Lichtenstein*. Alloway notes that Art Deco became a fad in the 1960s, but Lichtenstein was interested in its status as cliché more than as kitsch or camp. It is telling that Lichtenstein uses the term "hackneyed." Derived from "hackney," which was "a horse of middle size and quality" (and later a coach of the same status) available for hire, it became associated with hired laborers and prostitutes, and eventually came to mean "used so frequently" as to be "trite and commonplace" (*OED*).

42. Again, see my "Pop Pygmalion" in Bader, *Roy Lichtenstein*. Like his later painting, his sculpture tends to be overlooked because it is taken to be derivative or repetitive of his breakthrough work; obviously, that is not my view.

43. For example, his 1967 modular paintings contain design imagery à la Léger, and in 1975, Lichtenstein produced several paintings after Le Corbusier and Ozenfant. His Neo-Deco paintings were inspired in part by motifs at Radio City Music Hall. Relevant here is his own background in design: in the 1950s in Cleveland, Lichtenstein worked intermittently as an engineering draftsman at Republic Steel and for Hickok Electrical Instrument Company; he also decorated display windows for Halle's Department Store and made models for an architecture firm. See the excellent chronology compiled by Claire Bell in Cowart, *Lichtenstein: Beginning to End*, and in other Lichtenstein catalogues.

44. Walter Benjamin, "Paris, Capital of the Nineteenth Century," *Arcades Project*, 9.

45. At some point, Lichtenstein wrote out a list of such utterances: "Thwack, Thung, Ratat, Varoom, Pling, Beeow" (see Michael Juul Holm, Martin Caiger-Smith, and Poul Erik Tøjner, eds., *Roy Lichtenstein: All about Art* [Copenhagen: Louisiana Museum of Modern Art, 2003], 29). Onomatopoeic terms are often mistaken for the most natural of words; like Ed Ruscha (as we will see in chapter 5), Lichtenstein suggests that they are conventional in their own way—and, at least in the context of comics, commodified as well.

46. See André Malraux, *The Voices of Silence*, trans. Stuart Gilbert (Princeton, N.J.: Princeton University Press, 1978). Lichtenstein produced several studios and interiors after Matisse in the 1990s, but they are less reprises of his art à la Matisse than arrangements of his art (and others) as modish décor.

47. These propositions can be extracted, respectively, from Peter Bürger, *Theory of the Avant-Garde*, trans. Michael Shaw (1974; Minneapolis: University of Minnesota Press, 1984), and Baudrillard, *Political Economy of the Sign* (1972). "One is no longer the truth of the other," Baudrillard writes of image and object as treated

in Pop; "they coexist *in extenso* and in the very same logical space, where they 'act' as signs (in their differential, reversible, combinatory relation)" (*La société de consommation: Ses mythes, ses structures* [Paris: Gallimard, 1970], 175).

48. Allan Kaprow quoted in Avis Berman, "The Transformations of Roy Lichtenstein: An Oral History," in Holm, Caiger-Smith, and Tøjner, *Lichtenstein: All about Art*, 126.

49. Sylvester, *Interviews with American Artists*, 222–23. As we will see, Ruscha is also interested in this doubleness of the standard.

50. Ibid., 226–27. Lichtenstein did not classicize his commercial images either (as Le Corbusier and Léger were wont to do); rather, he suggested how classical idioms—from columns to the criterion of compositional unity—had become clichés in their own right, more on which below. This clichéd classicism almost reads as a riposte to postmodern style before the fact.

51. Coplans, "Talking with Lichtenstein," 201. In his 1966 conversation with Sylvester, Lichtenstein implied that cartoonists were indeed informed in this way. On the modernist sophistication of the comics, see Scott McCloud, *Understanding Comics* (New York: Harper Perennial, 1994).

52. Cowart, *Lichtenstein: Beginning to End*, 118–19.

53. Coplans, "Talking with Lichtenstein," 199.

54. In this desire to compete with spectacle, there is a relation to Léger more important than any stylistic connection. In this move "from cliché to archetype," there is also a relation to McLuhan, who published a text with this title in 1970.

55. Lichtenstein is again close here to Ruscha, as we will see. This defamiliarization places both, unexpectedly, in the lineage of Russian formalism.

56. The cross on the side might recall the Suprematist cups that Kazimir Malevich designed in the early 1920s.

57. Gombrich, *Art and Illusion*, 42.

58. See Krauss, *Picasso Papers*, and Lobel, *Image Duplicator*, 148–50.

59. Waldman, *Roy Lichtenstein*, 28. The dots are the stuff sometimes of his figures (or faces), sometimes of his grounds, and sometimes of both. Lichtenstein also activated this semiotic dimension in his first Pop objects: though already three-dimensional, his heads and cups are also covered with dots and stripes that signify the modeling of an object in light and shadow. The redundancy of these signs for volume and depth further underscores their conventional status.

The early 1960s saw a revival in semiotic analysis, and in his review of the 1963 Lichtenstein show at Castelli, Judd proposed that his paintings "suggest metalinguistics" (*Complete Writings*, 101). For a semiotic account of a comic strip contemporaneous with early Pop, see Umberto Eco, "A Reading of Steve Canyon" (1964), reprinted in Sheena Wagstaff, ed., *Comic Iconoclasm* (London: Institute of Contemporary Arts, 1987). Eco also offered a semiotic account of Pop in "Lowbrow Highbrow, Highbrow Lowbrow," *Times Literary Supplement* (October 1971), 1209–11.

60. Lichtenstein sometimes points to his differential way of working, as he does here: "My emphasis was in forming the relationship of mark-to-mark" (Lichtenstein, "A Review of My Work Since 1961," in Bader, *Roy Lichtenstein*, 60). Or again here: "Every mark you make, every line you put down, can't bear any relationships to representation or representational space at the moment it's being put down" (quoted in Waldman, *Roy Lichtenstein*, 26). Technically, if a language is understood, in Saussurean terms, as a system of differences with no positive values, there is literally nothing to harden or to reify. However, Lichtenstein accepts the visual positivity of the cliché and uses the semantic negativity—or at least the semantic mobility—of the sign to open up the cliché. Apposite here is Fredric Jameson on the prose of Wyndham Lewis: "His 'method,' if we can call it that, is to use the cliché against itself—or better still, to pit clichés on the level of gestural images against the verbal clichés with which the sentences themselves are hopelessly corroded. In this way, a kind of perceptual freshness is reinvented out of the unexpectedly virulent interaction of stale and faded substances" (*Fables of Aggression: Wyndham Lewis, the Modernist as Fascist* [Berkeley and Los Angeles: University of California Press, 1979], 73).

61. Waldman, *Roy Lichtenstein*, 26. There is a related wresting of the creative out of the commodified in his onomatopoeic terms.

62. Daniel-Henry Kahnweiler, "Preface," in Brassaï, *The Sculptures of Picasso*, trans. A.D.B. Sylvester (London: Rodney Phillips, 1949). Also see Kahnweiler, "Negro Art and Cubism," *Présence africaine* 3 (1948): 367–77. In "Kahnweiler's Lesson," Yve-Alain Bois explicates the semiotic dimension in Cubism brilliantly (see *Painting as Model* [Cambridge, Mass.: MIT Press, 1990]), as does Krauss in *Picasso Papers* and other texts, but Lichtenstein had already explored this dimension in his art.

63. While, as Krauss argues, Picasso was reactive about abstraction and photography, Lichtenstein embraced both (*Picasso Papers*, 141–54).

64. Sylvester, *Interviews with American Artists*, 231. "I am more interested," Lichtenstein commented in 1971, "in making a new meaning of an old meaning" (Waldman, *Roy Lichtenstein*, 26). In *Picasso Papers*, Krauss describes this process, with reference to Stéphane Mallarmé, as follows: "When stripped of its commodified exchange value, this coin [in the sense here of cliché] was instead endowed by

the modernist artist with the substitutional condition of the sign in its continual play of circulation" (76).

65. As noted at the outset, Lichtenstein layers manual and mechanical procedures in a way that mitigates reification. Other doubles in his work might have a similar effect, including some not mentioned above, such as affective content verses cool technique, visual impact versus narrative duration, and pictorial singularity versus sculptural mutability of perspective.

66. Lichtenstein quoted in Alloway, "Lichtenstein's Period Style," 145; Lichtenstein, "Review of My Work," 66. On the other hand, as Alloway notes, the revival of Art Deco in the 1960s made it "visible, even conspicuous again." Lichtenstein directs his parodies less at the original styles than at what "new contexts" have done to them (sometimes in a manner that calls up the old Marx maxim "the first time as tragedy, the second as farce"). In the process, historical insight might be gleaned, as Alloway intimates here: "The forms of the thirties are symbols of an antique period with a naïve ideal of a modernity discontinuous with our own" (145).

67. Steinberg, "'The Algerian Women' and Picasso," 128.

68. Ernst Gombrich discusses this fascination in *Aby Warburg: An Intellectual Biography* (Chicago: University of Chicago Press, 1986), 105–27. See the relevant papers collected in Warburg, *The Renewal of Pagan Antiquity*, trans. David Britt (Los Angeles: Getty Research Institute, 1999).

69. Karl Marx, "A Contribution to the Critique of Hegel's Philosophy of Right, Introduction" (1844), in *Early Writings*, ed. T. B. Bottomore (New York: McGraw-Hill, 1964), 47 (translation modified).

70. See Lobel, *Image Duplicator*, 136–44. In "Visual Pleasure and Narrative Cinema" (1975), Laura Mulvey argues that such Hollywood cinema aligns woman, surface, screen, and spectacle; see her *Visual and Other Pleasures*.

71. Coplans, "Talking with Lichtenstein," 202. Lichtenstein continues: "They put their lips on in a certain shape and do their hair to resemble a certain ideal. There is an interaction that is very intriguing. I've always wanted to make up someone as a cartoon." Of course, maquillage already preoccupied Baudelaire, who writes "in praise of cosmetics" for the artificial ideality it bestows on women (*Painter of Modern Life*, 31–34). It also figures importantly in Manet; see Jean Clay, "Ointments, Makeup, Pollen," *October* 27 (Winter 1983). Fried disputes Clay, and his remarks on "facingness" in Manet and his peers are also suggestive here; see *Manet's Modernism*.

72. Swenson, "What Is Pop Art?" in Madoff, *Pop Art*, 109. "What liberates metaphor, symbol, emblem from poetic mania, what manifest its power of subversion,"

Barthes writes, "is the preposterous" (*Roland Barthes by Roland Barthes* [New York: Hill and Wang, 1977], 81).

73. Deitcher and Lobel also discuss these connections. In chapter 3, I return to the postwar training and testing of the subject.

74. This association is implicit elsewhere in other modernist art, as Deitcher points out; think, for example, of how Moholy-Nagy developed his idea of "the new vision," produced by the spread of photography and film in the 1920s, into a pedagogy of design in his New Bauhaus in Chicago in the 1940s. These ideas were in turn elaborated by the Moholy associate Gyorgy Kepes in *Language of Vision* (1944) and other texts, which Sherman read closely. This continuum between "art vision" and "machine vision" is a particular concern of the work of Paul Virilio.

75. This aggressivity has become patent in our video-gaming present.

76. Swenson, "What Is Pop Art?" in Madoff, *Pop Art*, 108.

77. Sylvester, *Interviews with American Artists*, 224. Also see Lobel, *Image Duplicator*, 49–50, and Clearwater, *Roy Lichtenstein Inside/Outside*, 32–33.

78. Solomon, "Conversation with Lichtenstein," 67.

79. On targeting, see Samuel Weber, *Targets of Opportunity: On the Militarization of Thinking* (New York: Fordham University Press, 2005).

80. As Lobel notes, Warhol does not efface the brand names, but, as I suggest in chapter 3, he finds his own ways to distress the image.

81. Lobel, *Image Duplicator*, 120.

82. Ibid., 42–55, here 47. On the other hand, Kirk Varnedoe and Adam Gopnik claim that his early paintings make "the comic images more like the comics than the comics were themselves" (*High and Low: Modern Art and Popular Culture* [New York: Museum of Modern Art, 1991], 199). Sylvester suggested much the same thing in 1965.

83. Lobel, *Image Duplicator*, 73.

84. Coplans, "Talking with Lichtenstein," 198.

85. See Benjamin H. D. Buchloh, "Residual Resemblance: Three Notes on the Ends of Portraiture," in Melissa Feldman, ed., *Face-Off: The Portrait in Recent Art* (Philadelphia: Institute of Contemporary Art, 1994). In *Hall of Mirrors*, Bader reads these mirror paintings as forms of self-presence realized through self-negation.

86. Bruce Glaser, "Oldenburg, Lichtenstein, Warhol: A Discussion," *Artforum* (February 1966), reprinted in Madoff, *Pop Art*, 145 (the conversation was first presented on the radio in 1964). Here I disagree in part with Buchloh, who, in "Parody and Appropriation in Francis Picabia, Pop, and Sigmar Polke" (1982), sees

such parody "as a mode of ultimate complicity and secret reconciliation." Certainly, there is no "transgression of the code" in Lichtenstein, but a space of difference is also opened up. See Buchloh, *Neo-Avantgarde and Culture Industry: Essays on European and American Art from 1955 to 1975* (Cambridge, Mass.: MIT Press, 2000), 353, 363.

87. However, this is less the case when these same masters begin to flood his work in the late 1970s; indeed, in his late still lifes and studio scenes, Lichtenstein often lapses into the eclecticism of pastiche, which, in its mix of styles and signatures, is styleless, even subjectless, in implication. On the difference between parody and pastiche in this respect, see Fredric Jameson, *Postmodernism* (Durham, N.C.: Duke University Press, 1993).

3   Andy Warhol, or the Distressed Image

1. Jean Stein, *Edie: An American Biography* (New York: Knopf, 1982), 245–46.

2. See my "Death in America," *October* 75 (Winter 1996), reprinted in Annette Michelson, ed., *Andy Warhol* (Cambridge, Mass.: MIT Press, 2001), where I develop the notion of "traumatic realism." The next seven paragraphs are adapted from that text.

3. Swenson, "What Is Pop Art?" reprinted in Kenneth Goldsmith, ed., *I'll Be Your Mirror: The Selected Andy Warhol Interviews, 1962–1987* (New York: Carroll and Graf, 2004), 18.

4. Ibid.

5. I hesitate between "production" and "consumption" in part because Warhol was formed during the shift in dominance from the first order to the second: born in 1928 and raised in industrial Pittsburgh (his father was a construction and mine worker), Warhol became active in both advertising and art worlds on his arrival in New York in 1949.

6. In chapter 2 we saw that Lichtenstein practices a mimesis of the "hard" and "deadening" aspects of the culture, but Warhol takes it to the limit. Since his time, many artists (e.g., Jeff Koons, Damien Hirst, and Takashi Murakami) have adopted this strategy, perhaps playing it out. For more on mimetic exacerbation, see my "Dada Mime."

7. Undated statement by Warhol quoted in McShine, *Andy Warhol*, 457.

8. Andy Warhol and Pat Hackett, *POPism: The Warhol '60s* (New York: Harcourt Brace Jovanovich, 1980), 50. Lichtenstein provides an instructive contrast to Warhol on the question of transformation.

9. Swenson, "What Is Pop Art?" in Goldsmith, *I'll Be Your Mirror*, 19.

10. This distinction is drawn, of course, from Sigmund Freud, "Mourning and Melancholia" (1917).

11. In effect, Warhol elaborates on the notion of the "optical unconscious" introduced by Walter Benjamin to evoke a new order of visuality, beyond the naked eye, opened up by modern instruments of seeing and imaging. Benjamin proposed the notion in the early 1930s in response to technical advances in photography and film; Warhol updated it thirty years later in response to the postwar society of the spectacle, its image factory of mass media, technological disasters, tabloid exposés, and the like. In Benjamin, however, the optical unconscious is mostly a matter of the unseen, and he advocates its exploration with a modernist faith in new media; in Warhol, on the other hand, it approaches the unconscious precisely because it touches on the traumatic. Especially in the "Death and Disaster" paintings, we glimpse what it looked like to dream in the heyday of black-and-white television, *Life*, and *Newsweek*; or rather, what it looked like to suffer nightmares then, like so many shock victims who struggle to prepare for disasters that have already come. But, it must be acknowledged, these repetitions can sometimes generate pleasure, even in the case of the most gruesome images: traumatic repetition, Warhol suggests, is not always "beyond the pleasure principle," at least not in a society of spectacle that has learned to turn even "death and disaster" to its profit. See Benjamin, "Little History of Photography" and "Art in the Age of Its Technological Reproducibility" (both in *Selected Writings*, vol. 3).

12. See Lacan, *Four Fundamental Concepts*, 17–64.

13. See my *Compulsive Beauty*.

14. Lacan, *Four Fundamental Concepts*, 50.

15. Warhol introduced the device of "the blank" with *Silver Electric Chairs* (1963), giving as a flip reason that selling more painting meant getting more money. For Benjamin Buchloh, these blanks void the exalted ambition of the modernist monochrome (see "Warhol's One-Dimensional Art," 21–22). Certainly, the putative presentness of such modernist canvases is put in question, but it is not voided so much as turned toward its opposite—absence, death or (to use the word that hovers above the electric chairs) "silence." The blank in Warhol sometimes serves as a correlative of a blanking or blackout of the subject in shock.

16. Roland Barthes, *Camera Lucida*, trans. Richard Howard (New York: Hill and Wang, 1981), 26, 55. For an account of the connection between Barthes and Lacan, see Margaret Iversen, "What Is a Photograph?" *Art History* 17, no. 3 (September 1994), 450–64.

17. "I am trying here to grasp how the *tuché* is represented in visual apprehension," Lacan states. "I shall show that it is at the level that I call the stain that the tychic point in the scopic function is found" (*Four Fundamental Concepts*, 77). This point, then, is not in the world but in the subject, but in the subject as an effect, a shadow or a "stain" cast by the gaze of the world. Lacan argues that this gaze "qua *objet a* might come to symbolize this central lack expressed in the phenomenon of castration" (ibid.). In short, the gaze asks à la Warhol, "Where Is Yo__ Rupture?" (Here the break in the pronoun seems weirdly appropriate.)

18. The question was also prophetic, for after his shooting, Warhol was compelled to wear a corset. I return to the relation of image to subject in Warhol below.

19. Gretchen Berg, "Andy: My True Story," in Goldsmith, *I'll Be Your Mirror*, 90.

20. According to Freud, it takes two traumas to make a trauma. That is, for a trauma to be registered as such, a first event must be revived by a second event that the subject, now older, can understand; this is what Freud meant by the deferred (*nachträglich*) action of the traumatic. A related temporality seems to be embedded in some Warhol canvases, such as *White Burning Car*.

21. Barthes: "It is acute yet muffled, it cries out in silence. Odd contradiction: a floating flash" (*Camera Lucida*, 53). "Floating flash" calls to mind the famous Lacanian anecdote of the sardine can told in "The Gaze as *Objet Petit a*," a seminar that, again, is roughly contemporaneous with the *Tunafish Disasters*.

22. The real, Lacan puns, is *trou*matic; it pokes a hole in the subject, as it were, or, rather, it probes one that is already there. Again, the stain in *Ambulance Disaster* is a correlative of such a tear for me; it appears almost anamorphic, and so might recall the anamorphic skull in *The Ambassadors* (1533) by Hans Holbein, a memento mori that Lacan reads as a phallus—that is, a figure of castration—as well (see *Four Fundamental Concepts*). According to this association, then, death is again the subject here, and not only at the level of manifest content. There are other quasi-anamorphic stains in Warhol that are "punctal" in this sense, but not linked to death, thematically, at all.

23. Warhol and Hackett, *POPism*, 22.

24. Lacan, *Four Fundamental Concepts*, 54.

25. Warhol, *Philosophy of Andy Warhol*, 81. In "Warhol's One-Dimensional Art," Buchloh argues that consumers "can celebrate in Warhol's work their proper status of having been erased as subjects" (57). This is the opposite of the position argued by Thomas Crow, namely, that Warhol exposes "complacent consumption" (see his "Saturday Disasters: Trace and Reference in Early Warhol" [1986], reprinted in Michelson, *Andy Warhol*). Yet, rather than choose between the two, we might think of them together, as I attempt to do in "Death in America."

26. De Antonio recounts the story to Patrick S. Smith in Smith, *Andy Warhol's Art and Films* (Ann Arbor: UMI Press, 1986), 293. Warhol also tells it in *POPism*.

27. Warhol had his nose altered in 1956 and was disappointed by the result.

28. On the rupturing of language in Warhol, see the smart analysis in Wayne Koestenbaum, *Andy Warhol* (New York: Viking, 2002). Early as well as late, Warhol would project these images from ads and comics and paint them in directly on the canvas.

29. Just as the *Close Cover*s might be seen to parody the color fields of late-modernist abstraction, so the *Dance Diagram*s might be taken to mock the aesthetic of the spontaneous and the participatory, from Pollock to Happenings; see Buchloh, "Warhol's One Dimensional Art," 21–22. Warhol shows a persistent interest in damage. For example, in 1970 he curated a show called "Raid the Icebox" at the Rhode Island School of Design, in which he exhibited pictures from the collection that were stained or punctured, and he prized some *Marilyn* silk screens that had been shot by a Factory intruder.

30. Apart from the forty *Oxidation*s, there are some paintings drizzled with semen, the so-called *Come* paintings. The early *Piss* paintings are now lost, and the documentary evidence is scant (they are represented by one photograph in the catalogue raisonné). When asked about his nonrepresentational work in a 1976 interview, Warhol replied: "The only ones I know about are the piss paintings; I have a couple. That was a long time ago. Then there were canvases I used to leave on the street and people used to walk on them; in the end I had a lot of dirty canvases. Then I thought they were all diseased and so I rolled them up and put them somewhere" (*Unmuzzled Ox* 4, no. 2 [1976], 44, as quoted in Georg Frei and Neil Printz, eds., *Warhol: Painting and Sculpture, 1961–1963* [London: Phaidon, 2002], 469).

31. On desublimation in Warhol, see Krauss, *Optical Unconscious*, and Benjamin Buchloh, "A Primer for the Urochrome Painting," in Mark Francis, ed., *Andy Warhol: The Late Work* (Munich: Prestel Verlag, 2004); also see Michael Moon, "Screen Memories, or, Pop Comes from the Outside: Warhol and Queer Childhood," in

Jennifer Doyle, Jonathan Flatley, and José Esteban Muñoz, *Pop Out: Queer Warhol* (Durham, N.C.: Duke University Press, 1996).

32. Contrary to the common understanding of Benjamin, mechanical reproduction does not automatically sap the uniqueness and authenticity of the original; rather, especially in "Art in the Age of Its Technological Reproducibility," the very concept of "an original" depends on the existence of "a copy." Here again, Warhol qualifies Benjamin, for his copies often do erode his originals.

33. This paradoxical release of difference through repetition makes Warhol a suggestive example for the philosophy of Gilles Deleuze.

34. As we will see in chapter 4, this devaluation of the image through sheer proliferation is also performed at times by Gerhard Richter.

35. See Rainer Crone, "Form and Ideology: Warhol's Techniques from Blotted Line to Film," in Gary Garrels, ed., *The Work of Andy Warhol* (Seattle: Bay Press, 1989).

36. Indexical procedures qualify the role not only of the sender but also of the receiver. Charles Sanders Pierce, who developed the concept of the index, argued that indices are less in need of the "interpretant" than other signs (his example, suggestive vis-à-vis Warhol, is a bullet hole). See C. S. Peirce, "Logic as Semiotic," in *Philosophical Writings of Peirce,* ed. Justus Buchler (New York: Dover, 1955), 102.

37. On dedifferentiation, an influential notion in American art of the late 1960s, see Anton Ehrenzweig, *The Hidden Order of Art* (Berkeley and Los Angeles: University of California Press, 1967). We say that Warhol returned to abstraction in his last decade, but that term suggests a stability of picturing that this work does not possess; it is more like "decreation."

38. Oddly enough, Warhol is close here to Max Horkheimer and Theodor Adorno in *Dialectic of Enlightenment* (1944); the *Diamond Dust Shoes* do suggest a holocaust of the glamorous. (Ironically, too, Warhol produced the *Reflected* paintings with the Speer image for the 1982 "Zeitgeist" show in West Berlin, curated by Norman Rosenthal to promote Neo-Expressionist painting.) Moreover, the early optical paintings suggest an undoing of the "opticality" of Color Field abstraction affirmed by Clement Greenberg and Michael Fried, one that undercuts the self-possessed viewer whom such abstraction was said to support.

39. Sigmund Freud, "Psychogenic Visual Disturbance According to Psychoanalytical Conceptions" (1910), in *Character and Culture*, ed. Phillip Rieff (New York: Collier, 1963), 55.

40. Fried, "Three American Painters," 228. Also see "Torn Screens" in my *Prosthetic Gods*.

41. Lacan, *Four Fundamental Concepts*, 89, 109.

42. Ibid., 96. The association of jewels and genitals would not be lost on Warhol, who did both drawings and silk screens of penises.

43. Duchamp, *Essential Writings*, 32.

44. Duchamp in Pierre Cabanne, *Dialogues with Marcel Duchamp* (London: Thames and Hudson, 1971), 61. Duchamp was in Buenos Aires at the time.

45. Andy Warhol, *America* (New York: Harper and Row, 1985), 129; *Philosophy of Andy Warhol*, 113. In large part, this is precisely a performance: there is a subject "behind" this blank figure who presents it *as* a figure. Yet part of the fascination of Warhol is that one never feels certain about this subject "behind": is anybody home, underneath the silver wig and the thick glasses, inside the automaton? (In his *Myth* series (1981), Warhol used a self-portrait for the image in *The Shadow*, and his 1986 *Self-Portrait*s show him effectively decapitated.)

46. Koestenbaum, *Andy Warhol*, 2. In general, Koestenbaum argues, the typical Warhol move was to embed a "lurid subject" in a "cool presentation" in order to "embalm" it (152). Perhaps it was in the service of this same ambiguous end of control by gathering that, after 1974, Warhol diarized the bric-a-brac of his life in "time capsules," cardboard boxes filled with mementos and ephemera (there were more than 600 left in his estate).

47. It is a query that might also be related to multiple perplexities of his youth—about childhood trauma (his father died suddenly when Warhol was thirteen), gender identity ("Masculinity was a subject he failed from the start," as Koestenbaum puts it [*Andy Warhol*, 20]), and social position (the Warholas were persistently poor). Warhol also experienced a multitude of little ruptures—chorea, bad skin, premature baldness, and so on. See Karin Schick, "'The Red Lobster's Beauty': Correction and Pain in the Art of Andy Warhol," in Mark Francis, ed., *Andy Warhol: Photography* (Zurich: Edition Stemmle), 1999.

48. Perhaps in compensation, Warhol imbued his illustrations of the 1950s with an elegant nonchalance.

49. Henry Geldzahler, his longtime friend and Metropolitan Museum of Art curator, used the term "baffle" in relation to Warhol, as quoted in Stephen Koch, *Stargazer: Andy Warhol's World and His Films* (New York: Praeger, 1973), 25; and Peter Wollen considers it briefly in "Notes from the Underground: Andy Warhol," in *Raiding the Icebox: Reflections on Twentieth-Century Culture* (Bloomington: Indiana University Press, 1993), 165. The *OED* defines "baffle" as a plate that regulates passage in and out, and "to baffle" as "to reduce to perplexity"; both are fitting vis-à-vis

Warhol. In an homage to Warhol, Robert Rauschenberg touched on his iconic-ghostly doubling: "In his stardom Warhol became capable, as his own shadow, to control his mass" (in McShine, *Andy Warhol*, 429).

50. For more on this imaging, see Buchloh, "Residual Resemblance," and Candace Breitz, "The Warhol Portrait: From Art to Business and Back Again," in Francis, *Andy Warhol: Photography*.

51. See Benjamin, "On Some Motifs in Baudelaire," in Hannah Arendt, ed., *Illuminations* (New York: Schocken, 1968), 174–75. Benjamin made these comments vis-à-vis film in a manner also relevant to Warhol, as we will see below. For a classic text on mechanization, see Siegfried Giedeon, *Mechanization Takes Command: A Contribution to Anonymous History* (Oxford: Oxford University Press, 1948). The shock of this "snapping" is diminished with digital cameras.

52. Benjamin, "On Some Motifs in Baudelaire," 175. In a mock interview in 1963, Gerard Malanga asked Warhol, "What is your occupation?" and he replied, "Factory owner" (in Goldsmith, *I'll Be Your Mirror*, 48).

53. Benjamin, "On Some Motifs in Baudelaire," 176.

54. Philip Johnson, the commissioner of the New York State Pavilion, used this out-of-dateness to justify the suppression of the work at the 1964 World's Fair, where it was first shown on the pavilion façade, only then to be effaced, by order of Johnson, with silver paint. Other rationales were given (such as possible offense to Italian constituents!), but the effective reason seems evident enough (criminality is not the best advertisement for spectacle). Urban legend has it that Warhol offered, in a superb piece of deadpan irony, to substitute a portrait of Robert Moses, the president of the fair, but no such work has come to light.

55. See Richard Meyer, "Warhol's Clones," *Yale Journal of Criticism* 7, no. 1 (1994).

56. As we saw in chapter 1, Richard Hamilton also underscores this anxious selectivity of image in *My Marilyn* (1965).

57. By the early 1980s, Warhol had developed an archive of these parts, which he used freely in his silk screens.

58. I have in mind Freud on narcissism and Lacan on the mirror stage, among other texts (see note 17 in the Introduction). "I usually accept people on the basis of their self-images," Warhol writes in *The Philosophy of Andy Warhol*, "because their self-images have more to do with the way they think than their objective-images do" (69). However, many of his silk screens play on the gap between objective-image and self-image, body and ideal body, ego and ideal ego—a gap in which many of

the "untitled film stills" of Cindy Sherman operate as well. On this point, see my *Return of the Real*.

59. Edgar Morin, *The Stars: An Account of the Star-System in Motion Pictures* (New York: Grove, 1960; originally published in 1957), 137. On commodification and or as personification in Warhol, see Jonathan Flatley, "Warhol Gives Good Face: Publicity and the Politics of Prosopopoeia," in Doyle, Flatley, and Muñoz, *Pop Out: Queer Warhol*.

60. Michael Warner, "The Mass Public and the Mass Subject," in Bruce Robbins, ed., *The Phantom Public Sphere* (Minneapolis: University of Minnesota Press, 1993), 250. In a gloss on Jürgen Habermas on the public sphere (in which, in principle, we are treated as equal because we do not appear as marked bodies), Warner describes the partial reembodiment that occurs in mass culture as follows: "Where printed public discourse formerly relied on a rhetoric of abstract disembodiment, visual media—including print—now display bodies for a range of purposes: admiration, identification, appropriation, scandal, and so forth. To be public in the West means to have an iconicity, and this is true equally of Muammar Qaddafi and Karen Carpenter" (242). It is this relation between publicity and iconicity, and its volatility for mass subject and mass icon alike, that Warhol reframes from his *Marilyns* to his *Maos* and beyond. Of course, Warhol not only evoked the mass subject but also incarnated it, and did so precisely in its guise as witness. This witnessing was not as neutral or impassive as it appeared; it involved an erotics, both voyeuristic and exhibitionistic, both sadistic and masochistic. This is where the principle that "the mass subject cannot have a body except the body it witnesses" must be qualified. For we members of the mass also retain our individual bodies of desires, fears, and fantasies in a way that allows us to customize mass objects in personal or group ways—in the case of Warhol and friends, to camp images of Elvis, Troy, Warren, Marlon, and other wanted men as objects of gay desire.

61. Ibid., 250.

62. Berg, "Andy Warhol: My True Story," 90. Given how Warhol identified with these products, there might be an implicit connection between these images and his own body image.

63. Benjamin, "Little History of Photography," 510.

64. In a sense, the sitter is laid bare to the same extent that Warhol is self-protected (or self-baffled).

65. Letitia Kent, "Andy Warhol, Movieman: 'It's Hard to Be Your Own Script'" (1970), in Goldsmith, *I'll Be Your Mirror*, 187. This being-your-own-script might

be less difficult in our age of MySpace, Facebook, and so on (as the latter-day Warholian videos of Ryan Trecartin suggest), but it is also more insistent.

66. As Callie Angell writes, "Some subjects seem overcome with self-consciousness, squinting into the bright lights, swallowing nervously or visibly trembling, while others rise to the occasion with considerable force of personality and self-assurance, meeting the gaze of Warhol's camera with equal power. As the collection of *Screen Tests* grew, these provoked responses gradually became the overt purpose or content of the films, superseding the original goal of the achieved, static image" (Callie Angell, *Andy Warhol Screen Tests: The Films of Andy Warhol, Catalogue Raisonné, Volume 1* [New York: Abrams, 2006], 14). This volume is a treasure for Warhol studies.

67. "Some later *Screen Tests*," Angell writes, "seem to have been deliberately staged to make things as difficult as possible for the subjects" (ibid., 14).

68. For example, Jonas Mekas barely blinks, yet in time his eyes water, he gulps awkwardly, etc.

69. Angell, *Andy Warhol Screen Tests*, 206.

70. Ibid., 150. This is a suggestive formulation, but what does it mean? Imagining your own image, trying to shape it, to project it, to sustain it, and to interpret it all at the same time? (Warhol produced his own *Rorschach* paintings in 1984, more on which below.) One might see the *Screen Tests* almost as police interrogations in which both the police and the interrogation are internal, i.e., roles assumed by the superego.

71. Ibid., 109.

72. See Benjamin, "Art in the Age of Its Technological Reproducibility," 111.

73. Ibid.

74. Indeed, as Christopher Phillips has argued, Warhol "moves toward a symbolic identification with the position of the technological apparatus—with the 'gaze of the machine'" ("Desiring Machines," in Gary Garrels, ed., *Public Information: Desire, Disaster, Document* [San Francisco: San Francisco Museum of Art, 1995], 45). My reading that Warhol is intent on exposing individual "ruptures" keyed by sexual difference might contradict my reading that a shared "humanity" also exists in the distress in question here, but this contradiction is in the work, and it is not resolved there. In a personal communication David Joselit suggested that pleasure might also be found in this testing, especially it if is seen as a "tournament of gazes" that allows for desire.

75. Some films suggest a semi-sadomasochistic theater that was sometimes extended to the Factory at large. Certainly there was a psychological volatility to the

Factory roles, with Warhol as a director who was by turns kind and cold, passive and aggressive (he was called "Drella," a fitting contraction of Cinderella, dreaming of the ball, and Dracula, sucking the blood of others), with a great tension between inhibition and excess, withdrawal and exhibitionism, deathly stillness and sexual motility, narcissism and aggressivity. For a view of the Factory as a social microcosm in Bakhtinian reversal, see Annette Michelson, "'Where Is Your Rupture?' Mass Culture and the *Gesamtkunstwerk*," in Michelson, *Andy Warhol*. For a view of the Factory as a new space of gay relationality, see Douglas Crimp, "Misfitting Together," *October* 132 (Spring 2010). In the end, the *Screen Tests* were not the most intense assaults on the ego orchestrated by Warhol. In this respect, first prize must go to the Exploding Plastic Inevitable events, in which the immersive aspects of spectacle were exacerbated. See Branden Joseph, "'Mind Split Open': Andy Warhol's Exploding Plastic Inevitable," *Grey Room* 8 (Summer 2002).

76. Angell, *Andy Warhol Screen Tests*, 14. In this regard, these "stillies" do break down the distinction between film and photograph upheld by Barthes (and others), as here paraphrased by Raymond Bellour: "On one side, there is movement, the present, presence; on the other, immobility, the past, a certain absence. On one side, the consent of illusion; on the other, a quest for hallucination. Here, a fleeting image, one that seizes us in its flight; there, a completely still image that cannot be fully grasped. On this side, time doubles life; on that, time returns to us brushed by death" ("The Pensive Spectator" [1984], in *Wide Angle* 9, no 1. [1987], reprinted in David Campany, ed., *The Cinematic* [Cambridge, Mass.: MIT Press, 2007], 119).

77. In a personal communication, Jeremy Melius made this important point: "The films are about wanting to—consenting to—this rigorous scenario, and as if by necessity failing to live up to it. What might it mean, and what might it take, to make oneself present to a camera—make oneself be *there* for a full three minutes? And, perhaps even worse, what might it mean to discover that you simply can't, not *even* for three minutes? I read this as a weird analogue to the viewer's experience of watching someone not really there—not quite present enough to be really there."

78. Different though they are, these two types of representation evince the deep interest that Warhol had in repetition as such, an interest that is as formal and structural as it is psychological and social (after all, he puts his human referents—friends and acquaintances—in the service of repetition rather than the reverse). As with the silk screens, then, one can read the *Screen Tests* strictly for the content—as so many minidocumentaries of New York bohemians in the mid-1960s—but that would be to miss what is most provocative about them.

79. Peter Galison reads the Rorschach cards as "a technology of the self": "In the world of Rorschach's inkblots, subjects makes objects, of course: 'I see a woman,' 'I see a wolf's head.' But objects also make subjects: 'depressive,' 'schizophrenic.' Properly understood, the now canonical Rorschach test system measures but also reinforces a particular (and specifically modern) integrated, interior self" ("Image of Self," in Lorraine Daston, ed., *Things That Talk* [Cambridge, Mass.: MIT Press, 2004], 258–59). Although the shapes in the Rorschach cards were calculated, Rorschach wanted them to "register as undesigned designs, unpainted paintings . . . In order for the subject to speak, the card, and the card's author, had to find a perfect silence" (270–71). The Warhol *Rorschach*s are also undesigned, given that they are mostly black blots doubled by folding the half of canvas with wet paint back on itself. But the subject-effect is quite different from that of the Rorschach cards. For Galison, the Rorschach test "marks a shift in the logic of the self: *from* aggregate powers manipulating specific contents *to* a framing disposition in which experience is necessarily situated—self as form, not content . . . To describe the card (on the outside) *is exactly* to say who you are (on the inside) . . . That historical apperceptive self is picked out by its insistence on relations of depth and surface, inner and outer life, and the inseparability of ideation and affect." Warhol challenged each of these relations, inverting, indeed flattening, this psychology. For example, concerned that he might have nothing to say, Warhol asked others to read the *Rorschach*s on his behalf, and even the idea for the series is said to have come from an assistant.

80. See Luc Boltanski and Eve Chiapello, *The New Spirit of Capitalism*, trans. Gregory Elliot (London: Verso, 2005). Also see Avital Ronell, *Test Drive* (Urbana: University of Illinois Press, 2005). In a personal communication, Kevin Hatch pointed out that many of us have more than one subject to oversee; for example, we contrive avatars in video games (and other arenas), which are also tests—often tests of our aggressivity above all.

81. Boltanski and Chiapello, *New Spirit of Capitalism*, 93.

82. Karl Marx, *Grundrisse*, trans. Martin Nicolaus (New York: Vintage, 1973), 92.

83. This inquiry might be extended along two lines. First, the Factory can be seen as an early version, even a vanguard, of "the firm as network," which Boltanski and Chiapello see as fundamental to "the new spirit of capitalism": "*lean* firms working as *networks* with a multitude of participants, organizing work in the form of teams or *projects*, intent on customer satisfaction, and a general mobilization of workers thanks to their leaders' *vision*" (*New Spirit of Capitalism*, 72–73; emphasis in the original). Moreover, "the qualities that are guarantees of success in this new spirit" are ones

broadly associated with contemporary art à la Warhol: "autonomy, spontaneity, rhizo-morphous capacity, multitasking (in contrast to the narrow specialization of the old division of labour), conviviality, openness to others and novelty, availability, creativity, visionary intuition, sensitivity to differences, listening to lived experience and recep-tiveness to a whole range of experiences, being attracted to informality and the search for interpersonal contacts." In short, in this capitalism there is "an instrumentalization of human beings in their most specifically human dimensions" (97–98).

Second, Warhol was a pioneer of both "talk" and "reality" television: between 1979 and 1987, he conceived forty-two broadcasts for cable channels, usually with an interview format. Yet "talk" and "reality" here might be misnomers; both genres are forms of "test" television, for talk and reality are construed in such shows as matters of adaptability, even survivability, and what is tested is the capacity of the subject to project an image, to maintain a presence, through semiscripted situations of stress. It is this kind of television, this sort of reality, that Warhol pioneered.

84. See Louis Althusser, "Ideology and Ideological State Apparatuses" (1969), in *Lenin and Philosophy*, trans. Ben Brewster (New York and London: Monthly Review Press, 1971).

85. The views of cinema as hypnotic and as fetishistic are associated with Ray-mond Bellour and Christian Metz respectively.

86. As I suggested above, in Lacanian terms it is as though Warhol mobilizes the real against both the symbolic and the ideological. Some critics have searched for a Brechtian criticality in Warhol; if it exists at all, it is in this distress. In a personal communication, Gordon Hughes suggested that Barthes might have written the last pages of *Camera Lucida* in part with Warhol in mind. There Barthes writes of "two ways of the Photograph": "to subject its spectacle to the civilized code of perfect il-lusions [which he elsewhere calls 'making Photography into an art'], or to confront in it the wakening of intractable reality" (119). As we will see in chapter 4, Richter attempts both.

4 Gerhard Richter, or the Photogenic Image

1. Gerhard Richter, *Writings, 1961–2007*, ed. Dietmar Elger and Hans Ulrich Obrist (New York: DAP, 2009), 180; hereafter in the chapter, page numbers in the text refer to this volume.

2. These subjects had this unquiet status for Richter, too: "I had kept a number of pictures for years," he said of this suite in 1989, "under the heading of unfinished business" (*Writings*, 226). Also in 1989: "I tried to open it up again—to make a funeral again—but without a solution. The whole case, the entire complex of events, was not dispatched. Sometimes I have the feeling that we forgot, or that we are forgetting—throwing the entire thing away from us like garbage" (221).

3. See Robert Rosenblum, *Modern Painting and the Northern Romantic Tradition: Friedrich to Rothko* (New York: Harper and Row, 1975). According to Rosenblum, Friedrich and his peers faced this dilemma: "how to express experiences of the spiritual, of the transcendental, without having recourse to such traditional themes as the Adoration, the Crucifixion, the Resurrection, the Ascension, whose vitality, in the Age of Enlightenment, was constantly being sapped" (15). Although Rosenblum mentions Richter, the historian presumes a continuity that the artist problematizes, though Richter is typically ambiguous on this point. Here he is in February 1973: "What I'm lacking is the spiritual foundation that supported Romantic painting. We have lost the feeling of 'God's omnipresence in nature.' For us, everything is empty. And yet, those paintings are still there; they speak to us. We continue to love them, use them, and need them" (*Writings*, 82). In a letter to the curator Jean-Christophe Amman, also in February 1973, Richter restates his belief that "a painting by Caspar David Friedrich is not a thing of the past" (72), an allusion to the famous pronouncement of Hegel that "art is, and remains for us, on the side of its highest destiny, a thing of the past" (*Introductory Lectures on Aesthetics*, trans. Bernard Bosanquet [London: Penguin, 1993], 13).

4. In 1986, Richter was asked about the statement by Theodor Adorno that poetry after the Holocaust is barbaric, and he responded directly: "There is lyric poetry after Auschwitz" (*Writings*, 75). For a meditation on the fate of lyric painting in the postwar period, see T. J. Clark, "In Defense of Abstract Expressionism," in *Farewell to an Idea: Episodes from a History of Modernism* (New Haven: Yale, 1999).

5. Here is a sampling of pertinent statements. In 1973: "I refuse to limit myself to one single option—to an exterior resemblance or to a unity of style that cannot exist" (*Writings*, 72). In 1985: "I want the painting to be very heterogeneous, but nevertheless everything has to be of one mould, as contradictory as it may be. The contradictions have to be there but must coexist, must converge" (145). And in 2002: "I always hated those artists who were so consistent and had this sort of unified development; I thought it was terrible" (384).

6. See Michael Kimmelman, "An Artist Beyond Isms," *New York Times Magazine*, January 27, 2002. Buchloh draws his account from the younger Richter; in keeping with his own (neo) avant-garde commitments, he has stressed the critical aspect of the project. Robert Storr, the curator of the MoMA retrospective, identifies with the older Richter, who, however troubled by the historical straits of painting, is seen to fly its flag from first to last; see Robert Storr, *Gerhard Richter: Forty Years of Painting* (New York: Museum of Modern Art, 2002). At times, Storr is so concerned to refute Buchloh that he is distracted from the art (the very charge he levels at Buchloh) and so misses its aporetic nature. His exhibition not only played down the Duchampian moments in Richter (e.g., only a few glass pieces and Color Charts appeared) but also elided important shifts within the painting. Why did Richter turn to gray monochromes after several years of photo-based paintings? Are the early Color Charts as affirmative of painting as the later gestural abstractions? Are these later abstractions so affirmative? Are all the landscapes and the portraits equally second-degree, distanced from world and self alike? Such questions were raised, but not addressed, by the 2002 retrospective. In his catalogue interview, Storr is dismissive of the reading of the painting as rhetorical, to which Richter responds simply, "There has to be some truth to it" (429).

7. Benjamin Buchloh, "Gerhard Richter's *Atlas*: The Anomic Archive," *October* 88 (Spring 1999). Also see Iwona Blazwick, ed., *Gerhard Richter: Atlas; The Reader* (London: Whitechapel, 2003). In *Archive Fever: A Freudian Impression* (trans. Eric Prenowitz [Chicago: University of Chicago Press, 1996]), Jacques Derrida argues that "archive fever" is bound up with the repetition compulsion and the death drive, a provocative thesis that is more pertinent to Warhol than to Richter. *Atlas* might also be considered "stuplime," a neologistic conjunction of "stupid" and "sublime" defined by Sianne Ngai as an "aesthetic experience in which astonishment is paradoxically combined with boredom" (*Ugly Feelings* [Cambridge, Mass.: Harvard University Press, 2005], 271).

8. For Richter, there is no great contradiction between the relative and the selective. Here he is in 2005: "I see many landscapes, take photographs of hundreds of them, and paint one or two. This is proof to me that I know what I want—a fact that seems to give me a certain sense of self-assuredness" (*Writings*, 499). In a manner apposite here, Fredric Jameson once opposed Godard to the German filmmaker Hans-Jürgen Syberberg as representatives of postmodernist and modernist relations to the truth-value of cultural representations—the former treating them as "sheer text," the latter treating them as carriers of "some authentic vision of the

world" ("'In the Destructive Element Immerse': Hans-Jürgen Syberberg and Cultural Revolution," *October* 17 [Summer 1981], 111). Richter entertains aspects of both positions.

9. This is not to say that the paintings are mere tricks, or that the eggs are empty, though this is how they are viewed by some critics. However, a cuckoo's eggs are not innocent; beyond the element of deception, there is, especially in the German phrase (*"legt jemandem ein Kuckucksei ins Nest"*), the implication of harm visited on the rightful occupant of the nest.

10. Aleksandr Rodchenko, "Working with Mayakowsky" (1939), in Krystyna Rubinger, ed., *From Painting to Design: Russian Constructivist Art of the Twenties* (Cologne: Galerie Gmurzyska, 1981), 191.

11. Sometimes these abstractions suggest the meandering marks in late paintings by the ill Willem de Kooning.

12. For Buchloh, the *Silicate* paintings evoke both "computer cells and mass structures" in a way that "articulates a deep skepticism, not to say hopelessness," about "seriality and control" (Richter, *Writings* 486). In a sense, they update the *Urformen der Kunst* (1928) of Karl Blossfeldt: his close-up photos of plants suggest formal analogies between man-made and natural design, whereas the patterns in the *Silicate* paintings eradicate such an exchange; here, all that is left, at both micro and macro levels of cell and mass, is "technoanimalistic" organization.

13. For Simmel, this effect occurs at the level of the nerves, so stimulated are they by the capitalist marketplace "that they finally cease to react at all." In his account, "money, with all its colorlessness and indifference, becomes the common denominator of all values; irreparably it hollows out the core of things, their individuality, their specific value, and their incomparability." See "The Metropolis and Mental Life" (1903), in *The Sociology of Georg Simmel*, ed. and trans. Kurt H. Wolff (New York: Free Press, 1950), 414; also see Simmel, *The Philosophy of Money* (1900), trans. Tom Bottomore and David Frisby (London: Routledge, 1990). As we will see in chapter 5, the blasé is also pronounced in Ruscha.

14. Although they are often conflated, "arbitrary" is not the same as "random." Like "arbiter," "arbitrary" derives from the Latin *ad* and *betere*, "to go to" and, by extension, "one who goes to see," i.e., to examine and to decide. In the first instance, the term describes such decisions "relating to, or dependent on, the discretion of an arbiter." To my mind, then, the arbitrary implies a subject who decides, while the random suggests a displacement of such authority. Only in the next instance in the *OED* does the familiar connotation of "arbitrary" as "derived from mere opinion or

preference" come into play. In this sense, the decisions in Richter might be arbitrary, but they are not random.

15. Duchamp used the term in relation to his *Three Standard Stoppages* (1913–14). See "The Green Box" (1934), in Duchamp, *Essential Writings*, 33.

16. In his notes, Richter often quotes the Cage aphorism "I have nothing to say, and I am saying it." Richter is keen to the high degree of control at work in "Cage's method of coincidence": "He devised an ingenious system to build structures from dumb abundance. And he devoted even more skill to giving form to this succession of sounds. That is the absolute opposite of chance, nature and rubbish" (*Writings*, 446, 461).

17. Richter in 2000: "I said this thirty years ago: I have no opinions, I'm indifferent. I said it to protect myself" (*Writings*, 358). That such indifference might support an aesthetic was explored by Moira Roth in "The Aesthetic of Indifference," *Artforum* (November 1977), where she links its emergence in the 1950s to the political paralysis produced by McCarthyism.

18. Richter cites this story twice in his notes from the period, which suggests that it might be a set piece (*Writings*, 21, 30). Might this memory screen another scene, his traumatic encounter with images of the camps? I return to this question below.

19. Siegfried Kracauer, "Photography," in *The Mass Ornament: Weimar Essays*, ed. and trans. Thomas Y. Levin (Cambridge, Mass.: Harvard University Press, 1995), 59 (emphasis in the original). Buchloh also brings Kracauer to bear in his "Gerhard Richter's *Atlas*."

20. Kracauer, "Photography," 59.

21. As we saw in chapter 2, "banality" was a fraught term in the early 1960s, at the moment that Pop art was received and Richter emerged—a pejorative term for most critics, a positive one for some artists. For many, the notion threatened the very possibility of moral and metaphysical profundity—whether of art, in the case of Pop or, in the controversy surrounding Hannah Arendt upon the publication of her *Eichmann in Jerusalem* (1963), of evil. Paul B. Jaskot discusses this controversy in "Gerhard Richter and Adolf Eichmann," *Oxford Art Journal* 28, no. 3 (2005).

22. In his 2002 conversation with Storr, Richter alludes to the Arendt thesis of the banality of evil, then comments: "The chandelier [*Flemish Crown*] is a monster. I don't need to paint a monster; it is enough to paint this thing, this shitty, small, banal chandelier. That thing is terrifying . . . That is what makes the banal more than just banal" (*Writings*, 407). In this passage, Richter refers specifically to the

vulgarity of petit bourgeois culture, as crystallized in the chandelier, but then resists this class reading: "I refuse to discuss it in those terms because now it turns into social criticism" (408). For Richter, it seems, the banal has become general, even natural in its own way: "I have used the so-called banal," he commented in 1985, "to show that the banal is the important and the human" (152).

23. As suggested in note 51 to chapter 3, this effect might be transformed with digital cameras. Unlike Warhol, who sets up this effect, especially in his photo-booth pictures and *Screen Tests*, Richter reflects on it, at a remove, in painting.

24. If Warhol highlights the difficulty of this (self) imaging, Richter highlights the desire to achieve it.

25. These obliterated girls might be seen as the obscure others of the illustrious men of *48 Portraits* (1971–72), but then these men are no less subject than the girls to the regime of photographic appearance and banal seriality. Richter updates others well-known paintings, too. *Ema (Nude on a Staircase)* (1966), for example, is a play on the Duchamp paintings of the subtitle, but in this instance there is no travesty: the nude is his wife at the time, and the blurring is almost auratic in effect.

26. There are other examples based on family snapshots: *Family* (1964), *Family at the Seaside* (1964), *Swimmers* (1965), etc.

27. Here is Richter first on his gray: "For me gray is the welcome and only possible equivalent for indifference, for the refusal to make a statement, for lack of opinion, lack of form." And then on his blur: "I blur things to make everything equally important and equally unimportant" (*Writings*, 37). We might compare Warhol on the effects of repetition (again, in Warhol as in Richter, the aesthetic of indifference seems to have a traumatic core): "I don't want it to be essentially the same—I want it to be exactly the same. Because the more you look at the same exact thing, the more the meaning goes away and the better and emptier you feel" (Warhol and Hackett, *POPism*, 50). The Richter gray recalls the gray in James Rosenquist; both painters evoke the photographic, but to different effects (e.g., the Rosenquist gray is more nostalgic than indifferent in effect).

28. See Jean Laplanche, *New Foundations for Psychoanalysis*, trans. David Macey (Oxford: Blackwell, 1989).

29. The *OED* does not acknowledge this colloquial sense of "photogenic." It defines the word in these ways: "produced or caused by light"; "an earlier word for *photographic*"; "photogenetic," i.e., "having the property of producing or emitting light." In my Kracauerian inflection, there might be a circularity in this photographic semblance, as already captured by Edgar Morin not long before Richter emerged:

"Everything that is photogenic aspires to be photographed. Everything that has been photographed resembles everything that has been filmed. Everything that has been filmed is multiplied by photography" (*The Stars*, trans. Richard Howard [London: Calder, 1960], 62).

30. This note by Barthes on grisaille is suggestive here:

> The grisaille, figure that could be called the "color of the colorless," points to another way of thinking the paradigm as the great principle of organization. Model of the paradigm: the opposition of primary contrasted colors . . . the monochrome (the Neutral) substitutes for the idea of opposition that of the slight difference . . . of nuance: nuance becomes a principle of allover organization (which covers the totality of the surface, as in the landscape of a triptych) that in a way skips the paradigm: this integrally and almost exhaustively nuanced space is the shimmer . . . The Neutral is the shimmer: that whose aspect, perhaps whose meaning, is subtly modified according to the angle of the subject's gaze. (Barthes, *The Neutral*, trans. Rosalind E. Krauss and Denis Hollier [New York: Columbia University Press, 2005], 51)

I return to the notion of the neutral below.

31. In a way that suggests why his blur is multivalent, Richter notes that, technically, paintings "are never blurred." Instead, "what we regard as blurring is imprecision, and that means that they are different from the object represented. But, since pictures are not made for purposes of comparison with reality, they cannot be blurred, or imprecise, or different (different from what?). How can, say, paint on canvas be blurred?" (*Writings*, 60).

32. Different theoretical associations are keyed here (I mention the Freudian resonance below). On the one hand, the subject-effect of the Richter blur might be thought in Derridean terms of the *pharmakon*, Greek for "drug," which is both poison and remedy. On the other hand, its signification might be thought in Barthesian terms of "the third meaning," defined, saliently here, as an "obtuse meaning" ("*obtusus* means *that which is blunted, rounded in form*") that allows for both "a certain emotion" and a certain drifting of sense. As we will see in chapter 5, this blunting is also active in Ruscha. See Jacques Derrida, "Plato's Pharmacy" (1973), in *Dissemination*, trans. Barbara Johnson (Chicago: University of Chicago Press, 1981); and Roland Barthes, "The Third Meaning" (1970), in *Image-Music-Text*, trans. Stephen Heath (New York: Hill and Wang, 1977).

33. Jacques Lacan sees this "taming of the gaze" (*dompte-regard*) as the primary function of all painting (*Four Fundamental Concepts*, 17–64). Again, Richter highlights this taming, but unsettles it too, as do Hamilton and Warhol. For more on this unsettling in postwar art, see my "Torn Screens." Johannes Meinhardt argues that the Richter blur suppresses the *studium* of the source photograph, its repertoire of cultural meanings, in a way that strengthens its *punctum*, or traumatic dimension ("Illusionism in Painting and the *Punctum* of Photography" [2005], in Benjamin Buchloh, ed., *Gerhard Richter* [Cambridge, Mass.: MIT Press, 2009]).

34. Questioned in 1992 about his early interest in indifference, Richter responded: "That was an attempt at self-protection—saying that I was indifferent, that I didn't care, and so on. I was afraid my pictures might seem too sentimental. But I don't mind admitting now that it was no coincidence that I painted things that mattered to me personally—the tragic types, the murderers and suicides, the failures, and so on" (*Writings*, 283).

35. Paul Klee, "Creative Credo" (1920), in Herschel B. Chipp, *Theories of Modern Art* (Berkeley and Los Angeles: University of California Press, 1968), 182. Here is Richter in 1988: "Art makes artificial reality perceptible, and the other [natural reality] as well" (*Writings*, 205).

36. Typically, Richter is self-contradictory, or at least elusive, on this point. In 2002, he told Storr: "I was never interested in light. Light is there and you turn it on or you turn it off, with sun or without sun. I don't know what the 'problematic of light' is. I take it as a metaphor for a different quality, which is similarly difficult to describe" (*Writings*, 404).

37. For Richter in 1986, "the artist's productive act . . . has nothing to do with the talent of 'making by hand,' only with the capacity to see and to decide *what* is to be made visible" (*Writings*, 169). And again in 2001: "The main link and common ground of both the figurative and abstract paintings is that they have the same intent: to give a picture, a visible description, to represent an image, to produce appearance, like a photo" (373).

38. This note is from 1964–65; in 1971, Richter said much the same thing about vision: "Our sense of sight causes us to apprehend things, but at the same time restricts and partly precludes our apprehension of reality" (*Writings*, 57).

39. Lukács elaborates the concept in *The Theory of the Novel* in 1916 (trans. Anna Bostock [Cambridge, Mass.: MIT Press, 1971]) and then, in explicitly Marxist terms, in *History and Class Consciousness* in 1923 (trans. Rodney Livingstone

[Cambridge, Mass.: MIT Press, 1971]). Adorno also develops it in "The Idea of Natural History" (1932), printed in *Telos* 60 (Summer 1984).

40. For an artist like Godard, twentieth-century history is mediated by film above all, as he makes explicit in *Histoire(s) du cinema* (1988–98), the terms of which he flips—"the history of cinema" is "the cinema of history" too—which is to say that, in part, we see twentieth-century history through a cinematic lens. For his contemporary Richter, this mediation is mostly photographic and partly tele-visual. On a related topic, Buchloh has written of his "successful bid to outdo the industrialization of chromatic experience on its own terms" ("Richter's Abstractions: Silences, Voids, and Evacuations" in *Gerhard Richter: Paintings from 2003–2005* [New York: Marian Goodman Gallery, 2005], 22).

41. Lukács: "The second nature, the nature of man-made structures, has no lyri-cal substantiality . . . It is a complex of senses—meanings—which has become rigid and strange, and which no longer awakens interiority; it is a charnel-house of long-dead interiorities" (*Theory of the Novel*, 63–64). Richter attempts to find a modicum of lyrical substantiality in this second nature; that is part of his unlikely quest. Yet sometimes Richter wants to have it both ways. For example, in 1988, Richter agreed that he plays to "a [predetermined notion of a] landscape" (*Writings*, 210; brackets in the original); yet in 1993, he remarked of this pervasive mediation, "I don't know what the 'second degree' means" (307).

42. See Baudrillard, *Political Economy of the Sign*. Walter Benjamin sees the emergence of this condition of "semblance . . . consolidated in commodities" al-ready in the period of Baudelaire (see "Central Park" [1938–39], in Michael W. Jennings, ed., *The Writer of Modern Life: Essays on Charles Baudelaire* [Cambridge, Mass.: Harvard University Press, 2006], 146). Although he is not consistent on this subject, one of his formulas is the following: "The dissolution of semblance [*die Scheinlosigkeit*] and the decay of aura are identical phenomena" 148). Richter revises this equation: semblance and aura do not dissolve or decay outright; rather, they are transformed—as indeed Benjamin suggests in another note in "Central Park": "With the new manufacturing processes that lead to imitations, semblance is consolidated in commodities" (146).

43. On this point, see my "The Crux of Minimalism" in *Return of the Real*. A philosophical reflection from the early moment of Pop is useful here. In *This Is Not a Pipe* (1963; trans. Richard Miller [Berkeley and Los Angeles: University of California Press, 1984]), Michel Foucault argues that the privileged terms of representation are "affirmation" and "resemblance": the reality of the referent is

affirmed through the resemblance of the image to it. In modernist art, this paradigm is eroded in two fundamental ways, which Foucault associates with Kandinsky and Magritte respectively. In his abstractions, Kandinsky frees affirmation of reality from resemblance to it, and resemblance is mostly abandoned. Yet reality, now located *beyond* resemblance in another realm (seen as spiritual or Platonic), is still affirmed, indeed all the more so—and the same is true, in different ways, of the abstractions of Malevich, Mondrian, and many others. In his simulations, Magritte does the more radical converse: he frees resemblance from affirmation. Resemblance is maintained, but no reality is affirmed, and the referent, its reality, evaporates: "Magritte allows the old space of representation to prevail," Foucault writes, "but only on the surface . . .; underneath, there is nothing" (16). In Magritte, representation only seems to reappear; rather, it returns, transformed, as a subversive simulacrum. In its cancellation, abstraction preserves representation, whereas the simulacrum unfounds representation, pulls reality out from underneath it, as it were. Indeed, the simulacrum confounds the opposition of representation and abstraction, often considered to control modern art. Foucault ends his essay with an invocation of the Warhol soup cans, which, it is implied, go Magritte one better. This is the conclusion that Richter seems to reach as well; at the same time, he revises Kandinsky, Magritte, and Warhol alike. For unlike Kandinsky's, his abstractions do not affirm any transcendental reality; and unlike Magritte's and Warhol's, his representations are not merely simulacral—they rehearse its appearance in a way that reflects upon it.

44. Kracauer, "Photography," 52. Kracauer continues: "For in the artwork the meaning of the object takes on spatial appearance, whereas in photography the spatial appearance of an object is its meaning. The two spatial appearances—the 'natural' one and that of the object permeated by cognition—are not identical."

45. Adorno, *Aesthetic Theory*, 78.

46. Clement Greenberg, "After Abstract Expressionism" (1962), in *Collected Essays*, vol. 4, 125. Thomas Crow also refers to this Greenbergian term in "Hand-Made Photograph and Homeless Representation" (1992), reprinted in Buchloh, *Gerhard Richter*. In *The Theory of the Novel*, Lukács writes of homelessness as one motive of the novel: "The old parallelism of the transcendental structure of the form-giving subject and the world of created forms has been destroyed, and the ultimate basis of artistic creation has become homeless" (40–41).

47. See, for example, Terry Eagleton, *The Ideology of the Aesthetic* (Oxford: Blackwell, 1990).

48. The aesthetic ideal of harmony can also be held up as a critical foil to reflect on its lack elsewhere—a Schillerian line of reflection that runs from Marx to Herbert Marcuse and beyond. Here, too, the example of Richter is relevant.

49. "Yes, a lot of nonsense can be created with the word 'beauty,'" Richter remarked in 1986. "When it's exalted, it can be quite unpleasant. The Nazis are the worst example of this. A beautiful body, a beautiful mind, and all that crap. That was a particularly one-sided, pestilent form of beauty that is simply wrong. But this doesn't mean that beauty no longer exists! Nonetheless it remains a dangerous word" (*Writings*, 191). The years 2001–10 witnessed a return to the moral discourse of beauty, as if this tradition had never been challenged artistically or compromised historically; see Suzanne Perling Hudson, "Beauty and the Status of Contemporary Criticism," *October* 104 (Spring 2003). This might be the place to note my admiration for the provocative reading of affective analogies in Richter provided by Kaja Silverman in her recent *Flesh of My Flesh* (Palo Alto, Calif.: Stanford University Press, 2009), but I fail to see the paintings in the redemptive light that she sheds on them there.

50. It is true that some paintings of his family members appear distressed (and he hardly presents his infant son in the most attractive guise). On "hackneyed," see note 41 in chapter 2; the original German is *abgedroschen*. From the mid-1990s through the early 2000s, Richter oscillated between images suggestive of faith (e.g., his paintings of mother and child) and of resignation (e.g., his *Silicate* paintings). "That's my home," he remarked of "our Christian culture" in 2002; "those are my roots, it's a tradition I have the highest regard for" (*Writings*, 448). And lately he has produced several commissions for churches, including a large stained-glass window for the Cologne cathedral. "My conservative side," Richter commented in 2000, "has become more important over the years" (368).

51. See Fried, *Art and Objecthood*, especially the introduction. Richter has often attested to this fragility, especially lately. Here he is in 2002: "Traditional art is practically dead, by which I mean this huge, complicated entity—with all its wonderful aesthetic and moral aspirations—that used to be called art. That's been sidelined completely, and doesn't have any sort of public relevance any more; on the contrary, it's increasingly denigrated . . . I am the exception that is tolerated; perhaps not even that" (*Writings*, 445). And again in 2004: "I belong to a field of art that has become very unimportant and has hardly anything left to say" (493). And yet when asked in 2002 how he "would like to be understood," he responded, "Maybe as the keeper of tradition [laughs]" (439). His ambivalence about tradition rises when it

comes to the German line. "I'm very happy to be counted as part of that," Richter commented in 2006 (510), and then stepped back when asked whether there is a specifically "German spirit" in painting: "I believe so, yes. But I'd rather not know the details" (516).

52. Richter does not quite deny this note of the spurious or the specious; here he comments on his positive reception in the 1980s: "There was a demand for paintings that I satisfied, and at the same time there was this conceptual notion against painting—and so I served both sides. That was rather smart, a legitimation to enjoy them. Yes, pleasure without remorse" (*Writings*, 397). Here he is less than Adornian, and often he does not maintain the difficult dialectic associated with Adorno.

53. "Yes, it was my wish to be neutral," Richter said to Storr in 2002 regarding his "early statements"; "I saw it as an opportunity. It was the opposite of ideology" (*Writings*, 418). "The fact is that I can't see that as a flaw," he commented to his daughter Betty, also in 2002, concerning "the view, the accusation, that I am non-committal verbally and in my work, meaning that I am politically indifferent, neither left-wing nor right-wing, but maybe both at the same time"; "it shows that nothing is as clear and simple as people like to believe" (441).

54. Barthes, *The Neutral*, 6–7. We encountered "baffle" vis-à-vis Warhol in chapter 3, and we will encounter the neutral again with Ruscha in chapter 5.

5 Ed Ruscha, or the Deadpan Image

1. Ed Ruscha, *Leave Any Information at the Signal* (Cambridge, Mass.: MIT Press, 2002), 307; hereafter in the chapter, page numbers in the text refer to this volume.

2. Again, his relative uninterest in the East extended to Europe, where Ruscha traveled for seven months in 1961, only to remark later that as far as his own inspiration was concerned, "there was no art anywhere except in America" (*Leave Any Information*, 121). This is in keeping with other statements by American artists of this generation (e.g., Donald Judd) and must be read as part provocation, part blague, and part space clearing.

3. See Lisa Turvey, "Ed Ruscha and the Language That He Used," *October* 111 (Winter 2005), reprinted in Turvey, ed., *Ed Ruscha* (Cambridge, Mass.: MIT Press, 2011).

4. This convergence is not a resolution; the juxtaposition of painting and design remains disjunctive (more so than in Roy Lichtenstein), more on which below. One could pick other examples of this convergence of abstraction and design in early Ruscha, such as *Talk about Space* (1963), where the word "space" appears in Superman font in yellow capitals on a blue field that reads equally as pure painting and a comic-book version of outer space. The pencil depicted at the bottom and the "talk" announced in the title point to the late-modernist discourse about pictorial space, a discourse that, for Leo Steinberg, also collapsed abstraction and design, but in a way that Ruscha questions through his very different combination of the two. Steinberg: "In formalist criticism, the criterion for significant progress remains a kind of design technology subject to one compulsive direction: the treatment of 'the whole surface as a single undifferentiated field of interest.' The goal is to merge figure with ground, integrate shape and field, eliminate foreground-background discontinuities; to restrict pattern to those elements (horizontals or verticals) that suggest a symbiotic relationship of image and frame; to collapse painting and drawing in a single gesture, and equate design and process (as Pollock's drip-paintings do, or Morris Louis's Veils); in short, to achieve the synthesis of all separable elements of paintings" ("Other Criteria," 79).

5. Were these "collections of readymades" influenced by such examples as the Warhol cans at the Ferus Gallery in 1962? As Thomas Crow has suggested (in a lecture on Ruscha), there is a secret history of LA in these books. On the art scene there at the time, see Alexandra Schwarz, *Ed Ruscha's Los Angeles* (Cambridge, Mass.: MIT Press, 2010).

6. Yve-Alain Bois, "Thermometers Should Last Forever," in *Ed Ruscha: Romance with Liquids, 1966–1969* (New York: Rizzoli, 1993), 8; reprinted in Turvey, *Ed Ruscha*. Bois mentions in particular "the size and scale of letters, the phonetic flutter, the grammatic alliteration—but also the pattern of oil dripping on parking lots, the vacant real estate opportunities in the urban landscape, the metaphors in the robotized language of mass media" (12). Ruscha thus flies in the face of assumptions about the easy legibility of the Pop image, but then so do other key Pop artists.

7. Here I differ from Lisa Turvey (in her excellent essay cited in note 3). In my view, Ruscha stresses the materiality of his words less to motivate them than to contradict the assumed immateriality of communication (this is in keeping with the nonidealist tendency in Conceptual art such as that of Mel Bochner).

8. Bois relates this aspect of Ruscha to the Russian formalist project to de-automatize language: for them, the object was clichéd poetic language; for Ruscha,

the object is clichéd commercial language. As we saw in chapter 2, Lichtenstein was also drawn to onomatopoeic terms, whose conventionality he, too, stressed.

9. Aleksandr Rodchenko used a related form to signify "shout" in his 1925 agit-prop poster in support of literacy.

10. Ruscha painted his own version of the ancient legend of trompe l'oeil told by Pliny the Elder in his *Natural History* (c. 77–79), concerning a picture of grapes, by the artist Zeuxis, so lifelike that it attracted birds. *Angry Because It's Plaster, Not Milk* (1965) shows a bird "angry" at its deception by a glass of milk; the milk, the title tells us, is actually plaster, but of course it is not that either.

11. Foucault, *This Is Not a Pipe*, 19–31, here 20, 21, 25.

12. Ibid., 28, 25. There might be a connection here, too, to Raymond Roussel, whose interest in entropic messages and devolved sentences was passed on to Duch-amp—and perhaps, via Duchamp, to Ruscha as well.

13. Sometimes, as in his stained works of the early 1970s, Ruscha treats language materially. His play with denotation takes other forms in images of words presented in fonts they might be associated with stereotypically, such as a pseudo-Gothic script for "Church" and "German," or a faux-calligraphic script for "Foo."

14. Ruscha quoted in Turvey, "Ruscha and Language," 96. "Almost leaving its body": it seems that for Ruscha, words are not only like pictures but also like people, more on which below.

15. Here Ruscha is close to Johns, who, in a well-known sketchbook note c. 1963–64 regarding method, wrote, "One thing working one way/Another thing working another way/One thing working different ways *at different times*" (*Jasper Johns: Writings, Sketchbook Notes, Interviews*, ed. Kirk Varnedoe [New York: MoMA, 1996], 54). Although the epistemological significance of this ambiguity might be deeper in Johns, its critical edge might be sharper in Ruscha, who disturbs the image-word conjunction fundamental to the smooth operation of captioned photographs, advertisements, and so on. To take a recent example: by the mid-1990s, a particular category of distressed words came to predominate in his work; these are paintings, on monochromatic fields, with "censor strips," or rectangular blocks of phrases, that, like so many scratched-out messages or redacted letters, are usually effaced. In each case, the titles present the putative messages, which soon turn menacing, like so many lines from gang and prison movies of the 1940s and 1950s, such as "Agree to Our Terms or Prepare Yourself for a Blast Furnace" (most boil down to the succinct "Your a Dead Man"). There are multiple ambiguities and ironies here. Some of the strips are ragged, as if done in an angry afterthought by the would-be perpetrator;

others are neat, as though executed by the policing authority—newspaper, cop, court, or government. And as we match up phrases and strips, we, too, are caught between these positions of expression and erasure, exposing and withholding. Yet all this is a fiction, of course, and we don't have to believe any of it: why trust that the messages correspond to the titles, or the strips to the messages? We could simply see them as slightly odd abstractions. But then it becomes apparent that what is in question here is precisely belief and trust. This is made clear in a singular work, *In God We Trust* (1994), which can also be read as an abstract circle, except for the censor strips placed where the title phrase is placed on American coins. What constitutes value, this painting invites us to ask (in a way that recalls Warhol), and by whose authority?

16. Defined as that which is "left over when the rest have been distributed or divided into pairs" (*OED*), the odd can be seen to disturb given oppositions and distinctions. Here what is "odd" for Ruscha might be related to what is "obtuse" for Roland Barthes, who (as we were reminded in chapter 4) uses this term to describe a "third meaning"—"evident, erratic, obstinate"—that troubles more direct kinds of meaning, such as communication (or message) and signification (or sense); see Barthes, "The Third Meaning," 53.

17. For this relay between the common and the odd in more recent work, see my "Evening in America," in *Ed Ruscha: Catalogue Raisonné*, vol. 5 (New York: Gagosian Gallery, 2010).

18. This is a large topic in Pop, especially in its British incarnation. As we saw in chapter 1, the egalitarianism of the Independent Group, for example, challenged both the elitist notion of civilization (as represented by Kenneth Clark) and the academic status of modernism (as represented by Herbert Read); it also rejected the sentimental regard for a folk worker culture (as represented by Richard Hoggart). "American films and magazines were the only live culture we knew as kids," Reyner Banham remarked of his IG associates. "We returned to Pop in the early fifties like Behans going to Dublin or Thomases to Llaregub, back to our native literature, our native arts" ("Who Is This Pop?" 13). Here, in effect, Banham signals the partial displacement of folk by Pop as the basis of a "common culture," more on which below.

19. This common touch is evident in other ways, too, as in the font Ruscha invented c. 1981 for his word images, which he calls Boy Scout Utility Modern. His own persona also mixes a hipness with a folksiness.

20. His first group show, curated by Walter Hopps at the Pasadena Museum of Art, was titled "New Painting of Common Objects" (1962), and it included other

connoisseurs of the common, such as his friend Joe Goode, as well as Warhol, Lichtenstein, and Jim Dine, among others. Duchamp influenced Ruscha well before his 1963 Pasadena retrospective, as is evident from *Three Standard Envelopes* (1960), an early work that plays on *Three Standard Stoppages* (1913). As for Johns, all his subjects "up to 1958" are "commonplaces of our environment," as Leo Steinberg indicated long ago (*Other Criteria*, 26); for the specifics of this environment, see the second chapter in Joshua Shannon, *The Disappearance of Objects: New York Art and the Rise of the Postmodern City* (New Haven, Conn.: Yale University Press, 2009). Much of Ruscha hovers between "genre" and "generic," as though in an attempt to extract the general from both.

21. Ruscha underscores the commodification of script as well (see note 13), and so points to our distance from the modernist ambition, pronounced in the Bauhaus and elsewhere, to render type transparent.

22. See note 36 to chapter 2.

23. Here the subordination of image to word is less a tactic of proto-Conceptual art than a fact of consumerist life. Ruscha suggests that the word-image conjunction of the typical brand has trumped any avant-garde version of this combination.

24. Early paintings like *Dublin* (1960) and *Box Smashed Flat (Vicksburg)* (1960–61), in which the names of Southern towns are juxtaposed with a Little Orphan Annie fragment and a Sun-Maid Raisins box respectively, combine folk and Pop elements, as do paintings that combine different emblems of the West (e.g., a western comic and a gas station). A kind of folk Pop is also active in contemporaries like Robert Indiana, but without the edgy ambiguity in Ruscha.

25. The second category resonates with political concerns of the period, such as the prescient warning delivered by Dwight D. Eisenhower in 1959, in his final State of the Union address, about the "military-industrial complex." In a later text, "The Information Man" (*Los Angeles Institute of Contemporary Art Journal*, no. 6 [June–July 1975], 21), Ruscha mocks another kind of reified language that is statistical and bureaucratic in nature.

26. Ruscha anticipates the concern with administered language that was voiced by Herbert Marcuse in *One-Dimensional Man* (1964), and yet meaning and affect are not simply stripped from his words, as is sometimes argued. Indeed, Ruscha has remarked how he is drawn to his terms when, as it often happens, he first hears them in the street, on the radio, or elsewhere (his notebooks are peppered with such words and phrases, some of which return in the work). The subject seized by found language is a familiar topos of Surrealism, but the interest for Ruscha stems less

from any Surrealist revelation of desire than from the enigmatic appeal of oddity. For example: "The first book came out of a play of words," Ruscha said in 1965. "I like the word 'gasoline' and I like the specific quality of 'twenty-six'" (*Leave Any Information*, 23).

27. "Standard" is an ambiguous word, with nearly antithetical meanings of the distinctive and the uniform; e.g., on the one hand, a standard is a "distinctive flag"; on the other, it is a "weight or measure to which others conform" (*OED*). Some authorities refer to such words—those with opposed meanings—as "contronyms." Two common examples are "cleave" (split from, hold to) and "dust" (sprinkle with, or remove, small particles).

28. Appositely here, Walter Benjamin once suggested that the "salvation" of the word is to be sought where it is most commodified—in the newspaper (see "The Newspaper" [1934], in *Selected Writings*, vol. 2, 741–42). For Ruscha, commodified words pervade the entire environment, and sometimes he treats them almost as if they were "foreign" in the sense developed by Theodor Adorno in his 1959 text "Words from Abroad":

> Language participates in reification, the separation of subject matter and thought. The customary ring of naturalness deceives us about that. It creates the illusion that what is said is immediately equivalent to what is meant. By acknowledging itself as a token, the foreign word reminds us bluntly that all real language has something of the token in it. It makes itself language's scapegoat, the bearer of the dissonance that language has to give form to and not merely prettify. Not the least of what we resist in the foreign word is that it illuminates something true of all words: that language imprisons those who speak it, that as a medium of their own it has essentially failed. (*Notes to Literature*, ed. Rolf Tiedemann, trans. Shierry Weber Nicholson [New York: Columbia University Press, 1992], 2:189)

Duchamp, too, was interested in language that is anomic or (as he might have put it) "anemic."

29. Guillaume Apollinaire, *Les peintres cubistes* (Geneva: Editions Pierre Cailler, 1950), 76. The ratio of naïveté to irony in this statement is incalculable.

30. Swenson, "What Is Pop Art?" in Madoff, *Pop Art*, 103. The notorious statement reads in full: "Someone said that Brecht wanted everybody to think alike. I want everybody to think alike. But Brecht wanted to do it through Communism, in a way. Russia is doing it under government. It's happening here all by itself without

being under a strict government; so if it's working without trying, why can't it work without being Communist? Everybody looks alike and acts alike, and we're getting more and more that way." For important reflections on modern art and common culture, see Crow, *Modern Art in the Common Culture*, and Molly Nesbit, *Their Common Sense* (London: Black Dog, 2000).

31. Antonio Gramsci, *Selections from the Prison Notebooks*, ed. and trans. Quintin Hoare and Geoffrey Nowell Smith (New York: International Publishers, 1971), 326.

32. As Dave Hickey has written of these works, "It wasn't a standardized station but a station which dispensed standards, like a restaurant which serves norms, or a museum which did both ("Available Light," in *The Works of Edward Ruscha* [San Francisco: San Francisco Museum of Modern Art, 1982], 24).

33. Jean-Paul Sartre, introduction to Nathalie Sarraute, *Portrait d'un Inconnu* (1957), reprinted in *Portraits*, trans. Chris Turner (London: Seagull, 2009), 5–6. Sartre continues: "To appropriate [the commonplace] requires an act: an act by which I strip away my particularity in order to adhere to the general, to become generality. Not in any case *similar* to everyone, but, to be precise, the *incarnation* of everyone. By this eminently social adherence, I identify myself with *all* others in the indistinctness of the universal" (6).

This reading of the common has to do less with Kant (who, in *The Critique of Judgment*, discusses "common sense" in the sense both of *Gemeinsinn*, which supports the supposed universality of judgments of taste, and of *sensus communis*, which governs the understanding) than with Marx, who, in a passing reference in the *Grundrisse*, speaks of "the general intellect" (or "general social knowledge") as "a direct force of production" in its own right (706). Recently, Paolo Virno has developed this notion as follows: "The contemporary multitude is fundamentally based upon the presumption of a One which is more, not less, universal than the State: public intellect, language, 'common places'" (*A Grammar of the Multitude* [Los Angeles: Semiotexte, 2004], 43). Virno acknowledges that contemporary aspects of this public intellect might be unsavory (he mentions opportunism and cynicism in particular), but insists that it is a key resource in leftist politics. Others on the Left are skeptical: Jean-Luc Nancy questions the common in *The Inoperative Community* (1986; Eng. trans., 1991), for example, and even in Sartre, the commonplace is associated with the inauthentic.

In a personal communication regarding this section, Lisa Turvey adds:

The flip side of those words or sayings held in common are phrases so idiosyncratic that they seem to hint at a private language or code—possessed not by everyone but by no one. The first few words of many of Ruscha's depicted phrases seem to begin like a familiar cliché, or exhibit the structure of a joke or saying, but then veer off-course: *Faster Than a Speeding Beanstalk, Sand in the Vaseline, Industrial Strength Sleep, Mind If I Laugh, Bolts of Anger*, etc. Linguistically, this is the odd as opposed to the common, or the odd side *of* the common—yet another doubleness the work holds in tension.

34. Ruscha: "It's more like I'm painting ideas of ideas of ideas of mountains. The concept came to me as a logical extension of the landscapes that I've been painting for a while: horizontal landscapes, flatlands, the landscape I grew up in. Mountains like this were only ever like a dream to me; they meant Canada or Colorado" (quoted in Elisabeth Mahoney, "Top of the Pops: What Warhol Was to New York, Ruscha Is to L.A." *Guardian*, August 14, 2001).

35. In this way, the mountain paintings in particular hold yet another double in tension—the sublime and the banal. Some of the aforementioned ideals— mercy, purity, etc.—might be more Catholic than common (Ruscha was raised a Catholic). As for the commons, Daniel Heller-Roazen provides this helpful gloss on relevant Roman law: Objects with respect to ownership "may be 'universal' (*universitatis*), belonging to an entire community; they may be 'no one's' [*nullius*], still to be acquired by a private individual; finally, they may be 'common to all' (*communis omnium*). . . . Both common things and public things are 'outside our patrimony' (*extra patrimonium*), which no individual may own: the first [e.g., air, flowing water, the sea], because they cannot be joined in any way to the city, the second [e.g., streets and squares], because, with perfect symmetry, they may not all be disjoined from it" (*The Enemy of All: Piracy and the Law of Nations* [Cambridge, Mass.: Zone, 2009], 62–63). In our time of heightened enclosures, pervasive pollution, and global warming, the commons have become a renewed site of political contestation. For a history of the notion, see Peter Linebaugh, *The Magna Carta Manifesto: Liberties and Commons for All* (Berkeley and Los Angeles: University of California Press, 2008).

36. The suburban, eastern complement of the real-estate photo books is the Dan Graham piece *Homes for America*, published in the December 1966–January 1967 issue of *Arts Magazine*. In 2005, Ruscha updated *Every Building on the Sunset Strip* in a book documenting Hollywood Boulevard: *Then & Now*.

37. The "City Lights" paintings from the mid-1980s might seem an exception, for here the urban grids, also seen from above but at night, are illuminated with car lights

that glow intensely (especially at the intersections). Yet this life is entirely anonymous, and the city appears mostly as an abstract ground for disconnected texts.

38. One also feels this animation in Pop prose, especially in the "gonzo journalism" of Hunter S. Thompson and Tom Wolfe, but also in the criticism of Richard Hamilton and Reyner Banham (see note 62 in chapter 1).

39. See Georg Lukács, "Reification and the Consciousness of the Proletariat," in *History and Class Consciousness*, and chapter 1 of the present work.

40. Simmel, "The Metropolis and Mental Life," 410, 409, 411, 412. In part, the essay is an abstract of his monumental *The Philosophy of Money* (1900).

41. On the one hand, Simmel writes, "money, with all its colorlessness and indifference, becomes the common denominator of all values; irreparably it hollows out the core of things, their individuality, their specific value, and their incomparability" (see note 13 to chapter 4); on the other hand, in reaction the metropolitan type "seizes upon differentiation," even "adopts the most tendentious peculiarities." Finally, Simmel claims, "it is the function of the metropolis to provide the arena for this struggle and its reconciliation" ("The Metropolis and Mental Life," 414, 421, 423). At the extreme, the deadpan might be understood as an apotropaic mask turned toward the face of death. (This is evoked in a famous scene in *Steambat Bill, Jr.* [1928] in which Buster Keaton stands, impassive and untouched, as a building façade falls over and around him, a scene reprised by Steve McQueen in his short film *Deadpan* (1997). Aron Vinegar discusses the deadpan in Ruscha in *I Am Monument: On "Learning from Las Vegas"* (Cambridge, Mass.: MIT Press, 2008), but not as I do here.

42. Simultaneously to drain and to charge, to reify and to animate: such is also the paradoxical operation of fetishism, the effect of which Walter Benjamin once described as "the sex appeal of the inorganic," and as suggested, this, too, is pertinent to Ruscha (see Benjamin, "Paris, the Capital of the Nineteenth Century," in *Arcades Project*, 8). Another studio note condenses a related thought into an artistic credo: "Core of my aesthetic is the shape of 48 Ford gearshift knob vs 48 Chevy gearshift knob" (*Leave the Information*, 399). In this overlap of art and design, Ruscha suggests, aesthetic discrimination and fetishistic detailing are difficult to distinguish. Such fetishization is especially active in a subculture that has long intrigued Ruscha, that of customizers of cars, surfboards, and other products in LA. "'Hollywood' is like a verb to me," he has commented (in a phrase that also recurs in his work). "They do it with automobiles, they do it with everything that we manufacture" (221). Ruscha affirms this Hollywoodization ("they" here is also "he"), in both its

subcultural and its mass-cultural versions, in part because it promises another connection between "Art and the People." Such customizing has influenced his LA artist peers, too, as in "the finish fetish" practiced by Billy Al Bengston, Ron Davis, and Craig Kaufmann (among others), who have experimented with lacquers, polymers, fiberglass, and Plexiglas. For more on this subculture, see the title essay in Tom Wolfe, *The Kandy-Kolored Tangerine-Flake Streamline Baby* (New York: Farrar Straus & Giroux, 1965); also see Reyner Banham, *Los Angeles: The Architecture of Four Ecologies* (New York: Harper and Row, 1971).

Some Ruscha paintings, such as *Birds, Pencils* (1965), which imagines a combination of the two things in the title, recall some fantasies of related hybrids by the mid-nineteenth-century French caricaturist Grandville, which, as Benjamin remarks, "confer a commodity character on the universe" ("Paris, the Capital of the Nineteenth Century," 18 (translation modified). In this regard, Ruscha is matched, in contemporary fiction, by George Saunders; see, for example, his *In Persuasion Nation* (2006). Finally on this score, many of his words are also double in this way, both blunted and refined, administered and peculiar (see note 26). Often, as suggested in note 16, they appear "obtuse," both literally (*obtusus* means "blunted") and figuratively ("evident, erratic, obstinate"), in a manner that sometimes evokes a disruptive "third meaning" à la Barthes (see note 32 in chapter 4).

43. Benjamin, "Art in the Age of Its Technological Reproducibility," 119, 120. In an important reflection on this essay that is also pertinent to this aspect of Ruscha, Susan Buck-Morss writes: "Under shock the [synaesthetic] system reverses its role. Its goal is to *numb* the organism, to deaden the nerves, to repress memory: the cognitive system of synaesthetics has become, rather, one of *an*aesthetics . . . The simultaneity of overstimulation and numbness is characteristic of the new synaesthetic organization of anaesthetics" ("Aesthetics and Anaesthetics," *October* 62 [Fall 1992], 8).

44. On the Pop affinity with the simulacral, see note 43 in chapter 4.

45. One might think of James Rosenquist here, who drew on his experience as a billboard painter in his Pop practice. But Rosenquist used the billboard association to explode the scale of painting and to exploit a Surrealistic collage of images, whereas Ruscha remains within the size parameters of the tableau tradition and works to superimpose formats, not to juxtapose contents.

46. See, among other texts, Jaleh Mansoor, "Ed Ruscha's One-Way Street," *October* 111 (Winter 2005), and Cecile Whiting, *Pop L.A.: Art and the City in the 1960s* (Berkeley and Los Angeles: University of California Press, 2006), 61–105. Mansoor refers to the Benjamin essay "One-Way Street" (written 1923–25, published 1928), a meditation on Berlin roiled by economic transformation and

political turmoil (see note 68 in chapter 1). At one point, Benjamin sketches a vast history of the architectural orientation of the visual sign from ancient inscriptions to contemporary billboards: "If centuries ago [script] began gradually to lie down, passing from the upright inscription to the manuscript resting on sloping desks before finally taking to bed in the printed book, it now begins just as slowly to rise again from the ground. The newspaper is read more in the vertical than in the horizontal plane, while film and advertisement force the printed word entirely into the dictatorial perpendicular" (*Selected Writings*, vol. 1, 456). As we saw in chapter 1, Hamilton engages this "dictatorial perpendicular"; so does Ruscha, despite his favoring of the horizontal in his painting, and along with his revised window paradigm, this perpendicular distinguishes his work, too, from the flatbed model of the picture explored by Robert Rauschenberg, Johns, and others.

47. This is not the place to develop the connections between these aspects of Ruscha and the car-centered, commodity-inflected architecture and urbanism advanced by Robert Venturi, Denise Scott Brown, and Steven Izenour in *Learning from Las Vegas* (Cambridge, Mass.: MIT Press, 1972), who there acknowledge the influence of Pop in general and Ruscha in particular. To note just one connection: his attention to storefronts, with "almost like nothing behind the facades" (*Leave Any Information*, 223) and to billboards, with signs becoming spaces, clearly bears on their advocacy of "the decorated shed" as a "conventional shelter that applies symbols" (*Learning from Las Vegas*, 87). The great difference is that Venturi and Scott Brown tend to naturalize this condition of "the ugly and the ordinary," whereas Ruscha works to de-automatize it. This is also true of the distraction of the car-commodity subject: Venturi and Scott Brown assume it, even embrace it, whereas Ruscha invites us to reflect on it. Finally, whereas Venturi and Scott Brown present the commercial *as* the common (indeed, as the only such language), Ruscha seeks to reclaim the common *from* the commercial. For more on these matters, see my "Image Building" (*Artforum*, October 2004); for a different account, see Vinegar, *I Am a Monument*.

48. Incidentally, it is by this allusion to cinematic space that Ruscha trumps the fabled tension in painting between actual surface and illusionist depth (discussed in chapter 2). Just as Johns had "resolved" this problem, highlighted by Greenberg, by recourse to vernacular forms like flags and targets once deemed to be outside modernism proper, so Ruscha does so by recourse to a medium, the movies, also once deemed to be outside.

49. Dietrich Diederichsen in Marika Magers, ed., *Ed Ruscha: Gunpowder and Stains* (Cologne: Walter König, 2000), 9. Ruscha: "I have a very locked-in attitude

about painting things in a horizontal mode. I think I'm lucky that words happen to be horizontal." Already in Oklahoma, "everything was horizontal" (290, 300).

50. In his classic essay "The Structural Study of Myth" (1955), Claude Lévi-Strauss argues that the raven and the coyote are seen as tricksters in part because they lie outside or between the given oppositions of agriculture and hunting, "herbivorous animals" and "beasts of prey" (*Structural Anthropology*, trans. Claire Jacobson [New York: Basic Books, 1963], 224). Much in Ruscha is similarly tricksterish.

51. Franz Kafka, *The Complete Stories* (New York: Schocken, 1971), 230. In a sense, the silhouette is to Ruscha what the figment is to Warhol. Lisa Saltzman writes of the silhouette in Kara Walker in a way germane here: "Neither trace nor tracing . . . these silhouetted figures emerge from and concretize the bodies that haunt the historical imagination and its contemporary inheritors. The material fact of these cut-out images is not the body depicted through the visual strategy of the silhouette, but instead, the body as understood though the social system of stereotype" (*Making Memory Matter: Strategies of Remembrance in Contemporary Art* [Chicago: University of Chicago Press, 2006], 68).

52. Ruscha quoted in Dietrich Diederichsen in Magers, *Ed Ruscha: Gunpowder and Stains*, 9.

53. In 1985, Kim Gordon (of Sonic Youth) wrote this about Ruscha: "L.A.'s lush landscaping only begins to make sense when you realize that underneath it is a desert. *L.A. is Ed Ruscha's desert on fire*" ("American Prayers," *Artforum* [April 1985], 73–78; emphasis in the original).

54. One building is named "Tool & Die"; the message of the sequence overall is "Retool or Die." The ten paintings were first shown as a group at the 2005 Venice Biennale; in the exhibition catalogue, Ruscha has this to say about his "boxes with names on them": "You know, I never visit industrial parks, but my mind lives in one." The paintings might be taken as a riposte to the appropriation of his work by postmodern architects from Venturi and Scott Brown to the present.

Pop Test

1. Baudelaire: "I would be happy not only as a victim; it would not displease me to play the hangman as well—so as to feel the revolution from both sides! All of us have the republican spirit in our blood as we have syphilis in our bones; we have

a democratic and syphilitic infection" (*Oeuvres,* ed. Yves-Gérard Le Dantec [Paris: Pléiade, 1931–32], 2:728). In "The Paris of the Second Empire in Baudelaire," Walter Benjamin quotes this note, and comments: "What Baudelaire expresses thus could be called the metaphysics of the *provocateur*" (*Charles Baudelaire: A Lyric Poet in the Era of High Capitalism,* trans. Harry Zohn [London: New Left Books, 1973], 14). In my view, this line of the dandyish-diabolical provocateur runs through Dada on to Pop (among other stops). It is pronounced, for example, in the Zurich Dadaist Hugo Ball, who consciously performs this Baudelairean persona often in his diary, as in this entry dated September 20, 1915: "I can imagine a time when I will seek obedience as much as I have disobedience: to the full" (*Flight Out of Time,* ed. John Elderfield, trans. Ann Raimes [New York: Viking Press, 1974], 28). On another front, Benjamin positions Baudelaire already as the "last" lyric poet, but, except for Richter, the lyrical is not at issue in Pop; however, an engagement with modernity certainly is, and that is what I have stressed here.

PHOTOGRAPHY AND COPYRIGHT CREDITS

Permission to reproduce illustrations is provided by the owners and sources as listed in the captions. Additional copyright notices and photography credits are as follows. All Lichtenstein images © and courtesy of the Estate of Roy Lichtenstein. All Richter images courtesy of the artist and Marian Goodman Gallery, New York / Paris. All Ruscha images courtesy of the artist. 0.1, 0.2 courtesy of the artist. 0.3 © Scala / Art Resource, NY. 1.2–1.8 courtesy of the artist. 1.11 courtesy of the artist. 1.13–1.22 courtesy of the artist. 3.42, 3.43, 3.44, 3.45 film stills courtesy of The Andy Warhol Museum.

SUBJECT INDEX

Consult the title index to locate specific works by title.

TITLE INDEX

Illustrations are indicated with **bold.** See the subject index for concepts and artists.